The West and the Third World

HISTORY OF THE CONTEMPORARY WORLD

Consultant Editors: Dr Peter Catterall and Professor Lawrence Freedman

This series aims to provide students of contemporary history, politics and international relations with concise, critical overviews of the major themes and the development of key geographical regions that have dominated discussion of world events in the twentieth century. The emphasis in the regional histories will be on the period since the Second World War, but coverage will extend to the earlier twentieth century wherever necessary. The books will assume little or no prior knowledge of the subject, and are intended to be used by students as their point of entry into a wide range of topics in contemporary international history.

Published

The Causes of the Second World War
Andrew J. Crozier

The West and the Third World
D. K. Fieldhouse

The Communist Movement since 1945
Willie Thompson

Forthcoming

South Africa in the Twentieth Century
James Barber

Decolonization and its Impact
Martin Shipway

The West and the Third World

Trade, Colonialism, Dependence and Development

D. K. Fieldhouse

BLACKWELL
Publishers

First published 1999

2 4 6 8 10 9 7 5 3 1

Blackwell Publishers Ltd
108 Cowley Road
Oxford OX4 1JF
UK

Blackwell Publishers Inc.
350 Main Street
Malden, Massachusetts 02148
USA

British Library Cataloguing in Publication Data

A CIP catalogue record for this book is available from the British Library.

Library of Congress Cataloging-in-Publication Data

Fieldhouse, D. K. (David Kenneth); 1925–
    The West and the Third World: trade, colonialism, dependence and development/D. K. Fieldhouse.
      p. cm. – (History of the contemporary world)
    Includes bibliographical references and index.
    ISBN 0-631-19438-X (alk. paper). – ISBN 0-631-19439-8 (alk. paper)
    1. International economic relations.   2. OECD countries – Foreign economic relations – Developing countries.   3. Developing countries – Foreign economic relations – OECD countries.   4. Developing countries – Economic conditions.   5. International trade.
6. Imperialism.   7. Decolonization.   I. Title.   II. Series.
HF1359.F536   1999
337 – dc21   98-34507
                                CIP

Typeset in $10\frac{1}{2}$ on 12 pt Bembo
by Newgen Imaging Systems (P) Ltd, Chennai, India
Printed in Great Britain by MPG Books Ltd, Bodmin, Cornwall

This book is printed on acid-free paper

For Howard Johnson

Contents

Acknowledgements

I have been helped by many people, notably Dr John Lonsdale, who vetted my interpretation of the book he wrote jointly with Professor Berman, *Unhappy Valley*, and which is central to the argument of my chapter 6; by Professor Forbes Munro, who read the whole book in draft and made many helpful suggestions, most of which I have attempted to incorporate; and by Drs Hal Hill and Heather Smith of the Australian National University, who read and commented on an earlier draft of chapter 11. I am most grateful to Hilary Walford for her expert editing of the typescript. The Research School of Social Sciences, Australian National University, gave me a visiting fellowship and excellent facilities for revising the book between January and April 1998; and Jesus College, Cambridge, was throughout my academic sheet anchor. My wife, Sheila, as always, has been a tolerating partner.

D. K. F.
Cambridge, 1998

Tables

Abbreviations

ACP	African, Caribbean and Pacific (states)
AID	Agency for International Development
BKPM	Capital Investment Coordinating Board (Indonesian)
CD	Colonial Development Act 1929
CD&W	Colonial Development and Welfare Act 1940
CFA	African Colonial Franc
cif	cost–insurance–freight
CMB	Cocoa Marketing Board
CSES	Colonial Sterling Exchange Standard
DAC	Development Assistance Committee (of OECD)
DFI	direct foreign investment
EC	European Community
ECLA	Economic Commission for Latin America
EEC	European Economic Community
EFF	Extended Fund Facility
ERP	effective rate of protection
ESAF	Enhanced Structural Adjustment Facility
EU	European Union
FAO	Food and Agriculture Organization (of UN)
FDI	foreign direct investment
FIDES	*Fonds d'Investissement pour le Développement Économique et Social*
FM	French metropolitan franc
fob	free on board
GATT	General Agreement on Tariffs and Trade
GDCF	gross domestic capital formation

GDI	gross domestic investment
GDP	gross domestic product
GNP	gross national product
GSP	Generalized System of Preferences
HCI	Heavy and Chemical Industries
HPAE	high–performing Asian economy
IBRD	International Bank for Reconstruction and Development (the World Bank)
IDA	International Development Association (of the World Bank)
ILO	International Labour Organization
IMF	International Monetary Fund
ISI	import-substituting industry
ITO	International Trade Organization
LDC	less-developed country
MDC	more–developed country
MNC	multinational corporation
NDP	net domestic product
NEP	New Economic Policy (of Malaysia)
NICs	newly industrialized countries
ODA	Official Development Assistance
OECD	Organization for Economic Cooperation and Development
OEEC	Organization for European Economic Cooperation
OPEC	Organization of Petroleum Exporting Countries
QRs	quantity restrictions (on trade)
R&D	research and development
SAF	Structural Adjustment Facility
SAL	Structural Adjustment Lending
SAL	Structural Adjustment Loan
SECAL	Sectoral Adjustment Loan
TEAM	World Bank, *The East Asian Miracle* (Oxford, 1993)
TNC	transnational corporation
TNE	transnational enterprise
UN	United Nations
UNCTAD	United Nations Conference on Trade and Development
UNESCO	United Nations Educational, Scientific and Cultural Organization

Note on the Text

All dollars are US dollars unless otherwise stated.

The term *billion* is used in the US meaning of one thousand million.

In Indian currency Rs 1 crore = ten million rupees.

Introduction

Both the title and the subject matter of this book require explanation.

First, the title. Both the 'West' and the 'Third World' are, of course, terms of art, not accurate definitions of anything. The West is a long-standing concept, historically used to distinguish Christian Europe from the East, as in Kipling's over-quoted poem. But in modern development-studies terminology it has expanded to include the United States, Japan, and potentially all other relatively affluent industrialized states, those which the World Bank designates as 'high income market economies which are members of the Organization for Economic Cooperation and Development' (OECD). Conversely, until about 1990, the West had also contracted, to exclude the USSR and its eastern European satellites, which the World Bank described collectively as 'planned economies'. These became the 'First' and 'Second' worlds, though these terms were never in fact used.

So the West is now simply shorthand for the relatively rich countries. There are synonyms, such as 'industrialized economies' or the 'North', a term adopted by the Brandt Commission Report of 1980. In this book West is preferred and is used in its most indefinite sense to distinguish the few relatively rich economies from the 'Rest'.[1] But, whatever one calls it, the West was and is not homogeneous. Onion-like it has many

---

[1] The shape of this book is based on lectures I gave in the History Faculty in Cambridge under the title 'The West and the Third World'. Predictably the topic was always referred to by undergraduates as 'The West and the Rest'. I was tempted to use this for the title of this book, but it was deemed too frivolous.

concentric rings, with the richest and technically most advanced – now the USA and Japan – at the centre, shading off to much less rich and advanced economies at an indeterminate circumference.

The Third World is a more difficult concept to pin down; and, in any case, it has now lost any specific meaning it may once have had. The genesis of the term has been much debated. Some have traced it back to the 1920s, when 'third way' was used to suggest the possibility of an alternative to both capitalism and socialism. Others have seen in it a reference to the 'Third Estate' of pre-Revolutionary France.[2] A more realistic terminological genesis is a British Labour Party pamphlet of 1947, *Keep Left*, which argued, among other things, for the establishment of a 'Third Force' in world affairs, to avoid polarization of the capitalist West and the socialist East. 'Third Force', in this sense, seems to have been widely used in left-wing and anti-imperialist circles in that period, notably by (Lord) Fenner Brockway.[3] Thus the concept of 'third' seems to have become established as designating the non-capitalist and non-imperialist countries and colonies. But its final form 'Third World' seems to date from the Bandung Conference of non-aligned states in 1955, when Alfred Sauvy coined the term *tiers monde*, deliberately using the archaic *tiers* to relate to the *tiers état* of pre-1789 France, the underprivileged.[4] Thereafter it passed into general discourse to indicate those Latin American, African and Asian countries that were politically detached from both the United States and the USSR, and were economically less developed than either of these.

But by the 1990s 'Third World' had lost any specificity it might once have had. With the end of Soviet domination and the cold war, and the decline of socialism in eastern Europe and many other parts of the world, the dichotomy between West and Third World, or capitalism and communism, virtually disappeared: only China and a few small islands of socialism remained, and China was apparently determined to develop into a capitalist economy under communist party political control. Even if it had ever been so, the world was no longer divided into two superpowers and their satellites, with the Third World sandwiched between them. There remained only a single spectrum of countries, diversified mainly by their relative affluence and the degree of their industrialization.

Why, then, continue to use Third World? The 'South' is no more definitive than Third World, since there are affluent and industrially

[2] J. Toye, *Dilemmas of Development* (2nd edn, Oxford, 1993), p. 26.
[3] S. Howe, *Anticolonialism in British Politics: The Left and the End of Empire, 1918–1964* (Oxford, 1993), pp. 168, 173, 178–9, 302, 310.
[4] J. E. Goldthorpe, *The Sociology of Post-colonial Societies* (Cambridge, 1996), pp. 15–16.

advanced countries south of the equator. Since the 1950s 'less-developed countries' (LDCs), or the more optimistic 'developing countries', have been widely used, particularly by the United Nations and other international organizations. 'LDC' will occasionally be used here as shorthand. But, as none of these is more specific, since the Third World is still commonly used to point to the generality of poorer countries, and because its wider implications are so widely understood, it will normally be used in this book. It will be accorded upper-case initial letters as a reminder that it is merely a term of art, not an economic definition.

Secondly, the subject of the book. It is about a debate that has raged for a very long time and will continue to do so because it concerns an issue over which no general consensus is conceivable. The issue can be stated very briefly. Have Third World countries ('the Rest' in vulgar parlance) benefited or suffered from close economic relationships with the more developed countries of the West? Conversely, would the Rest have done better if they had been able to maintain an arm's-length relationship with the West, taking a long spoon to sup with the devil?

The fundamental idea behind the modern form of this debate, as developed by Immanuel Wallerstein and others from earlier Marxist and liberal thought, is that until the sixteenth century the world consisted of quite distinct and largely autonomous economic regions, each with its own characteristics and possessing unlimited potential for development. From that period, however, Europeans were able to use their exceptional maritime mobility, their increasingly superior military resources, and in course of time also their more developed economic power, to overcome distance and to link the Third World countries with Europe. Their motives were frankly selfish: the West needed minerals and crops which were available only, or most economically, from other parts of the world. Because of their increasingly superior power, Europeans were able to reorder the international system. In place of a world consisting of largely unrelated regional units there developed a pattern resembling a wheel. Europe became the hub; other countries lay on its circumference, each linked as by spokes to the centre. The result was, in Wallerstein's terminology, a single 'world system' possessing a 'core' and a 'periphery', plus perhaps an intermediate 'semi-periphery'.[5]

To this point few would dispute this as a generalized description of the historical process, at least to the later nineteenth century – though thereafter the geographical unity of the central 'core' was broken by the emergence first of the United States, then of Japan as part of the collective hub of the world system. In fact, in different terms this has been a central theme of the literature on European expansion for centuries.

[5] I. Wallerstein, *The Modern World System* (3 vols, New York, 1974, 1980, 1989). Other works in the same tradition are discussed in ch. 2.

It is, however, at this point that the debate with which this book is concerned starts.

Putting it in the crudest terms, was it a good thing for the less-developed 'peripheral' countries that they should lose their conceptual autonomy and become an integral part of a world system? Broadly two positions have been adopted. On the one hand, there have always been those who have claimed that integration was beneficial because it provided a wide range of benefits to Third World countries which they could not, at least in any predictable future, have provided for themselves. On the other hand, there have always been others who have argued that any benefits obtained by these countries were outweighed by penalties, so that their ultimate condition was less satisfactory than it had been originally, or than it might otherwise have become. In this book I have called the first group the optimists, their opponents the pessimists. Their contrasting arguments are surveyed in part I.

This debate has tended to be conducted at a fairly high level of generality. In order to attempt to clarify the argument it is necessary to look much more closely at what integration actually meant. This differed from one part of the world to another; but for most countries other than China, Japan and Thailand it had two main phases. The first involved political subordination to a state in the West; the second, after independence gained at various times from the late eighteenth to the mid-twentieth centuries, different forms of relationship, though possibly still involving subordination. This book is concerned primarily with the twentieth century. It does not, therefore, describe the processes of colonization in earlier centuries. But colonialism was a major factor for the first half of the twentieth century. Part II of the book therefore analyses the instruments of colonialism, part III trade and colonialism as they affected the welfare of Third World countries during the first half of the present century. Part IV then examines the character of the West–Rest relationship after the transfer of political power, during the second half of the century. A final chapter attempts to pull the argument together and suggest a synthesis.

Few people have the width of knowledge and technical expertise fully to cover so wide an area and so many issues. I am not one of those. As is obvious in the text, my professional interests lie mainly in two areas: in the theory and practice of European imperialism and colonialism, and in the theory and practice of multinational companies (alternatively transnational enterprises). Conversely I am not an economist or sociologist, and I have ignored the dynamic current debate over cultural imperialism, both for lack of space and because I have read too little of the huge recent literature on post-colonialism. Nor have I attempted to read all the vast number of specialist texts available on each of the topics I discuss. I have had to rely on a limited selection of those that appeared to offer the most reliable guidance in little-known territories. Hence any regional or subject specialist will be able to point to publications or information which I have missed or misunderstood, and which throw a different light on my argument. Perhaps the most serious gap is that of Japan and China, whose development patterns are highly relevant to the argument of the book. Japan would provide perhaps the best example of a non-western economy that escaped western political and military dominance by a thorough-going internal transformation and an enthusiastic embracing of the international economy. China was a large 'continental' economy that experienced some 'enclave' development, but also retained a large degree of autonomy, and therefore served as an implicit model for dependency theorists when arguing for 'disengagement'. For their omission there were three main reasons. Neither was ever a western dependency, whereas much of the argument of the book relates to the effects of colonialism and its aftermath. Space restrictions would have made it impossible properly to discuss either. Finally, I have no specialized knowledge of either country.

The book may therefore best be seen as the attempt of a conventional historian to examine issues which are of great importance, but which in some cases lie on or beyond the margins of his professional competence. Moreover, the level of analysis and the amount of detailed information provided are conditioned by the facts that this book is one of a series designed for students, not academic specialists, and that it has a tight word limit. My justification for making the attempt is that it seems to me that the issues involved are very important and that, so far as I know, no one else has yet attempted such a synthesis at this level.[6] I do not claim to provide an answer to the huge underlying questions posed above, merely to examine the arguments and marshal some evidence by which they may be assessed.

[6] I understand that David Landes has recently published *The Wealth and Poverty of Nations* (New York, 1998), but I was unable to read this before going to press.

Part I

The Debate over
an Integrated World System

1

The Optimists

In the broadest terms one can distinguish two main theoretical approaches to the consequences of closer relations between the West and the Third World, between North and South, 'core' and 'periphery'. The first can be designated 'optimistic', the second 'pessimistic'. Optimists are those who hold that the creation of a single world economic system has been and remains on balance beneficial to both the core and the periphery. Pessimists are those who deny this, at least for the periphery. They argue that, for a variety of reasons, any international politico–economic system contrived by a greater power and imposed on the lesser will necessarily tend to the disadvantage of the latter. These are very broad categories: the reasons for optimism or pessimism vary greatly. But they are useful organizing concepts. Chapter 1 surveys the two main groups of optimists, chapter 2 the greater variety of pessimists. In each case the basic arguments stem from before the twentieth century, but they must be traced back to their origins because they are for the most part still in current debate.

The common denominator of all optimistic theories of global integration is that each society can benefit from what another can offer. Where these theories most obviously differ is over how the relationship is best organized. There is much common ground, but a crude distinction can be drawn between arguments based on an open international market (or free trade) and those based on some form of exclusive cooperation, commonly through protection or tariff preferences. The first of these stems from Adam Smith and the classical economists of the early nineteenth century, and in the later twentieth century is most clearly expressed in the principles underlying the General Agreement on Tariffs and Trade (GATT) and the strategies pressed on less-developed countries (LDCs) by the World Bank and the International Monetary Fund (IMF). The second grew from the protectionist devices adopted by states and empires since the later Middle Ages, commonly called mercantilism or neo-mercantilism, and in modern times is reflected in partially exclusive organization such as the European Union (EU) and its associated states (the so-called ACP countries of Africa, the Caribbean and the Pacific) which receive important commercial and financial advantages with Europe under the successive Yaoundé and Lomé conventions. Section 1 outlines the main themes of the free-trade tradition, section 2 those of exclusive cooperation and protectionism.

1   Free-trade Theory and Comparative Advantage

The core of free-trade theory is the belief that both individuals and societies are most prosperous if they are free to produce and consume without artificial restriction. This in turn requires an open market for selling and buying. In an ideal world there would, therefore, be no obstacles to trade or investment and the world would constitute a single system of production and exchange. But why should this promote prosperity? The early classical economists provided two closely related answers: the benefits of specialization and the theory of comparative costs or advantage.

There are two fundamental arguments in favour of an open international market as a basis for increasing wealth to be found in Adam Smith's *The Wealth of Nations*, first published in 1776: specialization of function and what J. S. Mill later called a 'vent for surplus'.[1]

Specialization was a precondition of all economic progress. At the very beginning of the book Smith nailed his colours to the mast: 'The greatest improvement in the production powers of labour, and the greater part of the skill, dexterity, and judgement with which it is anywhere directed, or applied, seem to have been the effects of the division of labour.'[2] This division, or specialization, of labour, which Smith illustrated in the manufacture of pins, helped by the accumulation of capital and the development of new skills and techniques, enabled each worker, and, by extension, each community or country, greatly to increase its productivity.

[1] A. Smith, *An Inquiry into the Nature and Causes of the Wealth of Nations* (1776). References are to the Everyman's Library edition (2 vols, London and New York, 1964); hereafter *WN*.
[2] *WN*, vol. 1, p. 4.

But specialization, whether by an individual or a country, was dependent on exchange of productions. The specialized pin-maker must sell his product to buy the food and clothing which he had no time to produce himself. Hence the all-importance of trade – local, regional and international. At the global level such trade enabled any society to develop its own specialities, depending on its available resources and conditions. Conversely, Smith ascribed the relative lack of economic development in inland Africa and other regions to their inaccessibility to trade and therefore inability to specialize. Nations should, therefore, specialize in what they could produce best and buy other things from other countries. As Smith summed it up:

> It is the maxim of every prudent master of a family never to attempt to make at home what it will cost him more to make than to buy. . . .
> What is prudence in the conduct of every private family can scarce be folly in that of a great kingdom. If a foreign country can supply us with a commodity cheaper than we ourselves can make it, better buy it of them with some part of the produce of our own industry employed in a way in which we have some advantage.[3]

So far as it went, this was a compelling general argument in favour of specialization at all levels. But it left open at least one major question. Unless a country had an absolute advantage over all others, how was it to decide on what things to specialize in producing and trading with another country? An answer was provided by David Ricardo in his concept of 'comparative costs' or advantage. His classic example was the trade between Britain and Portugal, which was peculiarly useful because the Methuen Treaty of 1703 provided for favourable trade conditions between the two countries.[4] Ricardo suggested that Portugal needed to spend 80 hours on each unit of wine and 90 hours on each unit of cloth, whereas Britain needed to devote 120 hours per unit of wine and 100 hours per unit of cloth. That might suggest that Portugal had an absolute advantage in both categories. But Ricardo argued that, since Portugal had an advantage of 80 to 120 against Britain on wine but only of 90 to 100 on cloth, it should concentrate on producing and exporting wine while Britain should specialize in making and selling cloth. In this way a Portuguese wine producer could obtain 1.2 units of British cloth for one unit of his own wine, but could obtain only eight-ninths of a unit of Portuguese cloth for his unit of wine. Generalizing from this

---

[3] Ibid., p. 401.
[4] The treaty provided for Portuguese wines to enter Britain at one-third lower duty than French wines and for the removal of obstacles to the entry of British woollens to Portugal. It was largely responsible for the huge consumption of port in Britain until the French treaty of 1860.

model, Ricardo concluded that:

> Under a system of perfectly free commerce, each country naturally devotes its capital and labour to such employments as are most beneficial to each.... It is this principle which determines that wine shall be made in France and Portugal, that corn shall be grown in America and Poland, and that hardware and other goods shall be manufactured in England.[5]

The implication of this is that, if a country correctly judges its priorities, international trade cannot be harmful to either party and must contribute to the wealth of both. Ricardo's theory, however, as is obvious from the examples he gave, assumed that each country involved was fully employing its natural resources of land labour and capital. It had, therefore, to make a choice how best to allocate these resources. By contrast, Smith had produced an alternative model to his specialization argument which was more applicable to countries with less-developed economies and whose resources were not already fully committed: indeed, America and possibly Poland fell into this category when Ricardo published his book in 1817.

This model is commonly known as the 'vent-for-surplus' theory, though the label was attached only later by J. S. Mill. The essence of the theory is that many societies produce more of certain types of goods than they can consume at home, presumably because they lack the capacity (owing to specificity of factors) to transfer productive capacity in line with the principle of specialization. Alternatively, because of the lack of an adequate domestic market for things that a country is well suited to produce, a society may not fully employ its available factors. Either way, one solution is for that country to export whatever it is best equipped to produce. As Smith wrote:

> When the produce of any particular branch of industry exceeds what the demand of the country requires, the surplus must be sent abroad and exchanged for something for which there is a demand at home. Without such exportation a part of the productive labour of the country must cease, and the value of its annual produce diminish.... It is only by means of such exportation that this surplus can acquire a value sufficient to compensate the labour and expense of producing it.[6]

And again:

> between whatever places foreign trade is carried on, they all of them derive two distinct benefits from it. It carries out that surplus part of the produce of their land and labour for which there is no demand among

---

[5] D. Ricardo, *Principles of Political Economy and Taxation* (1817; ed. M. P. Fogarty, London, 1969), p. 81.
[6] *WN*, vol. 1, p. 333.

them, and brings back in return for it something else for which there is a demand. It gives a value to their superfluities, by exchanging them for something else, which may satisfy a part of their wants, and increase their enjoyments. By means of it the narrowness of the home market does not hinder the division of labour in any particular branch of art or manufacture from being carried to the highest perfection.[7]

This 'vent-for-surplus' theory has been much criticized. J. S. Mill thought it crude and a survival of mercantilist thinking. Its weakness as a universal nostrum is that it is not compatible with the Ricardian principle that a society reallocates its domestic production so as to specialize in what it can exchange most profitably with other countries. Under 'vent-for-surplus', by contrast, a country enters international trade with a surplus of productive factors and therefore does not need to reallocate them. The function of international trade is to put unused resources – in a less-developed country probably mainly land and labour – to profitable use by expanding production for export of whatever it already produces and can find a market for. The return to such exports is thus largely a net gain, enabling the exporting society to import and consume goods which it would not otherwise have been able to enjoy.[8]

Whatever its theoretical defects and incompatibility with both Smith's specialization argument and Ricardo's doctrine of comparative costs, the 'vent-for-surplus' concept has exerted wide influence. This is mainly because in a rough-and-ready way it has seemed to fit the conditions of many of the extra-European countries which were opened up to international trade from the sixteenth century onwards. This was particularly clear for those temperate territories which were 'opened up' by European settlers and which had relatively small indigenous populations but ample land. Even if capital and labour were initially in short supply, the land offered the opportunity to produce primary exports at a price which, even given the costs of sea transport, could not be matched in Europe. It was, therefore, natural for the settlers to produce a 'surplus' of agricultural and pastoral products for export which enabled them to buy the manufactured imports they could not economically produce for themselves. In this case, indeed, there was no real opportunity to reallocate factors of production: either one exploited the land for exports, or one lived a very primitive Robinson Crusoe existence.

The point was made repeatedly in the early nineteenth century by that intellectual magpie and great propagandist for colonization,

---

[7] Ibid., p. 392.
[8] The standard critique of 'vent-for-surplus' is by H. Myint, 'The "Classical Theory" of International Trade and the Underdeveloped Countries', *Economic Journal*, 68 (1958), pp. 317–37.

E. G. Wakefield. Thus, in his book, *A View of the Art of Colonization*, he summarized the argument as follows:

> Colonies, therefore, are ... naturally exporting communities: they have a large produce for exportation.
>
> Not only have they a large produce for exportation, but that produce is peculiarly suited for exchange with old countries. In consequence of the cheapness of land in colonies, the great majority of the people are owners or occupiers of land; and their industry is necessarily in great measure confined to the producing of what comes immediately from the soil: viz., food, and the raw materials of manufacture. In old countries on the other hand ... it may be said that manufactured goods are their natural production for export. These are what the colonists do not produce. The colony produces what the colony wants. The old country and the colony, therefore, are, naturally, each other's best customers.[9]

While this argument of complementarity was well suited to the early history of settlement societies from early Spanish America to nineteenth-century Australia, New Zealand and Canada, it was also applicable, in a modified form, to other parts of the world, notably tropical Africa and South-east Asia, which came under greatly increased European commercial influence during the later nineteenth century. As Myint has argued, many parts of Africa, however well developed their internal and regional trades might be, lacked markets for greatly expanded production, particularly of bulk commodities. The establishment of overseas markets for existing products, such as palm oil or groundnuts, or innovations such as cocoa, rubber and coffee, provided a stimulus to expand land and labour utilization. This type of development, which was found also in the expanded rice production of parts of South-east Asia, did not normally require radical change in modes of production or costly new equipment. It was, therefore, potentially cost-free to these societies, unless concentration on an export crop resulted in dependence on imports of foodstuffs that had been replaced by cash crops for export.

Up to a point, then, application of the principle of 'vent-for-surplus' in these 'new' economies appeared to contribute to a quite substantial growth in their wealth. But precisely because this did not necessarily involve any change in modes of production or significant investment, other than the labour of clearing and planting vacant land, such a strategy did not necessarily result in indefinite economic growth. As the 'pessimists' were to argue, continued increase in wealth depended on two main conditions: an overseas market that expanded with production, and additional supplies of factors (mainly land and labour) to keep up the increase of output. Ultimately these two problems were to lead to the concept of 'arrested development'.

[9] E. G. Wakefield, *A View of the Art of Colonization* (1849; Oxford, 1914), p. 83.

There were, however, other elements in classical economic thought, typically summarized in J. S. Mill's *Principles of Political Economy*, which supported an optimistic view of the gradual creation of a single world economy. First, specialization and increased output for the market are likely to result in improved techniques, even if in no revolutionary change. Secondly, the introduction of new foreign artefacts could stimulate demand for them and so encourage greater productive effort. Thirdly, the movement of people as part of the commercial process was certain to disseminate new ideas of all kinds and in all directions. Fourthly, even the commodity trades of West Africa were bound to result in the injection of capital by foreign merchants, which in turn might help the process of capital accumulation in the LDC. This was even more obvious when foreigners invested in mines, factories or railways. In short, classical and neoclassical economics suggest that trade increases wealth and welfare, both by specialization and by a 'vent-for-surplus'.

To this point of the argument the doctrines of the classical economists might be applied to any form of international economic system – to a 'mercantilist' empire of the pre-nineteenth-century type or to the 'neo-mercantilist' systems to be considered in section 2 below. Specialization, vent for surplus and complementarity were and are very flexible concepts, grist to almost any mill.

But in classical thought there was one essential condition for gaining maximum advantage from these principles and particularly from international trade. That was free trade. A substantial part of the writing of Adam Smith and his successors was devoted to attacking any form of interference with freedom of trading, what Smith called 'mercantilism' and 'monopoly'. The reason was that the benefits of specialization, comparative costs and 'vent-for-surplus' could be obtained only if each economy was able to find out, probably by experience rather than calculation, which things it was best equipped to produce. When Smith wrote *Wealth of Nations*, all European countries and their overseas possessions were encased in a web of regulations and customs duties that almost completely obscured their real economic potential. The most obvious of these restrictions related to trade between overseas colonies, their parent states and the rest of the world. In principle at least (though there were many exceptions and loopholes), European states aimed to hold a monopoly of their colonial markets, either for their own exports or for re-exports, to be monopsonic buyers of colonial products, and to be the sole carriers of intra-imperial trade. While many at the time accepted that such restrictions might harm the colonies (though some argued that such cooperation was mutually beneficial), most assumed that they benefited the parent states. Smith attacked such notions root and branch. In one famous passage he denounced the whole system as bad for all parties. The exclusive trade of the mother countries, he argued, was:

> a deadweight upon the action of one of the great springs which puts into motion a great part of the business of mankind. By rendering the colony produce dearer in all other countries, it lessens its consumption, and thereby cramps the industry of the colonies, and both the enjoyments and the industry of all other countries.... By rendering the produce of all other countries dearer in the colonies, it cramps, in the same manner, the industry of all other countries, and both the enjoyments and the industry of the colonies.[10]

Although Smith was here referring specially to the intra-imperial trades, the argument relates to all international trade. Any attempt artificially to interfere with the operation of the market is bound to involve costs. Thus to protect a domestic manufacturer or agriculture against foreign competition would raise that firm or farmer's profits but would have at least two undesirable effects on others. Consumers would pay more for the protected product than they would have to pay if the market was open to potentially cheaper imports. On the national level, capital and labour would be invested in that protected product (because of its higher profitability), which might be more productively invested in something else. Either way, such interference with the 'natural' course of events would slow up the process of economic growth because it was inconsistent with the principles both of specialization and of comparative costs.

This doctrine was and remains austere and challenging. At the time conservatives argued that to throw open the markets of a metropolis and its colonies might put important parts of their economies out of production. Conversely, a developing economy, which might benefit in the long run from establishing industries already operating elsewhere, was likely to find its nascent enterprises undersold by imports. These two reactions – the desire to preserve existing forms of production and to launch new and initially vulnerable industries – were expressed at the time of Smith and his early disciples and remain the main objections to free trade in the late twentieth century. They underlie the converse approach to economic development, some form of monopoly or cooperative protectionism, which is considered in section 2. In principle, however, it is clear that these two objections to free trade can be answered as follows.

---

[10] *WN*, vol. 2, p. 89. It is important for the later argument of this book that for Smith free trade alone was not sufficient for development. This required good government which was uncorrupt, could see the national interest beyond purely sectional ones, avoided arbitrary actions and policies, and taxed the population lightly.

First, the establishment of an open market in a country with protected production is likely, indeed certain, to reduce or destroy those sectors of the economy which cannot compete with imports. The result will be that individuals and firms will go out of business. Conservatives, along with these vested interests, will naturally regard this as a disaster, and it will almost certainly cause considerable hardship. But the free-trade response must be that such short-term destruction is beneficial in the long run because it enables the principle of comparative costs to operate. Once the ground has been cleared, those factors of production (land, labour, capital) no longer employed as before can and should be reallocated to other forms of production in which that country has a comparative advantage. In advance this will (as it did in the period when Britain was adopting free trade between the 1820s and 1840s) require an act of faith. But in the longer term the result can only be an increase in economic efficiency for the country as a whole. This in turn will contribute to the process of economic growth and development.

The second issue, the problem of starting up new enterprises in the face of established overseas competition, has always been a major difficulty for proponents of free trade. Rigorous free-traders have tended to adopt the position that any new enterprise will have some advantages to offset its inexperience: for example, access to cheaper raw materials or labour, the transport costs of imports, or the special consumer preferences of its own market. If, after a reasonable period of experiment, these prove insufficient to provide profitability, then the enterprise should be written off.

This was and remains a hard doctrine for aspiring manufacturers in 'new' economies. J. S. Mill, while otherwise a committed believer in free trade, attempted to soften the blow by introducing what came to be called the 'infant-industry' argument as the one major exception to the general rule.

> The only case in which, on mere principles of political economy, protecting duties can be defensible, is when they are imposed temporarily (especially in a young and rising nation) in hopes of naturalizing a foreign industry, in itself perfectly suitable to the circumstances of the country. The superiority of one country over another in a branch of production, often arises only from having begun it sooner.... A country which has this skill and experience yet to acquire, may in other respects be better adapted to the production than those which were earlier in the field.... But it cannot be expected that individuals should, at their own risk, or rather to their certain loss, introduce a new manufacture, and bear the burthen of carrying it on until the producers have been educated up to the level of those with whom the processes are traditional. A protecting duty, continued for a reasonable time, will sometimes be the least inconvenient mode in which the nation can tax itself for the support of

such an experiment. But the protection should be confined to cases in which there is good ground of assurance that the industry which it fosters will after a time be able to dispense with it; nor should the domestic producers ever be allowed to expect that it will be continued to them beyond the time necessary for a fair trial of what they are capable of accomplishing.[11]

He did, however, subsequently admit that 'an annual grant from the public treasury, which is not nearly so likely to be continued indefinitely, to prop up an industry which has not so thriven as to be able to dispense with it', would be preferable.[12]

This 'infant-industry' argument was to become a mainstay of modern protectionism, particularly in colonial and post-colonial situations. But Mill's warning that such protection should be only for 'a reasonable time' was taken seriously by free-traders. To convey the rigour of the doctrine as held by the British authorities in the later nineteenth century, here is part of a letter from the Board of Trade to the Colonial Office in response to a proposal by the New Zealand government to impose a temporary import duty on refined sugar in support of a planned manufacture of beet sugar.

> If an artificial stimulus is given to a particular industry in the hope of making it take root, the result is likely to be the loss of what is paid for the stimulus, the creation of a weak industry which will always need to be protected, and the diversion of industry and capital from enterprises which being more natural would be stronger and more healthy. It may be doubted if there is any case on record of an industry having been successfully established by means of protective duties and then flourishing without the aid of such duties, and even if there had been such instances, there has been no attempt to prove that the communities affected are better off than they would be if they had left matters alone.

Sir Robert Herbert, the permanent under-secretary at the Colonial Office, responded in a marginal note of possible examples of successful protection of infant industries, 'France and probably in the future Germany and the United States'.[13]

---

[11] J. S. Mill, *Principles of Political Economy* (1848; London, 1898), p. 556.
[12] Quoted in L. Robbins, *The Theory of Economic Development in the History of Economic Thought* (London, 1968), p. 115, from a letter written by Mill in 1868, in H. Elliot (ed.), *John Stuart Mill: Letters* 2 vols, (London, 1910), vol. 2, p. 119.
[13] T. H. Farrer, Board of Trade, to the Colonial Office, 28 Dec. 1876, Public Record Office, Colonial Office 209/235. Herbert, in an accompanying minute, expressed doubts about so dogmatic a statement 'on what is generally allowed to be a most extremely difficult question' and refused to send the report to New Zealand.

Herbert's doubts about the universal relevance of free trade did not reflect British official policy. Free trade had been imposed on the whole empire by stages, culminating in the abolition of preferences between 1846 and 1853. The empire was to be rigorously free-trading. But simultaneously the evolution of 'responsible government' in the colonies of white settlement made it impossible to forbid them to protect their own nascent industries, though British commercial treaties banned the use of preferences. New Zealand, as a self-governing colony, along with Canada and the Australian colonies (known as Dominions from 1907), could, if it wished, experiment with protection; and by the early twentieth century all these three (Australia having federated in 1901) had substantial protective duties. But the dependent empire had no such freedom. With one or two minor exceptions, no dependency was allowed to protect a domestic industry until 1923. From that year the Indian government was permitted (largely because it could claim the need for increased revenue from import duties) to impose protective duties for industries if the Tariff Board then created was prepared to assert that such duties would need to be only temporary: the infant-industry argument. Similar freedom was given to Ceylon (Sri Lanka) in the 1930s; but the rest of the colonial empire remained obligatorily free-trading until after 1945.

This fact lies at the heart of much of the modern debate over the effect of free trade, and indeed global economic integration, on LDCs. The evidence of the British colonial empire is central to any assessment of this process. In fact, however, as will be seen in chapter 4, Britain itself began to slide away from free trade after 1914 and adopted fully-fledged protection for itself in 1932. It also negotiated or imposed a complex structure of imperial preference with its Dominions and colonies. In broad terms Britain provided either free or preferential entry for empire products and received the same for its exports to the empire. It did so largely in response to the dramatic increase in protectionism in other countries, sparked off by the very high tariffs of 1922 and 1931 in the United States and intense protectionism throughout Europe. It seemed as if free-trade theory and practice had been destroyed by the economic crises of the post-war world.

Yet this did not last. As the recession of 1929 eased, the United States began to look for a general reduction of tariffs internationally: Congress passed a Reciprocal Trade Agreements Act which enabled the President to reduce tariffs by up to 50 per cent on a reciprocal basis. From then on the United States, now the world's leading industrial and agricultural power, aimed to negotiate the general reduction of import tariffs and other obstacles to freedom of trade (notably quotas on specified goods). The major achievement was the General Agreement on Tariffs and Trade of 1947, which committed the signatory countries gradually to reduce tariffs and other obstacles to freedom of trade. Despite much resistance, through a series of 'rounds' of negotiations this aim has been pursued, and with the completion of the 'Uruguay Round' in 1993 an International Trade Organization (ITO) was set up to oversee and promote this process. Meantime the US-dominated IMF and the International Bank for Reconstruction and Development (The World Bank), both set up in 1944 on the recommendation of the Bretton Woods conference of 1944, were committed to the same objectives. By being able to offer loans and investments respectively to countries with economic or financial problems, they were intended to offer alternatives to protectionism or other economically undesirable practices.

In the later twentieth century, in fact, the World Bank and the IMF were the main proponents of free trade and other related principles in the less-developed world. They thus filled the same role as Britain had done a century earlier. Their policies will be considered later as they affected particular Third World countries. But essentially their message had two parts.[14]

First, Third World countries should concentrate on production and export of those things in which they had a comparative cost advantage and not attempt to make things to which they were unsuited behind prohibitive tariff and regulatory barriers.

Secondly, every country should have a currency whose exchange rate accurately reflected the real cost of its domestic production and imports. The arguments deployed in favour of these principles and the practical steps pressed on Third World countries almost precisely embody the principles of Adam Smith, Ricardo and the classical economists. After two centuries the wheel had turned full circle.

The general consensus among modern development economists who adopt classical and neo-classical (post-Marshallian) principles can, therefore, be summarized as follows. The most profitable strategy for LDCs

---

[14] There is a huge World Bank literature, which provides information on global and territorial economic performance and proposes remedies for economic problems. For Africa, much of which was in economic crisis in the 1980s and 1990s, three widely known general surveys, which spelled out an essentially free-trade prescription for economic recovery through the so-called adjustment programmes negotiated with individual countries that called for financial help, were: *Accelerated Development in Sub-Saharan Africa: An Agenda for Action* (Washington, 1981: usually known as the Berg Report); *Toward Sustained Development in Sub-Saharan Africa* (Washington, 1984); *Adjustment in Africa: Reforms, Results, and the Road Ahead* (Oxford, 1994). Such strategies have not been popular with what can broadly be described as the Left, since they embody conventional capitalist assumptions. For a typical critique of World Bank strategies, see M. B. Brown, *Africa's Choices: After Thirty Years of the World Bank* (London, 1995).

of the Third World to adopt is to rely on the benefits of expanded trade. The export of commodities in which such countries have a comparative or absolute advantage should provide at least the following benefits.[15]

1 There should be some transfer of skills as indigenous producers learn the techniques of modern international trading and accounting. This may also involve improved methods of production caused by market pressure for higher-quality products and information on new strains, etc.

2 Foreign capital will be drawn in to finance the export and import trades. Initially this will provide essential credit for indigenous traders, middlemen and producers, and help at least some of those involved in the trade to accumulate capital.

3 Trade will result in the establishment of more sophisticated forms of currency, banking, business organization, ports and inland communications, which should contribute to the general development of the economy.

4 The greater availability and variety of goods on the market, both from other parts of the same region and from abroad, should and normally will stimulate consumer demand and therefore production as a means of satisfying that demand.

5 Successful commodity production for the market, contrasted with the extreme and largely hypothetical case of mere subsistence production, should (through its greater efficiency and exploitation of factors of production) generate a surplus in the hands of the producer and the merchant. Part at least of this should be available for investment rather than consumption. And, since such capital formation is the necessary basis for genuine economic growth, trade may make a major contribution to growth and development.

This, of course, is all theory, and it is one purpose of this book to investigate whether such optimism is justifiable. But, before leaving the free-trading optimists, it may be worthwhile to indicate very broadly

[15] Some of the standard critiques of export-led growth are: E. J. Chambers and D. F. Gordon, 'Primary Products and Economic Growth: An Empirical Measurement', *Journal of Political Economy*, 74 (1966), pp. 315–32; R. Findlay, 'Primary Exports, Manufacturing, and Development', in M. Lundahl (ed.), *The Primary Sector in Economic Development* (London, 1985); R. Findlay and M. Lundahl, 'Natural Resources, "Vent-for-Surplus", and the Staples Theory', in G. M. Meier (ed.), *From Classical Economics to Development Economics* (London, 1994); D. Lal, 'In Praise of the Classics', in Meier (ed.), *From Classical Economics*; W. A. Lewis, 'Economic Development with Unlimited Supplies of Labour', *Manchester School* (May 1954); Myint, 'The "Classical Theory"'; W. A. Lewis, *The Theory of Economic Growth* (London, 1955); L. Robbins, *The Theory of Economic Development in the History of Economic Thought* (London, 1968).

the most likely strengths and weaknesses of the case for saying that to maximize specialization and international exchange under free-market international conditions is likely to generate economic development.

The strongest pragmatic evidence in favour of the classical theory of growth through trade lies in the extraordinary economic success of the so-called settler communities of the nineteenth and twentieth centuries, some of which will be examined in chapter 5. Australia, New Zealand, Canada, and also Argentina, Chile and the United States, were countries which created very substantial wealth and established the foundations for sustained development, initially by exploiting the principle of comparative costs.

But such success has not proved universal. The experience of most parts of Black Africa, South and South-east Asia and China, at least until after 1945, proved different. Apart from China and Thailand, virtually all these regions came under colonial control during or after the nineteenth century. All those that were dependencies of Britain, the Netherlands and Belgium were subject to rigorous free trade, at least until India was permitted controlled protection in 1923. All attempted, in varying ways and degrees, to follow the path of development through specialization and comparative costs. All became proportionately large exporters and importers. Yet by the mid-twentieth century none was affluent, few (apart from India) had developed a significant industrial sector, and most remained heavily dependent on foreign capital and services such as shipping.

This suggests that, for them at least, the classical model had not worked, or had worked only up to a certain point. Alternative explanations from the 'pessimists' of why this might have been so will be considered later. But at this stage it is possible to point to some common symptoms of limited economic success in a free-trade environment.

1 The trading system was largely controlled by expatriates, from the roots of commodity production to the ultimate overseas markets. In South Asia this was commonly through the managing agencies at the ports, leaving the inland operations in the hands of indigenous middlemen. In Black Africa expatriate enterprise penetrated much more deeply and had greater control over the whole export/import economy through firms such as the United Africa Company.

2 Because these trading firms were foreign, they provided little opportunity for indigenous employment at the higher levels, and so little transfer of skills could occur. Moreover, the large scale of these foreign trades and the amount of capital they required meant that indigenous traders were squeezed out.

3 Because ultimate selling prices were, and are, set by international market forces, the country exporting primary commodities was

peculiarly vulnerable to price fluctuations. Historically, also, the terms of trade tended, at certain periods though not consistently, to move strongly against commodity producers. When this happened, the absolute or comparative advantage commodity producers possessed was of little benefit, since they had to export far more of their products to purchase the manufactured imports they needed.

4 Because the foreign trading company had so dominant a role in buying and selling, it might also be able to manipulate what it paid the indigenous producer and what it charged the consumer. How significant this was depended largely on the degree of monopoly (in selling imports) and monopsony (in buying local products) these foreign firms possessed. In certain parts of Black Africa this might seriously affect the benefits the indigenous people got from specialization in export production.

5 Because the export production sector was highly specialized, it might constitute a partly insulated 'enclave' detached from the rest of the local economy. This was particularly likely in the case of plantations or mining operations, whose products were entirely for export and whose skills had little or no relevance to the indigenous society. In such cases there was likely to be little transfer of skills or capital from the enclave to the rest of the economy.

6 Because the main trading and other enterprises were foreign owned, their profits were largely exported, and so made little or no contribution to the development of the host country.

7 International, and in some cases also internal, transport was controlled by monopolistic firms or cartels, so that a significant share of the profits of trade accrued to the foreign firms that owned these networks. Conversely, indigenous entrepreneurs were unable to enter these fields.

8 Because under free trade the local market was wide open to imported manufactures, which could often (though not invariably) undersell local products on cost or quality, in the early stages much of the indigenous manufacturing base was destroyed. Conversely, because of the relatively high costs of manufacturing with 'modern' techniques for limited local markets, it was very difficult for anyone, foreign or indigenous, to establish competing modern industries. The general effect was to 'de-industrialize' these economies and leave them excessively dependent on commodity exports. Alternatively, excessive specialization on a limited range of commodity exports might result in inadequate local production of food, so that a country might come to depend on imports.

The sum of these allegations is that in a free-trade environment specialization on production and exchange of what any country can most efficiently produce for what it needs to import may not have worked satisfactorily for a majority of the tropical and subtropical countries which have been linked to the more developed western world since the time of the classical economists. Briefly, even if the principles were and are sound, contingent factors which Smith, Ricardo, Mill and others did not foresee or take into account may have neutralized the benefits they predicted.

In fact, by no means all of these adverse results of the adoption of classical principles of free trade and specialization affected all LDCs or at all times. This list may best be seen collectively as a 'worst-possible' scenario. Some of these assertions mainly reflect the prejudices of critics of free trade and commodity production. They also pose the problem of why, if these disadvantages were endemic to any system of open trade, the colonies of white settlement seem, for the most part, to have faced the same dangers but to have achieved considerable wealth and development even before they adopted protection for their industries. These problems are central to the purpose of this book. But in the first instance the evident hazards of a free-trading open-market system help to explain why the second group of 'optimists' concerning the benefits of global integration chose to put their faith in protectionism and a regulated rather than an open market.

2   Exclusive Cooperation: Protectionism and Preferences

Although the battle between the free-trade doctrines of Smith and his successors and traditional protectionists, whom he called mercantilists, seemed by the mid-nineteenth century to have been won by the free-traders, this was an illusion. Classical economics might have gained the intellectual high ground, but in the real world there were many who remained unconvinced. What these doubters lacked was a doctrine with which to fight the new political economy. There had never been a protectionist equivalent of Adam Smith, merely a number of pragmatic commentators who pointed to specific benefits from a variety of largely *ad hoc* commercial devices. In the nineteenth century the nearest thing to a general rationale was Friedrich List's *The National System of Political Economy*,[16] which argued for a planned national economy for Germany, including protective tariffs, until it had caught up with Britain. But he did so on broadly pragmatic grounds, as part of a scenario for a greater German empire, including possession of a navy and colonies overseas. Neither he, nor the many later continental and British proponents of

[16] F. List, *The National System of Political Economy* (1841; Eng. trans., London, 1904).

protectionism and imperial preference, were ever to argue that such a system would increase wealth on a global level. Their aims, in common with earlier protectionists, were primarily nationalistic and defensive: to redistribute wealth rather than to maximize it.

It has been suggested above that adoption of a free-trade, open-market strategy involved an act of faith. In particular, it meant taking the risk that the sacrifice of existing industries and activities because they were not competitive would result in the growth of new enterprises that would more than compensate for what was discarded.

This was a risk the British were prepared to take by the 1840s and on which they based their economic and imperial strategies until the 1930s. For them it seemed to work. But critics of the strategy could and did point out that British success was contingent on the unprecedented industrial and commercial lead that Britain had then established over all other countries. The British might, for example, safely throw open their colonial ports to foreign trade on equal terms because for the most part they did not then fear foreign competition. Equally the British merchant marine could dominate the trades not only of the empire but of much of the rest of the world: between 1890 and 1914 Britain built two-thirds of the world's new ships, and in the 1890s over 70 per cent of tonnage passing through the Suez Canal was British.[17]

Things were seen differently by other countries. Those with overseas colonies, notably France, Spain and the Netherlands, were reluctant to open colonial trades and ports to the British or other foreign states. They were later joined by Germany and the United States when, in and after the 1880s, they too acquired overseas territories. Without attempting here to trace the course of each country's policies, which fluctuated with time and circumstance and are outlined in chapter 4, it may be said that all these, except for the Netherlands (which nevertheless attempted to exclude British Shipping from Indonesia in the 1880s), used a variety of devices to protect the trade of their dependencies in favour of the goods and ships of the parent state. In this account it is proposed to concentrate on the French example, because it was the most consistently protectionist of all the imperial powers of the modern period, and because its initially self-centred practices were later transformed into a cooperative system of relations between the modern European Union (EU) and a large part of the Third World.

France had never been fully converted to the principles of free trade. It paid nominal allegiance to them in 1860 with the Cobden treaty with Britain, which reduced protectionism at home and threw French colonies open to foreign trade on low or nil tariffs. But the reaction came

[17] D. R. Headrick, *The Tentacles of Progress: Technology Transfer in the Age of Imperialism, 1850–1940* (Oxford, 1988), p. 28.

by about 1880, and the drift back to protectionism and imperial preference reached a first climax in 1892 with the Méline tariff, whose aim was to enclose all overseas territories not otherwise excluded by treaties within the metropolitan tariff. One effect, coupled with restrictions, bounties and other stimulants for French shipping, was to give French goods a share of French colonial markets far greater than they might have had in a free-market system. Thus between 1900 and 1935 the percentage of French exports going to French African territories rose from 8.9 to 26.9, while French Africa's imports to France rose from 5.0 to 20.9 per cent of the total.[18] For the French overseas empire as a whole, excluding Algeria, imports to France from the colonies rose from 10.82 per cent in 1904 to 25.21 per cent in 1934, while exports from France to the colonies (excluding Algeria) rose from 12.54 to 30.87 per cent.[19] More significant for the effect of the protectionist system was the share of the trade of individual colonies with France. To take one example, imports to French West Africa from France rose from 44.5 per cent in 1905 to 69 per cent in 1938, while that federation's exports to France rose from 60.2 to 82 per cent of total exports in the same period.[20]

Another effect was, of course, to raise the price of foreign imports in French possessions to the extent of the differential import duties, just as protectionism increased prices in France itself. But there was one major inequity in the Méline system. While French colonial goods paid the standard import duties on entry to France (to protect domestic French agriculture), French exports to the colonies entered duty free. This inequity became the basis of a long-running French debate over the ethics of French colonial policy that began around 1900 and continued until basic changes were made in French policy in the 1930s.[21] For the present purpose its significance is that, as a single example, it highlights the critical question underlying modern neo-mercantilism: could it be beneficial to both the metropolis and the dependency, core and periphery?

At first sight it would seem that this sort of imperial economic system was merely a replica of the old *pacte colonial* of the eighteenth century,

---

[18] Quoted in D. K. Fieldhouse, 'The Economic Exploitation of Africa: Some British and French Comparisons', in P. Gifford and W. R. Louis (eds), *France and Britain in Africa* (New Haven and London, 1971), p. 642.
[19] G. Clarke, *The Balance Sheets of Imperialism* (New York, 1936), table 31, p. 65. Similar figures are given in other studies, notably J. Marseille, *Empire colonial et capitalisme français* (Paris, 1984), p. 44, and H. Brunschwig, *French Colonialism 1871–1914* (London, 1966), p. 90.
[20] Fieldhouse, 'The Economic Exploitation', p. 643.
[21] For an early denunciation of the inequity of this system, see J. Harmond, *Domination et colonisation* (Paris, 1910).

a system of exploitation that had nothing to offer the colonies. Indeed the early proponents of a French colonial policy from the 1880s made no bones about it: the empire existed to benefit France, not its colonies. Yet many imperialists, particularly from the early 1920s to the 1950s, argued, and sincerely believed, that an autarkic imperial economy could also offer a great deal to underdeveloped colonial economies: that it was better for them than to be exposed to the open world market. How could a protectionist empire be said to provide cooperative benefits to its Third World components?

The basic case made out by French and other protectionist imperial states during the earlier part of the twentieth century to justify their claim that an autarkic imperial system could generate growth and development in Third World dependencies can be summarized in five simple assertions.

1 Relatively weak economies must protect their producers against their entrenched rivals overseas by all the techniques traditionally available: tariffs, bounties, shipping controls and physical regulation of trade. Only when and if a country had caught up with its competitors could these defences be dismantled.
2 Colonies were essential to all but the world's dominant producers as preferential markets and secure, possibly cheaper, sources of raw materials. Free trade was a luxury for the dominant world power.
3 Conversely, a protected imperial economic system provided the less-developed dependencies with a vital buffer against the vagaries of market forces in the international jungle. These dependencies relied heavily on export of a limited range of raw materials, for which the world market was both inelastic and unstable. Since the metropolis needed these raw materials, it must, in its own interests, help the colonies to produce them and provide a secure market for them. Also, since the metropolis needed markets for its exports it was in its own interests to increase the wealth of the colonies to enable them to buy metropolitan exports. Thus the colonies could find a secure market for exports which might not be competitive in the wider market.
4 Such an empire could, therefore, constitute a mutual cooperative unit, enabling the most efficient use to be made of scarce resources, such as capital. In particular, metropolitan capitalists and taxpayers would be encouraged to invest in the colonies because they could be certain that their investment would be safe and profitable.
5 In this way both the more- and less-developed components of the system could flourish. The metropolitan and colonial economies would become more interdependent over time, each specializing in those things in which it had a comparative advantage, but within the

imperial, not the international economy. If this meant that the colonies were forced to remain primary commodity producers, at least the prices paid for their products could, in principle, be fixed at such a level that they received a reward comparable to that of a more-developed economy. If New Zealand could become a wealthy 'developed' economy, although essentially Britain's farmyard in the Antipodes, why should not francophone Africa wax fat as the protected source of French cocoa, coffee, vegetable oils and bananas?

This doctrine of complementarity was, of course, very similar to that propounded by Wakefield in a free-trade context. Indeed, early French theorists such as Paul Leroy-Beaulieu, who published his *De la colonisation chez les peuples modernes* in 1874, followed Wakefield closely. The difference was that to both these writers international market forces must decide what a 'new' economy should produce; whereas to the neo-mercantilist such decisions would be taken within an imperial context. The key to modern neo-mercantilism is the fact that such decisions were taken by the imperial state rather than by economic forces; and that the benefits the free-traders claimed would accrue to the colonies naturally as a result of specialization were to be provided artificially by state action.

The French case is the clearest example of the operation of modern protectionism claiming to operate to the advantage of less-developed dependencies. A moral turning point came after the First World War. In Britain the dominant concept of the two decades after about 1918 was the 'trust', or what Lord Lugard called the 'mandate', of the developed countries for the LDCs. That is, the alleged exploitation of colonies since their annexation must be replaced by deliberate measures to improve them. In Lugard's famous words, 'Our present task is clear. It is to promote the commercial and industrial progress of Africa, without too careful a scrutiny of the material gains to ourselves ...'.[22]

Lugard still assumed a free-trade environment for such development. His French equivalent, Albert Sarraut, minister of colonies for many years in the 1920s and 1930s and also an ex-colonial governor, naturally thought in protectionist terms. But he also, in a book published in 1923, argued for a reciprocal development policy in the French empire.

France, as a colonial power, is going to organize the development, for its own benefit no doubt, *but also for the general advantage of the world*, of those territories and resources which the indigenous races of these backward countries cannot or do not know how to develop, and whose benefits are thus lost both for themselves and for the generality....

[22] (Lord) F. D. Lugard, *The Dual Mandate in British Tropical Africa* (1922; 3rd edn, London, 1926), p. 61.

The pattern is no longer one-sided: it is designed to benefit both parties. It is not exploitation of one race by another, but *association*, to adopt the happy formula which has become the basis of our colonial policy.[23]

Neither statement should be taken too literally, and Sarraut in particular clearly had in mind an autarkic imperial system whose main beneficiary would be France. But in the early 1930s, as the slump in world commodity prices hit colonial producers and colonial government revenues, the French state felt bound to step in. Despite severe criticism from many sections of metropolitan France, which felt that their interests as consumers of colonial products or as producers of competing goods were being sacrificed to those of the colonies, France at last developed a commercial system designed to promote the economic interests of the colonies.[24]

This system, of *surprix*, or protected prices for selected colonial exports entering France, which provides the main ground for seeing imperial protectionism as beneficial to the colonies and ex-colonies, will be described in chapter 4. France was not, of course, the only imperial power to experiment with intra-imperial cooperative arrangements in the twentieth century. The British followed the French example from 1932 with the system of imperial preference that stemmed from the Ottawa Agreements of that year.[25] The British system was based on the same assumption as that of France half a century earlier: that a relatively weak metropolitan power and its colonies both needed defences against the competition of a hostile world and that collaboration within a partially closed economic system would benefit all parties. The British also developed similar institutions to those of France to support the colonies: free entry to Britain for colonial produce, bypassing tariffs on foreign goods; quotas on trade both ways; and aid under the 1929 and later Colonial Development [and Welfare] Acts. From 1939, moreover, the sterling area acted like the franc zone to regulate trade through control of the common imperial currency. Unlike France, however, the British ran down the system after about 1950, and, when the colonies achieved independence, they were free of all formal commercial or

---

[23] A. Sarraut, *La Mise en valeur des colonies françaises* (Paris, 1923), pp. 87–8; trans. author.

[24] For a detailed analysis of one such debate, over a proposal to help the producers of groundnuts in French West Africa, see Marseille, *Empire colonial et capitalisme français*, ch. 12.

[25] The classic treatment of the Ottawa system is in W. K. Hancock, *Survey of British Commonwealth Affairs*, vol. 2, part 1, *Problems of Economic Policy 1918–1939* (London, 1942). See also I. M. Drummond, *Imperial Economic Policy 1917–1939: Studies in Expansion and Protection* (London, 1974).

monetary links with Britain. Other imperial powers tended to follow the same protectionist course before 1945: the United States, Portugal and Spain throughout, the Dutch and Belgians only partially and from the early 1930s.

It is not intended at this point to evaluate the economic consequences for Third World countries of such protectionist or protective systems. But, as in the case of free trade, a short comment is necessary on the possible negative effects of such close economic relationships between core and periphery, in this case within a hothouse preferential economy rather than as part of an open international economy. That is, should one be optimistic about the likely effects of such a system on Third World countries? Three effects are likely to have been particularly significant.

First, as was seen above, the basis or justification of all these protectionist systems was belief in complementarity of interest. This, of course, was equally true of free-trade doctrine and the theory of comparative costs or advantage. The difference lay in the fact that in protectionist systems the balance was artificially adjusted, perhaps manipulated. For example, it might well be true that the Ivory Coast had a natural advantage in producing coffee or cocoa rather than manufacturing textiles. Under free-trade conditions, as in the Gold Coast, this operated naturally. But in the French case Ivory Coast coffee was given an artificial advantage in its main, French, market by being exempt from duties on foreign coffee. The extent or reality of comparative advantage was thus partly concealed, and it therefore became less likely that the Ivory Coast would consider possible alternative forms of production should changing comparative costs dictate a change. In this way a protected imperial or post-imperial system was likely to perpetuate an economic orientation which might be in the best interests of both metropolis and colony (core and Third World country after decolonization) at one stage, but was no longer so later on. It was also likely to result in higher prices in both the core and periphery of the system owing to protection against external competition, and therefore in reduced ability by both parties to compete in the international market.

Secondly, a tied or common currency system, such as those described in chapter 4, might have similar effects. The British system of colonial currencies tied to the metropolitan pound until decolonization, or the French device of the franc zone, which continued into the 1990s for most one-time French dependencies (at their own choice), offered considerable potential benefits for Third World countries. It made it unnecessary for them to manage their own currencies; it ensured relatively stable prices, immune to the huge inflations common in, for example, many Latin American countries; it encouraged foreign investment; and it ensured convertibility into international currencies.

On the other hand, from the standpoint of the dependency or Third World country it also meant that its international exchange rate, and therefore its competitiveness, was determined by the economic fortunes of the metropolis. If, for example, the French franc was strong, a West African state using the CFA franc (CFA50 = 1 French franc, changed to CFA100 = 1 French franc in 1994) would find its exports overpriced by comparison with those of a neighbouring state whose freestanding currency had been devalued. To take a single example in the 1980s, when Nigeria devalued its Naira, the Ivory Coast found that its wax print cotton textiles were no longer competitive with those of its main West African rival, Nigeria.[26]

Thirdly, a complementary system of this kind, particularly when backed up by guaranteed aid and at least some insurance against international market fluctuations, was likely to be habit-forming. So long as a developing country could sell all its main commodities under favourable conditions to the core of the organization, it was less likely either to want to diversify into other forms of production or to attempt to sell its goods outside the ring. To those who believe that such countries should not continue to concentrate on cash crops or mineral exports this is undesirable: it perpetuates 'dependence' on the industrialized West. On the other hand, there is no reason why continuation of export production should not run in harness with industrialization, as both Senegal and the Ivory Coast have shown since independence. Moreover, since much local manufacturing was essentially uneconomic in such limited markets, its costs were largely borne by profits from commodity exports.

These issues remain hotly debated and will be considered in the concluding chapter. But one thing at least is clear. All Third World states which were allowed to join the post-1958 group of ACP states as associate members of the EU have done so, including several with 'socialist' economies. Clearly they believed in the principle of regulated cooperation. Whether membership will be to their advantage in the longer term remains an open question. But they at least can be listed among the optimists.

---

[26] For details of one example of this, the Uniwax factory in the Ivory Coast, see D. K. Fieldhouse, *Merchant Capital and Economic Decolonization: The United Africa Company 1929–1987* (Oxford, 1994), p. 587.

2

The Pessimists

Although, as suggested in chapter 1, there has been and remains a substantial body of opinion which holds that the relationship between core and periphery, metropolis and colony, within a global economy may, and probably will, contribute to economic growth and development in the Third World, there have also, at all stages since the expansion of Europe in the fifteenth century, been those who qualified or denied this. These doubters are here loosely labelled and lumped together as 'pessimists'. But they are not homogeneous, because their doubts vary widely in two ways: first, in their reasons for not accepting the arguments of the optimists; secondly, in the depth of their pessimism.

In this chapter the pessimists of the modern period are divided into five broad categories, in descending order of pessimism. The first is a miscellaneous group whom I have roughly labelled humanitarians and liberals; secondly, there are the development economists of the 1950s and thereafter; thirdly, the Marxists and neo-Marxists, including Marx himself; fourthly, those who can broadly be labelled 'dependency' theorists; and, finally, proponents of 'unequal exchange'.

1 Humanitarian and Liberal Critics of Imperialism

Criticism of the impact of the West on the Third World is as old as European expansion itself. Broadly it falls into two categories: humanitarian and economic.

The humanitarians

Humanitarian criticism began in the sixteenth century and its main target was Spanish treatment of Amerindians. There was an important academic debate in Spain over the rights of Spaniards and Amerindians, led by the Dominican jurist Francisco de Vitoria. But the most influential and vehement critic of Spanish practices was the Dominican settler turned missionary Bartolome de las Casas, who published extensively to denounce the abuse of Indians by settlers.[1] This type of criticism, not anti-imperialist but concerned to ameliorate the conditions of non-Europeans under colonial rule, continued for the next three centuries. Its foundations were Christianity and respect for the concept of law. The former imposed the moral obligation to treat non-Europeans as if they were one's neighbours, the latter to do so with due respect to legal principles, both those of the imperial state and the laws of nature. Edmund Burke linked the two together in one of his speeches during the impeachment of Warren Hastings in 1794, though admittedly there were strong political elements in the trial.

> The law is the security of every person that is governed. It is the security of the people of India; it is the security of the people of England. There is but one law in the world, namely, that law which governs all law – the law of our Creator, the law of humanity, justice, equity, the law of nature and of nations.[2]

This line of thought ran continuously from the later eighteenth century to the age of decolonization after 1945, including, in the late eighteenth century, the Abbé G. T. F. Raynal[3] and the whole campaign against the slave trade and ultimately slavery. In the nineteenth century the British Aborigines Protection Society kept the theme going, and it was taken up by the Congo Reform Association of the early twentieth century, led by E. D. Morel and Roger Casement. Thereafter criticism of colonialism on moral and ethical grounds swelled to a flood, promoted

---

[1] There is a large literature on this. See, in particular: L. Bethell (ed.), *The Cambridge History of Latin America* (5 vols, Cambridge, 1984–6), vol. 1; D. Brading, *The First America: The Spanish Monarchy, Creole Patriots, and the Liberal State, 1492–1867* (Cambridge, 1993); A. Pagden, *Spanish Imperialism and the Political Imagination* (New Haven and London, 1990); J. H. Parry *The Age of Reconnaissance* (London, 1963), ch. 19.

[2] Speech on 28 May 1794, quoted in P. J. Marshall, *Problems of Empire: Britain and India 1757–1813* (London, 1968), p. 177. For fuller records of Burke's very influential speeches on the morality of empire in India, see P. J. Marshall (ed.), *The Writings and Speeches of Edmund Burke*, vol. 5: *Madras and Bengal, 1774–85* (Oxford, 1981).

[3] See, in particular, G. T. F. Raynal, *A Philosophical and Political History of the Settlements and Trade of the Europeans in the East and West Indies* (London, 1798).

in the 1920s by writers such as André Gide and leading to such publicists of the case for indigenous rights and independence after 1945 as
(Lord) Fenner Brockway and Basil Davidson. In short, there has never
been a period when some Europeans did not challenge the character of
domination over other societies on broadly ethical grounds.

Except inferentially, however, such critics were seldom, until the
mid-twentieth century, overtly hostile to the fact of European domination and colonial rule. Nor were they much concerned with the
nature of the economic systems imposed by the imperial powers
on the Third World, unless these could (as in the case of slavery or
the *encomienda* system in Spanish America) be shown to be contrary
to moral principles. Thus criticism of the international economic
system developed by Europe followed different paths. Chronologic-
ally it divides into two, before and after the rundown of the old
'mercantilist' system.

The liberal economists

The earliest and strongest critics of the economics of empire were the
classical economists, led by Adam Smith and ending with J. S. Mill in
the mid-nineteenth century. Their target, as was seen in chapter 1, was
not international trade and investment, which they regarded as wholly
desirable for all parties, but any form of artificial manipulation of these
things. By the 1850s their victory was won in Britain, though it took
time for all European states to follow the British example, and for some
this lasted only for a couple of decades.

The real genesis of modern pessimism concerning international trade
and integration starts from that point, and took the form of reaction to
the effects of an open market. Apart from the theories put forward by
Karl Marx and early Marxists, probably the first considered critique of
the integration of the world market came from India. This began in the
1890s and was first publicized by the Parsi businessman and founder of
the Indian National Congress, Dadabhai Naoroji, and by the Bengali
R. C. Dutt, an early Indian member of the elite Indian Civil Service,
who resigned his post to attack British policies.[4] These writers, and others
who followed them, made two basic assertions about the economic
effects of British rule in India, and at the same time about the causes

---

[4] See D. Naoroji, *Poverty and Un-British Rule* (London, 1901); R. C. Dutt,
The Economic History of India in the Victorian Age (London, 1906). For a general
account of the rise of the Indian critique of free trade as it affected India, see
B. Chandra, *The Rise and Growth of Economic Nationalism in India* (New Delhi,
1966). See also M. Kidron, *Foreign Investments in India* (London, 1965); A. K.
Bagchi, *Private Investment in India 1900–1939* (Cambridge, 1972).

of continuing Indian poverty. First, free trade had largely destroyed much of Indian industry, particularly that in cotton textiles, resulting in the 'de-industrialization' of the country for the benefit of British manufacturers and traders. Moreover, the development of modern industry in India was blocked by rigorous free trade, which provided no protection for infant industries. Secondly, and unconnected, there was a 'drain' of real resources from India to Britain as a result of obligatory payments by India for British military expenses, salaries of British officials, and interest due on British loans and investments in India. The combined effect was to condemn India to perpetual poverty as a nation forced to remain a primary producing country that was bled of the surplus which might have provided investment for modernization.

These assertions were to be taken up by many of the theorists on the Left who will be considered below. But, while Indians were developing these arguments against an international free-trade economy and imperial rule, others were mounting a parallel attack on the effects of what was coming to be called 'economic imperialism' on the metropolitan countries and the Third World alike. This new critique developed mainly in Britain during the 1880s and 1890s and was a liberal reaction to the recent surge in British colonial expansion and its attendant costs and wars. Its most famous exponent was J. A. Hobson, whose *Imperialism: A Study* was first published in London in 1902.[5] He denied that the empire was an economic benefit to Britain as a whole. He was less concerned with its strictly economic effects on the colonies, but wrote at length about the disastrous social and moral consequences of alien rule in Africa and Asia. A very similar line was adopted by Leonard Woolf (husband of Virginia) in a book written for the Labour Party in 1920, *Empire and Commerce in Africa*.[6]

There were, therefore, well-established intellectual and moral traditions that, from different standpoints, challenged the assumption that an integrated world economy and European domination were necessarily or historically beneficial for non-Europeans. What was lacking in any of these ideas or movements was a positive economic alternative to free

[5] There is a very large literature on Hobson and his associates. See, in particular: P. Clarke, *Liberals and Social Democrats* (cambridge, 1978); N. Etheringon, *Theories of Imperialism* (London, 1984); D. K. Fieldhouse, '"Imperialism": An Historiographical Revision', *Economic History Review*, 2nd ser. 14 (1961), pp. 187–209; J. Pheby, *J. A. Hobson after Fifty Years: Freethinker of the Social Science* (London, 1994); B. Porter, *Critics of Empire* (London, 1968); E. Stokes, 'Late Nineteenth Century Colonial Expansion and the Attack on the Theory of Economic Imperialism: A Case of Mistaken Identity?', *Historical Journal*, 12 (1969), pp. 285–301.
[6] L. Woolf, *Empire and Commerce in Africa: A Study in Economic Imperialism* (London, 1920; 2nd edn, London, 1968).

trade or an imperial economy of the sort practised by the French as a route to development. Thus it was the function of the mostly liberal development economists of the mid-twentieth century to lead on from these unsophisticated foundations and establish a new 'scientific' critique of poverty in the Third World and the way to escape from it.

2   Development Economics and its Background

The starting point of the school of thought, commonly known as development economics, that evolved from the 1940s and reached its peak in the 1950s and early 1960s was the evident fact of the intense poverty of much of the non-European world. The obvious question was why this was so: why there was so great and apparently widening a gap between the poor and rich countries; in particular, why, after a long period of close contact with the richer West, the principle of comparative advantage appeared not to be working. Development economics set out to explain this gap and to evolve strategies to close it. Its practitioners can, therefore, be described as part pessimistic, part optimistic.

There were probably two main reasons for the character of this form of economics specifically related to the Third World as it evolved after about 1945. The first was the experience of the international recessions between 1920 and 1939. Until 1914 it had been generally assumed that the integration of LDCs into the international economy, under either free trade or protectionist conditions, had greatly increased their welfare and that this improvement would continue indefinitely. The First World War severely shook the international trading system on which these beliefs were based: the recession of the early 1920s, and still more the slump of the early 1930s, seemed to demonstrate that this beneficial process had ended – if, indeed, it had ever existed. The contraction of international demand for Third World commodities led to a serious deterioration in Third World terms of trade: an African or Asian farmer now had to produce and export considerably more than before 1914 to buy the same quantity of imported goods. The Second World War merely intensified these problems. By the early 1940s few remained confident that a return to the open market would be sufficient to restart the process of growth and development. Something more positive was needed, more particularly as many in Europe predicted (falsely as it emerged) that there would be another major depression once the immediate post-war boom was over.

The second and more problematic root of the new development economics was what may broadly be called Keynesian economics. Keynes's main work was not specifically concerned with problems of LDC development: his concern was with employment in developed countries. But his work, particularly the *General Theory of Employment, Interest and Money*, published in 1936, suggested among other things a much more positive governmental role in economic life than the classical economists had wanted or than most western governments before the 1930s had adopted. Moreover, it suggested as a general principle that public investment might be necessary, even through deficit financing, to overcome a low-level equilibrium or liquidity trap.

These ideas became building blocks of the new development economics. So also did two other concepts evolved in the 1930s or 1940s. First, the multiplier effect of investment, originated by R. F. Kahn at Cambridge in 1931 and taken up and developed by Keynes and others: broadly, investment has a greater effect on income and employment than the actual sum invested. Secondly, the so-called Harrod–Domar principle, originally published in 1939 by Sir Roy Harrod at Oxford and added to by the American economist Evsey Domar, which set out the conditions under which additions to productive capacity, generated by new investment, would be absorbed by the additional income generated by the same investment.

The wider significance of these new economic concepts was that they stimulated the idea that governments should have an active role to play in economic processes and that, by means of intelligent planning, any economy could escape from low levels of investment, income and production.

There were two other major stimuli after 1945 for the evolution of development economics and for the planning that became an integral part of it. First, as is described in chapters 3 and 8, the colonial powers and other states, such as the United States, were now ready to make substantial financial contributions to the welfare of the Third World, particularly those parts that were still colonies. There was, therefore, money available for development.

Secondly, economists, and also the nationalists of the Third World, had a model of a totally planned economy to see and admire: the USSR. The USSR was then seen as a country that had pulled itself up from being near-feudal to being a major industrial society in some two decades, and this had enabled it to withstand the assault by Germany in and after 1941. Moreover, many later Third World leaders, such as Nehru, along with western intellectuals such as Beatrice and Sidney Webb and Bernard Shaw, had visited the USSR before 1939 and had been deeply impressed.

These were the starting points of the new development economics of the post-1945 period. In practice it grew in response to demand by reformist late-colonial governments, their successors as indigenous rulers, and the international aid-giving community to be given specific principles on which investment could be based. Briefly, the economists' response was as follows.[7]

Their first concern was to identify why the LDCs of the Third World remained so poor. Among the reasons offered in the 1950s were the following.

1 Development requires investment. The inducement to invest is limited by the size of a market, and savings (as Keynes had argued) were determined by per capita incomes. So a poor small country had both small investment resources and limited demand for investment, leading to a vicious circle of poverty.[8]

2 Such societies were caught in what Leibenstein called 'a low level equilibrium trap'.[9] If average incomes increased because of some fortunate circumstance, the result would be population increase rather than sustained growth through increased savings, and the old condition would recur.

3 Gunnar Myrdal[10] and others rejected the doctrine of comparative costs for modern LDCs. Market forces would tend cumulatively to accentuate international inequalities. Singer had already (in 1949[11]) argued that since 1870 there had been a secular deterioration in the terms of trade of LDCs, and this (though heavily criticized) became a basis for much of the later thinking about commodity exporting. Singer suggested that such exports were a poor basis for development because the commodity markets were too volatile, and also that specialization in commodities resulted in excessive inflexibility in LDC economies. A decade later (in 1959) Nurkse added other explanations.[12] The income elasticity of demand for commodities was lower than for manufactures. The more-developed countries (MDCs) were substituting synthetics for commodities. MDCs adopted protectionism

---

[7]   The best critical outline account of the evolution of development economics in this period is I. M. D. Little, *Economic Development: Theory, Policy, and International Relations* (New York, 1982). See also the shorter account in T. Killick, *Development Economics in Action: A Study of Economics Policies in Ghana* (London, 1978), ch. 2.

[8]   See, in particular, R. Nurkse, *Problems of Capital Formation in Underdeveloped Countries* (Oxford, 1953).

[9]   H. Leibenstein, *Economic Backwardness and Economic Growth* (New York, 1957).

[10]   G. Myrdal, *Economic Theory and Underdeveloped Regions* ((London, 1957).

[11]   Published as H. Singer, 'The Distribution of Gains between Investing and Borrowing Countries', *American Economic Review*, Papers and Proceedings, 40 (1950), pp. 473–85.

[12]   R. Nurkse, *Patterns of Trade and Development* (Wicksell Lectures; Stockholm, 1959), reproduced in Nurkse, *Equilibrium and Growth in the World Economy* (Cambridge, Mass., 1961).

against both commodities and manufactures that competed with domestic products.

4 Walt Rostow saw limited technical innovation as a key obstacle to growth.[13] This imposed a ceiling on 'attainable output per head' and therefore to capital accumulation and investment.

For these and similar reasons the classical theory of development and the concept of comparative costs stood condemned. They might have worked once, for the now-developed and industrial countries, but times had changed. That way was now closed. Hence the profound retrospective pessimism of most (though by no means all) the economists of this generation.[14]

It is not central to the present argument what the development economists proposed to put in place of the discredited classical prescription; but a brief summary of the typical proposals of the 1950s serves to highlight the reasons for both their rejection of classical prescriptions and their optimism about a future based on new principles.

Their primary concern was to break through the perceived inertia of the past. To do this seemed to require destruction of the apparent obstacles to growth and development. These were seen as 'structural' — that is, inherent in the nature of these societies as then constructed. Ian Little has written that 'there is no such thing as a structuralist theory of growth: it may be called into play to explain why other theories do not work very well, but it primarily seeks to provide a reason for managing change by administrative action'.[15] Administration was, indeed, the key to the new approach. Its central feature was the need to plan rather than trust to economic forces and the price mechanism, because the market could not provide adequate information on the long-term consequences of investment decisions. The object was the obverse of comparative advantage through commodity production and export. LDCs must industrialize, whatever their cost disadvantage, and almost everything else followed from that.

But why industrialize? At one level the answer was simple: all the richest societies were then industrialized, so that this was clearly the key to affluence. But more sophisticated arguments were produced to show why it was essential in LDCs.

The most influential theoretical argument derived first from P. N. Rosenstein Rodan[16] and later from A. Hirschman.[17] The first

---

[13] W. Rostow, *The Stages of Economic Growth* (Cambridge, 1960).
[14] Nonconformists include (Lord) Peter Bauer and Prof. S. H. Frankel.
[15] Little, *Economic Development*, p. 21.
[16] P. N. Rosenstein Rodan, 'Problems of Industrialization of Eastern and South-Eastern Europe', *Economic Journal*, 53 (1943), pp. 202–210.
[17] A. Hirschman, *The Strategy of Economic Development* (New Haven, 1958).

suggested that, while individual industries in an LDC might make little impact on poverty, many industries would have a multiplier effect. What was needed, Rosenstein Rodan later added, was a big push to bring in the capital that would provide the infrastructure for such industrial development.[18] To this Hirschman added the concept of linkages. By means of state planning, industries could produce backward and forward linkages, thus stimulating both upstream production of raw material and intermediate inputs, and downstream further production, transport, trading, etc. In this way an underdeveloped economy could break through the bonds of the low-level equilibrium trap and achieve what Rostow later described as a take-off into sustained growth.

But the creation of such a virtuous industrial spiral required specific conditions. Three things in particular would be necessary.

First it required capital. This could be generated by taking part of the surplus of the agricultural sector which might otherwise be used by producers to buy imported goods. Alternatively it could be acquired by increased taxation. The second option was clearly difficult in most LDCs because of administrative limitations. But, as it happened, in anglophone Africa at least, a means already existed of taxing peasants who could not be taxed directly – the marketing board to which they had to sell their produce at prices fixed by the state. In the 1950s and 1960s most development economists regarded this as a legitimate and harmless way of doing things. Beyond that, in the first place at least, the LDC could borrow abroad or look for grants from the affluent West.

Secondly, industries needed labour. The general assumption was that most LDCs had considerable underemployment on the land, what (Sir) Arthur Lewis described in his very influential paper 'Economic Development with Unlimited Supplies of Labour'.[19] The argument was that 'at the prevailing wage, more labour can be taken on in modern sectors of the economy without raising the wage, and without loss of output in the traditional sectors'.[20] Although there was little empirical evidence for this, it remained a basic assumption of most development economics. Moreover the considerable and accelerating drift from country to town in many LDCs in this period suggested that ample labour for industry was available: indeed, the need to provide work for these migrants was a significant political factor in the adoption of industrializing strategies.

Finally, however, it was necessary to provide a market for the products of the new industries; and the problem was that many societies provided

[18] In H. S. Ellis (ed.), *Economic Development for Latin America* (London, 1961), quoted in Little, *Economic Development*, p. 38.
[19] Sir W. A. Lewis, 'Economic Development with Unlimited Supplies of Labour', *Manchester School* (May, 1954).
[20] Little, *Economic Development*, p. 87.

too small a market for large-scale modern industrial enterprises. In the classical model the solution was to export the surplus. But in the mid-twentieth century it was accepted that many of the proposed new industries of the LDCs would not be able to compete in the international market. Therefore, it was necessary to create closed markets, cutting these countries off as far as possible from the international economy. The means would be protectionism, through either tariffs or physical controls on imports. This strategy was in any case in line with the then dominant argument concerning the secular deterioration in the terms of trade, used to denigrate export-oriented economic activities. This, as was seen above, was being publicized by Singer and R. Prebisch of the Economic Commission for Latin America (ECLA) and taken up, among others, by the very influential Gunnar Myrdal, who saw import controls as a necessary complement to the cost of importing essential goods for industry: 'import restrictions in underdeveloped countries are primarily necessitated by the effects on the foreign exchange balance of the increased demand for imported goods. This, in turn, is the direct or indirect result of the increased investment implied by an economic development policy.'[21]

Thus, seen in the round, the development economists of the post-1945 period, and down to the later 1960s, rejected all traditional formulas for economic development in the Third World on the grounds that what had once worked for the West had clearly not worked elsewhere and now could never work. In their place they constructed a complex structure of ideas which ultimately boiled down to the proposition that such development depended on a highly artificial system whose basic feature was planning within a partially closed national economy rather than within the world economic system. The economic rationality of these ideas cannot be discussed here;[22] The economic outcome of their application will be considered in part 4 of this book.

3   Marx and the Neo-Marxists

There is a fundamental ambivalence about the attitude of Karl Marx, along with his colleague and posthumous editor, Friedrich Engels, and still more about that of the many subsequent writers who regarded themselves as 'Marxists', to the character of the relationship between the West and the Third World. As will be seen, in one sense all were and are pessimists in the sense that they deplore many aspects of the impact of the

[21] G. Myrdal, *Development and Underdevelopment* (Cairo, 1956), p. 275, quoted in Little, *Economic Development*, p. 72
[22] See Little, *Economic Development*, for a continuous and very critical assessment of these economic ideas.

core on the periphery. On the other hand, Marx himself and some of his followers saw the impact of the West, which he regarded as synonymous with capitalism, as not only inevitable but ultimately a necessary and beneficial stage on the path to a better socialist future. In this account Marx will be considered separately from later Marxists on the assumption (following Bill Warren) that the later Marxist theories of imperialism were based on a false interpretation of Marx's basic teaching.[23]

Marx and the Third World

Marx never published an explicit theory about imperialism (a word he did not use) or the relations between the West (which for him meant primarily Britain) and the less-developed world. The reason was, presumably, that such a theory was not necessary for his general analysis of the origins and nature of capitalism. Its genesis could be accounted for satisfactorily within the confines of Britain or Europe and its evolution was mainly autonomous: it was potentially a closed economic and social system. Nevertheless, there is a sufficient amount of information available on his attitude in a variety of his publications to pinpoint the dualism of his views.[24]

First, there was Marx the humanist and humanitarian, and this Marx was profoundly pessimistic about the western impact. Historically he saw the role of Europeans in America, Asia and Africa as destructive and despoiling. Marx regarded the initial conquest of peripheral countries as a contribution, though a minor one, to the initial breakthrough of Britain from feudalism to primitive accumulation, which in turn would lead on to modern industry.

> The discovery of gold and silver in America, the extirpation, enslavement and entombment in mines of the aboriginal population, the beginning

---

[23] B. Warren, *Imperialism: Pioneer of Capitalism*, ed. J. Sender (London, 1980). Other useful accounts of Marx's approach to West–Third World relations include: A. Balinsky, *Marx's Economics: Origin and Development* (Lexington, Mass., 1970); A. Brewer, *Marxist Theories of Imperialism: A Critical Survey* (London, 1980).
[24] Some of the best-known statements of his position were contained in articles he wrote for the *New York Daily Tribune* in 1853. There is also his argument concerning 'The Law of the Falling Tendency of the Rate of Profit and its Counteracting Causes'. In addition to 'Foreign Trade', Marx included 'Raising the Intensity of Exploitation', 'Depression of Wages below their Value', Cheapening the Elements of Constant capital' and 'Relative Overpopulation', as factors counteracting the tendency of the rate of profit to decline. See *Capital*, ed. F. Engels, (1894; Eng. edn, Chicago, 1909), vol. 3, pp. 272–280. In addition to *Capital* there are several collections of relevant writing by Marx, notably: S. Avinieri (ed.), *Karl Marx on Colonialism and Modernisation* (Moscow, 1971): K. Marx and F. Engels, *On Colonialism* (Moscow, n.d.).

of the conquest and looting of the East Indies, the turning of Africa into a warren for the commercial hunting of blackskins, signalised the rosy dawn of the era of capitalist production. These idyllic proceedings are the chief moments of primitive accumulation.[25]

And again, when describing the effects of free imports of British machine-made cottons on the Indian spinners and weavers of muslins, he wrote:

India, the great workshop of cotton manufacture for the world since immemorial times, became now inundated with English twists and cotton stuffs. After its own produce had been excluded from England, or only admitted on the most cruel terms, British manufactures were poured into it at a small and merely nominal duty, to the ruin of the native cotton fabric once so celebrated.[26]

This destructive process was, moreover, part of a wider trend by which the industrialized West was forcing the rest of the world into its economic orbit. Basically, Europe now saw the periphery as a market for its manufactures and as a source of raw materials for its industries.

Importing raw materials from the periphery had a further advantage for Britain and other industrialized countries. In an apparently throw-away passage in the third volume of *Capital* Marx put forward an idea that was to play a large role in late-twentieth-century left-wing thinking. On the basis of Ricardo's labour theory of value, he suggested that an 'advanced country' could obtain a profit by selling its goods to an LDC because machine-made goods contained a smaller labour value than those of a pre-capitalist society. This was later to be called 'unequal exchange' and to imply that advanced countries were exploiting the less advanced through the medium of trade. Yet Marx immediately pointed out that the bargain was not entirely one-sided. Indeed, he apparently accepted the principle of comparative advantage and made international trade equivalent with any capitalist transaction.

This [less-advanced] country may offer more materialized labour in goods than it receives, and yet it may receive in return commodities cheaper than it could produce them. In the same way a manufacturer, who exploits a new invention before it has become general, undersells his competitors and yet sells his commodities above their individual values, that is to say,

[25] K. Marx, *Capital*, (1867; Eng. edn., Moscow, 1954), vol. 1, ch. 32, p. 751. Marx briefly defined primitive accumulation as follows: 'We know that the means of production and subsistence, while they remain the property of the immediate producer, are not capital. They become capital only under circumstances in which they serve at the same time as means of exploitation and subjection of the labourer' (*Capital*, vol. 1, ch. 33, p. 767, quoted in Brewer, *Marxist Theories*, p. 43).
[26] Marx and Engels, *On Colonialism*, p. 52.

he exploits the specifically higher productive power of the labour employed by him as surplus-value. By this means he secures a surplus-profit.[27]

One could, therefore, sum up this side of Marx's thinking on the economic and social consequences of international integration and colonialism as initial pillage followed by methodical destruction of indigenous manufacture through imposed free trade, and finally exploitation of cheap labour in the process of exchanging raw materials for manufactures. If that was all, Marx would have to be seen as an unqualified pessimist.

But there was a totally different side to Marx's thinking. What differentiated him from most later Marxists, humanitarians and Third World nationalists was that he never sentimentalized or enthused over the non-European and pre-capitalist societies and their methods of production which capitalism casually destroyed in its onward march. Much of his comment related specifically to Asia, and above all to India, on whose recent history he had apparently read virtually all that was then available in Britain. From this emerged his concept of the 'Asian mode of production', which was characteristic of 'Oriental despotisms', and which were incapable of evolving by themselves into capitalist societies. Thus:

> Now, sickening as it must be to human feeling to witness these myriads of industrious patriarchal and inoffensive social organizations disorganized and dissolved into their units, thrown into a sea of woes, and their individual members losing at the same time their ancient form of civilization and their hereditary means of subsistence, we must not forget that these idyllic village communities, inoffensive though they may appear, had always been the solid foundation of Oriental despotism, that they restrained the human mind within the smallest possible compass, making it the unresisting tool of superstition, enslaving it beneath traditional rules, depriving it of all grandeur and historical energies.... We must not forget that this undignified, stagnatory and vegetative life, that this passive sort of existence, evoked on the other part, in contradistinction, wild, aimless, unfounded forces of destruction, and rendered murder itself a religious rite in Hindostan. We must not forget that these little communities were contaminated by distinctions of caste and by slavery, that they subjugated man to be the sovereign of circumstances, that they transformed a self-developing state into never changing natural destiny, and thus brought about a brutalizing worship of nature, exhibiting its degradation in the fact that man, the sovereign of nature, fell down on his knees in adoration of Hanuman the monkey and Sabbala the cow.
>
> England, it is true, in causing a social revolution in Hindostan, was actuated only by the vilest interests, and was stupid in her manner of enforcing them. But that is not the question. The question is, can mankind fulfil its destiny without a fundamental revolution in the social state of Asia? If not, whatever may have been the crimes of England, she was the unconscious tool of history in bringing about the revolution.[28]

---

[27] Marx, *Capital*, ed. Engels (Eng. edn, Chicago, 1909), vol. 3, p. 279.

Little of this description of Hindu society would be acceptable to modern historians. The point, however, is that, much as he hated capitalism, Marx saw it as a necessary agency for creating what we now call development in India and, by inference, most parts of the Third World. In the West the historic function of capitalism was to create a society which was both technically advanced and socially divided between capitalists and workers. so that in course of time a proletarian revolution would overthrow capitalism and give birth to socialism. Only capitalism could do this: there was no short cut to socialism.

The same was true of the rest of the world. Wealth and civilization could come only through the advance of capitalism, even though this caused immediate misery. India offered the only example of this process in action. Marx described it thus in the most famous of his dispatches to the *New York Daily Tribune* of 8 August 1853.

England has to fulfil a double mission in India: one destructive, the other regenerating – the annihilation of old Asiatic society, and the laying of the material foundations of Western society in Asia. . . .

The political unity of India, more consolidated, and extending further than it ever did under the Great Moguls, was the first condition of its regeneration. That unity, imposed by the British sword, will now be strengthened and perpetuated by the electric telegraph. . . . The free press, introduced for the first time into Asiatic society, and managed principally by the common offspring of Hindoos and Europeans, is a new and powerful agent of reconstruction. . . . From the Indian natives, reluctantly and sparingly educated at Calcutta, under English superintendence, a fresh class is springing up, endowed with the requirements for government and imbued with European science. Steam has brought India into regular and graphic communication with Europe, has connected its chief ports with those of the whole south-eastern ocean, and has rev-indicated it from the isolated position which was the prime law of its stagnation. . . .

The ruling classes of Great Britain have had, till now, but an accidental, transitory and exceptional interest in the progress of India. The aristocracy wanted to conquer it, the moneyocracy to plunder it, and the millocracy to undersell it. But now the tables are turned. The millocracy have discovered that the transformation of India into a reproductive country has a vital importance to them, and that, to that end, it is necessary, above all, to gift her with means of irrigation and of internal communication. They intend now drawing a set of railroads over India. And they will do it. . . .

I know that the English millocracy intend to endow India with railways with the exclusive view of extracting at diminished expenses the cotton

---

[28] Marx, 'The British Role in Indian', *New York Daily Tribune*, 25 June 1853, quoted in Warren, *Imperialism*, pp. 40–1, from Avinieri (ed.), *Karl Marx on Colonialism*, pp. 93–4.

and other raw materials for their manufacturers. But when you have introduced machinery into the locomotion of a country, which possesses iron and coal, you are unable to withhold it from its fabrication. You cannot maintain a net of railways over an immense country without introducing all those industrial processes necessary to meet the immediate and current wants of railway locomotion, and out of which there must grow the application of machinery to those branches of industry not immediately connected with railways. The railway system will therefore become, in India, truly the forerunner of modern industry.

Modern industry, resulting from the railway system, will dissolve the hereditary divisions of labour, upon which rests the Indian castes, those decisive impediments to Indian progress and Indian power.

The Indians will not reap the fruits of the new elements of society scattered among them by the British bourgeoisie till in Great Britain itself the now ruling classes shall have been supplanted by the industrial proletariat, or till the Hindoos themselves shall have grown strong enough to throw off the English yoke altogether. At all events, we may safely expect to see, at a more or less remote period, the regeneration of that great and interesting country.[29]

Marx, of course, was a notoriously poor prophet. On India he was wrong on some aspects of this prediction, at least concerning its timing. It was long before what would now be called the backward linkages of the railway system generated a basic iron and steel industry or advanced secondary industries other than textiles. Nor did communications or other aspects of modernization ever destroy Indian castes or social divisions. It is also arguable that India began to enjoy some of the fruits of modernization long before it became politically independent, and certainly before Britain experienced a proletarian revolution. Yet the message of these and other comparable writings is clear. Marx was only a partial pessimist concerning the impact of the West on the Third World. He believed that colonialism and the injection of Western habits of mind and technology were the only way in which pre-capitalist peoples could move from what he regarded as their static and deplorable condition to progressive capitalism and ultimately to technically advanced socialism.

It is important to emphasize this because it has commonly, and for obvious reasons, been underemphasized or ignored both by most later writers in the socialist tradition, whom we may broadly label neo-Marxists, and by nationalists in the Third World. The former treated imperialism as purely exploitative and destructive. The latter have often argued that countries such as India might, and probably could, have carried out

[29] Marx, 'The Future Results of British Rule in India', *New York Daily Tribune*, 8 Aug. 1853, quoted in Warren, *Imperialism*, pp. 41–4, from Avinieri (ed.), *Karl Marx on Colonialism*, pp. 132–7.

their own industrial and social development without European intrusion by building on their own unreconstructed craft industries. This is why Marx, arguably the clearest thinker of them all, must be considered in a class of his own and only a qualified pessimist concerning the impact of the core on the periphery.

The Neo-Marxists

The modern socialist view of imperialism, colonialism and the broader impact of the core on the periphery owes little to Marx himself. Rather it derives from the writing of would-be disciples a generation or more after his death in 1883, and is based on a number of assumptions which are either absent from or at variance with his own arguments. In particular, most of these writers based their analysis on a factor that Marx ignored: the necessity for the West to export 'surplus' capital to the Third World and its impact on these societies. This section will provide a short account of the evolution of this argument from the first decade of the twentieth century to the 1940s, after which it lost much of its force and was overtaken by other interpretations of Third World poverty.

Before 1914 a major stimulus for the production of new socialist ideas on the character of imperialism and its possible cure was the Second International, founded in 1889. Until 1914, and again after the First World War, this collection of national socialist groups and parties provided a forum for debate over the 'correct' interpretation of Marx's doctrines and their application to the specific problems of the period. Among these was the fact of overseas empire. Out of the often bitter controversy that this question generated emerged what were to become the classic texts of modern socialist theory, most written or published in the six years between 1910 and 1916. Here it is proposed to consider only those parts of the argument that relate specifically to the problem of the economic and social impact of the West on the Third World, and mainly arguments put forward by the four most influential Marxist theorists of the period: Rosa Luxemburg, Rudolph Hilferding, N. I. Bukharin and V. I. Lenin. Although Luxemburg's *The Accumulation of Capital* was published in 1913, three years after Hilferding's *Finance Capital*, it is taken first because it stands apart from the other three in important respects.[30]

Rosa Luxemburg and the imperialism of trade   Luxemburg's primary purpose in this book was to correct what she saw as a fault or gap in Marx's

---

[30] Luxemburg replied to criticisms of her original arguments in her *Anti-Critique*, written in 1915 but not published until 1921.

theory of capitalist reproduction. Briefly, she could see no way that the capitalist could sell all of that part of industrial production that accrued to him as surplus value (profit), since the worker could not afford to buy all he produced, and capitalists as a class did not want to do so, either for reinvestment or for their personal consumption. Her conclusion was that this surplus had to be sold to 'such social organizations or strata whose own mode of production is not capitalistic'.[31]

This argument has been severely criticized, then and later,[32] but that is not important here. What matters are the deductions Luxemburg drew from it on relations between the West and the Third World. Essentially she argued that this surplus had to be sold either to peasants, in the form of consumer goods, or to governments, in the form of capital goods (such as railways), in each case outside the world of modern capitalism. Either way, the effect would be to draw these places into the orbit of western capitalism. In order to pay for consumer goods or pay interest on loans for railways, etc., the LDC would have to produce and export commodities that the capitalist world needed. Thus an Indian peasant might grow and export raw cotton in exchange for Lancashire cotton goods. Indeed, capitalism depended heavily on such raw materials and foodstuffs, because, as both the classical economists and Marx had recognized, cheap non-capitalist imports reduced the cost of constant capital (the means of production) and kept down variable capital (wages), so maximizing the profits of the capitalist. Thus capitalism depended heavily on its relations with pre-capitalist societies, a process often now described as 'articulation'.

So far this is not very different from the concept of comparative costs, at least so far as the capitalist society was concerned. But Luxemburg's Marxist assumptions turned that theory on its head so far as the non-capitalist world was concerned. Briefly, because access to the markets and raw materials of the Third World was so crucial to the West, and because there was a finite supply of these assets, competition between the capitalist societies had evolved into imperialism. Thus:

> Imperialism is the political expression of the accumulation of capital in its competitive struggle for what remains still open of the non-capitalist environment. Still the largest part of the world in terms of geography, this remaining field for the expansion of capital is yet insignificant as against the high level of development already attained by the productive forces of capital. . . . On the international stage, then, capital must take appropriate measures.[33]

[31] R. Luxemburg, *The Accumulation of Capital* (1913; Eng. edn, London, 1951), p. 352; hereafter *AC*.
[32] e.g. by Brewer, *Marxist Theories*, pp. 63–9.
[33] *AC*, p. 446.

This explained the imperialism of the forty or so years before the First World War: it was a scramble for exploitable non-capitalist territories. It is significant that for Luxemburg it is the need to export goods and import raw materials, rather than the need to export capital, that is the driving force behind imperialism; and this was to mark her off decisively from the other Marxists of this period. But from the present point of view the really interesting thing is her analysis of the effects of this process of commercial expansion and consequential territorial annexation on the societies of the Third World. Did she see the impact of western capitalism as progressive, as Marx had done, or as merely immiserating?

The answer stems largely from her lack of interest in capital investment, which, for Marx, was the means by which the West would transform India. Because there was little capital investment, the impact of western power was largely negative and destructive: there would be no colonial industrial revolution. At the same time, the very act of incorporating the non-capitalist peoples of what she called 'natural economies' – in her thinking, peasants – into the capitalist system was bound to change their character. Essentially they would gradually cease to be non-capitalists and become proletarians. But the process would be uneven and prolonged. Thus:

> Capitalism needs other races to exploit territories where the white man cannot work. It must be able to mobilize world labour power without restriction in order to utilize all productive forces of the globe – up to the limits imposed by a system of producing surplus value. This labour power, however, is in most cases rigidly bound by the traditional pre-capitalist organization of production. It must first be 'set free' in order to be enrolled in the active army of capital. The emancipation of labour power from primitive social conditions and its absorption by the capitalist wage system is one of the indispensable historical bases of capitalism. . . . Obtaining the necessary labour power from non-capitalist societies, the so-called 'labour problem', is ever more important for capital in the colonies. All possible methods of 'gentle compulsion' are applied to solving this problem, to transfer labour from former social systems to the command of capital. This endeavour leads to the most peculiar combinations between the modern wage system and primitive authority in the colonial countries. This is a concrete example of the fact that capitalist production cannot manage without labour power from other social organizations.[34]

The general thrust of this argument is that the aim of capitalism, using colonial rule as its agent, was to separate the peasant from his land (by whatever means) and to force him to become a wage labourer, presumably on plantations, in mines, or in factories. The effect was

[34] Ibid., pp. 362–4.

clearly immiseration of the non-European workers as they lost their independence as peasants. There is no hint here of Marx's belief that capitalism improves living standards. Indeed Luxemburg wrote that 'The more ruthlessly capital sets about the destruction of non-capitalist strata at home and in the outside world, the more it lowers the standard of living for the workers as a whole . . .'. In short, she is a profound pessimist. The effect of capitalist penetration, at least in the short term, was the creation of what would now be called an agro-proletariat in the Third World, worse off than it had been previously, with no prospect that capitalism would create an industrial society capable of providing benefits or generating the socio-economic process that might eventually lead to a proletarian revolution. As to the ultimate result, she was ambivalent. The logic of her economic argument was that western capitalism must, eventually, lose its momentum because it would have destroyed the non-capitalist environment on which its accumulation depended. Yet, in line with current Marxist political correctness, she provided an alternative scenario. 'But even before this natural economic impasse of capital's own creating is properly reached it becomes a necessity for the international working class to revolt against the rule of capital.'[35]

The interest of Luxemburg for this study is that, however incorrect her analysis is by Marxist criteria, she proved a far more accurate predictor of the effect of the western impact on the periphery than other neo-Marxists who dominated later thinking. Since she could see no benefits from the creation of a single world economy until an eventual proletarian revolution, she stands as a precursor of much later but equally pessimistic commentators, notably the 'dependency' theorists of the mid-twentieth century. Her influence can also be seen clearly in chapter 6, on modern analysis of the impact of colonialism and capitalism on colonial Africa.

The classical Marxist writers: Hilferding, Bukharin and Lenin   The common denominator of these three Marxist theorists of the pre-1916 world was their emphasis on the importance of capital investment by the capitalist core in the periphery. In this they followed Marx. Where they differed from him was that they regarded this investment as essential for the capitalist economies, whereas he had not; in the explanations they gave for such investment; and, finally, in their estimate of its impact on the rest of the world.

Their common and basic principle was that the West had capital that it found necessary to invest overseas. Imperialism was primarily the product of the need for territories in which to make this investment, safely and profitably. There was no hint of this need in Marx. The argument

[35] Ibid., pp. 466–7.

stemmed mainly from Hilferding, a Viennese intellectual, and from his concepts of 'monopoly capitalism' and 'finance capital', which were then taken up by Bukharin and Lenin.

Briefly, Hilferding's argument was that since Marx's time the process of concentration of capitals had progressed very fast. Industrial enterprises had coagulated to secure monopoly prices by eliminating competition. To finance their expansion they had become close allies of the banks which, in Germany, Belgium and America (though not in Britain), made medium to long-term investments in industrial companies. The result was 'finance capital', a final concentration of money and industrial power in the same hands through the development of the joint-stock company, the 'combine'. By these means individual combines, or cartels of such combines, could control the domestic market of any state, and by their monopoly raise the prices they could charge. And, in order to make their monopoly secure, these enterprises had persuaded their states to erect high external tariffs that kept out foreign competition.

But one effect of such monopolistic pricing was that the workers, the final consumers, could no longer afford to buy as great a volume of goods as previously, since their wages did not rise with prices or in line with the profits of the big firms. These monopolies had, therefore, to find overseas markets. In the first instance they exported goods, if necessary at marginal cost, since they could make their main profit in the protected home market. Even if some of the foreign markets erected protectionist barriers, these monopolies could penetrate their defences by cutting prices. But in time international competition in overseas markets had grown more intense, and this was one reason why the advanced economies had taken to investing in them: by manufacturing inside these tariff walls they could obtain a higher rate of profit in the same way as in their home countries.

There were, however, other reasons for the accelerating export of capital since the 1870s. Hilferding did not accept the argument that such investment was made necessary by a tendency for the rate of profit to decline at home and did not talk of 'surplus' capital. What, then, was the connection between finance capital and capital export? Primarily that the very size of these monopoly enterprises and their integration with the world of finance made it relatively easy for them to raise money and move it round the world. But there were other attractions abroad. In LDCs shortage of capital meant that interest rates were higher, so that loans could obtain a better return. Above all, less-developed territories offered the attraction of low wages, ample land at low prices, and, therefore, the chance to produce goods, such as tropical raw materials, which were needed by the advanced countries.

Such investments could be and were made in any part of the world. But there were special benefits to be had from political control of places in which the investment was made, where this was possible. Annexation provided security for property, protection against foreign competition, and, where necessary, compulsion on the indigenous people to work in plantations, mines or factories. Hence the export of capital had intensified the division of the world between the great capitalist states, each determined to create what Hilferding called its 'national economic territory'. This was a primary explanation of the imperialism of the period.

Hilferding admitted that, at least in the short term, this process had beneficial economic and social effects in the developed countries, though it was also arousing intense and base nationalistic fervour in Europe which might (though Hilferding did not definitely predict this in 1910) result in international conflict and possibly the end of capitalism. But the effects of capital investment in the Third World were very different. Particularly when it was placed in the less-developed territories in order to increase production of raw materials, it would have much the same effects as Rosa Luxemburg predicted. That is, it would be destructive and brutal. 'These violent methods are of the essence of colonial policy, without which it would lose its capitalist rationale. They are just as much an integral part of it as the existence of a propertyless proletariat is a *conditio sine qua non* of capitalism in general.'[36]

So the general effects on the Third World were immiseration rather than progress. Yet there is also a gleam of hope, not economic but political, which echoes Marx.

> In the newly-opened countries themselves, however, the introduction of capitalism intensifies contradictions and arouses growing resistance to the invaders among the people, whose national consciousness has been awakened, which can easily take the form of policies inimical to foreign capital. The old age-old bondage to the soil of the 'nations without a history' is disrupted and they are swept into the capitalist maelstrom. Capitalism itself gradually provides the subjected peoples with the ways and means for their own liberation. They adopt as their own the ideal that was once the highest aspiration of the European nations; namely, the formation of a unified nation state as an instrument of economic and cultural freedom.[37]

Thus Hilferding stands somewhere between Marx and Luxemburg in his attitude to the impact of capitalist imperialism on the Third World: no real progress or amelioration in the short term, but the possibility of ultimate revolution through the creation of a potentially revolutionary proletariat.

[36] R. Hilferding, *Finance Capital* (1910; Eng. edn, London, 1981), p. 319.
[37] Ibid., p. 322.

Hilferding's work was comparatively little known at the time, but it provided the essential basis for the much more influential subsequent writings of Bukharin and Lenin. Both adopted his concepts of finance capital and the monopoly stage of capitalism. Both regarded the export of capital as the latest and most influential force determining the strategies of the advanced countries and the partition of the world. Both described imperialism as the necessary result of the process of monopoly in the West: it was not an optional strategy but an unavoidable expression of the nature of these societies. They had to export capital and therefore to control territories in which it was invested and which produced the essential raw materials the West needed. For Lenin in particular the need to export capital was explained in terms of Hobson's doctrine of under-consumption rather than in strictly Marxist terms. This process generated intense rivalries, first between the great international cartels and monopolies, then between the nation states in which the finance capitalists were based. To quote Lenin's own most abbreviated definition of imperialism:

> Imperialism is capitalism in that stage of development in which the dominance of monopolies and finance capital has established itself; in which the export of capital has acquired pronounced importance; in which the division of the world among the international trusts has begun; in which the division of all territories of the globe among the great capitalist powers has been completed.[38]

In fact, for Lenin, this meant the present. The end result was the war that was in progress when these authors wrote and which they confidently predicted would end in the destruction of capitalism and the victory of the proletariat.

Lenin's pamphlet, largely because of his political victory in Russia in 1917, became the textbook of the communist movement for the next thirty years. All socialists had to adopt his definition of imperialism. Unfortunately he seems not to have been very interested in the effects of imperialism on the Third World: from occasional phrases it must be assumed that he simply accepted the general immiseration argument of Hilferding, which would end only when imperialism and capitalism themselves ended. And this was the tradition that dominated socialist thinking down to at least the 1940s.

The Marxist tradition, 1917–1945

It is clear from this that the inheritance of the European left between the two world wars was a neo-Marxist doctrine that saw the impact of

---

[38] V. I. Lenin, *Imperialism: The Highest Stage of Capitalism* (1917; Eng. edn, Moscow, 1947), p. 109.

the West on the Third World in terms of economic and social exploit-ation. The West was there only for what it could get. It would promote industrialization in LDCs where this was profitable for monopoly capi-talists, and this implied some degree of development and the rise of local capitalisms, including the rise of an indigenous bourgeoisie. But the overwhelming power of western capitalism meant that there could be none of the beneficial effects for the Third World perceived by the classical economists, nor even the limited potential advantages described by Marx himself. Since this Marxist tradition ran side by side with the liberal and humanitarian tradition of Hobson, Woolf and others and was reinforced by the general anti-colonialism of the liberal intellectuals of the United States,[39] pessimism seemed to have triumphed in academic and liberal circles.

But it was a remarkably unfocused and uninformed pessimism. Just as few of the pre-1920 Marxists had any direct or expert knowledge of conditions in the Third World, so, between the wars, the later Marxist tradition fed on dogma rather than knowledge. Moreover, precisely because the Leninist doctrine had been adopted by the Third Interna-tional, the Comintern, and enforced by Stalin after Lenin's death, it was deemed unnecessary, perhaps improper, for the Left to work out new concepts. The only substantial innovation of the 1920s was, in fact, the adoption by the Sixth Congress of 1928 of the proposition that imperial-ism positively discouraged industrialization in colonies and that India in particular was therefore being kept in a state of underdevelopment. This was clearly contrary to the arguments of Marx, Hilferding and even Lenin in his *Imperialism*, and appears to have been adopted to serve current Soviet interests.[40] The effect was to stultify orthodox Marxist thinking for at least two decades: it was stuck with the proposition that monopoly capitalism was largely responsible for underdevelopment in the Third World and had no beneficial consequences.

This assumption was clearly reflected in *The Theory of Capitalist Development*, published in 1942 by the Harvard economist Paul Sweezy,[41] which became a textbook of orthodox Marxism. For the colonies and

---

[39] See e.g. the widely read book by P. T. Moon, *Imperialism and World Politics* (New York, 1926); Grover Clark, *The Balance Sheets of Imperialism* (New York, 1936).
[40] See Warren, *Imperialism*, pp. 84–107, for an analysis of the background to this decision. See also S. Howe, *Anticolonialism in British Politics: The Left and the End of Empire, 1918–1964* (Oxford, 1993), pp. 53–67, for an account of the contrary views of the Communist Party of Great Britain on this issue, particularly as expresssed in R. Palme Dutt, *Modern India* (London, 1927).
[41] P. Sweezy, *The Theory of Capitalist Development* (New York, 1942; 2nd edn. London, 1946).

Third World Sweezy adopted an uncompromising immiseration position. Taking India as his model, he made two main assertions. First, following the earlier Indian nationalists and R. C. Dutt, he argued that British industrial imports and the partial industrialization of India had destroyed Indian 'handicraft producers'. This caused 'a swelling of the ranks of the peasantry, increased pressure on the land, and a deterioration of the productivity and living standards of the agricultural masses': that is, what the 'de-industrialization' argument already stated. Secondly, and consequentially, 'the colonial economy stagnates, and living conditions for the great majority of the people tend to become worse rather than better. All classes of the colonial population, with the exception of the landlords and a few relatively small groups which are in effect agents of imperialist rule, are therefore thrown into the struggle for national independence.' His dogmatically correct prediction was that the Indian bourgeoisie would lead the struggle to independence in alliance with the 'colonial working class', but would later be unable to decide whether to break finally with its imperialist allies. So the working class, in alliance with 'the more advanced sections of the peasantry', would take the lead in forcing independence, and the colonial workers would then make common cause with the proletariat of the developed countries in promoting the world revolution.[42]

This doctrine of immiseration through the operations of monopoly capitalism, based on the injection of foreign capital, the pauperization of the indigenous artisans and peasants, unequal development through the promotion of commodity exports, and the extraction of surplus value, dominated left-wing thinking and writing until the later 1950s. It was reflected very clearly in, for example, the pioneering historical study by Jean Suret-Canale, *Afrique noire: L'Ère coloniale*.[43]

The main limitation on these and most other contemporary Marxist writings was that their evidence was taken from colonial situations and mostly (though not those by Suret-Canale) assumed massive capital exports to the Third World from the West. They therefore had little or no resonance for other parts of the world, or even for countries that had become independent long before. Above all they did not take account of the fact that many places had received very little foreign investment. The way was, therefore, open for new and more realistic applications of basic Marxist concepts to the Third World as a whole, particularly to independent countries. This reassessment began in the later 1950s and was to lead to that most pessimistic of all concepts, dependency theory.

[42] Ibid., pp. 326–8.
[43] J. Suret-Canale, *L'Afrique noire: L'Ère coloniale* (2 vols, Paris, 1964; Eng. edn, *French Colonialism in Tropical Africa*, New York, 1971).

4   Towards a General Dependency Theory

By the later 1950s it was becoming clear, even to some orthodox Marxists, that conventional post-1928 versions of Leninism would not explain Third World poverty in the post-colonial age. In particular, in addition to the long-independent Latin American countries, the newly independent countries of South and South-east Asia were clearly not following the scenario of socialist revolution led by an indigenous pro-letariat; moreover, in many cases neither their poverty nor their economic dependence on the West appeared to be decreasing. Another factor was the growth of early development economics, which was described above. The way was, therefore, open for new hypotheses, and these came from two sources: revisionist Marxists and Latin Americans.

It is arguable that on the European and North American side the breakthrough into new concepts of West–Third World relations came in 1957, the year when Gunnar Myrdal and Paul Baran both published very influential books. Although different in many respects, their common denominator was that they rejected the traditional Marxist view that the poverty of the Third World was due to the export of surplus capital by the West, and that they looked for other explanations of lack of development in the Third World.

Myrdal's views as a development economist have been considered above. Seen as a Marxist, however, the important thing about his book *Economic Theory and Underdeveloped Regions* was that he discounted the influence of foreign capital investment in the process of immiseration. Rather, he described a process of cumulative polarization between those countries that industrialized first and the rest. Because of this technical gap, the more developed countries were able to exploit the LDCs by destroying their handicrafts through cheaper imports, by removing their accumulated wealth by political power, and by restructuring their economies so as to provide the raw materials needed by foreign industry at prices held artificially low by foreign capital. Precisely because very little investment was made by foreign capitalism, Myrdal rejected any possibility that the poor countries could make real economic progress; and, because he ignored the distinction between formal colonization and economic subordination, he could generalize his argument throughout the whole non-western world.

Baran, Sweezy's colleague at Harvard, also followed conventional Marxist arguments up to a point. Underdevelopment was the outcome of a historical process by which Europeans used an accidental and temporary power advantage to remove much of the accumulated wealth from countries such as India, destroyed local manufactures and forced the indigenous peoples to produce primary export commodities. He also accepted the need of advanced capitalist states to export 'surplus' capital. But there he broke with the Leninist tradition. In fact very little capital was exported to the underdeveloped world, because it was not capable of absorbing it. Indeed he correctly pointed out that 'The increase of Western assets in the underdeveloped world is only partly due to capital exports in the strict sense of the term; it is primarily the result of the reinvestment abroad of some of the economic surplus secured abroad.'[44] Thus there was relatively little capitalist investment in typical Third World countries. There was, however, sufficient foreign investment to enable foreign firms, typically trading rather than manu- facturing, to gain effective control of segments of the host economy, often with the support of sections of the indigenous middle and upper classes and the backing of their overseas government. This control enabled the foreign firms to dominate the host economy without neces- sarily owning much of it. Above all it enabled them to control a sub- stantial part of the 'economic surplus' all societies generate in the form of profits and send them abroad.

This was the key to Baran's concept of 'underdevelopment'. Economic growth is always dependent on the use of this surplus. In a planned, Soviet-type economy it will be maximized by correct planning. In a western advanced economy it will be applied at random, but at least it will be devoted mainly to domestic investment. But in Third World countries it was not used to the best local advantage. There was, of course, a surplus, possibly small in international terms, but significant and potentially the basis of growth. Baran suggested two main reasons why this surplus was not used effectively. First, much of it was drained away by foreign firms or wasted by the indigenous middle and landed classes in buying imported luxuries. But, secondly, there was very little incentive for either foreign or local capitalists to invest in industrial expansion, the key to growth. One reason was limited local demand, itself due to low productivity and wages in the dominant agricultural sector. But, in addition, such domestic industries as existed would be monopolistic, whether owned by foreign firms or the indigenous bour- geoisie, because both groups could count on the support of the state through tariffs and other controls. Moreover, in this way international monopoly capital could secure its economic stranglehold over the rest of the world without the cost or inconvenience of maintaining formal colonial empires. Thus these Third World countries were caught in a vicious circle of poverty from which they could be released only through the destruction of capitalism, both indigenous and foreign, and the imposition of a Soviet-style state and economy in which the surplus was correctly applied.[45]

[44] P. Baran, *The Political Economy of Growth* (New York, 1957), p. 179.
[45] Ibid., *passim*, esp. pp. 140–2, 178–84, 249–64.

Baran's arguments in 1957 were tentative, short on facts about the realities of the Third World, and therefore prone to fall back on rhetoric. But they marked a significant break with the rigidities of post-Leninist theories of imperialism by rejecting the view that imperialism was bound to lead to the development of capitalism throughout the world through the export of capital from the West, and therefore to the convergence of western and Third World economies and societies. By contrast, Baran pointed towards what was to become the dominant concept of the next twenty years – that the impact of foreign capitalism was not to narrow but to widen the gap between the capitalist West and the pre-capitalist Third World, making underdevelopment a potentially permanent condition which expressed the 'structural' weakness of these economies.[46] This doctrine of 'underdevelopment' was taken much further in the following decade, primarily by theorists writing about Latin America and bringing to bear a considerable body of relevant information that had not been available to Baran.

It is significant that it was Latin Americans who brought down Marxist theory on underdevelopment from the highly theoretical level at which it had tended to float and applied it to the facts of their own history. An obvious reason for their primacy is that in the 1950s and early 1960s Latin America provided the only evidence available (apart from that of the United States and other societies dominated by European settlers, such as Canada, Australia and New Zealand) on the long-run economic performance of one-time European colonies after they had become independent. Moreover, by this period even those Latin American countries, particularly Argentina, which had once appeared to be in the same category as these economically successful settler states, seemed to have lost their momentum. The question the theorists posed was why this was so and how it might be remedied.

Their starting point owed much to Baran and little to the classical Marxists.[47] Far from tending towards the integration of the West and the Third World into a single capitalist system through the operation of capital investment, western economic dominance had in fact divided the world into two parts. Within what would later be called a 'world system'[48] the 'core' states of the West (and later Japan) had restructured

---

[46] C. Leys, (*Underdevelopment in Kenya* (London, 1957), p. 4), suggested that Baran 'has good claims to be regarded as the most influential founder of contemporary "underdevelopment theory"...'.

[47] The most convenient short account of the genesis of Latin American dependency theory is by P. J. O'Brien, 'A Critique of Latin American Theories of Dependency', in I. Oxall et al. (eds), *Beyond the Sociology of Development* (London, 1975), pp. 7–27.

[48] The phrase in this sense was publicized mainly by I. Wallerstein, notably in his first volume of *The Modern World System* (New York, 1974), and in a number of other books and articles.

the 'peripheral' countries to suit their own needs, mainly as markets and sources of raw materials. In doing so, they had developed only those parts of the peripheral economy which served their purposes – typically mines, plantations, communications, banking – leaving the rest of the economy and society virtually unaffected and unimproved.

This implied a form of economic dualism, an idea that had been running for some time.[49] In the words of Celso Furtado, one of the most influential of the Latin American economists, a 'dualistic economy' contained a 'capitalist wedge' driven into a surrounding pre-capitalist economy. This resulted in a 'hybrid structure' and a 'static equilibrium' at a low overall level, because the capitalist wedge had very little impact on the rest of the economy and because those who owned it transferred much of their profits (Baran's surplus) overseas. This pattern became ossified because it was not in the interests of those who benefited to change it.[50] Crucially, the beneficiaries were not merely the foreign capitalists and traders, but also segments of the indigenous population who were in alliance with them, particularly local manufacturers, politicians and owners of large estates, *latifundia*. The result was not a negative or transitional stage to the higher levels of capitalism, but a concrete and potentially permanent condition of 'underdevelopment'.

These ideas were taken up by many radical theorists in the 1960s and 1970s. One of the most influential was Andre Gundar Frank. Thus, in his *Capitalism and Underdevelopment in Latin America*,[51] his argument, much criticized by others, was that underdevelopment was not the product of modern capitalism but, in the Americas, was as old as European colonization there. 'My thesis is that these capitalist contradictions and the historical development of the capitalist system have generated underdevelopment in the peripheral satellites whose economic surplus was appropriated, while generating economic development in the metropolitan centers which appropriate that surplus – and, further, that this process still continues.' Thus he concluded that 'economic development and underdevelopment are not just relative and quantitative ... [They] are relative and qualitative, in that each is structurally different from, yet caused by its relation with the other.'[52]

---

[49] See, in particular: J. H. Boeke, *The Evolution of the Netherlands Indian Economy* (New York, 1942), and *Economics and Economic Policy of Dual Societies* (New York, 1953); J. S. Furnivall, *Colonial Policy and Practice* (Cambridge, 1948); Lewis, 'Economic Development with Unlimited Supplies of Labour'.

[50] C. Furtado, *Development and Underdevelopment* (Eng. edn, Berkeley and Los Angeles, 1964; Harmondsworth, 1973).

[51] A. G. Frank, *Capitalism and Underdevelopment in Latin America* (London and New York, 1967; 2nd edn, London and New York, 1969). Among his many other publications, *Dependent Accumulation and Underdevelopment* (London and New York, 1978), provides one of the broadest expression of his views.

[52] Frank, *Capitalism and Underdevelopment*, pp. 3, 8.

Such arguments were widely accepted and developed. In 1968, for example. T. Dos Santos published an article in which he took the basic concept of 'dependence' one stage further, basing it firmly in the domestic rather than the external condition of a Third World country.[53] Latin American economic development was different from that of Europe because its dualistic character 'neither permitted nor stimulated full development of capitalist relations of production but rather based itself upon servile forms of work or slavery'. Dependence was, therefore, a perpetuation of what might have been a transient colonial stage of economic development, 'a *conditioning situation* in which the economies of one group of countries are conditioned by the development and expansion of others.... Dependence ... is based upon an international division of labour which allows industrial development to take place in some countries while restricting it in others, whose growth is conditioned by and subjugated to the power centers of the world.' Thus there was no possibility of genuine development under these conditions: the only hope for these peripheral countries was to break off relations with the capitalist world altogether, as China had done, and to make their own way. ' "External" domination, in a pure sense, is in principle impracticable. Domination is practicable only when it finds support among these local groups who profit by it.' So 'the only solution would be [for a country] to change its internal structure – a course which necessarily leads to confrontation with the existing international structure'.

From that point in the 1960s dependency theory developed rapidly and was generalized from the specific experience of Latin America to the rest of the world. Immanuel Wallerstein, for example, developed his concept of a world economic system in which there were three concentric rings: the 'core' countries of the West, a 'semi–periphery' and 'periphery'. The distinctions were created by history. The core states industrialized first and acquired a commanding advantage over the rest of the world. The peripheral states are those that serve the needs of the core and are deliberately prevented from developing the higher industrial skills. The semi–periphery is an intermediate category of states that could be moving in either direction, and may include one-time core states which are losing their credentials. The whole system reflects an international division of labour and the process of transferring surplus from periphery to core.[54]

---

[53] English translation was published as T. Dos Santos, 'The Crisis of Development Theory and the Problem of Dependence in Latin America', in H. Bernstein, (ed.), *Underdevelopment and Development* (Harmondsworth, 1973), pp. 57–69.
[54] There is a useful summary of Wallerstein's arguments in Brewer, *Marxist Theories*, pp. 165–7.

The concept of dualism was further refined by a number of writers, notably by P. P. Rey, a French sociologist, who had done most of his research in Congo-Brazzaville.[55] His concept of the 'articulation of modes of production' was a much more sophisticated version of the dual economy. Rey argued that the reason for underdevelopment in some parts of the world, though not in the developed countries, reflected largely the character of the indigenous society. In the West, feudalism could and did lead to capitalism because of the attitude of the feudal upper class. In the rest of the world, where feudalism in a European sense did not exist, the effect of a society being drawn into the international economy through trade and investment was to reinforce the control of the existing dominant classes and to reinforce their resistance to the extension of capitalism – that is, the conversion of the mass of the people under their control into a capitalist proletariat. Thus foreign capital, during the colonial period, was able to obtain whatever it wanted, mainly primary commodities, and so lost its inbuilt impulse to extend the range of capitalist relations of production. The local economy became stagnant; and the colonial powers could safely decolonize, knowing that their interests were secure in the hands of their allied indigenous rulers. For the dependent country the only way out of this dead end was revolution and the simultaneous overthrow of the class structure and capitalism, to be replaced by socialism.

The dominant theme, therefore, of the dependency approach to Third World poverty is fundamental pessimism. Underdevelopment is not merely lack of development but the product of the failure of western capitalism to fulfil the functions Marx ascribed to it. The condition of the Third World is not transient, not merely a painful stage on the route to eventual industrialization and revolution by the new proletariat. It may prove permanent, sustained as much by the internal structural and social characteristics of a country as by external forces. This condition served the interests of the core countries well enough, since it enabled them to extract surplus at minimum cost. In particular, it benefited, and was partially sustained by, the multinational (or transnational) companies of the West, whose role as the main modern agents of capital export and economic exploitation was being investigated and publicized from

---

[55] See P. P. Rey, *Colonialisme, neo-colonialisme et transition au capitalisme* (Paris, 1971); *Les Alliances de classes* (Paris, 1973). Rey was one of a group of French Marxist anthropologists whose purpose was to bring the debate in Marxist circles back to the issue of distinctive Third World modes of production, as expressed by Marx in the 'Asiatic mode of production'. By focusing on articulation, they were able to argue that, despite what Marx had said about India, the capitalist 'mode of production' did not need to erode non-capitalist modes to extract 'surplus value'. For the influence of this idea, see ch. 6 below.

the 1960s at the same time as these theories of dependency. Their character and functions will be described in chapter 9.

But dependency theory did not prove the last stage in the evolution of radical pessimism. The bottom line came with the highly exotic theory of 'unequal exchange', developed by the French economist Arghiri Emmanuel, taken up by Samir Amin, and then publicized by Frank. Since this argument is based on entirely different premises from those of either classical Marxist or dependency theory, it requires to be treated separately.

5   Unequal Exchange

This last category of pessimists stands apart from the rest in that both capitalism and colonialism play a small, in fact sometimes negligible, part in their analysis of relations between the West and the Third World, and in their explanation of the relative poverty of the latter.

In a sense, the works to be considered here – primarily Arghiri Emmanuel's *Unequal Exchange: A study of the Imperialism of Trade*,[56] and more briefly Samir Amin's *Accumulation on a World Scale*,[57] and A. G. Frank's *Dependent Accumulation and Underdevelopment*, – are descended from the argument of Rosa Luxemburg: a modern orthodox Leninist from East Africa, D. W. Nabudere, makes this as an accusation.[58] Emmanuel and Amin have one important thing in common with Luxemburg: like her, they regard trade rather than the export of capital as the main engine of European imperialism and the means whereby the West exploits other countries and creates structural obstacles to Third World growth. Both accept the then conventional Wallerstein model of the gradual establishment of a single world capitalist economy, with its core and periphery; but neither is particularly interested in colonialism, or the so-called colonial mode of production, treating the colonial period as merely an expression of the growing predominance of the centre. Both, therefore, take for granted such things as specialization of different sorts in the centre and periphery; their concern is why this division of functions should not act as the Ricardian model of comparative costs predicted in that it perpetuated divergent levels of income in the centre and periphery. The main emphasis of this very abbreviated

[56] A. Emmanuel, *Unequal Exchange: A Study of the Imperialism of Trade* (Paris, 1969; Eng. edn, London and New York, 1972).
[57] S. Amin, *Accumulation on a World Scale* (Paris, 1970; Eng. edn, New York, 1974).
[58] W. Nabudere, *Essays on the Theory and Practice of Imperialism* (London and Dar es Salaam, 1979), pp. 35–41.

and simplified account will be on Emmanuel's explanation, since he really originated it, and because Amin, Frank and others accepted it with little alteration though much embellishment.

Emmanuel starts by rejecting the Ricardian principle that differentiation and specialization of production between more and less developed countries will be to their mutual advantage, even if one country is more rich and advanced than the other. The basis of Ricardo's argument was the assumption that there would be uniformity in the wages of labour (that is, subsistence wages) internationally, but that capital was relatively immobile and that profits would vary from one country to another. Thus a good would have an identical labour content wherever it was made, but would vary in cost according to its capital element. Since he (later followed by Marx) believed that the value of a good lay solely in its labour content, it followed that international exchange did not involve inequality of exploitation: that is, trade could not involve a transfer of real value unless it was done under compulsion, when market values were ignored. Differences in the level of profits would result from different capital elements and environmental factors.

The basis of Emmanuel's argument is that it is now no longer true that money wages are uniform internationally, though they may have been in the early nineteenth century. He argues that in fact wages may vary by a factor of 30 or more internationally.[59] Conversely, the great reduction in international transport costs means that prices of identical or substitutable goods tend to equalize everywhere. Finally, the rise of multinational companies has made capital completely mobile and its return is much the same throughout the world.[60] Thus, if prices and profits are much the same internationally, the main variable in exchange relations must be money wages (not real incomes). This is because workers, by contrast with capital, are not, in aggregate, mobile, so that workers in different countries are not directly in competition with each other. Hence the level of money wages can and does vary immensely.

Why is this? To oversimplify for brevity, it results from the effect of low money wages on the price of Third World exports. For the mass of LDCs Emmanuel postulates two alternative patterns.

---

[59] Emmanuel, *Unequal Exchange*, pp. 63–4. According to the World Bank (*World Development Report 1990: Poverty* (Oxford, 1990), table 1, pp. 178–9), in 1988 the weighted average per capita national product of the 'high-income countries' was 22 times that of the combined 'low- and middle-income countries'. While this is no indication of wage levels, it tends to support the argument for very large differential incomes.

[60] See S. H. Frankel, *Investment and the Return to Equity Capital in the South African Gold Mining Industry, 1887–1965* (Oxford, 1967), for a detailed examination of the tendency of the profits of capital to equalize.

1 Where any two countries with different wage levels make and trade the same things, but profit levels and the costs of producing the same goods are the same, wage differentials are accounted for by productivity differences. Exchange between these countries is therefore 'equal'.

This, in fact, is the conventional explanation of differential wages. But Emmanuel, in common with most dependency theorists, regards this situation as the exception, because, empirically, high wages are normally associated with relatively sophisticated forms of production, and low wages with commodity production or low-grade manufactures using low levels of technology. Instead he claims that there is an international division of labour in which countries, some advanced, others less advanced, specialize in producing different goods which are not in competition. This results in a second pattern.

2 Where any two countries produce wholly different things and are not in direct competition with each other, prices are determined by the money wage levels in each country. High-price goods are produced in high-wage countries, low-price goods in low-wage countries. Prices in the high-wage countries are dearer and the products of the low-wage countries cheaper than if wages had been the same in both countries.

This is what Emmanuel calls 'unequal exchange'. Exchange is 'unequal' because the low-wage country has to pay more for the goods it imports than it receives for the goods it export. It therefore has to export more in terms of hours of labour than it imports. A very simple example might be as follows.[61] Assume that a motor vehicle, which contains (hypothetically) 1,000 hours of labour, and was produced in country A by sophisticated machinery, has an international value of £10,000. It is exchanged for West African cocoa from country B, also with an international value of £10,000, but which represents, say, 20,000 hours of labour. In this case country A is exchanging 1,000 hours of labour for country B's 20,000 hours of labour, representing a wage ratio of 20:1. This, in turn, means that country B is transferring 19,000 man hours to country A; and, since these hours represent real resources which might otherwise have been used to increase the wealth of the poorer country, 'unequal exchange' is a main reason why the wealth gap exists and indeed widens.

Thus the world is divided into two segments: the high-wage, high-value economies, and the low-wage low-value economies. The former

---

[61] Emmanuel gives an example in *Unequal Exchanges*, pp. 367–8. Brewer, *Marxist Theories*, provides an alternative model on pp. 212–16.

exploit the latter, not by capital investment but through the terms of trade. The result is unequal development and a progressive widening of the gap between the two.

This pattern is almost immutable, at least for the majority of LDCs. The only solutions Emmanuel suggests in *Unequal Exchange* are (a) autarky: the poor countries simply stop international trading, though possibly trading between themselves, so putting a tourniquet round the haemorrhage of 'unequal exchange'; or (b) the formation by LDCs of alliances or cartels in order to raise traded prices artificially, by export duties, or by monopoly pricing (as of oil by OPEC in and after 1973).[62]

It is not possible here to consider the theoretical validity of 'unequal exchange'. After a sympathetic but fairly devastating critique of Emmanuel's argument, Brewer concludes that its 'major weakness ... is that he is unable to explain why all capital does not flow into low wage areas'.[63] From the very different standpoint of neoclassical economics, one leading American economist, P. A. Samuelson, in one of a number of published refutations of the argument, takes the same Ricardian formula for the England–Portugal trade relationship which Emmanuel used to demonstrate the fact of unequal exchange, and shows that, by adding profit rates, both countries would in fact benefit in the manner that Ricardo claimed. His conclusion is as follows:

> Of course wine is traded against cloth in the model. Anyone who wants to say that a certain number of high-wage hours of A has been traded against a certain larger number of hours of low-wage B is free to do so. (David Ricardo did). But that tautology does not mean that there is a meaningful par for such a ratio and that a deviation on one side from it represents 'unequal exchange'. Unequal exchange in this sense is not the result of wage differentials – nor is it the cause of wage differentials; rather it is tautologically a restatement of the fact of assumed wage differentials! It is a cruel hoax on the laborers in poor countries to pretend that there is some way of increasing their real incomes by 100% or 200% or even 2% by choking off trade, or by some other proposed way of eliminating unequal exchange. Indeed, romantic dilettantism

---

[62] But in his later book (A. Emmanuel, *Appropriate or Underdeveloped Technology?* (Paris 1981; Eng. edn, Chichester, 1982)), he developed a different argument. The way for underdeveloped countries to escape from poverty and the dilemmas of unequal exchange was for them to adopt the highest possible level of current industrial technology, if necessary by invoking the services of multinationals. In this way they could develop a capital-intensive and high-wage sector of the economy and cut out the long time lag which would be required if they were to develop their own 'appropriate technology', as was then being proposed by Schumacher and others.

[63] Brewer, *Marxist Theories*, p. 230.

been the enemy of social progress for the masses. Whether wrapped in Marxist symbolism or otherwise, logical nonsense is logical nonsense.[64]

In other words, a poor country benefits absolutely from specialization and trade, even if it benefits less relatively from these things than a richer country with higher levels of technology and labour productivity. Wage differentials are the product of a complex of factors, many historical, and the correct way to attempt to equalize wages is by equalizing other variables, such as technical efficiency.

For the present purpose, however, the significance of 'unequal exchange' is that in its pessimism it almost exactly balances the optimism of Adam Smith and Ricardo. Economic relations between more- and less-developed countries cannot be of any benefit to the LDCs once a technological gap had developed between the two. Trade will not be an engine for transmitting growth and affluence from the core to the periphery but rather a device for perpetuating the differentials and extracting value from the poor for the benefit of the rich. Thus the symmetry of the argument between optimists and pessimists is complete.

As was stated at the start, the primary purpose of this book is to survey the great debate over the relationship between the affluent West and the relatively poor Third World: the function of these two initial chapters has been to demonstrate the range of arguments still in play over this question. Despite the wide range of theories, at least one thing is common ground: at the end of the twentieth century the Third World, taken as a loose category, is on average very much poorer than the relatively affluent West. The question, then, is why this is so. How does the historical record relate to the assumptions of optimists and pessimists?

The problem will be approached from two directions, each suggested by some at least of these theorists.

First, how significant was the fact of colonial rule over much of the Third World as a cause of 'peripheral' poverty? Secondly, what was the relative significance of colonialism and normal economic relationships, notably trade and investment, during and after the colonial era?

Colonialism, of course, was only one of the mechanisms by which the Third World was brought within the international capitalist economy, and detailed examination of it may seem an abrupt break with the broader discussion of 'capitalism as a world system' in the previous two chapters. Some indeed have argued that colonialism was used only

---

[64] P. A. Samuelson, 'The Illogic of Neo-Marxian Doctrine of Unequal Exchange', in D. A. Belsey, E. J. Kane, P. A. Samuelson and R. M. Slow (eds), *Inflation, Trade and Taxes* (Ohio, 1976), pp. 106–7.

where other means of integration had failed, particularly when local or indigenous governments proved incapable of developing the necessary links with the West. Nevertheless, since a substantial proportion of the modern Third World was subject to western rule during the twentieth century, detailed examination of its mechanisms and their likely economic consequences is necessary. Colonialism, therefore, is the subject of parts II and III of this book. Part II concentrates on the instruments of colonialism: government and economic strategy. Part III then examines more loosely the contrasting economic impact of the West, and in particular trade, on independent or self-governing countries and dependent colonies, in order to pinpoint the economic impact of colonialism as contrasted with general economic factors. In short, how much difference did the imperial impact make?

That leaves the second half of the twentieth century, when virtually all Third World countries had political independence and when trade and other economic forces were able to have relatively free play. As was seen above, it was widely assumed that, if colonialism was responsible for underdevelopment, freedom might enable ex-colonies to join the ranks of the affluent West. Part IV, therefore, examines why this was true for some but by no means all states after the mid-century.

A final chapter attempts briefly to summarize the argument and to suggest whether the optimists or pessimists had the better of it.

Part II

Instruments of Empire

3

Imperial Government and the Development Imperative

There are at least three main standpoints from which one can examine the character of government in the modern colonial empires and its effects on Third World development: the nature of the central imperial government, the seat of sovereignty; the character of government in the colonies; and the attitude of both imperial and colonial governments to the economic and social development of the colonies. These issues will be considered in the three sections of this chapter.

1   The Institutions and Ideology of Imperial Government

The single, obvious, but critically important feature that distinguished imperial rule from self-government in a nation state was that it was external to each colony. Indeed, the essence of 'colonialism' lay in the fact that, by a quirk of the historical process, power to rule in these societies had been abstracted from them and vested in another state with which they had nothing in common. It was as if the ability to decide a country's destiny, its collective mind, had been cut out surgically and transplanted into another mind in London, Paris, Brussels, The Hague or Washington. This is also the sort of thing that enemies of a federal Europe are afraid of: that alien bureaucrats in Brussels would take over the power to determine critical aspects of life in each component state.

Of course, this analogy is false on two counts. First, in a normal federation or confederation each member country has the capacity to

influence decisions taken at the centre: it constitutes part of the collective mind. In the modern colonial empires this was never so, despite
some of the largely notional systems for colonial representation at the
centre of some empires. Colonies did not contribute Commissioners to
the central bureaucracy nor (with rare exceptions) have representatives
in a federal parliament. Moreover, those who actually ran government
in the colonies were aliens, whereas even in a federal Europe it is
assumed that ministers and other public servants in individual countries
would be indigenous.[1]

There is another major point of difference. A federal Europe would
consist of nation states, each of which had previously existed as a geographical and political entity, so each state would have to give up a
great deal of its previous identity. This has seldom been true of colonial
territories. There were exceptions. Egypt was effectively a political state
when the British occupied it in 1882, so was Ethiopia at the time of
the Italian invasion of 1936, and there were others; and the fact that
these had a previous history as states greatly affected their role as colonies
and their experiences after independence. But the majority of the
modern colonial units had not been states with the same boundaries or
had single governments before they became colonies. Nor, in any
meaningful sense, were they 'nations'. Most of the modern Third World
states took their present form only as colonies and were coagulations of
distinct social, ethnic, linguistic, religious and political territories. They
were put together by the imperial powers at the time of conquest or
by international agreement. They were, and often remain, artefacts.

This had important consequences, both during and after the colonial
period.

First, in terms of political ethics, the act of colonization did not
remove a single national mind. It transferred a large number of local
decision-taking capacities. The effect on the colonial subjects was much
the same: they simply lost their freedom of choice. But the loss was not
by a nation but by social and political groups which bore little relation
to the modern Third World states.

Secondly, this fact had considerable significance for the way in which
the colonial empires were run and for the successor states. The diversity
of these societies meant that a colony did not have a single united
consciousness, at least until one was created, often only momentarily,
in the course of a struggle for independence. Until then the imperial
power could deal with localities rather than countries: it could rule by
division without having to divide. Conversely, after the end of empire this
diversity meant that, when the new states were given back their 'minds',

---

[1] The concept of the northern 'carpetbagger' in the southern United States
after the Civil War reflects this type of situation in a western society.

they were, in most cases, given something they had never had before in that form, and which they found it very difficult to use. That is, they had never before had, or been able, to think collectively as a single nation or state. For many of them this remained a major problem at the very end of the twentieth century, as will be seen in chapter 10.

These are the basic facts of imperial government. Alien rule meant loss of freedom and responsibility. Colonial subjects were compulsory passengers in a vehicle whose direction they could not control. Where they went and how safely they were driven depended mainly, though not entirely, on the imperial driver. How good a substitute was government in the imperial centres for self-government in the localities? How much did the centre know about the dependencies? How much did it care about their welfare? Did it put the interests of the metropolis before those of the periphery?

Given that empire meant the transfer of the power of thought and final decision, there are two critical questions about how this power was used in the metropoles. First, how much attention did the imperial government give to the affairs of its colonies? Secondly, how selfishly did it use its power in pursuit of its own interests rather than those of the colonies?

The central fact about imperial government is that, whereas the affairs of India or Indonesia or Senegal were naturally central to those who lived there, they were extremely distant and marginal to people in London, The Hague or Paris. People in the colonies always tended to assume that their affairs were under constant consideration in the metropolis. They were wrong. As a rough rule of thumb, colonies impinged on the imperial government and population in proportion to the size and status of the metropolis, not of the colony. In a small country such as Portugal, Belgium or the Netherlands, overseas possessions were relatively important because they had considerable significance for the metropolitan economy (trade, investment, currency backing, etc.), and also for sections of society that looked to the colonies for employment. But for the major colonial powers – Britain, France, the United States – this was rarely so, despite the great importance of India for British trade, investment, employment and strategy. At a time of crisis – a colonial rebellion, international rivalry for a particular territory, in time of economic crisis, such as during the early 1930s or after 1945 – colonial matters might briefly reach the front pages of newspapers, arouse a parliamentary debate, even (though rarely) be placed on the agenda of a cabinet meeting. But for the most part and for most of the time colonies were very peripheral in every sense. Electorates invariably refused to show interest in them. Very few British electors in, say, 1945 could have named a single British colony; and colonial issues very seldom played a significant part in general elections, with the possible exceptions

of the 1902 'khaki' election in Britain at the end of the South African
War, and during the constitutional crisis in France after de Gaulle came
to power in 1958 over the Algerian issue. In short, empire was not a
primary concern of the imperial peoples and therefore not of their
governments.

The consequences of this can be traced through every aspect of
imperial government and ideology. Consider first the administration of
colonial affairs in the metropolitan capitals. In all modern states colonial
issues were of second- or even third-rate importance. Parliaments had
the ultimate power to legislate for the colonies, but they very seldom
debated them and chambers tended to empty when colonial business
was called. For their part, cabinets very rarely spent time on the colonies unless they were related to some larger issue, such as defence or
international relations.

This meant that responsibility for the colonies devolved onto the civil
servants who ran the British Colonial Office and India Office, the
Colonial Ministries of Paris and Brussels, or the Ministry for Overseas
in Lisbon. Significantly (because it showed how little they cared, and
also that Americans never admitted that they were an imperial power),
the United States never had a colonial ministry. Colonial matters were
handled variously by the State Department, the Navy, or the domestic
departments, according to the nature of the business.

A great deal depended on how efficient and responsible these colonial
departments were. All were headed by a minister, a politician, who was
commonly of cabinet rank. But with very rare exceptions – reflecting
the low political significance of his work – he was not a front-rank
politician, unless he was a young man who hoped to rise. In France,
Belgium and the Netherlands these ministers were often retired colonial
governors, who therefore knew some at least of their territories, though
their ideas on them might become out of date. This almost never happened in Britain: the only exception was Lord Milner, who was Colonial
Secretary from 1921 to 1922; and the only really front-rank British
politician who held that office in the twentieth century was Joseph
Chamberlain, from 1895 to 1903. This had important side effects.
A colonial minister seldom possessed the personal status or departmental
firepower to insist that his government adopt a particular policy, above
all when it involved significant expenditure of public funds. In Britain
the Treasury was always senior to the Colonial Office and there were
very few if any votes to be won by spending money on relieving poverty
or providing amenities in Africa or Asia.

In practice, therefore, thinking – policy-making so far as it existed at
all – was delegated to these colonial departments, and a great deal
depended on the ability and character of these officials. Did they accept
that the transfer of power from colony to metropolis obliged them to

undertake the positive thinking and planning role which, conceptually at least, an independent government in one of the colonial territories would be expected to take on? And how did they treat conflicts of interest between metropolis and colonies, between their fellow-countrymen and subjects overseas?

Take first the question of active thinking and planning. To oversimplify, the short answer is that the colonial offices did very little positive thinking or planning before about 1939: thereafter they became very active.

For the lack of much pro-active thinking before the Second World War there were perhaps two main reasons.

First, except for Belgium, these offices had too many overseas territories to control and insufficient staff to fulfil an active role for any of them. Secondly, it was not seen as part of the peacetime function of any government, at least before about 1945, and even in its home base, to take an active role in economic matters. The economic function of government was to ensure a sound currency, determine tariff policy, and provide a minimum of essential public services and infrastructure. It is, therefore, not surprising that, before the Second World War, which effectively started the era of central government economic planning in Britain and elsewhere, colonial ministries did not expect to direct colonial economic life or take responsibility for development. These things were left to market forces and the initiative of local colonial governments.

To illustrate the conventional frame of mind among at least British Colonial Office staff before the 1940s there is a story told in his later history of the Office by Sir Cosmo Parkinson, eventually its senior civil servant. In his early days as a very junior member of the Office staff, before 1914, he was approached by a Swiss national who wanted information about growing lucerne in the newly occupied British East Africa for feeding ostriches on a proposed ostrich farm: in those days every woman had ostrich feathers in her hat. Parkinson recalled that:

> Ostriches were not so bad. I had even seen some in the Zoo; and I knew about their mistaken ideas of concealment and their immunity to dyspepsia. But lucerne was a much more obscure thing. I had just heard of it; but a classical education had not included the study of grasses, and off-hand I could not recall a reference to it even in Virgil's *Georgics*.... Luckily I remembered Kew Gardens as a repository of knowledge concerning every herb bearing seed ... and I took refuge in passing the inquirer on to Kew. He never called again.[2]

This passage reflects two features of central colonial government in its earlier days: the mandarin character of most officials and their

[2] Sir Cosmo Parkinson, *The Colonial Office from Within, 1909–1945* (London, 1947), p. 26.

ignorance of and distaste for anything as vulgar as economic or business life. Much of that changed after 1945, and during the last fifteen or so years of the colonial era British and continental colonial ministries took a very much more informed and active role in the economic development of the colonies. For the first time, also, they had money to spend, the precursor of modern aid to the Third World. So at last there was dynamic use of the power held by the centres. This had many positive economic results and helped to produce the greatest boom period in African and Caribbean economic history during the 1950s and 1960s. Ironically, it was also counter-productive in terms of imperial control. What John Lonsdale and Anthony Low have called 'the second colonial occupation' (implying that for the first time imperial countries were then actively involving themselves in the detail of colonial affairs) aroused so much resistance in colonies who were unaccustomed to being told how to terrace their fields against soil erosion or to reduce their flocks of goats and cattle (essential in many places as a currency used to buy wives) that it greatly stimulated nationalistic movements.[3]

This suggests an important general conclusion. It was never practicable for an imperial government actually to use its power to think and decide for its dependencies to the full. Either it lacked the ability to do so at all, or it lacked the capacity to do so in a way acceptable to the colonial subjects. This meant that most of the real decision-making had to devolve back onto the colonies themselves, despite the fact that in principle they lacked the final power of decision.

But before examining how the colonies contributed to their own government we must consider briefly the question of conflict of interest. If one assumes, as many critics have done, that empire was necessarily intended as a means of exploiting colonies for the benefit of the metropolis, one would expect that the scales of justice would be heavily weighted on the imperial side. How far was this so?

It is impossible to provide a certain and short answer. But the case can be put in two ways.

On the one side, and for the most part negatively, it is probable that no metropolis ever adopted policies for the colonies, particularly economic policies, which were clearly harmful to itself. On some issues, notably trade, most empires imposed tariff systems that favoured their own interests rather than those of the colonies. This will be seen in chapter 4. Particular vested interests in the metropoles demanded, and sometimes succeeded in getting, their interests served at colonial expense: Lancashire cotton manufacturers and exporters, for instance, were able

[3] J. Lonsdale and D. A. Low, 'Introduction: Towards the New Order, 1945–63', in D. A. Low and A. Smith (eds), *History of East Africa*, vol. 3 (Oxford, 1976).

to insist for some forty years, from the 1880s to the 1920s, that India should not protect its own cotton industry against them. Again, in the 1930s, Britain and most other colonial powers imposed import quotas on Japanese textile imports to the colonies, again to protect metropolitan producers at the expense of colonial consumers. Much the same was true of imperial policy on currency and defence. In short, with very few exceptions, the general rule was that imperial interests came first and overrode those of the colonies if they conflicted.

But there is another side to this question. By and large those who were responsible for controlling the colonies – both the bureaucrats in the capitals and their agents in the colonies – tended to act as defenders of colonial interests as they saw them, if necessary against those of greedy compatriots. That is, they became professionally affiliated with the colonies in what has been described as the chameleon effect. This was true throughout most of the modern period. But, as will be seen in section 3, from the 1930s a new development occurred. During the last thirty or so years of the colonial era all the colonial powers, with the possible exception of Portugal, became more concerned to promote the interests of the colonies as well as their own, primarily through huge increases in loans and grants. The motives were mixed: there was a belief that what was good for the colonies was also good for the metropolis. There was also, perhaps until the early 1950s, hope that Africans and others could be weaned from nationalism and the demand for independence by kindness and generosity. But there was also a growing sense of guilt at past sins of commission or omission and a genuine concern to promote the welfare of the dependencies. In short, empires were never more virtuous than when they were about to expire – some would say a deathbed conversion and repentance.

2 Government in the Colonies

It is now necessary to turn to the other side of the picture and consider what went on in the colonies. To revert to the original concept, what sort of 'mind' was left there once the ultimate power of decision-making had been removed? How great a role was played in their own affairs by the indigenous subject peoples? How totally were these societies remodelled and their traditions and structures destroyed?

Here we come to two of the great paradoxes of empire. First, despite all that has been said about the loss of freedom by a colony, in practice most colonies had a great deal of autonomy. Secondly, despite the great weight of imperial authority and the desire of imperialists to destroy what they found inconvenient in indigenous societies and institutions, which Crawford Young has characterized with the phrase *Bula Matari* (he who crushes rocks),[4] in practice most indigenous societies retained much of their pre-colonial character and even their capacity to run their own affairs.

There was an obvious reason for the relative autonomy of colonial governments: imperial governments lacked both the capacity and the energy to run such vast empires from the centre. Nature abhors a vacuum. For most of the time and on most matters colonies therefore had to run their own affairs. The external control over them was mostly negative. The colonial authorities could not change imperial policies – for example, tariff structures or the basis of their currency. They could not have direct relations with foreign states or their colonies. Their legislation was subject to approval or disapproval by the centre. But for the rest – and that meant on most matters of purely domestic concern – colonies did their own thing.

That leaves the vital question: who actually ran the colonies? What were the relative roles of Europeans and the indigenous peoples? The special feature of a colony, of course, was that its government was not indigenous: it was alien and owed its authority to the metropolis. In most Asian and African dependencies this meant that the head of state, the governor, was British, French, etc., and that the heads of key departments were also expatriates. So also were the majority of whatever executive and legislative councils a colony might have, though British legislative councils almost always had a minority of nominated (rather than elected) indigenous members and, from different times (the 1890s in India, the 1940s in Black Africa), these bodies gradually came to have a majority of nominated or elected members. Overall, however, there is no question that government at the colonial capital (Lagos, Delhi, Batavia, Dakar) was predominantly official and largely expatriate.

So also were the higher levels of provincial administration. There were differences between each imperial system; but essentially administration outside the capitals was run by a hierarchy of European officials who ranged down from provincial governors or commissioners to district officers. There were not very many of them, because poor colonies could not afford their relatively large salaries and overheads; but they were responsible to the colonial centre for almost everything that went on, from collecting taxes to administering justice and building bridges.

At first sight, then, it would appear that even the subsidiary powers of decision-taking that were left to a colony were in alien hands: that the domestic 'mind' of a black society was white, and that Africans, Indians, etc. had no part in even the most trivial domestic decisions. But this is another of the paradoxes of modern (and also ancient and

[4] Crawford Young, *The African Colonial State in Comparative Perspective* (New Haven and London, 1994).

early modern) empires. Behind the façade of expatriate rule in the colonies there remained very considerable scope for indigenous autonomy and personality.

The reason was simply that there were never enough Europeans to run large colonies nor did these know enough about the territory or its people and traditions to be able to do everything on their own. There were, for example, never more than about 1,000 Britons in the Indian Civil Service, the elite corps that controlled an India of perhaps 400 million. And, because these people were alien, and deliberately maintained some distance from their subject peoples in order to preserve their status, they were largely ignorant of what the people they ruled were thinking.

There were two practical consequences. First, below the top veneer of foreign administrators, there was everywhere a vast majority of indigenous civil servants and other agents of the colonial government. Although these might have limited formal independence of action, they were essential to government, and it was through them that the alien rulers learned about what went on. Their information – or disinformation – was critical to the colonial state's existence. Moreover, over time, these people increasingly rose to the higher levels of the bureaucracy, so that, by 1947 for instance, the majority of the Indian Civil Service was Indian.

Secondly, and perhaps more importantly, alien government never reached down to the roots of society. Below the lowest level of foreign control there always survived indigenous units of society and their traditional rulers and modes of self-government. How autonomous these units and rulers were varied very widely, according to the style of foreign rule the imperial state adopted. Indian princes, Malayan sultans, Northern Nigerian emirs, and so on, down to much lower levels, retained much of their pre-colonial status and much of its reality. Even in British India, where such formal indigenous authorities had been abolished, at the level of the village and the town Indians ran local affairs. In most parts of Black Africa chiefs retained a lot of local influence, particularly over social and economic affairs. Moreover, indigenous chiefs and others with traditional authority could use power delegated to them by the colonial authorities to further their own ends in strictly traditional ways. Thus J.-F. Bayart, in his profound study of African political life, argued that: 'The indigenous intermediaries of the colonial State ... made free use of their privileges as auxiliaries of the administration to enrich themselves. In this sense "corruption", as it is called today, was an organic part of the system of "indirect rule", especially in Northern Nigeria.'[5]

[5] J.-F. Bayart, *The State in Africa: The Politics of the Belly* (Paris, 1989; Eng. edn, London, 1993), p. 71.

The general point, therefore, is that there was in all imperial situations a contrast between the theory and practice of empire.

The theory was that the act of imposing imperial rule implied the transfer of all power to govern and take decisions from the province to the metropolitan centre and then back to its expatriate agents in the colonies. This in turn implied that empire was positive and all-embracing: that it completely filled the gap left when a province lost its previous independence.

The reality was that imperial governments never really filled this gap. The metropolis could not be sufficiently bothered to provide all the thought and action government of a colony needed, while the expatriate agents in the colony were too thin on the ground, too alien to the local society, and also too restricted by the negative control of the imperial centre, to do all that the country needed. Conversely, although the indigenous people, one way or another, played a very active role in their own affairs, they were always too subordinate to be able to take major decisions. This paradox is examined in more detail in chapter 6.

Ultimately, however, the test of any political system must be its achievement; and, in the context of the relatively very poor Third World countries which made up most of the modern colonial empires, this meant economic and social development. The main economic strategies of the imperial powers will be considered in chapter 4 and some of the consequences in chapter 7. Here it is proposed to consider only their attitude to the needs of their colonies. Was there a will to develop? How far did the imperial states accept that, having taken over the full powers of sovereignty, it was their obligation to do what independent states might otherwise have done for themselves?

3   The Imperial Will to Develop: The Genesis of Aid

There was a basic paradox in the approach of all the modern colonial powers to the economic development of their colonies, taking 'development' to imply (as it normally did before the growth of modern development economics in the 1950s) making full use of factor endowment to increase production and consumption, which in turn should increase wealth in real terms. The paradox lay in a divergence between ends and means. Broadly, during the first thirty years of the twentieth century there was a growing belief in the need for colonial development, but an almost total lack of publicly funded means to do so. It was only during the last three decades before decolonization that means began to be available to realize actual 'colonial development'.

The concept of a public obligation to promote colonial development was itself almost new in the early twentieth century. One of the earliest

European proponents of such ideas was Joseph Chamberlain, who, as Colonial Secretary in London from 1895 to 1903, and as a businessman, pressed hard for imperial action to improve colonial economies. Even before taking office he told a Birmingham audience that 'it is not enough to occupy certain great spaces of the world's surface unless you can make the best of them – unless you are willing to develop them. We are land-lords of a great estate; it is the duty of a landlord to develop his estate'.[6]

Chamberlain was before his time. The British Treasury effectively blocked his attempts to obtain public funds for development in the colonies, though he at least obtained legislation that made it cheaper and easier for colonies to raise capital on the London money market.[7] But this quotation reflects the ambivalence of European attitudes to colonial development that lasted as long as the colonial empires. On one side there was recognition that imperial states had a moral obliga-tion to the colonies they controlled in the interests of their inhabitants. On the other was belief that such development would benefit the imperial power in three main ways.

First, it would increase production of commodities which were needed in the metropolis and which might be in short supply interna-tionally. In the early years of the twentieth century there was widespread fear, reflected in much of the early Marxist literature surveyed in chapter 2, that growing industrial demand for minerals and vegetable products such as oils was outstripping supply.[8] This suggested that political possession of a territory was important because it would ensure that the imperial owner had control over its commodity exports. But for them to be really valuable substantial investment in such territories was essential. This was what Chamberlain and others who succeeded him saw as the primary economic role of the imperial state.

---

[6] J. L. Garvin, *The Life of Joseph Chamberlain* (London, 1934), vol. 3, p. 19, quoted in M. Havinden and D. Meredith, *Colonialism and Development: Britain and its Tropical Colonies, 1850–1960* (London, 1993), pp. 87–8. See also R. M. Kesner, *Economic Control and Colonial Development: Crown Colony Financial Management in the Age of Joseph Chamberlain* (Westport, Conn., 1981), for a full treatment of Chamberlain's ideas and policies.

[7] The Colonial Loans Act 1899 and the Colonial Stock Act 1900.

[8] For a concrete example of this fear by an industrialist, William Lever, and the steps he took to safeguard his own source of vegetable oils, see C.H. Wilson, *History of Unilever* (2 vols, London, 1954), vol. 1, ch. 11. See also D. K. Fieldhouse, *Unilever Overseas: The Anatomy of a Multinational* (London, 1978), chs 8, 9. The theoretical literature on imperialism in the pre-1917 period was heavily influenced by this concern for sources of raw materials. See, in particular, V.I. Lenin, *Imperialism: The Highest Stage of Capitalism* (1917; Eng. edn., Moscow, 1947), and R. Luxemberg, *The Accumulation of Capital* (1913; Eng. edn, London, 1951).

Secondly, economic development was seen as increasing the colonial market for the exports of the metropolis. In a world of increasing protectionism from the 1880s to after 1945 there was great attraction in the concept of secure colonial markets, though they would only be really secure if protected from international competition: hence the development of the tariff and other regulatory devices which are described in chapter 4.

Finally, though less important, development of colonies was expected to benefit individual and corporate Europeans. It would widen the market for portfolio investment, and also provide opportunities for the more adventurous who were prepared to go out to Africa or Asia and establish plantations, mines, trading enterprises, banks and farms. But experience showed that few Europeans were prepared to venture much of their own capital until and unless the imperial state had provided the essential services. Thus development of infrastructure on public account was the necessary condition for private enterprise.

There were, therefore, many arguments and vested interests favouring the development of the colonies during the first decades of the twentieth century. The interest in fact declined during the decade before 1914, as more buoyant economic conditions seemed to make colonies less important to Europe than had seemed likely during the depressed last years of the nineteenth century. The First World War revived that interest. Commodity shortages stimulated colonial production and generated some elaborate and largely exaggerated ideas on the future value of their production to the imperial states.[9] These ideas proved short lived, but in the early 1920s they had sufficient momentum to produce the two famous statements of development strategy in Britain and France, by Lugard and Sarraut, which were quoted in chapter 1.

In retrospect it is clear that these expressions of a will to develop the colonies were a reflection of pre-1920 war time conditions. After 1921 the huge drop in commodity prices made it pointless to invest large sums in developing the productive capacity of tropical colonies. For most of the rest of the 1920s the imperial powers left colonies to undertake and finance their own development plans, and when positive schemes were revived it was largely in response to the effects of recession on the metropolitan economies.[10]

[9] See Sir W. K. Hancock, *Survey of British Commonwealth Affairs*, vol. 2, part 1, *Problems of Economic Policy 1918–1939* (London, 1942), ch. 1, sec. 5, for the classic account of the growth of neo-mercantilism in Britain during the First World War and proposals to exclude Germany from access to key raw materials after the war was over, which was fully supported by France and other allies at the Paris conference of 1916.

[10] The standard work on British public investment in the colonies is S. Constantine, *The Making of British Colonial Development Policy 1914–1940*

The turning point was 1929 and the beginning of the recession. The passage of the British Colonial Development (CD) Act in 1929 marked a symbolic new departure. This act stemmed primarily from hope that, by helping colonies to service borrowing to pay for public works such as railways and bridges, a stimulus would be given to the decaying British heavy industry. It was important because it was the first formal expression of a willingness to provide grants and cheap loans to help colonial development. At the time, however, it had little practical effect. During the decade 1930–9 a total of roughly £18 million was spent by the imperial government on colonial development, including funds under the CD Act.[11] This was minute compared with the amount colonies borrowed on the open market (though helped by the Guaranteed Loan Act and the Colonial Stock Act): £144,957,693 between 1919 and 1939.[12] All this borrowing had to be financed from colonial revenues, and was restricted by colonial poverty; it did not reflect a British will to develop.

Nor was private capital eager to invest in the colonies. Figures for this are very hard to come by, but for 1936 and British Africa alone Herbert Frankel estimated that total listed private capital was £413.5 million, of which only £102 million was in the whole of British Black Africa, excluding southern Africa and the Rhodesias with their huge mining investment.[13] A great deal more British money had been invested in other imperial possessions: for example, in 1934/5 British India's government sterling debt was £385.1 million.[14] But in 1938 estimated long-term private business investment in India (excluding banks and insurance), much of it British, amounted to a mere £180 million.[15]

Such statistics are highly conjectural. They merely suggest that the British colonial empire had aroused little enthusiasm for development on either public or private account before 1939. They also suggest that the greater part of British investment was on public account, mostly borrowing by colonial governments to meet the cost of infrastructure.

Much the same appears to have been true of France, though public investment in the colonies increased markedly in the 1930s, and the

---

(London, 1984). The most valuable study of French investment is J. Marseille, *Empire colonial et capitalisme français: Histoire d'un divorce* (Paris, 1984). Unfortunately this does not provide a subject index or list of tables.

[11] Constantine, *The Making*, table 7, p. 275; table 1, p. 203.

[12] Ibid., p. 295.

[13] S. H. Frankel, *Capital Investment in Africa: Its Course and Effects* (London, 1938), pp. 158–9.

[14] B. R. Tomlinson, *The Economy of Modern India, 1860–1970* (Cambridge, 1993), table 3.10, p. 153.

[15] Rs crores 235.08, converted at Rs13 = £1. B. R. Tomlinson, 'British Business in India', in R. P. T. Davenport-Hines and G. Jones (eds), *British Business in Asia since 1860* (Cambridge, 1989), p. 116.

Popular Front government set up the equivalent of the British Colonial Development Act system, *Fonds d'Investissement pour le Développement Économique et Social* (FIDES), in 1938. Again the sums invested by both the state and the private sector before 1939 were small, and do not suggest that the French state had responded enthusiastically to Sarraut's call for an energetic public development policy.[16]

Although these statistics relate only to the British and French empires, much the same general trends can be seen in those of other European states.[17] Clearly from 1920 to 1939 the will to develop European colonies was weak. Under conditions of general international recession metropolitan countries lacked resources and there seemed little point in increasing production of tropical commodities – which was what 'development' in effect then meant – when the commodity markets were overstocked and prices very low. But there were two other factors, related to the nature of colonial economies rather than those of the imperial power, which discouraged metropolitan initiative and capital investment.

First, it was difficult to invest in tropical agriculture. In countries where plantations were suited to the crops desired and where there was no political obstacle to establishing such enterprises, this was no problem. But in much of West Africa and some other places political and social factors made plantations impracticable, and it was impossible to invest in peasant agriculture except by financing production. Thus the main form of private European investment was necessarily in trade rather than production.[18]

Secondly, investment in industrial production was unprofitable in most colonies. There were two main obstacles, one economic, the other political. The economic obstacle was the absence of factors favourable to local manufacture rather than importing. The markets of most colonies, other than those of India and Indonesia, were very limited and few justified setting up a modern factory. It was rare that availability of raw materials overcame the higher costs of small-scale manufacture. Although wage levels were lower than in Europe, labour was initially unskilled and total labour costs usually above those in MDCs. By the twentieth century transport costs for imported manufactures were very small in relation to the value of goods. Clearly only high levels of import protection could make manufacture in most colonies viable.

---

[16] For French investment in this period, see Marseille, *Empire colonial* p. 105.
[17] For Belgian investment in the Congo, see Frankel, *Capital Investment in Africa*, pp. 167–70. G. Vandewalle (*De conjoncturele evolutie in Kongo en Ruanda-Urundi van 1920 tot 1939 en van 1949 tot 1958* (Antwerp, 1966), p. 68) gives similar estimates.
[18] For a recent study of this extensively examined subject, see A. Phillips, *The Enigma of Colonialism: British Policy in West Africa* (London and Bloomington, Ind., 1989).

Here the political factor was critical. It was intrinsic to colonial regimes that they expected colonies to provide markets for their manufactured exports. As will be seen in chapter 4, this could result in one of two strategies. France, Spain, Portugal and the United States all gave free entry of their own goods to their colonies, while placing import duties on those of other states. Conversely Britain, Belgium and the Netherlands remained free-trading until about 1932. They could not, therefore, protect their colonial trade from foreigners; but they could, and did, prevent colonies from protecting their own industries. From 1923 in India, during the 1930s in Ceylon and the Netherland Indies, protection was provided on a selective basis for some local industries, but largely on the argument that the duties were needed for fiscal purposes. These were the exception. Virtually no other colony belonging to these three powers was allowed to protect domestic industry until the 1950s.

Imperial reasons were to some extent selfish – safeguarding key domestic industries. But there were also strong and disinterested economic arguments against artificially stimulated local industries. For the economic reasons summarized above, such industries would largely benefit the protected producers – initially probably expatriate – at the expense of the poor consumer. Because they would be relatively inefficient, there would be negative value added. In much of tropical Africa, indeed, these predictions proved true after independence.

It was the Second World War and the economic crisis facing the European states during the decade after the war, plus the new need to attempt to win the hearts of colonial peoples, that changed these attitudes and at last generated a true development imperative.

The war and its aftermath had two main effects. First, shortages of raw materials for the British and later American war effort resulted in sustained attempts to stimulate production in the colonies, though until after 1945 British determination not to pay international prices to colonial producers tended to discourage production.[19] After 1945, as after 1918, all the colonial powers saw their colonies as a vital source of raw materials, both for their own use and for sale to earn hard currency. Thus development once again became the dominant idea.

The other main effect of the war was psychological. Even before 1939 there was a growing acceptance in London and Paris that colonial poverty and the absence of economic growth were a serious threat to the future of these empires: the riots of 1937 in the British West Indies led to the appointment of the Moyne Commission of 1938. The change of heart and recognition that substantial imperial expenditure was essential

[19] For a detailed study of this and its effects in West Africa, see, D. K. Fieldhouse, *Merchant Capital and Economic Decolonization: The United Africa Company 1929–1987* (Oxford, 1994), chs 6, 7.

in at least these colonies was reflected in the statement in a Colonial Office memorandum for the Cabinet that 'any further, steady deterioration will prove very damaging to Great Britain's reputation as a Colonial Power. It is ... imperative that, at a time when the "colonial question" is being ventilated at home and abroad, we should ourselves be as far as possible above reproach.'[20]

Although this Commission did not report until 1940, when its evidence was concealed, the momentum for greatly increased imperial expenditure on the colonies was now irresistible. For a mixture of motives — guilt at colonial poverty, fear of colonial resistance to the war effort, desire to impress neutrals, particularly the United States, with Britain's good intentions — Britain passed the 1940 Colonial Development and Welfare (CD&W) Act. By later standards the provisions were modest: up to £5 million a year could be given to colonial governments to support both capital and recurrent development schemes, and £500,000 a year could be spent on research. Under wartime conditions, less than this was in fact available until after 1945. But the 1940 Act was a breakthrough in two main respects. First, it included 'welfare', thus accepting that Britain should subsidize current expenditure in the colonies; secondly, payments did not have to be approved by the hardheaded Advisory Committee, as had been necessary from 1929. In short, as extended by the CD&W Act of 1945 and later versions, this was the start of 'aid' as it later became understood.[21] Its later development is examined in chapter 8.

The war thus greatly increased the sense that empire now depended for its life on evidence that it was constructive. A major influence was the attitude of the United States, on whom Britain increasingly depended for its survival. Liberal Americans were conventionally hostile to imperialism and many saw little difference between the position of Britain in its colonies and Germany in occupied Europe. The issue came to a head over the drafting of the Atlantic Charter in August 1941.[22] The charter was primarily a publicity document, but the effect of American attitudes forced Britain to reconsider its whole attitude to the future of its

[20] Quoted in Constantine, *The Making*, p. 237.
[21] For the 1940 and later CD&W acts, see Constantine, *The Making*, ch. 9; D. J. Morgan, *The Official History of Colonial Development*, vol. 1: *The Origins of British Aid Policy, 1924–1945* (London, 1980), chs 10,15.
[22] Quoted in J. M. Lee and M. Petter, *The Colonial Office, War, and Development Policy: Organisation and the Planning of a Metropolitan Initiative, 1939–1945* (London, 1982), p. 118. For a fuller discussion of the background and significance of the charter and American attitudes to the British empire, see Wm. R. Louis, *Imperialism at Bay 1941–1945: The United States and the Decolonization of the British Empire* (Oxford, 1977).

colonies. Political decolonization for all but India and possibly Ceylon
was thought to be still in the distant future, but economic development
was now seen to be essential, both to satisfy American and neutral
opinion, and after 1945 also the United Nations, and also to persuade
colonial subjects that empire meant progress.

Actual economic investment on any scale was impossible during
the war, but from about 1943 there was a decisive change in British
attitudes to economic development: the Colonial Office accepted an
obligation to plan for the future. In an empire that had always assumed
that initiatives must come from the colonies, this was a profound change,
incidentally stimulated by the unprecedented degree of governmental
control over the British economy. In 1943 agencies were established
within the Colonial Office to acquire information and to prepare and
coordinate plans for each colony. But the British tradition that colonies
were autonomous polities that must take the initiative in economic
matters prevented the establishment of a dictatorial central planning
system of the type France was to set up after 1945. Thus the British
colonies were instructed to draw up their own plans, first in 1940, then,
more urgently, for ten-year periods, after the passage of the 1945 CD&W
Act, which increased the sum initially available to subsidize colonial
development to £120 million over ten years. This was the beginning of
the post-war belief that development required planning which was to
become the dominant feature of all states after decolonization.

From about 1945, then, Britain, followed by France and Belgium
after their liberation (the Netherlands lost what became Indonesia in
1949, so was unable to pursue the same strategy), was at last committed
to the principle that empire was responsible for ensuring economic
growth in its dependencies. During the 1950s in particular, with the
growth of nationalist movements in all remaining colonial possessions,
imperial economic aid became a device for persuading colonial politicians that it was to their advantage to remain as colonies or, after
political liberation, to retain close links with their one-time parent
states. On the British side the CD&W Act was renewed from time to
time and the allocations increased. By 1970, when the Act was finally
ended (to be replaced by aid under different assumptions), a total of
£343.9 million had been spent, at an average annual rate of £14.3 million.[23]
These were grants. In addition the colonies could and did borrow money
on the London market. Market loans plus Exchequer loans totalled
£282.5 million over the period 1948/9 to 1969/70, averaging £13.5
million a year.[24]

[23] Quoted in Havinden and Meredith, *Colonialism and Development*, p. 258,
from official reports.
[24] Ibid., p. 264.

These were, of course, very small amounts in relation to the size
and needs of the remaining British colonial empire. They were supplemented by other sources of money: local borrowing, foreign loans
and private direct investment. It is impossible to be certain of the size
of these capital injections, but it is clear that they fell far short of what
was needed or wanted.[25] In short, the development imperative had
proved too expensive to be sustained within the framework of the
British empire.

The French development effort was proportionately much greater
than that of Britain. Partly to strengthen the Union created in 1946,
but also because colonial investment was expected to strengthen the
franc by saving on and generating hard currency, France was prepared
to invest heavily in the colonies: it was also prepared to fight very
expensive wars in Indo-China and later Algeria. The French approach
was more centrist than that of Britain. Planning was dominated by a
department of the Treasury and by FIDES (FDES for North Africa) and
was far more indicative than that of the Colonial Office.

There has been much debate over the real value of the funds provided
for the colonies, since much was spent on the salaries of French 'technical' staff (a third of the total in 1965), much of which was repatriated
to France by its recipients. Moreover, virtually all materials were drawn
from France, at internationally inflated prices. The size of French aid
to the colonies after 1945 is also uncertain, but there is no doubt that
it was very large in relation both to the French economy (1.76 per cent
of the national income in 1962[26]) and compared to that of Britain.[27]

Finally, the Belgian Congo/Zaire is the classic example of a post-1945
colony that because of its booming economic condition, was able to
attract a very large amount of private capital, borrow on public account,
and rely very little on aid. Here too indicative planning proved seductive:
the Congo's first ten-year plan was drawn up in 1948. It proposed public
investment of some £178.5 million, but this was exceeded: between
1950 and 1958 fixed government investment, excluding parastatals,
amounted to some £242.8 million. Significantly only some £36.8 million
of this came from the Belgian government in the form of aid.[28] Most
was financed either from government revenue surplus or by borrowing
on the Brussels market or in the Congo itself, from the surplus profits of
the big mining and other companies. These companies also made a very

[25] The best statistics are in the *Board of Trade Journal*, 187 (July–Dec. 1964),
p. 293; 189 (July–Dec. 1965), p. 230.
[26] T. Hayter, *French Aid* (London, 1966), p. 45.
[27] For a comparison, see Marseille, *Empire colonial*, p. 105, and Havinden and
Meredith, *Colonialism and Development*, p. 257.
[28] Vandewalle, *De conjoncturele evolutie*, p. 146.

large investment. Vandewalle estimated that in the period 1950–8 new private investment amounted to nearly £600 million.[29] Until the recession of 1958–60 the Congo was one of the fastest-growing economies of Black Africa, even though heavily weighted towards mining and plantations, and though the bulk of the large-scale enterprises was owned and run by Europeans. Conversely the colony was not a financial burden on Belgium. There at least the development imperative was self-financing.

How then, did the modern colonial state stand as a substitute for an independent state? The argument of this chapter is that it was not so much bad, as was alleged by both colonial nationalists and western liberals and some later historians, as inadequate. Consider first some of its advantages, which may appear more significant in retrospect than during the critical later-colonial period.

Whether in the metropolis or the individual colony, officials believed in certain ethical values, above all impartiality and incorruptibility. This meant that they were immune to sectional pressures of the kind that bore heavily on later indigenous rulers: there was no 'politics of the belly', at least at the European level of colonial administration. They also possessed the administrative skills of advanced western societies – for example, in accounting and budgeting. Tight financial control might limit economic development, but it ensured that no colony incurred serious debts. Expatriate officials might be paid much higher salaries than those of indigenous officials, but there were relatively few of them and government was, by later standards, very cheap. Detached though they might be, most career colonial officials developed very strong affinities for the area in which they worked. In short, colonial government was likely, in the twentieth century at least, to be 'good government' within the limited meaning of the term and concept as it was understood in Europe in the first half of the twentieth century.

Why, then, has colonial government been so severely criticized? It was natural that colonial nationalists should be critical, since colonialism denied them the power and responsibility they desired. But what were the characteristic weaknesses and limitations of the late-colonial state?

Essentially these lay in what it could not do rather than in what it did. It suffered from three major disabilities. First, however well intentioned, it always had divided loyalties, between colony and metropolis. Secondly, because it was alien, it could never fully understand the needs and aspirations of its subject peoples. Finally, and most importantly, because it was alien, it could never mobilize the latent enthusiasms and resources of its dependent peoples: it lacked the legitimacy that

[29] Ibid., p. 107.

only voluntary support by the subject peoples could give. Because it was alien, it was also likely to be cautious and conservative, since, as a 'trustee' (to use the key concept of the period between the wars), it was likely to feel unable to gamble on the welfare of its subjects.

Here one comes to a fundamental fact of underdevelopment. It is due not only to lack of resources but also to weakness of the will to develop, if necessary at the cost of present inconvenience or sacrifice. Colonial governments were, on occasion, able to mobilize considerable indigenous support for projects which it could be shown were directly and demonstrably in the interests of those involved: the Gezira cotton scheme in the Sudan was a classic example. But the fundamental reconstruction of an economy and society required very large changes that might result in a revolution of lifestyles, redistribution of wealth, and changes in attitudes to work. Colonial governments did, of course, make some attempt to undertake this sort of social engineering – for example, by deliberately imposing forms of direct taxation so as to force people to produce or work for the market. The difficulty was that virtually all such efforts could be, were and still are denounced as 'tyrannical' and 'exploitative',[30] whereas much more drastic social engineering with far more disastrous consequences has been accepted as legitimate in post-colonial states.

It follows that, in principle at least, any independent successor regime in an ex-colony should have great advantages over its imperial predecessor. With its 'mind' returned from the old imperial metropolis, it could unify all aspects of decision-making. With no implicit conflict of interests, it should be free to pursue the new state's best interests. Based on the national will as expressed in free elections, it should possess the 'legitimacy' denied to all alien regimes everywhere. On the other hand, every new state was born with the confused inheritance of its own pre-colonial past and the more recent colonial impact. It was also vulnerable to all the weaknesses, self-seeking, corruption and incompetence found in any less-developed society Hence the balance of advantage after decolonization might go either way. The outcome of these conflicting tendencies in some states will be considered in chapters 10 and 11.

[30] For a recent example, see Young, *The African Colonial State*, pp. 124–40.

4

Imperial Economies and Third World Development

It was suggested in chapter 1 that 'optimists' who believe in the potentially beneficial effects of close economic relations between MDCs and LDCs have placed great emphasis on the precise nature of the economic links between them. In particular a basic distinction was made between the theoretical effects of an open free-trading international economy and closed or protectionist systems. In the present chapter it is proposed to examine in more detail the economic devices adopted by the main imperial powers in the twentieth century and to consider what effects these had on the LDCs under their control. Two main topics will be examined: methods of controlling trade and the regulation of currency. Both were critical for the relationship between metropolis and colony and for the economic consequences of colonialism. In both cases the underlying issue must be whether these imperial systems promoted development through interaction and cooperation, or whether they inhibited it through subordination of colonial to metropolitan interests.

1   The Control of Trade: Tariffs, Preferences and Quotas

In a normal independent state there are broadly two alternative trade strategies to choose between: free trade, in the sense that no import or export duties or other physical controls are imposed whose primary aim is to affect domestic production, though there may be substantial revenue-producing duties; and protectionism, which means that such controls are deliberately calculated to influence the character of an economy. But in an imperial system the options are more complicated because the normal bilateral relations between one country and any other are replaced by a series of relationships between the metropolis, any one colony and third parties outside that imperial system. Thus it was possible for a metropolis to use trade controls to guard its home market against both its colonies and third parties, thus treating the colonies as foreign states. Alternatively, the metropolis could give its colonies free or preferential access to its home market, while imposing controls on foreign imports to any part of the imperial system. Finally, the imperial power could vary the terms as between any two colonies. The possible permutations were almost infinite. There was nothing inherent in the mere fact of empire that would determine the commercial situation of a European colony.

Nevertheless, in the modern period imperial tariff policies fell into two contrasting patterns. First, there were empires that were generally free-trading, so that, with individual exceptions, both metropolis and its colonies rejected differential tariffs and other controls as a tool of economic and political policy. The best examples of this were Britain and the Netherlands until the early 1930s, and the Belgian Congo, tied by international treaties, throughout. Secondly, there were empires that were generally protectionist. In these, trade controls constituted a ring-fence surrounding the metropolis and its dependencies, segregating them, to some extent at least, from the world economy. France, the United States, Spain and Portugal conformed to this model at all times; Britain and to some extent the Netherlands from 1932 and 1933 respectively. It is proposed to outline the strategies adopted by only two of these states – Britain and France – and then to consider their consequences for the colonies.

Britain

Of all the modern imperial powers, Britain most nearly conformed to the model of a free-trade state and empire. Starting from the 1820s, Britain gradually dismantled the complex of 'mercantilist' controls on both ships and goods which had built up since the seventeenth century until, by the 1860s, Britain and its dependencies were open to the ships and goods of the rest of the world on precisely equal terms. Indeed, Britain committed itself by a series of 'most-favoured-nation' treaties not to receive from or give any advantages to its colonies that were not available to all others with whom it had commercial treaties. Britain's hope was that, by example and by putting pressure on others, it could create a free-trade world in which there were no obstacles to trade and the only import duties were for revenue purposes. Thus from the 1820s commercial treaties with the ex-Spanish and ex-Portuguese colonies in

America contained clauses along these lines. The Ottoman Empire, China, Japan and Thailand were all persuaded or compelled, usually by a consortium of western states, to sign treaties placing a limit, often 5 per cent, on import duties. Only the European states and the United States altogether escaped this 'empire of free trade',[1] though all managed to break the treaties imposing it in the course of time.

For Britain, the free-trading phase lasted until 1932, though long before then its self-governing colonies – the Dominions, as they were called from 1907 – had used their partial autonomy to reject free trade in favour of protection. India had been allowed to join them in the early 1920s. Why, then, did Britain change its strategy so completely in the 1930s? Three main influences can be pinpointed: demands by the self-governing Dominions for imperial preference; the effects of the First World War; and the world slump of the period after 1929.

Historically the roots of modern British imperial preference lay in the self-governing colonies, the Dominions. Once self-governing in the later nineteenth century, these had successively adopted protection for domestic manufactures. Since Britain was their main market, they wanted it to provide preferences on their key exports. Pressure began at the Ottawa Conference of 1894: the bribe was a preference for British imports, though this was done by increasing duties on foreign goods, not, as the British wanted, by reducing duties on British goods. Since it was clearly against Britain's interests as an international trader to alienate foreign states by discriminating against their imports, the Dominions had no success. In 1914 Britain gave no preferences and refused to impose them on the non-self-governing dependencies.

The recession proved the catalyst, though Britain had experimented with a few preferential duties on 'luxury' colonial imports between 1919 and 1923. For entirely domestic reasons Britain passed the Import Duties Act in 1932 which imposed a general import duty of 10 per cent ad valorem. That was purely protectionist: but the Act also gave a perpetual exemption to all the dependencies and exemption to the Dominions conditional on their providing reciprocal preferences. These were negotiated at the second Ottawa Conference in 1932.[2] The general result was that the Dominions promised increased preferences for British imports in return for advantages in the British market.

---

[1] To adopt the concept made famous in the article by J. Gallagher and R. E. Robinson, 'The Imperialism of Free Trade', Economic History Review, 2nd ser., 6 (1953), pp. 1–15.

[2] The best study of the conference remains I. M. Drummond, Imperial Economic Policy 1917–1939: Studies in Expansion and Protection (London, 1974). See also T. Rooth, British Protectionism and the International Economy: Overseas Commercial Policy in the 1930s (Cambridge, 1993).

The Dominions could not be dictated to, but the dependencies could. All colonies not prevented by international treaties were ordered to pass local legislation to generalize any preferences they already gave throughout the empire, and to give empire (mainly British) imports a preferential margin over foreign goods. This sweeping and arbitrary order was less extensive than it appeared. Relatively few colonies were affected because of international treaties covering West and much of East Africa: the main effect was on British Malaya, Ceylon and India. Conversely, since the British tariff imposed zero rates on most basic foodstuffs and raw materials, only those colonial products which, like sugar, coffee and tea, were subject to revenue-producing duties benefited, since these were reduced for colonial products.

This fact is the key to calculating the effect of imperial preference on the British dependent colonies: it did not create a genuinely cooperative pattern. Whereas the new system was directly beneficial to the Dominions, it was mainly harmful for those colonies affected.[3] On the one hand, they received no advantage in the British market for their primarily commodity exports: since there was no import duty, no preference could be given. The only significant beneficiaries were colonies which exported 'luxury' goods, above all sugar: the complex preference and quota system for empire sugar in fact saved the West Indies, Fiji and Mauritius from disaster, though Indian textile exporters also benefited from continued free entry to Britain and the dependencies. Overall the share of the tropical colonies in the British market increased only from 4.9 to 5.6 per cent between the late 1920s and later 1930s.[4]

As against this, imposed preferences, where they operated, were clearly against the interests of the colonial consumers. This was fully recognized in the dependencies. Preferences were normally established by raising the duty on foreign goods rather than reducing those on British imports. As a result, prices of standard consumer goods were increased without significantly increasing the absolute volume of British imports. In practice, however, imperial preference had little real effect on the major colonies, notably India. India had high import duties, and, even though British goods paid less than foreign goods, they were unable to compete with domestic products. Thus the British cotton textiles' share of the Indian market, which had been declining sharply before 1932 from about half in 1900–4 to 15.2 per cent in 1931/2, rose only momentarily in 1932/3 to 19.7 per cent, and then resumed its decline: in 1937/8 it was down to 10.5 per cent of total Indian consumption.[5]

[3] The standard study of this is F. V. Meyer, *Britain's Colonies in World Trade* (London, 1948).
[4] Calculated by M. Havinden and D. Meredith, *Colonialism and Development: Britain and its Tropical Colonies, 1850–1960* (London, 1993), p. 191.

Because so many colonies did not have to apply imperial preference, the new tariff system probably had limited economic effect. More significant was the system of quotas on textiles imports to the colonies introduced in 1934. From 1931 Japanese textiles, their low prices made possible by a drastically devalued yen and by lower production costs, were seriously penetrating British and other colonial markets. The 1911 Anglo-Japanese treaty barred preferences aimed at Japan, and specific duties on cheaper cotton textiles from 1931 failed to check the invasion. After negotiations for voluntary import restriction by Japan had failed, Britain ordered all colonies not excluded by treaty (mainly East Africa: Hong Kong was also allowed to opt out) to impose quotas on all cotton-textile imports, basing quotas on the average of 1927–9. Since that was before the Japanese surge began, this radically reduced Japanese imports. The main effect was to raise the average price of these goods in colonial markets, but also to benefit Indian cotton-textile exports. Nowhere were the quotas welcomed, except in Lancashire: colonial trading firms disliked them intensely and the poorest colonial consumers were worst affected. Textile quotas lasted until the Second World War made them irrelevant, though general import quotas were then used for virtually all goods.

Indeed, the most significant economic impact of empire trading controls on the colonies was during and after the war. The first main innovation, in fact a revival of techniques used during the First World War, was the introduction of bulk buying of colonial commodities. This began in 1939 and was steadily extended. The British government contracted to buy all or a fixed quantity of a colonial product at an upset price. Initially this began as a device to provide markets when disruption of international trade and shipping shortages might have left producers high and dry; and at the start prices paid bore some relation to immediate pre-war prices. This might indeed have qualified as beneficial cooperation. But over time benevolence hardened into a calculated policy of ensuring British supplies of vital raw materials and of earning foreign exchange by resale. Worse, London refused to increase the prices paid, despite rising international prices. This was justified on the argument that to pay higher prices would increase inflation in colonies that were unable to import trade goods to mop up increased spending power. The profit was held by the relevant British ministry or commodity marketing board.[6]

[5] B. R. Tomlinson, *The Economy of Modern India, 1860–1970* (Cambridge, 1993), pp. 107, 110.
[6] For the genesis of bulk buying in West Africa, see D. K. Fieldhouse, 'War and the Origins of the Gold Coast Marketing Board, 1929–40', in M. Twaddle (ed.), *Imperialism, the State and the Third World* (London, 1992), pp. 153–82;

Parallel with the growth of bulk buying came the rise of these marketing boards. Initially designed to operate state purchase of commodities in West Africa and, under different conditions, also in East Africa, these organizations took over the buying of agricultural products such as cocoa, coffee and oilseeds from the mainly expatriate trading companies. These firms were used as intermediary agents, now paid commissions and expenses, but the prices paid were set by the British government. Once the marketing boards were making large profits (the margin between the price paid to producers and that paid by the British ministries), they were believed to have a second function: to build up reserves so that after the war producers could be compensated for the predicted large fluctuations in commodity prices. Behind this in turn lay official reactions to the Gold Coast Cocoa hold-up of 1937–8 and the *Report of the Commission on the Marketing of West African Cocoa* of 1938, which had recommended a different form of state purchase and marketing. As a result, the system was continued after the war and control of the marketing boards passed to the colonial governments. While the original intentions were certainly honourable, if possibly misguided, once these boards came under the control of local politicians they were used to extract surplus from the rural producer, notionally for development purposes, in practice largely for party and personal advantage. Probably nothing the British did concerning agriculture in West Africa had more serious effects in the longer term than this system.[7]

These wartime devices probably had a worse effect on economic development in these colonies than all the preferences or quotas of the pre-war era. In effect, through the bulk-buying and marketing-board systems the British economy was being subsidized by the colonial producers. Cooperation had become exploitation. Moreover, one of the most serious by-products was that relatively very large amounts of money were held in blocked sterling accounts in London for more than a decade after the war. These sums represented real assets of the colonies which they were prevented from spending on investment or consumption because Britain was unable to provide either the goods that the

---

see also D. K. Fieldhouse, *Merchant Capital and Economic Decolonization: The United Africa Company 1929–1987* (Oxford, 1994), part three, for a full account of bulk buying and also of the evolution of the marketing boards of West Africa.
[7] The early and very critical study of the boards was by P. T. Bauer, in *West African Trade* (Cambridge, 1954), part 5. Much has since been written about them. Early favourable accounts, e.g. in G. K. Helleiner, 'The Fiscal Role of the Marketing Boards in Nigerian Economic Development, 1947–61', *Economic Journal* 74 (1964), pp. 582–610, have given way to denunciation, as in D. Rimmer, *The Economies of West Africa* (London, 1984), ch. 5, and his *Staying Poor: Ghana's Political Economy 1950–1990* (Oxford, 1992), pp. 199–205.

colonies needed, or the hard currency to buy them elsewhere. Thus in 1956, the last year before the independence of both Malaya and Ghana, sterling assets of £250 million were held in London on account of the marketing boards.[8]

On top of these trade controls during the war and the late-colonial period came regulation of shipping and of imports to the colonies. Shipping was a very scarce commodity and so were manufactured consumer goods. Both were rationed. The effect was that from 1939 to the early 1950s colonies could import only limited quantities of goods of all kinds, mostly from the sterling area, irrespective of the foreign exchange they earned through their exports. This rationing was inevitable during the war, but after 1945 it mainly reflected British domestic priorities: British exports went to non-sterling markets to ease the balance-of-payments problem. This was one reason why the colonies were forced to build up such large sterling balances. In addition, shortage of consumer imports caused much resentment in the colonies, in West Africa in particular fuelling political unrest which led to the Accra riots of February 1948 with their momentous effects on decolonization.

The late 1940s proved the climax of exploitative British neo-mercantilism. During the 1950s the whole complex of trade controls and shortages gradually disappeared and by the end of that decade imperial preference was no longer a significant economic factor as price changes eroded specific preference margins and as the GATT terms committed Britain to run down the whole system. Thus the period from about 1932 to the early 1950s constituted a unique period in British imperial trade policy. Its significance for a general assessment of the economic impact of empire will be considered at the end of this chapter.

France

French policy on trade with its colonies stood at the other end of the spectrum from that of Britain, at least until 1932. Although during the Second Empire, and largely for political reasons, Louis Napoleon had moved France towards free trade, this ran counter to fundamental French interests and attitudes. Under the Third Republic after 1871 the tide turned. From 1881 the course was clearly towards strong protective tariffs at home and imperial preference in the colonies. The Méline Tariff of 1892 established the general pattern until the Second World War.

In the early twentieth century France was, therefore, a conventionally protectionist country with a general tariff. Some raw materials were

[8] Taken from Havinden and Meredith, *Colonialism and Development*, table 11.14, p. 268.

allowed in duty free, but, wherever a domestic interest was involved, protection was provided. The average level of duties on protected agricultural products was 25 per cent *ad valorem*, on industrial products rather more: British manufactured imports to France after 1900 paid an average duty of 34 per cent *ad valorem*.

Inevitably the protectionist impulse affected the colonies. There was a political imperative behind French colonial protectionism that had no exact equivalent in Britain. The French overseas empire was politically contentious both because of the large cost of conquest and administration, and also because many believed it distracted France from its primary ambition of reversing the defeat at Sedan in 1871. Colonialists bolstered their case by attempting to give France a monopoly of its colonial markets by enclosing them within the metropolitan tariff wall.

This was not everywhere possible, given international treaties. But with exceptions (primarily the Ivory Coast, Dahomey, Togo and Cameroon after 1918, most of Equatorial Africa, the North African protectorates of Morocco and Tunis), the French empire was assimilated as nearly as possible to the French tariff. The effect was that French goods entered most colonies duty free, while foreign goods paid the same duties as if entering France. But the system was one-sided. Colonial exports did not necessarily enter France free of duty. Some colonial raw materials had free entry because the French duty on these was low or zero; but sugar, which competed with French beet sugar, paid the full foreign duty, because the French beet-sugar industry paid a countervailing excise.

This was the most vulnerable and criticized feature of French imperial commercial policy. It was deliberately one-sided, and in no sense cooperative; yet protectionists were unashamed: France was entitled to compensation for the costs of the colonies. Albert Girault, doyen of early French colonial historians, denounced the system on the ground that no tariff contrived to meet the needs of France, an advanced industrialized country, could conceivably benefit primary-producing colonies. These were in no position to develop modern industry on a large scale and the tariff merely forced them to pay more for French imports than for foreign goods. Ironically, as Girault pointed out, the system did not significantly help the French producer either, since the mere fact of political control was the greatest economic protection his exports to the colonies could have. Only the French cotton industry really benefited, because it had been able to destroy local producers and exclude British competition in Madagascar and Indo-China.[9]

This system, with minor changes, remained unchanged until 1939. The main and most important innovation was a system of support prices

[9] A. Girault, *The Colonial Tariff Policy of France* (Oxford, 1916).

on certain colonial commodities entering France, which at last implied a cooperative balance. During the recession of the early 1930s it became essential to provide a market for virtually unsaleable colonial primary products, so that the colonies could earn money to buy French manufactures and pay interest on their debts. Introduced in 1931, this system of *surprix* had two elements. First, quotas were imposed on foreign imports to France and the colonies of certain products available from French possessions, together with a ban on selected colonial exports to foreign markets and state contracts for the purchase of a quota of colonial commodities. Secondly, specific duties were placed on certain foreign commodities that competed with colonial imports entering on quota. These were intended to provide a reasonable margin above the disastrously low prevailing international price levels for goods for which there was insufficient elasticity of demand in France. For example, specific duties, calculated on the cif (cost–insurance–freight) value, amounted to 91 per cent on non-colonial coffee, less *ad valorem* duties. On cocoa they were 110 per cent, on palm oil 34 per cent, on groundnut oil 34 per cent, on palm kernels 20 per cent, and on bananas 11 per cent. The effect, of course, was that market prices of these commodities in France rose to the price of duty-paying foreign imports; and this in turn, allowing for market imperfections, gave a proportionately higher return to the colonial producer.

Although initially introduced as an emergency response to the conditions of 1931, this system of *surprix* lasted, apart from the war period, into the 1950s and was finally built into the structure of the EEC in 1958, later modified as part of the Yaoundé and Lomé conventions. How does this affect the critique of French protectionism as it affected the colonies? Does it justify using the term cooperative of this form of protectionism?

On the credit side the *surprix* system for the first time made French protectionism two-sided: the colonial consumer received some compensation for paying higher prices for French manufactures. Under slump conditions in the 1930s it kept French West and Equatorial Africa economically alive. After 1945 it encouraged expanded production to the limit of the French market and helped to produce the 'miracle' of the Ivory Coast and other places. In short, this was a classic example of the potential benefits of a cooperative economic system as outlined in chapter 1. *Surprix* was one method by which a metropolitan consumer could be forced to contribute to the welfare of producers in less-developed regions.

But there are strong arguments on the other side. First, as in any system of imperial preference, the metropolis took its return by ensuring that a large share of the colonial market was reserved for its manufactures at prices inflated by high discriminatory duties. It was a matter of luck which partner received most benefit.

A more serious objection is that the *surprix* system, in common with the British quota and preference on colonial sugar, had the effect of making the protected colonial industry less competitive in world markets. The combined effects of high expectations in the protected French (or British) market and the relatively high domestic price of imports meant that commodities receiving this protection were produced almost entirely for that market. This extreme dependence on a single market had obvious implications for the effective economic independence of the colony after decolonization. Indeed, the system can be quoted by dependency theorists as an example of how the core states 'locked' an economy into 'dependence' both on commodity production and the specific metropolitan market. Part of the 'locking' process was the creation of a stratum of beneficiaries ('compradors') on the periphery who had a vested interest in this particular commercial system and therefore in continued dependence on the centre.

Finally, there is the potentially adverse effect of a relatively profitable metropolitan commodity market on the general economic development of a poor country. The relationship can, in fact, cut two ways. On the one hand, it is possible, as the 'optimists' were seen to argue in chapter 1, that a profitable commodity export structure may provide foreign earnings which can be accumulated and used to purchase capital goods, thus financing a more diversified pattern of development. On the other hand, there is the danger that, so long as commodity exports provide a satisfactory return to the producers, the stimulus to invest in other enterprises, and especially manufacturing, may be weakened. If, moreover, high commodity export prices are conditional on reciprocal advantages for imported manufactures, the cards are stacked against the indigenous entrepreneur who wishes to establish local industrial enterprises which would compete with the privileged imports. Under colonial conditions there was no solution to this problem; but after independence the French colonies were free to combine continued access to a privileged French/European market for their commodities and at the same time to establish industries behind protective tariffs.

It is a remarkable feature of the post-1960 francophone world that this combination became possible. This had seemed unlikely after 1945. The French then had a genuine choice between a return to their neo-mercantilist system and adopting something nearer that of Britain. Unhesitatingly they chose the first. The main innovation was that the empire was restructured. The newly named 'overseas departments' (Algeria, the Caribbean colonies and other long-term possessions) became part of the metropolis and fully within the French tariff. Most other possessions became 'overseas territories'. In principle these had freedom to determine tariff policy, though French control over their governments ensured that (apart from the mandates/trust territories) they reimposed the pre-war preferential regime. But in 1954 all these were given free entry of goods to France, subject to some advantages for the overseas departments. This brought them into line with British tropical colonies and ensured that these places had a guaranteed market when France entered the European Economic Community (EEC) in 1958. Meantime the protectorates, and also Indo-China, became 'associated states', treated as foreign countries with complete tariff freedom, but in practice given special advantages for their exports to France.

The dissolution of the French Union and the entry of France into the EEC made remarkably little difference to this structure, mainly because the EEC itself was based on the same protectionist and cooperative concepts. The potential difficulty was that, if the French possessions, and later ex-colonies, retained their advantages in the French market, other member countries of the EEC would be forced to share France's burden of high commodity prices but were unlikely to share its advantages in the colonial markets. The French overseas possessions might have been excluded, but France would not accept this.[10]

The result was the very important compromise by which French possessions, after independence in 1960 and later, could, if they chose, become associate members of the EEC. The effect was that the special economic relationship between these countries and France was transformed into a relationship with the Community as a whole. The associate members gave all full members of the EEC the same tariff preferences as to France; and quotas for their imports to France were eventually shared between the six members of the EEC. In return, the associate members were exempt from the common external tariff of the Community. Development aid became the common responsibility of the Six. This was the genesis of the Yaoundé and Lomé conventions.[11]

The results were generally favourable both to France and to those of its African ex-colonies that chose to accept associate membership – initially all but Guinea. France had shifted part of the burden of paying above-market prices for tropical commodity imports onto its European partners. In principle it had lost its unique trade advantages in these overseas markets; but in practice established market mechanisms, language

---

[10] On French insistence on including its own, but not British, colonies, in the EEC, see C. R. Schenk, 'Decolonization and European Economic Integration: The Free Trade Area Negotiations, 1956–8, *Journal of Imperial and Commonwealth History*, 24, 3 (Sept. 1996), pp. 444–63.

[11] For a good critique of the system to the early 1980s, see A. Hewitt, 'The Lomé Convention: Myth and Substance of the "Partnership of Equals"', in M. Cornell (ed.), *Europe and Africa: Issues in Post-colonial Relations* (London, 1981), pp. 31–42. See also Rimmer, *The Economies of West Africa*, pp. 144–51.

and consumer preferences gave it a continued advantage. Its share of francophone African markets declined, but not drastically. For their part, the African countries retained an advantage in Europe against foreign competitors, particularly against anglophone African states until after 1975, when these states also became associate members under the new Lomé Convention. The common external tariff of the European Community (EC, as it was called after 1967) from which all these states were exempt was slightly lower than the old French tariff, but the essential principle of the *surprix* survived. The *surprix* themselves were phased out between 1965 and 1969; but from 1975 they were replaced by the Stabex system. Each time the Convention was renegotiated a fixed sum was set aside by the EEC/EC to compensate states which became associate members as ACP states for major falls in their commodity earnings which were due to a decline in market prices. A complicated formula took account of both the proportionate drop in prices and the relative importance of any of a specified list of major export commodities. For the poorest countries these payments were grants; for others interest-free loans over five years. Stabex applied in 1975 only to eleven agricultural products and iron ore. In 1979 a parallel scheme, Minex (or Sysmin), was set up to cover most major minerals, plus iron ore, though compensation was on a different basis and was intended to prevent decline of mineral production rather that to support the local economy as a whole.

In one sense, then, the post-independence relationship between Europe and the ACP states, numbering fifty-eight by the early 1980s, represented the continuation and victory of the French system of protectionism and cooperation as liberalized by the *surprix* system. But that is misleading. The French model was constructed to make France as far as possible autarkic, with its own protected markets and sources of raw materials. At its peak, in 1959, some 28.2 per cent of total French exports went to francophone Africa, and France drew 20.3 per cent of its imports from there.[12] After decolonization in the early 1960s this changed. From the standpoint of France, francophone Africa became very much less important. In 1960 its African colonies took 27.5 per cent of total French exports, by 1964 15.4 per cent, in 1978 7.9 per cent, and in 1984 7.8 per cent – only 28 per cent of the 1960 proportion. In the same years, imports from francophone Africa constituted 19.2, 22.3, 4.3 and 5.9 per cent of total French imports, a drop to 30.7 per cent of the 1960 figure. Moreover, the ACP states in Africa (the great majority) were always relatively unimportant for the EEC/EC as a whole, though the decline was less marked. In 1960 the ACP states as a whole took 7.2 per cent of EEC exports and provided 9.6 per cent

[12] *Annuaire statistique de la France* (Paris, 1966).

of EEC imports. In 1984 the figures were 4.6 and 5.5 per cent respectively.[13]

Conversely, however, Europe remained relatively very important for most of these ACP states. Thus in 1977 the trade (exports, imports and services) with the EC of a sample of seven of France's most important one-time Black African possessions was at least 50 per cent of what it had been in 1962 and in only one of these (Sudan) was it less than 29 per cent of the country's total trade. In one case, Central African Republic, it was actually 1 per cent higher. Much the same was true of the ex-British African colonies. Although the British share of their trade had declined in all cases in the same period, in only two countries – Nigeria and Tanzania – was the 1977 proportion less than 50 per cent of that in 1962.[14] Why was this? How far was it due to the protectionist features of the EC?

The general answer must be that the pre-independence institutional links between the ACP countries and their metropolitan states remained strong.[15] The fact of common language and continuing commercial organizations made for a large degree of continuity. So did the orientation of bilateral aid. But, most importantly, Europe provided for many commodities the best, and sometimes the only, market. Moreover, the EC guaranteed free entry for most ACP exports, though with quotas for some processed and manufactured goods. Preferences existed on some exports to the EC, but the general level of non-preferential duties, the Generalized System of Preferences (GSP), was so low on most of the typical ACP exports that they had little effect. Conversely, while ACP countries were not obliged to provide reverse preferences nor to offer free entry to EC goods, they had to provide most-favoured-nation status to the EC. Thus it seems that the dominant EC share of ACP trade was not primarily the result of continuing protectionism along French lines: exceptions were sugar and bananas, which faced particularly strong competition from Europe itself and from America respectively. Rather it reflected the fact of a uniquely open market for tropical commodities.

The EC/ACP system of the Lomé Conventions, still in existence near the end of the twentieth century, was clearly the outcome of earlier French protectionist policy, and the system retains much of its original

[13] IMF, *Direction of Trade* (Washington, 1963–).

[14] D. G. Morrison, R. M. Mitchell and J. N. Paden, *Black Africa: A Comparative Handbook* (London, 1989), p. 182.

[15] Much of the argument of the next paragraphs is taken from C. Stevens and J. V. van Themaat (eds), *Europe and the International Division of Labour: New Patterns of Trade and Investment with Developing Countries: EEC and the Third World: A Survey 6* (London, 1987), chs 2, 5, 6.

character. Essentially it claims to embody the principle that economic development in underdeveloped countries can best be stimulated by a structured cooperative relationship with richer industrialized countries. How far has this been true?

First, during the colonial period, the tariff and other trade-controlling policies were imposed on the colonies and, with rare exceptions, were conceived to further the perceived best interests of the metropolis rather than the colony. It would, therefore, be to some extent accidental if the effects on growth at the periphery were good or bad; and this in turn would depend on whether the interests of the metropolis happened to coincide with those of the colonies.

Secondly, however, the evolution of the ACP group after 1958 shows that the French ex-colonies, along with many one-time British, Belgian and Portuguese African colonies, Ethiopia and Liberia, once these were free to do so, chose to belong to the system. What were, and are, the attractions of the system?

Basically there were two. The first is the guarantee of trading access to the EC, critical in a highly competitive world economy, and especially for 'awkward' goods which compete with products of the EC, such as sugar, beef and textiles. The second is the special feature of the aid provided by the EC: by contrast with many other forms of international aid, it is guaranteed for five years at a time and is contractually binding on the donors. In principle, also, the allocation of aid is done neutrally by the commission in Brussels, and proposals for the use of these funds comes from the ACP members.

These are the positive aspects of ACP. There are perhaps two main negative features that are intrinsic to all special relationships of this kind between MNCs and LDCs.

First, in practice if not in theory, the system assumes that the bulk of the ACP production and export will continue to be in the traditional unprocessed or partly processed commodities. Thus of the twenty-five most valuable ACP exports in 1984, those which had the highest percentage share of the EC market were virtually all long-established commodities: coffee, cocoa, hardwoods, sugar, tea, aluminium oxide, copper ore and groundnut oil. The only innovative import was preserved tuna.[16] Much the same pattern would have been found fifty years earlier, which suggests that the EC system was tending to perpetuate heavy dependence on a few export commodities.[17] If it is assumed that true development requires diversification out of such products into manufacturing, the Community, despite its claimed liberalism, clearly did not

[16] Ibid., pp. 124–5.
[17] See World Bank, *World Development Report 1990: Poverty* (Oxford, 1990), app. table 16, for the structure of merchandise exports of all countries.

encourage this. Indeed, the EC from the start excluded Asian ex-colonies from the ACP states on the grounds that they would prove dangerous competitors in a range of industrial products; and the EC insisted on 'voluntary' restraint by ACP states, notably Mauritius, which proved embarrassing competitors in textiles. In short, the whole system, in common with protectionism under the colonial regime, depends on complementarity. If the ACP members join the ranks of newly industrialized countries (NICs), the whole rationale of the system would be at risk.

Secondly, seen simply in terms of economic performance, it is not clear that, under either French protectionism or the EC regime, these Third World countries did any better in times of economic crisis than other developing countries outside the system. During both the 1930s and the 1980s the effects of international recession on African economies was broadly similar, whether or not a country was within the French protected system or later the ACP system. Thus, whereas during the 1980s Black Africa, all inside the ACP system, had a negative per capita growth rate of minus 2.2 per cent, South Asia, which was not, had a per capita growth rate of 3.2 per cent.[18] There were many other reasons for this disastrous performance, among them the population explosion and the domestic policies of many African states. But it is at least clear that no cosseting within a partially enclosed cooperative system such as the EC (from 1993 the European Union (EU)) could provide sufficient shelter against the realities of the international economy.

Regulation of Currency

The significance of money as an element in modern colonialism and the relations between the West and the Third World is commonly underestimated or ignored. Yet money and the agencies through which it is distributed have been a very important element in the linking of the core to the periphery. It may even be said that it has been the most important single factor in the creation of an integrated global economy. Its importance can be considered under three main heads: first, the introduction of a western-style currency system into what Marxists have called 'natural economy'; secondly, the means used to provide and maintain a 'sound' currency in a colony or independent LDC; finally, the economic consequences of linking a colonial currency to that of the metropolis, both before and after decolonization.

The introduction of a western-style currency was not, of course, necessary for economic activity. All societies had their conventional measures of value − cowrie shells, copper bars, etc.; alternatively an economy

---

[18] Ibid., table 1.2, p. 11.

could thrive on barter. In short, domestic and international trade did not depend on a western–style currency system. Yet the inconvenience of not having one was considerable. Conventional metallic or fiduciary currencies provide a more definite, fixed and universal measure of value than anything else: indeed, even before such currencies were introduced into West Africa, many Africans chose to measure values in European coins, even if the final transaction took the form of barter. It was, therefore, natural for Europeans, once they had occupied these places, eventually to convert these values into actual currencies.

The introduction of a conventional European–style currency where one did not previously exist was likely to have two major consequences. First, it stimulated internal economic activity by facilitating exchange and encouraging saving, which is very difficult without a currency. Secondly, and more importantly, it tended to integrate the Third World economy into that of the West, because colonial products could more accurately be measured in terms of internationally accepted units of value. In particular, it was likely to maximize commercial links with the metropolis – or the source of the currency system in use (dollars, pounds sterling, francs, etc.) – since a common currency facilitated such bilateral links. In short, western currencies can either be regarded, optimistically, as a conduit through which trade, and therefore development, flowed in both directions; or, from a pessimist's point of view, as chains which tethered less to more developed economies and enabled the latter to exploit the former most effectively. Which effect this had depended to a large extent on how western money was introduced and then how it was controlled by the West.

Non–European countries, whether they became formal colonies or were merely drawn into the western economic orbit, fell into two distinct categories that required different treatment.

First, there were those, mostly in Asia, which possessed their own more or less western–style metallic currencies. Until after 1914 these presented few problems. Their currencies could be retained, and the only issue was whether they should remain totally autonomous, depending on the commodity value of their coins or the market rate of paper currency, or be linked at some definite rate of exchange with one or more western currencies.

Secondly, there were countries that did not possess a viable metallic currency. These posed greater problems. Given that it was desirable to introduce a western–style monetary system, should the currency be that of the metropolis or one designed to meet local conditions? How should the colony pay for its currency?

If the new currency contained bullion equivalent to its face value, this posed few economic problems. The introduction of a new currency would almost certainly stimulate trade, particularly with the metropolis whose currency was injected. But it would have a largely neutral economic effect on the colony, since each coin introduced to the colony would represent the export of goods and could pay for imports to the same value. But, if the colonial currency ceased to contain precious metals equivalent to its face value — if it became fiduciary — how should it be supported?

These are some of the main theoretical issues connected with currency in an imperial situation. How did each of the main metropolitan states of the twentieth century deal with them? What effects did money and banking have on economic development in the Third World, including countries that were not part of the formal colonial empires? It is proposed to deal very briefly first with the relatively minor empires, which present few interesting questions, before considering in more detail Britain and France and the wider economic significance of currency regulation and post-independence changes.

Money in the Belgian, Dutch, Portuguese and American empires

The common denominator of all these was that during the twentieth century the national currency of the metropolis became the currency of the dependencies. Thus the American dollar, the Belgian franc, the Dutch guilder and the Portuguese conto/escudo became the official currency, gradually replacing all local alternatives. In American and Belgian territories the coins and values in the colonies were identical with those of the metropolis; in the others, there were differences in how currency was managed.

The Netherlands Indies used the Dutch guilder. But from 1828 the local currency was issued and managed by the chartered Java Bank. It was under strict government control, so maintained the local guilder at par with that of the Netherlands until 1939. After independence the Indonesian guilder was renamed the rupiah. The Java Bank, nationalized in 1953, attempted to sustain the old parity but was unable to do so in the face of Sukarno's inflationary policies.

The two distinctive features of Portugal's colonial currency system were that, until the 1920s, bank notes in the colonies were issued by a private bank, the Banco Nacional Ultramarino, not by the government; and that the exchange value of the colonial currencies varied considerably from that of Portugal. From 1926, however, colonial currencies were brought under tight metropolitan control. The Portuguese escudo was stabilized and became a hard currency. Colonial escudos were given a fixed rate of exchange with the metropolitan escudo and could be converted only into that currency. From 1931 all foreign-currency earnings had to pay a high percentage into locally managed colonial funds: from 1948 such earnings were centralized in Lisbon. This system, very similar to the British Colonial Sterling Exchange Rate system described below, survived until the end of the Portuguese empire.

In all these places the only serious issue arising from use of the metropolitan exchange rate was that this allowed no adjustment for local conditions. This was particularly serious in the Netherlands Indies in the 1930s, when local industries were faced with intensified competition from Japanese imports, helped by devaluation of the yen. The only palliative was imposition of quotas on some Japanese imports.

British monetary policies

For Britain, imperial monetary policy was only a part of a much larger and more important pattern.[19] Since the earlier nineteenth century the pound sterling had been the chief international currency, based on its gold parity and Britain's consistently favourable balance of payments, though not of visible trade. Before 1914, and perhaps as late as 1931, the pound sterling was as much the universal measure of value as the US dollar became after 1945. Although the pound was the unit of currency only within certain parts of the British empire, almost all its components used the pound and the London banking system as the medium through which they exchanged their own currencies into other currencies to settle trade balances. States whose trade was primarily with Britain found it convenient to peg their currencies to the pound and some or all of their official assets in London. Thus in the 1930s foreign countries which were more or less completely tied to sterling included Norway, Sweden, Denmark, Finland, Latvia, Lithuania, Estonia, Eire, Portugal, Iraq, Egypt and Thailand.[20]

This was indeed an empire of money in addition to the 'formal' British empire. Before 1945, however, the fact that sterling was a dominant international currency largely determined monetary policy within the empire. Since a large proportion of the trade of the empire was with Britain, and in view of Britain's very large capital investments in the empire, it was necessary to relate the local currency to that of Britain. As with foreign countries within the sterling area, this did not necessarily mean use of an identical currency: the important thing was convertibility at a realistic and preferably fixed rate of exchange. In 1900 this was by no means universally so; by 1930 it was. The following account summarizes the process of integration.

[19] Apart from the very large specialized literature, the best overall account of the significance and evolution of sterling is in P. J. Cain and A. G. Hopkins, *British Imperialism* (2 vols; London, 1993).
[20] This list is given in ibid., vol. 2: *Crisis and Deconstruction 1914–1990*, p. 80.

At the start of the twentieth century the empire was divided into five main currency groups. First, there were the self-governing colonies – after 1907 Dominions – all of which except Canada and Newfoundland used the gold-based pound sterling at par but had their own mints for coins and issued their own paper money, which could be made legal tender by local legislation. Secondly, there were Canada, Newfoundland and British Honduras, which used dollars related to the US dollar. Thirdly, there was a very important group based on the Indian rupee, which included India, Burma, Ceylon (Sri Lanka), Aden, British Somaliland, Mauritius, the Seychelles, British East Africa and (from 1919 after its conquest from Germany) Tanganyika. Fourthly, there was a group of possessions in the East which used silver dollars, inherited from the predominance of the Mexican dollar: Malaya, the Straits Settlements, Borneo and Hong Kong. These dollars were minted in Britain but their exchange value fluctuated with that of silver. Finally, there were the largely new territories, mostly in Africa, but also in the Pacific, which did not possess any currency system. To create a viable imperial currency system involved finding a formula to bring all of these, except for the American dollar group, into a uniform though not necessarily identical pattern.

The Dominions were no problem. The only difficulty arose after Britain's devaluation in 1931. Would the Dominions follow suit? Australia had already devalued its pound to £1 = £A1.25 in 1931, and retained that parity. New Zealand devalued its pound in line with that of Britain in 1931, then in 1933 followed Australia to £1 = £NZ1.25.[21] South Africa initially refused to devalue with Britain, largely to demonstrate the country's autonomy; but the strength of the South African pound had a disastrous effect on exports, and it devalued to parity with sterling in 1933. Thereafter, with variations in their parity with sterling, the Dominions retained their sterling link until after the end of the sterling area in 1972.

But the rupee and silver countries presented major issues of monetary policy. There were no strictly economic reasons for changing their currency systems: they were perfectly viable and, especially in the case of India, exchange rates were managed with great sophistication. The problem was rather that, seeing the empire as a whole, the coexistence of these silver-based currencies with the British gold-based sterling amounted to bimetalism. This created few problems so long as the market prices of gold and silver remained roughly constant. But the effects of major changes in the ratio were that, if either metal rose in price, it would be exported and exchange rates would fluctuate violently, with adverse effects on commercial and other transactions.

[21] For a full treatment of the New Zealand decision, see G. R. Hawke, *The Making of New Zealand: An Economic History* (Cambridge, 1985), ch. 8.

Such problems are analogous to those arising from different currencies within a single economic area, such as the EU in the earlier 1990s. The logical solution is either a single currency or fixed ratios. But any such solution creates two problems: the rate at which the various currencies are initially fused or pegged; and the likelihood that differing economic developments subsequently make the original ratio unrealistic. The British therefore approached the problem by stages. In 1893 the value of the rupee was de-linked from that of silver and the sterling value stabilized, by conventional management, at Rs1 = 1s. 4d., as compared with the previous 2s., where it was kept, with variations, until 1914. For comparable reasons, the Straits dollar was related by management to sterling at $1 = 2s. 4d. from 1903.

At the time these links caused few problems, and provided solid benefits; though some Indian nationalists criticized the rate of exchange on the ground that it still overvalued the rupee and was therefore to the benefit of expatriate interests, making Indian exports less competitive, and also increasing the burden of the 'drain' of Indian resources.[22] But after 1914 management proved inadequate to maintain these ratios owing to wide variations in the gold–silver ratio and British devaluation. Finally, after the pound had returned to gold parity, it was decided in 1926 to peg the rupee to the new strong pound at Rs1 = 1s. 6d. The Straits dollar was also pegged to the pound. There they remained, despite the devaluation of the pound in 1931, until independence. In the 1920s this policy again caused an outcry in India on the familiar grounds that this strong rupee made Indian exports less competitive and was introduced simply to benefit British expatriates. Yet, ironically, independent India retained the 1926 ratio with sterling until 1966, despite strong evidence that the rupee was by then grossly overvalued.

In tropical Africa, the Pacific and other places where there was no inherited viable currency, British policy went through three distinct phases. During the first, which lasted until 1912 in West Africa and until the 1920s elsewhere, the aim was to establish sterling as the currency of account and actual British coins as the sole legal tender. During the second phase these colonies were given local currencies pegged to the pound but with coins of intrinsic silver value. During the third phase these colonial currencies were made fiduciary.

In the first period Britain did not endow any colony with a stock of British coins. British coins were provided for public purposes, such as paying officials and troops. For the rest importation was left to private enterprise – merchants, contractors and banks – which simply shipped it in like any other commodity. This did not preclude the continued use

---

[22] A good account of this criticism is in B. Chandra, *The Rise and Growth of Economic Nationalism in India* (New Delhi, 1996).

of earlier forms of currency, such as manillas or cowries for non-official transactions.[23] Banks could issue paper money, but this was not legal tender and no British colonial bank was chartered. Thus the imperial currency penetrated the new colonies only gradually.

The main problem with this imported British currency was that the denominations of these coins were not suited to very poor societies: hence the continued use of indigenous currencies. Moreover, the British Treasury was worried that a surge of repatriated coins from a colony might upset the ratio in Britain between token silver and its cover in the Bank of England. The solution adopted came to be known as the Colonial Sterling Exchange Standard (CSES). In 1912 a West African Currency Board was set up in London, with agents in each West African colony, whose function was to replace the banks and merchant houses as the sole supplier of coins to these colonies. The Board supplied a new West African currency, identical in value with British coins, though with smaller denominations, but legal tender only in these colonies. They could be exchanged for sterling at face value. During the following thirty years the CSES system was extended to most other ACP dependencies.

By the Second World War, therefore, most of the British dependent empire, excluding India, Ceylon, Burma, Malaya and other South-east Asian posessions, was united in the CSES, though their pegged currencies performed the same function. Ten years later the system began to come under attack from nationalists and development economists. Its benefits were that it provided the colonies with a currency as stable as that of the metropolis, without the need for sophisticated monetary management which they were unqualified to provide. These were substantial advantages. On the other hand, the CSES required colonies to maintain virtually 100 per cent cover for their money supply in the form of gold or British gilt-edged securities held in London. Although the securities provided interest, the effect was as if they were on a gold standard when Britain itself had a fiduciary currency. Moreover, a colonial trade deficit had to be financed by transfer of money or its equivalent

---

[23] A good example is the manilla, made of bronze or a mixture of copper, lead and tin. Widely used in West Africa, it was briefly made legal tender in Nigerian markets between 1902 and 1911, along with sterling coins, probably to encourage use of the latter. Although no longer legal tender, it continued to be widely used in the south-east of Nigeria until 1948–9, when the stock of manillas was redeemed by the colonial government. By 1949 the weight of manillas redeemed was 2,464 tons, with a metallic value of £153,000. The cost to the government at the upset price (which varied from one region to another according to the conventional weight of local manillas) was £401,000: the loss was carried by the colonial treasury. For details, see United Africa Company, *Statistical and Economic Review* (London, 1948–9), no. 3, pp. 44–56; no. 4, pp. 59–60.

in goods, and this automatically reduced the volume of currency in circulation, with deflationary effects. Finally, the system prevented manipulation of money supply as a tool of economic management.

But the most criticized feature of the CSES among the new breed of development economists of the 1940s and 1950s was that it tied up large sums which might otherwise have been used to finance investment, and so promote economic development. This fact has to be seen in conjunction with the wider range of controls operated by Britain from 1939 to the late 1950s. All colonial foreign-currency earnings had to be paid into the British Exchange Equalization Account and credited in sterling: colonies could buy outside the sterling area only by permission. Sterling credits also were tightly controlled because Britain could not afford to provide the goods the colonies wanted to buy with their credits. Thus in effect the colonies were forced to make large loans to Britain at a time when the commodity boom was earning them large sums. On top of this major colonial export, crops were bought by the British government through bulk purchase at prices often well below world levels. As a result of all these factors colonial credits in London amounted to some £411 million in 1945 and £1,281 million in 1955.

Such exploitation could not last indefinitely at a time of growing colonial nationalism. Colonial credits were gradually liberated during the 1950s; and from 1954 the colonies were freed from the need to maintain the previous 100 per cent cover. They were then able to adopt a fiduciary currency and encouraged to establish their own central banks – though in practice all retained parity with sterling, despite the 1949 devaluation, at least until political independence. Thereafter, however, the British colonies chose to break free from sterling, using London merely as a convenient intermediary for foreign-exchange transactions and keeping appropriate balances with the Bank of England. As will be seen below, in the longer term the pressure of internal demand for public expenditure persuaded most ex-colonies to adopt highly inflationary policies, which were financed mainly by printing money through their central banks. This, in turn, contributed to the disastrous economic condition of most anglophone African states from the later 1970s.

French monetary policy

The general aims of French monetary policy in the colonies were very similar to those of Britain: to have a uniform metropolitan franc as the common currency wherever possible, with free convertibility at fixed parities where this was impracticable. Again 1939 was a major watershed, leading to the end of convertibility into foreign currencies and close metropolitan control of colonial transactions.[24]

---

[24] The following section is based mainly on the following: A. Girault, *Principes de colonisation et de legislation coloniale* (5th edn, 3 vols, Paris, 1927–30; 6th edn,

By the early twentieth century the pattern of French currency policy and institutions was established in much the same form as it was to retain until 1939. Excluding Indo-China, which had to be dealt with separately, the system was based on two things: the universal metropolitan franc and the regional chartered bank.

In existing and newly acquired colonies the franc was imposed as the only legal tender in place of local tokens or barter, though no effort was made to provide a supply of metropolitan coins in Africa until 1908. After 1920 the new metropolitan nickel coinage gradually replaced the previous coins. Since there was no special colonial currency, the colonies automatically devalued with the metropolis in 1936, 1937 and 1938.

Indo-China was initially excluded from this franc system because it possessed its own quasi-currency and because its dependence on trade with China made it essential that its currency should be based on the Mexican silver dollar rather than gold. The French adapted to this situation. They struck piastres of the same silver content as the Mexican dollar, together with smaller coins in decimal denominations, and exported them to Indo-China.

Adoption of this silver standard inevitably raised the problem of exchange rates with the gold franc once silver depreciated in the 1890s. Pegging the piastre to gold, the British solution, was impracticable because of the China trade. Consequently the piastre remained autonomous, its relationship with the franc varying widely: in 1914 one piastre was worth only 2.5 francs; in 1926, as the franc devalued, 27 francs. The commercial inconvenience of this was clear; but it was not until the economic crisis of 1930, when Indo-China's imports from France had risen to nearly half the total, that the French adopted the British model. The piastre was then pegged to the gold franc, as stabilized in 1928, at 1 piastre = 10 francs. When France devalued in 1936 and subsequent years the ratio remained unchanged.

By 1936, therefore, the French imperial currency system was very similar to that of Britain: almost all dependencies used either the metropolitan franc or a currency pegged to it. The most important difference was that France used local monopoly chartered banks to provide both paper money and, after 1920, also token coins as legal tender. Moreover, the cover required for note issue was only one-third of metallic reserves of the bank and for notes three times the fixed capital plus reserve funds, plus any increase in the metallic reserve. Thus the French colonies possessed a partly fiduciary paper currency, and after 1914 the rules concerning reserves for note issue were further liberalized. Hence the French colonial monetary system was never as conservative as that of Britain.

vol. 4, Paris, 1933); A. Duchêne, *Histoire des finances coloniales de la France* (Paris, 1938); F. Bloch-Lainé, *La Zoné franc* (Paris, 1965); M. Leduc, *Les Institutions monétaires africaines, pays francophones* (Paris, 1965).

The Second World War radically changed this pattern. The new system had four main features: exchange control; the end of note issue by private institutions; fragmentation of the unity of the franc; and a system that ensured full convertibility of colonial into metropolitan francs at minimal cost to the colonies.

Exchange control was adopted in 1939 for the same reasons as by Britain: to use colonial foreign-exchange earnings for imperial purposes. Convertibility was suspended and all foreign-exchange holdings and bullion were concentrated in the metropolitan, and later Free French, agencies. The system remained intact for all territories under effective French control until the franc became fully convertible in 1958. As in the British case, this gave the metropolis dictatorial powers over the pattern of colonial trade and was used to bolster the franc as an international currency. The same criticism applies: being forced to buy from France restricted the colonies' range of choice, contributed to inflation due to high French prices, and probably held back economic development.

The second post-1939 innovation was to replace the chartered banks by government-controlled 'institutes' that performed the functions of a central bank, with full control over all aspects of money supply. Although these institutes were tightly controlled by the French government, they provided the successor governments with a means of using money supply as an instrument of economic policy.

The third feature of the period after 1939 was that the franc lost its carefully preserved unity. Cut off from France, the Free French pegged colonial francs to sterling and in 1944 attempted to reimpose a common franc in France and the empire at F200 = £1. This unity proved impossible to sustain, given the economic condition of France and frequent devaluations. For once the separate interests of the colonies were given proper weight, since to devalue them in line with France would have undervalued their currencies. In 1945, therefore, when the franc was devalued to F480 = £1, the overseas possessions were divided into three, plus Indo-China. The West Indies and North Africa had the metropolitan franc. The Pacific territories, the African colonies and Indo-China all had different ratios. As the metropolitan franc continued to devalue, the differentials widened, but in 1949 a halt was called and each of the three currency areas pegged to the franc. The most significant because the most enduring of these was the CFA for all African territories (except Somaliland, which was pegged to the dollar) at CFA1 = 2FM. There it stayed until the metropolitan franc was called down by 100, when the ratio became CFA50 = 1FM, surviving African decolonization. In 1994 the ratio was changed to CFA100 = 1FM, to improve the competitiveness of the overseas economies.

The last innovation of the post-war period was the adoption in 1952 of a new method of assuring the convertibility of colonial currencies at fixed parities without the restricting effects of the British CSES. The pre-war limit on a colonial chartered bank overdrawing on its account with the French Treasury when converting local into French francs was removed. Colonies could now convert local into metropolitan francs without restriction through an operating account in Paris, subject to paying 2.5 per cent on their overdrafts. From 1955 the institutes, which replaced the old banks in West and Equatorial Africa, were released from any obligation to keep money or securities in Paris as cover; and this was later extended to other overseas territories whose central banks conformed to the rules laid down by Paris. Conversely, the colonial banks continued to pay all foreign-currency earnings into the French Treasury. This meant that the colonial francs became entirely fiduciary and the previous cover became available for financing purchases in France or overseas.

Clearly the standing of these colonial currencies now depended entirely on French readiness to meet all calls for foreign exchange by the colonies. The danger was that, if the colonies and later ex-colonies inflated their money supply, while the exchange rate remained fixed, the metropolis might find itself providing relatively 'hard' French francs or foreign currencies in exchange for increasingly 'soft' colonial francs; this, in turn, implied that France would make loans at very low rates of interest. To meet this danger France insisted not only that the statutes defining the functions of these institutes/central banks should be approved by Paris, but also that at least half the members of their policy-making bodies should be representatives of the French Treasury.

The establishment of these exchange accounts and the support given to colonial currencies without cover was the final, and potentially most constructive, French achievement in the field of colonial currency. From a metropolitan standpoint, the system ensured full unity of the franc zone and helped to support the franc with the foreign-exchange earnings of the dependencies. In terms of colonial economic development, however, the system potentially cut both ways. On the debit side, it riveted very close economic relations with France: in particular it made it impossible to alter colonial exchange rates so as to make a territory's exports more competitive. It also imposed 'conservative' monetary policies. There were, however, overriding advantages for small and economically weak territories. The colonies and ex-colonies were provided with currencies as strong as the French franc without the need to maintain any cover or use methods of management that were beyond their technical resources. Since the CFA franc was entirely convertible, the stimulus for foreign investment was considerable. Since, moreover, these territories had a very large share of their trade with France and depended heavily on French aid, it was convenient for their currencies to be tied to the franc. On balance it seems probable that the French imperial and post–imperial currency system served the economic interests of the francophone territories better than any alternative system. This may be regarded as an example of constructive cooperation.

What, then, is the wider significance of these imperial currency and monetary systems for colonial economic development and the relationship of these Third World countries with the metropolitan core? Perhaps three main issues stand out: imperial motives, the effects on colonial modes of production, and the wider effects on the colonial economy.

As to imperial motives, there can be no doubt that currency was used deliberately to integrate the colonies with the metropolis for its own economic advantage. Currency was a means of embedding colonies into the imperial economy.

Secondly, there were two obvious effects of a western–style currency on the modes of production of LDCs. First, by helping to integrate the colony into the international market, it stimulated the restructuring of local modes of production to meet the demands of that market. Secondly, and particularly where western currency was a novelty (as in much of Black Africa and the Pacific), the fact that the colonial government commonly demanded hut or head taxes in cash forced people either to produce for the market or to take paid work to earn cash wages.

Finally, the larger effect of these currency systems was that they stimulated the evolution of an 'open economy' in the colony and links with the wider world system. Market forces had full play. Thus a colony which found itself losing its market overseas could not devalue in order to become more competitive: it had either to become more efficient or to turn to some other product. Nor could a colony stimulate domestic industrialization by devaluation in order to make manufactured imports artificially dear. In short, colonial monetary policy was critical for the incorporation of Third World countries into the international division of labour, and it also provided relative economic stability. Its opponents eventually asserted that this was the stability of economic death.

Currency strategies and development after decolonization

Once independent, the new states had a choice: to retain or to reject their inherited currency system. They responded in two ways. The great majority broke away from external monetary systems to adopt autonomous currencies, but a number of ex-French colonies chose to retain the franc as their currency and accepted its continuing discipline. What were the economic consequences for each group?

On independence all British, Dutch, Portuguese and Belgian dependencies sooner or later broke away from their metropolitan currency areas. All established their own central banks, supported renamed currencies in their own way, and adjusted international parities according to their estimate of the national advantage. An almost invariable early step was to end free convertibility, so that foreign exchange could be obtained only through the appropriate government agency at whatever rate of exchange the government chose to fix: often there were two or more differential rates, distinguishing between importers and exporters. Commonly there was also a black market or parallel rate, representing commercial opinion on what constituted a realistic rate, which varied widely from the official rate. The effect was that few Third World currencies bore any precise relation to real or international values, any more than those of eastern Europe before the end of the Soviet domination.

Nevertheless it is possible to divide those states which adopted their own currencies into two broad categories: those which made little or no attempt to control money supply and whose currencies therefore sooner or later became almost worthless; and others which adopted relatively austere policies and sustained high – often over-high – exchange rates.

A typical example of the first group was Ghana. Ghana adopted a £G in 1957 on parity with the pound sterling at £G1 = $2.80. The adoption of the cedi in 1965, at the rate of C2.40 = $1.17, did not alter the effective exchange rate. Thereafter, ignoring terminological and technical changes, the cedi had successively to be devalued, until by 1986 the official exchange rate was C1 = $0.011. Thereafter the cedi was allowed to find its own level, as indicated by weekly auctions of foreign exchange.[25]

By no means all ex-colonial countries, however, allowed their currencies to deteriorate in this way. Broadly, those in South and South-east Asia, apart from Indonesia before 1966, maintained a reasonable degree of currency stability by means of avoiding grossly inflationary policies. India, for example, managed to retain the pre-independence parity with the pound, following its devaluations against the dollar, until 1966. By that time, however, the rupee was clearly overvalued, maintained at the existing exchange rate only by a host of economic regulations and controls, and by making it non-convertible. Eventually, in 1966, and under pressure from the IMF, the rupee was devalued by 36.5 per cent. This, in fact, marked the beginning of a slow liberation of India's post-independence economic system, though the immediate economic results were disappointing.[26]

[25] Taken from D. Rimmer, *Staying Poor: Ghana's Political Economy 1950–1990* (Oxford, 1992), pp. xi–xii.
[26] For an analysis of Indian economic policy in this period and its relation with the rupee , see J. N. Bhagwati and P. Desai, *India: Planning for Industrialization: Industrialization and Trade Policies since 1951* (Oxford, 1970), esp. ch. 22.

The other option was for the new states to maintain their links with the currency of their former metropolis, and this was the choice of the majority of the one-time French dependencies. It was not universal. Indo-China, Guinea, Tunisia, Morocco (and also briefly, in 1962–7, Mali) broke all links with the franc, and established their own autonomous currencies after the manner of anglophone states, using Paris largely as a convenient market for international currencies. But the rest – most of the francophone states of West and Equatorial Africa, Madagascar, Algeria and the smaller territories – chose to remain members of the franc zone on much the same terms as before independence. Modifications in the system were made to reflect their new sovereign status: they joined the IMF independently and had separate foreign currency accounts in the French Office de Stabilisation. But continuity was more significant. These states continued to pool their foreign-currency earnings, accepted common external rates of exchange and fixed internal parities, and accepted the rules made by the Monetary Committee of the franc zone. They also accepted continued French representation on the boards of their central banks. In short, they surrendered some portion of their new sovereignty, and the freedom to manipulate money supply. Their reward was an operating account in Paris with unlimited drawing rights and currencies almost uniquely strong and convertible in the developing world.

The economic consequences are debatable.[27] Since the international exchange value of the franc was determined by the economic situation and strategy of France, it was fortuitous whether the economic interests of a new state were best served by that particular rate of exchange. This was of limited significance so long as the greater part of a country's trade was with the one-time metropolis, particularly if its major exports were given favoured status, as through the *surprix* system or in the EC. But this situation changed once Britain, France and other one-time imperial states in the EC ceased to command as large a share of the ex-colonial trade as they had done previously. The new states had then to compete in the international market, except in so far as the system set up by the EC continued to give them special advantages. How did the franc-zone system affect the francophone territories in this changed situation?

On the positive side, the CFA franc saved all of them from the grosser weaknesses of government financial manipulation. Unlike Ghana, Nigeria and many other developing countries, they did not need to use physical controls on trade and international transfers to maintain their

---

[27] Much of the data used in the following argument are drawn from the World Bank Policy Research Report, *Adjustment in Africa: Reforms, Results, and the Road Ahead* (Oxford, 1994).

currency. Most had low inflation throughout the post-decolonization period, and therefore they did not have to undergo the very painful experience of currency devaluation in and after the period of recession in the 1980s.

On the other hand, a 'sound' currency is no protection against either unwise domestic policies or international changes. On the domestic front it did not, for example, prevent franc-zone countries from over-expansion of economically inefficient manufacturing, imposing state monopolies on commodity production, underpaying agricultural producers, or borrowing heavily. Thus in 1982 three of the African states with the highest debt-service obligations as a proportion of the export of goods and services were members of the franc zone: the Ivory Coast (the highest of all at 36.9 per cent); the Congo People's Republic (22.6 per cent); and Cameroon (15.6 per cent).[28]

The more serious effect was on their international competitiveness. The prolonged decline in the terms of trade of commodity exports during the 1980s meant that exporters had either to devalue their currencies in line with market prices or, if their currency was fixed, to reduce domestic prices accordingly. The World Bank calculated that between 1980 and 1990 the real exchange rate of a group of non-African commodity-exporting countries depreciated by an average of 60 per cent, implying that African countries needed to depreciate by at least as much to remain competitive. Most African countries with flexible currency systems did this, often under pressure from the World Bank/IMF as part of the Structural Adjustment programmes, which are described in chapter 8. But real depreciation in the franc-zone countries averaged only 5 per cent in this period, as the franc appreciated against the dollar as a result of France's hard-currency strategy. The result was that the real effective exchange rate in all the African franc-zone countries appreciated, and that the growth rate of exports in most of them slowed down significantly.[29]

This does not necessarily mean that the fixed parity system is undesirable. The implication is rather that such a system needs to be more flexible. Ideally the CFA should be adjusted periodically to reflect changes between the economic circumstances of the developing and developed members of the franc zone. In fact, the first significant adjustment did not take place until 12 January 1994, when the exchange rate was fixed at one French franc to 100 CFA – that is, the CFA currency was devalued by 100 per cent. This should clearly have been done long before 1994 and it remained to be seen what effects this

[28] The World Bank, *Toward Sustained Development in Sub-Saharan Africa* (Washington, 1984), table 13, p. 69.
[29] World Bank, *Adjustment in Africa*, pp. 55–7; table A3, p. 226; table A4, p. 227; table A6, p. 229; table A16, p. 242; table A20, p. 246.

belated devaluation would have on the commercial fortunes of the franc countries.

Imperial and post-imperial currency policies formed only part of the wider strategy of imperial economic integration. It is now necessary to consider the strategy as a whole and its wider implications for the Third World components of these empires.

There is no doubt that the primary economic aim of the European powers, as later of Japan in the east, was to maximize the benefits they obtained from their colonies. A means to this end was the closest possible integration of the colonies into the western 'core' economies. As was emphasized above, colonialism was not a necessary means of such integration. During the nineteenth century in particular the overwhelming economic, financial and political pull of the newly industrialized West ineluctably drew other parts of the world into its orbit. The concept of 'informal empire', though difficult to use with precision, captures this pull. The power of sterling as the main international currency, the ability of the London and, to a lesser extent also, the French and German financial markets, to provide loans for development, and the availability of technology and people to apply it ensured that very many politically independent countries became intimately bound up with the West. Until the early twentieth century, with the rise of the United States and Japan as alternative sources of all these assets, Europe necessarily became the core of the emerging new world economic system.

The formal colonial empires and their systems of commercial and currency regulation must, therefore, be seen as empires within a larger worldwide quasi-imperial system. Yet colonialism provided the opportunity for far more planned and intensive integration of peripheral countries because they were subject to imperial sovereignty. The regulations and policies outlined above were the expression of this power. How much difference did they make? Ignoring for the moment the effects of this control on the colonies themselves, how completely did the metropolitan countries succeed in integrating the colonies into the imperial economies? Did their trade and currency regulations significantly distort the 'natural' economic patterns of these territories? Although it is only one measure, the proportion of the trade of colonies with their metropolis is probably the best single test of the extent of this integration. Since measures to integrate the colonies had reached a very advanced stage by the mid-1930s, even though these became more intensive during and after the Second World War, it is proposed to take this period as a test of the effectiveness of these measures and, to save space, to use the British empire as the model. Very similar patterns would, however, be seen in the other European empires.

First, how important was the empire to Britain? In 1934 44.0 per cent of British exports went to the empire. For a considerable range of important British manufactures the proportion was considerably higher: indeed, the empire was critical for many engineering goods and for cotton textiles, despite the recent reduction in Indian imports of British cottons. Conversely, in 1934 35.3 per cent of total imports to Britain came from the empire, including 49.2 per cent of foodstuffs and 36.8 per cent of industrial raw materials. These figures show a significant increase over those for 1913, when the empire had taken 37.2 per cent of British exports and provided only 24.9 per cent of its imports, though they were later to reach a peak around 1947, when the empire took 52.7 per cent of British exports and provided 45.2 per cent of British imports.[30] These high figures in the 1930s reflect both the longer-term effect of the various tariff and currency measures outlined above and the more immediate effects of the international recession. They suggest that, while the empire was in no sense autarkic, it had become a vital element in the British economy.

If the standpoint is reversed, it is clear that Britain was still more important as a trading partner for many of its overseas possessions, though not for all. This was most obvious for British Africa. In 1937 39.0 per cent of all British Africa's exports went to Britain: this had been much higher earlier – 85.3 per cent in 1905, for example – and it rose to 58.4 per cent in 1950.[31] For the self-governing Dominions Britain was also a vital market, its value increased by the concessions made in Ottawa in 1932. Thus, at one extreme was New Zealand, 80 per cent or more of whose exports went to Britain in the 1930s; at the other was Canada, whose main trading partner was the United States, but which sent about 38 per cent of its exports to Britain in the mid-1930s, up from 31.4 per cent in 1928/9.[32] India was the best test case of the effects of both tariff autonomy and the post-1932 preference system. In 1913/14 India had an adverse trade balance with Britain of some £39 million; by 1938/9, after it had adopted high tariffs and despite imperial preference, it had a favourable balance of about £9 million.[33] Nevertheless, Britain remained

---

[30] Figures taken from D. K. Fieldhouse, 'The Economic Exploitation of Africa: Some British and French Comparisons', in P. Gifford and Wm. R. Louis (eds), *France and Britain in Africa: Imperial Rivalry and Colonial Rule* (New Haven and London, 1971), p. 646, where the sources are shown.

[31] Ibid., pp. 647–52.

[32] N. Mansergh, *Survey of British Commonwealth Affairs: Problems of External Policy 1931–1939* (London, 1952). pp. 181, 109.

[33] *The Economist*, 30 Oct. 1937, quoted in R von. Albertini, *European Colonial Rule, 1880–1940: The Impact of the West on India, Southeast Asia, and Africa* (Oxford, 1982), p. 62.

a vital export market for India. The proportion of India's exports to Britain rose from 20.9 per cent in 1929 to 31.7 per cent in 1937.[34] Finally the eastern colonies, including Malaya, were much less closely tied to the British economy. In 1938 they took only 16.2 per cent of their imports from Britain and sent 19.8 per cent of exports there. For the small Pacific territories the proportions were 32.8 and 47.2 per cent, and for the Caribbean 36.3 and 49.2 per cent.[35]

It is dangerous to draw large conclusions from such data, but their broad implications seem fairly clear.

First, particularly during the testing conditions of the 1930s, the empire did constitute a cooperative trading organization which helped both Britain and the colonies to find markets for products which were difficult or impossible to sell on the international market.

Secondly, the fact of empire, and its commercial and monetary strategies and institutions, clearly had a significant effect in diverting the trade of its members from what might have been their 'natural' patterns, given their geographical situations and the availability of other potential trading partners. This must not be overemphasized, since in the 1930s much of the trade reflected the once unique and still significant position of Britain as one of the world's leading industrial exporters and as the largest single consumer of colonial commodities. Yet the influence of imperial rule on commercial patterns seems undeniable. As late as 1930/1 37.2 per cent of Indian imports came from Britain compared with 7.5 per cent from Germany and 9.2 per cent from the United States, while 23.5 per cent of its exports went to Britain, only 6.5 per cent to Germany, and 9.4 per cent to the United States.[36] By 1968, when the effect of preferential tariffs had virtually disappeared, when most one-time British possessions had autonomous currencies and were free to trade as they wished, the Commonwealth as a whole (then excluding South Africa) took only 22 per cent of British exports and provided only 22 per cent of British imports. In the same year the average percentage of Commonwealth exports destined for Britain was 14 and the average percentage of commonwealth imports coming from Britain was 12.[37]

This dramatic decline in the commercial importance of Britain to its colonies and ex-colonies in the period after the mid-1950s was not due entirely to the running-down of the imperial system. Major contributing

---

[34] Ibid., pp. 62, 64. The trade-balance figures have been converted from rupees at the prevailing rates of exchange with the pound sterling.
[35] Havinden and Meredith, *Colonialism and Development*, p. 249.
[36] D. Kumar (ed.), *The Cambridge Economic History of India*, vol. 2: c.1757–c.1970 (Cambridge, 1983), table 10.2A–B, pp. 864–5.
[37] Taken from J. D. B. Miller, *Survey of Commonwealth Affairs: Problems of Expansion and Attrition 1953–1969* (London, 1974), pp. 442, 445.

factors were the revival after the war of competing markets and sources of Commonwealth imports and the serious erosion of British industrial competitiveness. But it is at least arguable that the end of the imperial economy significantly increased the propensity of the one-time British colonies to look for and discover the role in the international economy that best suited their needs and interests. That is one measure of the effect the imperial economic systems had on incorporating Third World dependencies into the imperial and international division of labour.

That, of course, ignores the effects that these imperial systems had on the economic development of the colonies during the colonial period, and in particular how their condition compared with that of non-colonial territories in the Third World. That, and the question of how far imperial economic systems acted as agencies for cooperative development, is the main theme of part III of this book.

Part III

Trade, Colonialism and Development

5

Trade and Development in the Settler Societies

It was suggested in part I of this book that there are, broadly, two contrasting interpretations of the likely impact of the West on the economic development of the rest of the world. The 'optimists' have always argued that the impact would be favourable, basing their case mainly on the claimed benefits of trade, the transfer of technology, and the investment of capital. For their part the 'pessimists' have claimed that, while there may have been some benefits from these things, they were outweighed by related disadvantages. The aim of this and the following two chapters is to test these arguments against the facts for the twentieth century, roughly to the 1960s, which marked the end of colonialism in its nineteenth-century form and the start of the new international system of the second half of the century. But there are two major difficulties in doing this.

First, there is the difficulty that, before about 1950, there is very little reliable statistical information on the economic performance of most Third World countries. Modern practice is to assess a country's economic development in terms of its gross domestic product (GDP) or its gross national product (GNP), either in total or in relation to population.[1] For very few countries outside Europe and North America is accurate earlier information on GDP, or even population, available: indeed, for many Third World countries the figures on these and most

---

[1] GDP measures the total value of goods and services within a country. GNP takes account also of overseas transfers both ways.

other matters currently provided by governments for international organizations such as the World Bank must be regarded as highly speculative.

The second main problem is conceptual. To say that intimate contact between the West and the rest of the world was good or bad for the latter is to assume that, if such contact had not taken place, there was a possible alternative that was either worse or better than what actually occurred – that is, to construct a counter-factual proposition. Thus it could be argued that the creation of a single world economic system, and more particularly the imposition of colonial rule, stunted the natural development of Third World countries, creating 'underdevelopment' rather than development.

It is in the nature of such counter-factual propositions that they can very seldom be proved or disproved, and no attempt will be made to do either. The following account will use what evidence is available to answer the simpler question of what economic impact the West appears to have had on the Third World, and in particular whether the creation of a world trading economy, initially centred on western Europe and North America, had beneficial or damaging effects on Third World countries.

But in doing this an important distinction must be made between two forms this impact took. On the one hand, there was the general effect of economic integration, mainly through trade, investment and migration. On the other hand, there were the specific effects of the imposition of colonial rule. In this account it is, therefore, proposed to consider first, in this chapter, the evidence on the general impact of the West, using the examples of Latin American countries which had been politically independent from the 1820s, before western capitalism had much if any impact on them, and of British settler societies which were self-governing from the mid-nineteenth century.[2] Such an examination should provide reasonably clear evidence on the general impact of foreign trade, capital and settlement before we consider the more specific impact of colonialism in the following chapters.

But it is necessary first to state what criteria to adopt when measuring 'growth' and 'development', and how these can be measured, given the problem of reliable historical data.

'Growth' can be described simply as the increase of the real output of an economy over time. Although this ability to produce more goods and services may be the result of any one or more of a number of changes – typically an increase in the quantity and quality of its capital goods, its

---

[2] But A. G. Frank, in his well-known study *Capitalism and Underdevelopment in Latin America* (London and New York, 1967; 2nd edn, London and New York, 1969), argued that capitalism was imposed during the period of Spanish rule from the very beginning.

labour force, its exploited natural resources, a more efficient use of any of these things, or the development and introduction of innovative techniques – growth does not necessarily imply structural change. It can result simply from doing more of the same things rather better than before.

'Development', on the other hand, is usually taken to mean a process of economic transition, involving the transformation of an economy so that there is not only growth but the prospect of continuing and expanding growth based on higher levels of saving, investment and technical development. It is, therefore, possible to have 'growth without development'. This would imply that, while the more intensive use of existing forms of production and resources can increase the national product, it can do so only up to a point. Thereafter an economy can stagnate, or even regress, if population growth outruns production.

For long economists have tended to assume that the essential difference between mere growth and development lay in the combination of savings/investment and modern industry. From Marx, for whom history started with the evolution of capitalism, to the development economists of the 1950s and 1960s it has seemed self-evident that development depended on breaking out of the grip of agriculture, with its Malthusian implications, and into manufacturing, which offered higher and unlimited returns to the investment of capital and labour. A related hypothesis is that development, including industrialization, depended on raising a country's saving and investment level beyond a certain point, after which its capacity to save and invest would increase exponentially: in an influential popularization of this argument Walt Rostow called this 'the take-off'.[3] Moreover, since at least the later nineteenth century critics of imperialism have blamed lack of industrialization for the limited economic development of colonial and other Third World countries, seeing this as the deliberate policy of the already industrialized West which wanted to preserve Third World markets for its own products.

This, therefore, raises the double question of whether there is a fundamental difference between growth and development and whether both growth and development are possible without industrialization. To avoid this problem the American economist Lloyd G. Reynolds has evolved a different terminology. He distinguishes between 'extensive growth' and 'intensive growth', though without defining the conditions for either. 'Extensive growth' is described as 'A situation in which population and output are growing at roughly the same rate, with no secular rise of per capita output . . .'. He points out that growth is growth, even if it only keeps up with population increase, and that increase itself implies some growth to sustain larger numbers. For many societies

[3] W. W. Rostow, *The Stages of Economic Growth* (Cambridge, 1960).

this process may continue for many centuries without substantive change. But for some, and now most, societies there has come a 'turning point', and the start of 'intensive growth'. He defines this as 'the beginnings of a sustained rise in per capita output ... sustained in the sense that, although year-to-year growth rates are uneven, per capita output does not fall back to its initial level'. This, however, is not an irreversible condition: by contrast with the implications of a once-and-for-all 'take-off', 'the turning point is not an insurance policy for all future time'.[4] Notable subsequent economic changes are indicated by the end of a natural increase in population, the start of a decline in the absolute size of the labour force, and a rise in real wages owing to the end of a surplus pool of labour.[5]

The value of these concepts is that they are flexible. The turning point does not, as did Rostow's take-off, depend on a particular rate of savings. It can be based on the export of agricultural products or the products of handicrafts and small workshops. Moreover, it can be roughly measured, using available data which would be inadequate for a more precise definition of the start of development.

Reynolds's definitions are open to challenge, but they offer a stimulating approach to the nature of modern Third World economic development. It is, therefore, proposed to summarize his general argument before examining evidence by which it can be tested.

Applying his criteria Reynolds first (in chapter 2) examines the character of 'extensive growth'. He rejects terms such as 'traditional' and 'subsistence', because, as all modern research has shown, virtually all pre-industrial societies had manufactures and traded. Rather, the defining feature of such societies was that most production was 'household' or 'handicraft', not excluding highly specialized and skilled craft industries. What kept these as 'extensive-growth' economies was that output only kept up with population growth, in agriculture by expanding the area under use and greater use of organic fertilizers and double-cropping, in industry by greater sophistication in the same techniques of production. Thus there must have been significant economic change, otherwise production could not have kept up with population increase, which Kuznets estimated at perhaps 0.35 per cent per annum from 1800 to 1850 and 0.56 per cent per annum from then to 1900.[6]

What, then, enabled a large number of Third World countries, many of them European colonies, to move to 'intensive growth' even before 1900: Reynolds lists twenty-two of them. His basic explanation

[4] L. G. Reynolds, *Economic Growth in the Third World, 1850–1980* (New Haven and London, 1985), pp. 7–8.
[5] Ibid., p. 9.
[6] Ibid., p. 23.

(in chapter 3) is the great world economic boom of the period 1850–1914 whose effects were transmitted from Europe and North America to much of the rest of the world via trade. The unprecedented expansion of industrial production, coupled with faster population growth in the West, created a huge demand for food and raw materials from the periphery. The sum of world trade (exports plus imports) grew at an average rate of 50.3 per cent per decade from 1850 to 1880 and at 30.5 per cent in the decades before 1913. By 1913 the ratio of world trade to world output had reached 33 per cent.[7] In response, tropical exports grew at an average of 3.6 per cent a year between 1883 and 1913, with no secular changes of importance in the terms of trade.[8]

This world boom had a huge impact on much of the Third World – indeed on any area that had or could generate exports needed by the West. Around 1900 there was even widespread concern in the West that the expansion of tropical products could not keep up with the demand, generating the sort of theorizing among Marxists about imperialism as a search for sources of these things that was described in chapter 2, and also attempts by industrialists such as William Lever to establish plantations to increase the output of industrial raw materials.[9] The significant thing is that this crisis of supply never happened. Largely through the expansion of peasant production, but also through large-scale foreign-owned capitalist enterprises in mining and plantations, the Third World met the demands of the industrial West. In the course of doing so those countries which were able and willing to make the effort obtained the economic benefits of an international market and were able to exploit the two possibilities to which the classical economists had pointed, comparative advantage and vent for surplus.

It was because of this long boom that Reynolds and others argue that trade created the possibility of LDCs moving from 'extensive' to 'intensive' growth. But between 1913 and about 1945 conditions in the international economy changed for the worse. The average growth rate of the West dropped from 3.6 per cent before 1913 to 2.7 per cent from 1913 to 1929, and to 1.3 per cent from 1929 to 1938. In the same period the rate of growth of the value of tropical exports fell from 3.7 to 3.2 and then 1.9 per cent, while the terms of trade, roughly constant

[7] Ibid., pp. 32, 33.
[8] Ibid., p. 34.
[9] About 1900 the young J. Maynard Keynes was predicting deterioration in the West's terms of trade with the Third World (see ibid., p. 45). William Lever established coconut plantations in the Solomon Islands, attempted to start oil-palm plantations in the Gold Coast and Nigeria, and, when rebuffed there, did so in the Belgian Congo. See D. K. Fieldhouse, *Unilever Overseas: The Anatomy of a Multinational* (London, 1978), chs 8, 9.

before 1913, turned very strongly against the Third World exporters. This, of course, was also the period when belief in the possibility of sustained development through trade was first seriously called into question. In the 1950s and early 1960s Marxist historians were still arguing that deterioration in the terms of trade between the world wars proved that this was impossible.[10]

Developments after about 1950 seemed to prove them wrong. The Second World War was followed by what Reynolds calls 'the greatest boom', lasting from the later 1940s to 1973, the year of the OPEC oil-price rise. In these years average GNP of the developed countries grew at an average of 4.9 per cent per annum, and the volume of exports by the developed (OECD) countries by an average of 8.6 per cent. Exports from LDCs grew rather less fast, since the trade of the developed countries was increasingly between themselves, so that the Third World's share of world trade fell from 25.3 to 17.7 per cent. But, in absolute terms, between 1950 and 1970 the exports of most Third World countries grew at least as fast as before 1913. Perhaps more significantly, the share of manufactures in Third World exports rose from 7.6 per cent in 1955 to 16.7 per cent in 1970, while the share of foodstuffs fell from 36.7 to 26.5 per cent, implying a welcome diversification of many.[11]

This post-war boom, the result, among many other factors, of restocking and initially stimulated by the Korean War of 1950–2, ended in 1973 with OPEC's oil-price increase of some 400 per cent, followed by a near doubling of the price in 1979. While the small minority of oil-exporting countries benefited, the international economy suffered nearly as severe a blow as was caused by the First World War. The growth of world exports dropped to around 4 per cent, prices for Third World commodity exports fell in real terms, and many LDCs were forced to borrow on the international money markets to meet the obligations incurred during the boom period. The result was a period of serious hardship for many of these countries. This, in turn, led to renewed questioning of the value for Third World countries of specialization in the export of both commodities and manufactures and the popularization of some of the 'pessimistic' arguments that were surveyed in chapter 2.

For the present discussion, however, the main significance of Reynolds's argument is that he pinpoints the growth of external trade as probably the most important single factor in the development of peripheral countries from 'extensive' to 'intensive' growth, both before 1913 and again after 1950, though he qualifies this by suggesting that political factors, such as the achievement of stable government after a period of domestic

---

[10] See, in particular, J. Suret-Canale, *L'Afrique noire: L'Ère coloniale* (2 vols, Paris, 1964; Eng. edn, *French Colonialism in Tropical Africa* (New York, 1971)).
[11] Reynolds, *Economic Growth*, pp. 36–7.

disorder or (in the case of colonies) of independence' might have a significant influence. To test this hypothesis sections 1 and 2 will survey the
experience of the major Latin American countries and two self-governing British settler colonies, all of which were politically free to determine
their own economic strategies and most of which adopted a growth-
through-trade strategy with varying degrees of success. The following
two chapters will then consider the special case of non-self-governing
European colonies to investigate how far colonialism might affect the
'growth-through-trade' hypothesis.

1 Trade and Development in Latin America

The Latin American countries,[12] are among the few non-European
states, other than the United States and, after about 1860,[13] the group
of British settler colonies, called Dominions from 1907, whose experience
can be used to test the extent to which independent or quasi-independent
countries could benefit from an economic strategy based on export of commodities. Their common denominator was that in the mid-nineteenth
century all except the United States were relatively poor societies with
very little industry, heavily dependent on agriculture and mining, distant
from the main centres of economic development in Europe; yet before
1913 a number of the larger Latin American states and all the British
Dominions (though these were not included in his list) had passed
Reynolds's 'turning point'. What light does their comparative success throw
on the concept of development through trade in export commodities?

Consider first the main Latin American republics. Although several
of these one-time Spanish or Portuguese possessions had huge natural
resources, including gold and silver, and had developed substantial
commodity production, notably of sugar and later coffee in Brazil, until

---

[12] The main argument here is based on C. Furtado, *Economic Development of
Latin America* (1970; 2nd edn, Cambridge, 1976).
[13] The date is chosen as symbolic because in 1859 the Canadian government
imposed a new set of import duties which, though nominally revenue producing, had the effect of protecting some nascent Canadian industries against foreign
and British competition. Protests by the British government were rejected.
Thereafter all colonies with 'responsible government' had effective freedom to
adopt their own economic and fiscal policies. Most had adopted protectionist
tariffs by 1900 and the British consulted them before including them in British
commercial treaties. In 1897, on the demand of these colonies, Britain abro-
gated her long-standing commercial treaties providing most-favoured-nation
status for foreign trade with British possessions. These colonies were, therefore,
for all practical purposes independent economic actors and could opt into or
out of the international trading economy.

independence in the 1820s their overseas trade, despite liberalization during the eighteenth century, was handicapped by metropolitan controls, market limitations in Europe, and the high cost of transport, both internally and across the sea. Political freedom, though in many countries followed by economically debilitating political instability, coincided with the beginnings of the great economic development of Europe. In combination these provided the first opportunity for substantial Latin American economic development.

By the mid-nineteenth century industrializing Europe, initially mainly Britain, offered Latin America the three things its economic growth needed: an expanding market for food and minerals; capital investment to pay for internal communications and other infrastructural improvements; and increasingly cheap and fast maritime transport. In combination these enabled Latin America to become part of the new international division of labour.

The response by the larger Latin American countries varied according to their natural endowment. They fell into three main groups. First, Argentina and Uruguay, with temperate climates and vast reserves of potentially exploitable land, developed in much the same way as British settler colonies of the nineteenth century. They borrowed capital from Britain to create extensive networks of communications to open up their hinterlands. They adopted western, particularly US, agricultural techniques in stock rearing and processing and in grain production. In the later period, between about 1880 and 1914, they accepted very large numbers of European immigrants. By 1914 Argentina had a rail network of 31,000 km, and exported 5.3 million tons of cereals and 376,000 tons of frozen meat. It has been estimated that real GDP grew at an average rate of at least 5 per cent between 1880 and 1914, and at 6.3 per cent in the decade before 1914, which, despite population growth of 4.3 per cent in the later period, still implied a substantial rise in real per capita incomes.[14] Its per capita GDP was then one of the highest in the world.

In view of the importance often placed on manufacturing in development, it is, however, significant that manufacturing output was only about 15 per cent of GDP in 1900 and was still only 19 per cent in 1929.[15] Much of this industry was related to the agricultural export sector – meat-packing plants, flour mills and wool-washing enterprises. There were some import-substituting industries, but textiles, later to become important, were very underdeveloped. In short, in 1914 Argentina was a highly successful commodity-exporting economy, closely integrated into the European economy and the international division of labour.

[14] Quoted in Reynolds, *Economic Growth*, p. 88, based on C. F. Diaz Alejandro, *Essays on the Economic History of the Argentine Republic* (New Haven, 1970), p. 3.
[15] Reynolds, *Economic Growth*, p. 88.

It seemed a classic example of the value of comparative advantage and 'vent-for-surplus'.

A different model can be seen in the tropical regions of Latin America – Brazil, Colombia, Ecuador, the Central American Republics, parts of Venezuela and Mexico – and the Caribbean islands. For these comparative advantage dictated concentration on tropical agricultural products, notably sugar, coffee, cocoa and tobacco. Since prices, and therefore wages, were conditioned by competition with producers in other parts of the world, in the case of tobacco those in the United States, the economic value of these exports was less than those of Argentina. Moreover, their production usually involved limited investment in infrastructure and less social change. Responding to the international trading boom of this period greatly stimulated the trade and production of most parts of tropical America; yet even by 1914 it was clear that such a response had dangers and limitations. Brazil's dependence on the coffee market laid it open to the growth of foreign competition, while for the smaller Central American producers concentration on such tropical crops as bananas made them dangerously dependent on large foreign companies which controlled the international market.

Finally, there were states which concentrated on extractive industries, notably Mexico, Chile, Peru, Bolivia and (from the 1920s) Venezuela. In the later nineteenth century the combination of increased overseas demand for metals and, in the case of Chile, nitrates for agricultural fertilizers, plus cheaper transport, led to major investment and expansion of exports. Because of the high capital costs of large-scale exploitation of these assets and the geographical concentration of the ores to be exploited, much of this development was undertaken by foreign firms, British for nitrates, American for copper, silver, petroleum and other minerals. The result, according to Furtado, was that the main benefits accrued to these foreign firms and that the modern extractive sectors of these economies became partial enclaves with very limited impact on the rest of the economy. He nevertheless shows that in the period 1877 to 1910 the population of Mexico grew from 9.4 million to 15.3 million; that between 1900 and 1910 real per capita incomes grew at the very high rate of 3.1 per cent a year; and that during that decade exports of minerals and petroleum grew at an average rate of 7.7 per cent.[16]

There can, in fact, be no doubt that the growth in international trade and the consequential demand for commodities before 1914 had a dynamic effect on much of Latin America. Moreover, before 1914 there was already evidence that expanding imports, increasing affluence and growing population could generate modern domestic industries, though these were strictly import substituting. Furtado estimated that the industrial sector in

[16] Furtado, *Economic Development*, p. 49; Reynolds, *Economic Growth*, p. 32.

Argentina contributed as much as 18 per cent of the domestic product as early as 1905. In Mexico conditions were rather less favourable, yet at that time its industrial sector contributed some 14 per cent of GDP.[17]

For the international economy as a whole the First World War proved a major turning point. The most important effect for LDCs as a whole and for Latin America was the decline in the external trade coefficient (the ratio between trade and GDP) of the industrial countries: that of Britain, for example, fell from about 30 per cent before 1913 to 25 per cent in 1927–9 and to around 17 per cent in the 1930s. In the other major industrial countries the coefficient became static in the 1920s and declined in the 1930s.[18] At the time few realized that the change was fundamental: hence, for example, the determination to return to currency parities related to gold which was a feature of the mid-1920s. Moreover, the growth rate of tropical exports fell only from 3.7 to 3.2 per cent between 1913 and 1929.[19] Indeed, total exports from Latin America rose, from $1.6 million in 1913 to $3.1 million, in 1928 and their imports from $1.4 million to $2.4 million in the same years, providing a substantial surplus on visible trade to service their overseas debts.[20] Although many economic historians, following League of Nations and later United Nations publications, have claimed that there was a secular deterioration of the terms of trade in this period, Bairoch has argued forcefully that this belief was based on misinterpretation of crucial evidence and that in fact the terms of trade of primary produce actually improved by 3 per cent between 1896–1900 and 1926–9.[21]

Maynard Keynes was one of the few who seem to have realized that the war had ended an era of the international economy.[22] In his *The Economic Consequences of the Peace* (1919) he suggested that the classical economists and their successors had been wrong in thinking that the international economy of the nineteenth century could last indefinitely. In Keynes's view this economy had been based on a 'complicated and artificial system': in particular on currencies related to gold, increasing free trade, freedom of movement for capital and people, a balance

[17] Furtado, *Economic Development*, p. 105.
[18] Reynolds, *Economic Growth*, p. 35.
[19] Ibid., p. 36.
[20] P. Bairoch, *The Economic Development of the Third World since 1900* (London, 1975), table 30, p. 97.
[21] Bairoch (ibid, ch. 6) argues the case at length. Major elements in earlier miscalculations were: the use only of British prices for exports and imports to and from the Third World; ignoring the huge decline in transport costs; and failing to take account of the gap between cif and fob prices.
[22] This account is based on Lord R. Skidelsky, *John Maynard Keynes*, vol. 2: *The Economist as Saviour 1920–1937* (London, 1992), esp. ch. 7.

between both capital and labour and savings and consumption, and the balance of trade and capital transfers between Europe and America. The precarious balances on which this system had depended had been at risk before 1914 and had been shattered by the war.

Many economists thought Keynes wrong, but developments during the 1930s proved him right. The stock-market crash of 1929 delivered what seemed a final blow to the old international economy. Between 1929 and 1933 world exports dropped by 25 per cent and the prices of exports by 30 per cent, implying a fall in the value of world trade of over 50 per cent. During the peak of the crisis, from 1931 to 1932, Britain, France and the United States became net importers of capital by repatriation, and during the 1930s provided very little new long-term capital for the Third World. In Latin America the average quantum of exports, compared with 1925–9, fell by 8.8 per cent from 1930 to 1934 and by 2.4 per cent in 1935–9.[23] If one accepts the conventional measurement, the terms of trade of Latin America deteriorated even more sharply in these periods – by 24.3 per cent in the first and 10.8 per cent in the second – very seriously reducing the capacity to import.

Whatever the precise statistics, the crisis of the 1930s proved the major watershed in the history of the international division of labour and the process of world economic integration. The general lesson appeared to be that LDCs were vulnerable to the extent that they were most closely integrated into the world economy. The problem was how best to minimize these risks without losing the residual benefits of an export–import economic system. Short of extreme autarky there appeared to be only two main options.

First, these exporting countries could attempt to redress the adverse trends in the international prices for their commodities by various forms of restrictive practices. Where a country controlled the major part of the world supply of a commodity, as Brazil did for coffee in the 1930s, the world price might be raised by destruction of part of the crop. Yet real coffee prices did not recover until the later 1940s.[24] In principle a better way might have been to form international producer cartels to control prices. Some attempts at this were made between the two wars, but it was not until the success of the OPEC organization in 1973 that such commodity cartels proved really effective.

The main alternative to such schemes was diversification. This might take the form of evolving alternative export crops, producing more food for the home market, or even returning to subsistence production. To some extent Latin American countries tried all three in and after 1929. But, since the main purpose of exporting was to earn foreign exchange

[23] Furtado, *Economic Development*, pp. 54–5.
[24] Ibid., pp. 185–6.

to pay for imports, the most significant development of this period was the increase of local manufacturing, mainly for import substitution rather than export. This development is of critical importance in the study of Third World development then and later since industrialization was to become the central focus of most development strategies after 1950. The important questions are how did modern industry start in Latin America, what stimulus did the recession give it, and what were the longer-term economic consequences?

The key to the development of modern manufacturing in Latin America, as in virtually all Third World countries since, lay in development of the exporting sector. Exports increased incomes (through greater productivity) and so expanded the domestic market for consumer goods. Up to a point this demand could be met by expansion of local, mainly artisan, production; but urbanization and relatively high urban wages generated demand for more sophisticated and often cheaper imports. Given sufficient state help, mainly in the form of protective tariffs, this market might also provide encouragement for local manufacture of previously imported consumer goods. The export economy helped industrialization in two other ways. First, where, as in Argentina, exporting involved extensive modern communications, utilities and processing works, it generated a nucleus of technical skills and a managerial class. Secondly, provided much of the export industry was domestically owned, its profits were available for investment in industry.

In different ways and degrees these factors generated local industries in at least the three most prosperous Latin American countries before 1929. In Argentina industry was closely linked with the export economy, and was led by its needs. Meat processing and packing, flour milling and wool washing were the three early developments, coupled with building and maintaining the transport network and urban utilities. After them came a number of light consumer industries, such as tobacco, foodstuffs and beverages, which in 1914 constituted 56.5 per cent of manufacturing output. But as late as 1929 manufacturing still represented only 19 per cent of Argentina's GDP.[25]

In Mexico also there was considerable growth of manufacturing before 1914, encouraged by high external tariffs and the reduced value of the peso, which increased the cost of imports. During this period manufacturing grew at an estimated 3.6 per cent annually, faster than the growth of GDP. There was considerable import substitution, again mainly in light consumer goods. There was a similar pattern in Brazil, again reflecting export success. With substantial tariff protection many consumer goods industries grew up, led by textiles. By 1915 Brazil had 240 cotton-textile mills employing over 82,000 workers, and supplying over 85 per cent

[25] Reynolds, *Economic Growth*, p. 88.

of domestic textile consumption.[26] These were the best examples of export-induced manufacturing, but on a lesser scale similar developments took place in several other Latin American countries before 1929.

Before 1914 this may be described as the import substitution of affluence. It was not economically necessary, because there remained the alternative of importing without serious consequences for the balance of payments. During the 1920s, moreover, the growth of domestic industries began to slow up. Furtado argues that this was because import substitution of this kind was intimately linked to and circumscribed by the export economy. Domestic manufacture was merely substituting, at a higher cost, for consumer goods otherwise imported. The range of goods was very limited: expansion involved only making more of the same things. There was no diversification backwards into intermediates or capital goods. Growth was directly related to the export market: when that slowed up, as it did in the 1920s, the domestic market also flattened out. Thus Furtado concludes that the industrial sector could overcome its dependence on the export market only 'if it became sufficiently diversified to generate its own demand. In other words, it required the establishment of machine-making and other industries whose output could be absorbed by the industrial sector itself and by other productive activities.' This had not occurred by 1929. Most machines and intermediates were still imported. There was very limited domestic technical skill and the lack of a genuine industrial outlook or managerial ability.[27]

After 1929 circumstances changed radically: there followed the import substitution of poverty. As the international commodity markets collapsed, the ability of the Latin American states to import declined sharply. Import-substituting industry (ISI) grew to fill the gap left by reduced capacity to import. Thus between 1929 and 1937 industrial production in Argentina grew by 23 per cent; in Mexico by 46 per cent; in Brazil by 42 per cent; in Chile by 16 per cent; and in Colombia by 90 per cent.[28]

This industrial expansion was not planned in the sense that post–1950 industrial growth was planned in many developing countries. It was a spontaneous response by existing industries to the two new stimulants of the post-1929 economic situation, acting in addition to the long-established protective tariffs: higher import prices due to devaluation of local currencies and domestic inflation caused by the fiscal and monetary policies of Latin American governments. This inflation, which was to become the endemic characteristic of most Latin American countries, resulted largely from government measures to offset the serious decline in their income from import and export taxes. Internally the results

26 Ibid., pp. 100, 93.
27 Furtado, *Economic Development*, pp. 107–10.
28 Ibid., pp. 111–12.

were to maintain the domestic market for manufactures but at the same time to stimulate inflation. Externally the main effect was continuous devaluation of floating currencies, state licensing of foreign exchange, and the increase of foreign public debt through further overseas borrowing and the increased cost of servicing it.

The experience of these Latin American countries is critical for any analysis of the benefits and limitations of later Third World development based on the export of commodities and the expansion of light consumer goods ISIs. Furtado argues that this phase of rapid industrialization was 'strictly a phenomenon of the 1930s and the war period, that is, the period when the decline of the capacity to import permitted the intensive use of an industrial nucleus formed in an earlier period'.[29] By the later 1940s this process was again slowing down, because it was reaching the limits of the market for its narrow range of products. Between 1947 and 1957 the industrial coefficient of the main Latin American countries grew relatively slowly as a percentage of GDP.[30] Furtado argues that it could proceed further only as a result of radical restructuring of these economies to remove 'structural' obstacles.

This conclusion ties Furtado into the school of Latin American 'structuralists' who were dominant during the 1950s and 1960s and whose arguments were outlined in chapter 2. Their fundamental assumption was that beyond a certain point commodity exports cease to provide sufficient foreign exchange to pay for necessary imports, initially of consumer goods, then, after ISI has reached a certain point, of essential intermediate and capital goods for industry. The shortfall is commonly attributed to deterioration of the terms of trade, which plays a large role in dependency theory. But an alternative explanation is that these once-dominant exporting countries lost much of their comparative advantage in international markets through the growth of competition and the decline of their export efficiency. Thus in the mid-1970s Argentina's exports were only half as large per capita as they had been at the beginning of the century. In 1950–4 its per capita production of cereals was only 46 per cent of that in the later 1930s, and in those two decades total agricultural production per capita fell by 11 per cent.

The reasons seem to lie mainly in the deliberate fostering by successive Argentinian governments of an economy based on inflation, urbanization and industry, with agriculture subordinated and paid deliberately low prices so as to keep down urban food prices. The combined effect of protected industrialization, high inflation and reduced exports was the fall of Argentina from the ranks of the affluent states to those of the better-off Third World. Thus, while in 1928 the per capita income of

[29] Ibid., p. 117.
[30] Ibid., p. 111.

Australia, with which Argentina was often compared, was only one-third above that of Argentina, by 1988 it was almost five times as high. Moreover, between 1965 and 1988 Argentina had a zero rate of per capita growth and between 1965 and 1980 an inflation rate averaging 78.2 per cent, rising to 290.5 per cent in the 1980s. By contrast, Australia's growth rate for the earlier period was 1.7 per cent and its inflation rate 9.3 per cent, dropping to 7.8 per cent in the 1980s.[31]

Argentina may have been an extreme example of the relative decline of a once-prosperous export-oriented country. But only one of the other main Latin American countries – Venezuela, benefiting from its oil exports – did better in the long run. None of the others had a higher per capita national product than Argentina in 1988, and in 1965–80 Chile's annual growth rate per capita averaged only 0.1 per cent. Such relative economic failure raises the crucial question of whether export-led development followed by ISI is necessarily a dead end.

For Furtado the answer seems to be that it may, but need not be. For the major Latin American countries his analysis of reasons for failure to continue development satisfactorily after about 1950 fall into two categories – domestic and international.

Internally a main cause of checked development was structural inflation, itself the product of more profound domestic factors.[32] There were also external constraints, particularly deterioration of the terms of trade and foreign ownership of dominant sectors of the Latin American economies. In the larger Latin American countries, while many smaller locally owned companies, making relatively unsophisticated products dating from the earlier ISI period, survived, by about 1970 most of the newer and larger companies making more sophisticated goods, notably pharmaceuticals, were foreign owned.[33] In this way dominant sectors of these Latin American economies were controlled by foreign firms, and a substantial proportion of both capital gains and profits was exported.

Furtado's general conclusion appears to be that the Latin American example suggests that development through incorporation into the international division of labour was generally beneficial at least up to 1929. Commodity exporting transformed non-progressive economies to dynamic economies and generated at least the start of modern industry. But the First World War, then the recession of the 1930s, seriously weakened that system. Commodity exporting alone could no longer assure relative affluence and economic growth. Latin America attempted to meet the challenge by unplanned development of local manufacturing

[31] World Bank, *World Development Report 1990: Poverty* (Oxford, 1990), table 1, p. 179.
[32] This paragraph is based mainly on Furtado, *Economic Development*, ch. 12.
[33] Ibid., pp. 205–8.

to compensate for lost export income and later by expropriating the main foreign-owned extractive industries and utilities. But it was unable to achieve sustained per capita growth comparable to that in the golden age before 1929. The export economy was no longer able to compete with other parts of the world and after 1945 found increasing competition from other Third World producers and from manufacturers of synthetic substitutes. Incompetent financial management led to high levels of inflation, increasing public debts and very high external debt-service costs.[34] Industrialization stopped short at relatively inefficient import substitution, unable to compete on international markets. In short, Latin America appeared to have failed to achieve sustained development through following the classical prescription of comparative advantage and vent for surplus.

How far was this the case universally? In the following section the evidence of two of the British settler societies which followed similar strategies will be considered more briefly. Countries that were colonies during the early twentieth century are examined in chapters 6, 7, 10 and 11.

2 The British Settler Societies: Australia and New Zealand

In his widely influential book *Settler Capitalism: The Dynamics of Dependent Development in the Southern Hemisphere*[35] Donald Denoon attempted to analyse the reasons for the relative prosperity before about 1914 of three of the Latin American countries included in Furtado's study – Argentina, Uruguay and Chile – in comparison with three British settler societies – Australia, New Zealand and South Africa. His argument was that they had many common characteristics, among them substantial areas of temperate grassland that was more or less 'vacant' for settler occupation, in four cases exploitable minerals, and a predominantly European immigrant population. All of them developed their economies on the basis of specialized production of export commodities for the European or US markets within an initially free-trade world economy, and all were able to expedite development by accepting foreign, initially mainly British, investment. At least until about 1914 all were relatively affluent societies, living evidence of the validity of the principle of comparative advantage and the value of concentration on efficient production and export of primary commodities.

[34] In 1988 the debt-service ratios (debt service as a percentage of the export of goods and services) for leading Latin American countries were: Chile, 19.1; Mexico, 43.5; Brazil, 42.0; Argentina, 36.0; Venezuela, 39.7 (World Bank, *World Development Report 1990*, table 23, p. 223).
[35] D. Denoon, *Settler Capitalism: The Dynamics of Dependent Development in the Southern Hemisphere* (Oxford, 1983).

By the 1990s, however, a substantial gap had emerged between them in terms of affluence. In 1994 World Bank estimates put their per capita incomes (in US dollars) as follows: South Africa, $3,040; Chile, $3,520; Uruguay, $4,660; Argentina, $8,110; New Zealand, $13,350; Australia, $18,000. For comparison, in that year the figure for Portugal was $9,320, the United Kingdom $18,340, France $23,420, and the United States $25,880.[36] Thus, alone of these 'settler economies', Australia and New Zealand remained near the end of the twentieth century among the 'high-income' economies, as defined by the World Bank, though no longer, as they had been at the start of the century, among the very richest. Moreover, although both had developed as commodity export-ing countries, apparently heavily 'dependent' on overseas trading part-ners, both had diversified their economies. In 1980 agriculture provided only 11 per cent of GDP in New Zealand, 5 per cent in Australia, and employed 11 and 6 per cent respectively of the labour force. Conversely in that year manufacturing constituted 22 per cent of GDP and 20 per cent of exports in New Zealand, 19 and 20 per cent in Australia.[37] In short, both countries had diversified away from overwhelming depend-ence on agriculture, while remaining two of the world's most efficient agricultural producers, and some at least of their initially import-substi-tuting industries had become internationally competitive. From the stand-point of the present argument the question is how they were able to do this and what light their success throws on the basic question with which this book is concerned – the benefits or disadvantages of a developing economy integrated into the international division of labour.

These two countries shared common features. They were at the fur-thest point from Europe. In neither was there an indigenous population that could provide profitable trade goods or was willing to act as an agricultural labour force, though both Aborigines and Maoris played an active economic role, notably as shearers, herders, etc., once the pas-toral industries were established. Although there were natural resources to be exploited in the early days, such as whales, seals, flax and timber, these could not provide a long-term basis for economic development. Nor was there any imperial economic design for either country. New South Wales may have been seen in terms of Britain's strategic position in the Pacific, but it was primarily a convict prison, chosen when the loss of the United States closed that depository for felons; while New Zealand was annexed in 1840 for a composite of reasons, including the presence of British beachcombers and the threat of French annexation. In short, in its early days – before about 1810 for Australia, as late as

[36] World Bank, *World Development Report 1996: From Plan to Market* (Oxford, 1996), table 1, p. 188.
[37] Ibid., table 12, p. 211; table 15, p. 217.

the 1850s for New Zealand – neither country had any obvious line of economic development. There was a real danger that they might become primitive peasant communities, largely dependent on their own production of essentials and finding it very difficult to pay for the imports which, as emigrants, they regarded as necessary.

Both societies were saved by discovering staples for export and by taking advantage of the demand for commodities in the more developed countries of Europe and later North America: that is, they were classic examples of the value of comparative advantage and vent for surplus. Both became affluent, among the richest countries in the world on a per capita basis before 1914, and, as was seen above, still in the top sector in the 1990s. The important question is whether, and how far, they were able to use the commodity trade to generate this wealth. At a theoretical level the question turns on the concept of dependence. If both these countries developed as satellites of Europe, and more particularly of Britain, did this imply exploitation of their dependence and, as some *dependentistas* have alleged, a limit to their development? If the answers to these questions are in the negative, then why did these countries not conform to the pattern? It is impossible here to describe their experiences in any detail. For Australia it is proposed to outline the growth of the economy mainly before about 1960, but to take the New Zealand story briefly down to the 1990s.

The Australian economy before 1960

There is no novelty in treating Australia as an economic dependency of Britain: it was, for example, the main theme of Brian Fitzpatrick's *The British Empire in Australia*, published in 1939,[38] long before the evolution of modern dependency theory. The case for dependence is obvious. There, in the early nineteenth century, were small communities deriving from the convict settlement of 1788, without an obvious economic future: no large indigenous population to provide a labour force or the foundations of a trading system; no markets nearer than South Asia; very little local capital, except that brought in by immigrants or saved by settlers. The colonists had only two options: to accept a Crusoe-like existence with a self-sufficient economy, or to discover some means of using the factor endowment of the continent to build up an overseas trade. In practice, of course, no such alternatives were considered. By reflex action settlers directed their effort towards the production and export of whatever commodities they could catch or produce in order

[38] B. Fitzpatrick, *The British Empire in Australia* (London, 1939). A more recent and valuable general study B. Dyster and D. Meredith, *Australia in the International Economy in the Twentieth Century* (Cambridge, 1990).

to pay for the European imports they regarded as essential. Since most exports went to Britain and most imports came from there, this was the basis of an export-oriented and potentially dependent economy.[39]

For most of the following century and well into the twentieth a very large proportion of Australian trade was indeed with Britain and the majority of its exports were commodities. In the period 1887–91 some 70 per cent of imports came from Britain, and the proportion was still 48 per cent in 1950/1, before dropping sharply to 25 per cent in 1965/6 and going on down. Exports followed much the same pattern. Britain took over 70 per cent of Australian exports in the 1880s and early 1890s and an average of 44.4 per cent between 1928/9 and 1932/3. By 1956 it was down to 31 per cent and by 1965/6 to 17.7 per cent. The composition of all Australian exports is not known before 1903; but in 1881 gold and wool combined constituted 72.4 per cent of Australian exports, and in 1928/9 all commodities, then including dairying, pastoral, agricultural and mining products, still amounted to 65.9 per cent of the value of Australian exports. The balance of exports consisted of 'manufactures', but the bulk of these consisted of processed or semi-processed primary products. In 1966 commodities still provided 39.7 per cent of all exports, agriculture 32.7 per cent.[40]

These statistics, coupled with heavy reliance on British capital investment and other services, seem to be the hallmarks of dependence. Yet in fact they led not to 'underdevelopment' as a subordinate peripheral economy but to growth, affluence and economic autonomy. This is what needs to be explained. Although full treatment would involve examination of many aspects of the Australian economy, it is possible here to examine only two: the organization of trade and control of money and credit.

The trading system   One of the characteristic features of many Third World countries has been that a large proportion of their trade, both internal and external, was in the hands of expatriates. In most cases the main export staples were controlled by foreign firms, which dealt directly with the producers or middlemen, and shipped the goods overseas for sale. In this way the staple trades tended to constitute an alien element in the local economy. In some cases the buying power of such firms approached monopsony, since the producer had to accept whatever price was offered, irrespective of world market prices. Conversely these firms

---

[39] For the genesis of the early Australian economy, see G. J. Abbott and N. B. Nairn (eds), *Economic Growth of Australia 1788–1821* (Melbourne, 1969); N. G. Butlin, *Forming a Colonial Economy: Australia 1810–1850* (Cambridge, 1994).

[40] Commonwealth Secretariat, *Commonwealth Trade 1966* (London, 1967).

controlled much of the import trade and internal distribution, and were thus able to dictate selling as well as buying prices. It can be argued that under such conditions much of the development potential of an export-oriented economy was destroyed, since the profits belonged overseas.

It is a key fact that Australia never experienced such alien dominance. From the start the import, distribution and sale of most goods was handled by settlers. Circumstances were very favourable to the growth of local wholesale and retail trading. London merchant houses specialized in consigning goods on order to all parts of the world, and any Australian merchant who could obtain some credit could set up as a wholesale importer. Conversely, British firms were reluctant to tie up capital and run risks by setting up branches in Australia. Hence the characteristic commercial institution of early Australia was the general merchant house in the bigger cities, and the stock and station agents, which bought and exported Australian and South Pacific commodities to Britain and imported a wide range of goods for local distribution through retail channels, usually also providing credit. A few of the more successful of these firms eventually came under metropolitan control, but this was commonly because the founder chose to return to Britain and run his business from there. The majority of the domestic wholesale and retail trade always remained in Australian hands.

Potentially, judging by other commodity-exporting economies, it might be expected that the main exception to this settler control of trade would lie in the export business. The reasons are that long-distance commodity trades tie up large sums of capital for long periods and that success depends on knowledge of the highly speculative international markets. These two factors dictated that, for example, West African producers and traders were unable to control the export and final sale of their product, so that much of the profit accrued to the European and American firms that bought, exported and speculated in cocoa, oilseeds, rubber and other tropical commodities.

For Australia the equivalent of Gold Coast cocoa or Nigerian palm oil was wool, which was extraordinarily important to the Australian economy.[41] As a proportion of the total value of exports it rose from 21.2 per cent in 1861 to 44.9 per cent in 1871 and was 46.1 per cent as late as 1954/5–1956/7. Wool was the staple on which the Australian export economy was built, even though in the mid-nineteenth century its dominance was briefly challenged by gold, and from the 1880s it was joined by products of the pastoral and sugar industries, and later by other minerals.

---

[41] Much of the following material on the wool industry is based on A. Barnard, *The Australian Wool Market 1840–1900* (Melbourne, 1958); A. Barnard (ed.), *The Simple Fleece: Studies in the Australian Wool Industry* (Melbourne, 1962).

We should, therefore, ask of Australian wool the same three basic questions commonly asked of tropical export staples. Was specialization in wool forced on Australia to serve the international economy? How far were production and the trade dominated by foreigners? Did marketing methods give the Australian producer and economy maximum advantage, so providing the surplus needed for economic development?

The answer to the first question is clear. The pastoral industry was a spontaneous reaction to the economic needs of the early settlements and in no sense forced onto the settlers. Indeed, pastoralism ran contrary to both the system of convict settlements and the later principles of 'systematic colonization' publicized by E. G. Wakefield in and after 1829. Large-scale wool production was developed by Australians who realized early on that, given the factor endowment of the continent – ample grazing land coupled with a shortage of both capital and labour – wool offered the best chance of developing a staple which could pay for imports. A crucial fact in the success of this strategy was transport costs. Wool had a relatively high value in relation to its weight and bulk, in sharp contrast with many other commodities. Given the great distance from European markets and the high cost of ocean freights until late in the nineteenth century, this alone made wool economically viable.[42] The industry was greatly helped by the huge increase in European demand for wool as the woollen industry mechanized. Yet Australians had first to establish their share of the market in competition with British, Spanish and Saxon wool producers, and then to break into the expanding worsted industry by breeding for different types of wool. Credit for successful specialization in wool lay therefore almost entirely with Australians, though they were helped by domestic factors and an international demand that, except for part of the 1880s and 1890s, was more consistent than for many other commodities.

It was, however, simpler to produce wool than to obtain the maximum return from selling it, and it was in financing its production and marketing that one might expect foreign firms and capital to play a major role. The vital question is, therefore, what role non-Australians, mainly from or in Britain, played in the processes of production and marketing; whether this gave them effective control over the trade; and whether their intervention seriously vitiated the economic value of wool to Australian development.

As with all export staples, the method of conducting sales was critical for the producer. A large commercial organization that bought outright from the pastoralist, and perhaps formed a ring with other buyers to hold down prices, would be in a commanding monopsonic position. This never happened in Australia. Initially much of the wool was sold

[42] This point was made by G. Blainey, *The Tyranny of Distance: How Distance Shaped Australia's History* (Melbourne, 1966).

by growers to general merchants to obtain credit at whatever price they could bargain for. But from the 1840s auctions became the almost invariable rule. At first these were mostly in the Australian centres, where the wool was bought by specialized buyers who speculated on the resale value in London. But increasingly the wool was consigned direct for auction in London by the growers themselves on the assumption that competition would be greater there and would ensure the best price. This was normally done on commission through a variety of merchant and credit firms in Australia, who sent the wool to importing firms in London. These provided bills of exchange against the expected sale price and, again on commission, arranged for the final auction by specialized wool-selling brokers, where the wool was bought on behalf of British and continental manufacturers by specialist brokers.

The key to this complex system was that at all stages the wool remained the property of the original producer. Although he took the risk, he could also expect to obtain a fair competitive international market price. In doing so he faced two problems common to all commodity producers: the need for credit, and transaction costs. First, he needed credit to tide him over the long period from shearing to final payment, which might be many months. It was inability to wait for a return that forced most small-scale tropical producers or middlemen to sell outright to an exporting firm, accepting whatever price they were offered. Australian wool-growers were more fortunate. The interest they were charged on loans on the credit of their wool, and also for capital invested in their farms, followed the current bank rate in Australia and was never exploitative. This was mainly due to the high level of competition for pastoral business between banks and a range of credit agencies; indeed, by the end of the nineteenth century pastoral credit was carried on mainly as a service to the grower in order to retain his business. Creditors were commonly very unwilling to foreclose on mortgages on land or stock until and unless the position was clearly irretrievable. Nor, secondly, was the pastoralist fleeced by the various intermediaries on whom he depended. The total commission charged by the Australian and British agents was normally between 2 and 2.5 per cent of the final price. In short, competition ensured that the grower received a fair price.

From an Australian point of view there were only two disadvantages in this operation of the international market economy: the length of time the grower had to wait for his return, and therefore pay interest on credit; and the loss of commission and profit to overseas agencies. The solution clearly lay in holding final auctions in Australia, yet attracting international buyers to ensure maximum competition and prices. This was not easy to achieve, but by the early twentieth century the big Australian stock and station agents had built up an organization to run such auctions in the main Australian centres, and they were helped by

the growing competition between European, American and other countries for high-quality raw wool. By 1900 some 50 per cent of wool was
sold in Australia; by the 1960s some 95 per cent.

The Australian wool industry provides solid evidence that both producers and their society can grow rich by specializing in a suitable export
commodity; and the subsequent development of meat and dairy products
for export from the 1880s, with the invention of satisfactory refrigeration
equipment on shore and at sea, supports this conclusion.

Money and credit   It was seen in chapter 4 that one of the hallmarks of
colonial systems was that money was dominated by the imperial power.
In the Australian case it might seem at first sight that the colonies were
heavily dependent on Britain. They were part of the sterling system
until the 1960s; they relied on Britain for long-term capital investment;
there were powerful British-based banks in Australia; there was no
Australian central bank until 1924; and Australian banks relied heavily
on British banks for credit. Yet it is also clear that the Australian economy was never dominated by British investors or banks, and the reasons
for this are critical for understanding the success of this export-oriented
economy.

First, use of sterling currency was never an inconvenience to Australia.
Until 1914 the fact that Australian-minted money was convertible at
par into sterling or gold provided great flexibility in international dealings. Thereafter the tie to sterling, though Australia in fact devalued in
1931 so that the exchange rate became £A1.25 = £1.00, provided a valuable discipline to prevent the indiscriminate printing of money which was
economically disastrous for many Latin American countries.

Secondly, although Australia, in common with most other settler
societies, borrowed quite heavily from Britain from the mid-nineteenth
century until the later 1920s, and was thus able to run a fairly consistent
adverse balance on current account, the debt burden never got out of
hand. This can be seen in two ways. First, between the 1860s and the
end of the 1930s debt service (interest and repayment) only twice – in
the recessions of the early 1890s and the early 1930s – rose above 6
per cent of Australian GDP: to an average of 6.3 per cent between 1891
and 1895, and 6.4 per cent between 1930/1 and 1934/5. Secondly,
although foreign borrowing, mostly from Britain, was considerable,
especially during boom periods and when the main infrastructure was
being built (in the 1860s and 1880s) and again during the 1920s, only
twice (1861–5 and 1886–90) did it amount to more that 50 per cent of
gross domestic capital formation (GDCF). For most of the period foreign
borrowing was very much less than domestic savings.

This in turn means that from early on Australia had a high rate of
domestic capital formation in relation to the domestic product. In no

period between 1861 and 1939 was GDCF less than 11 per cent of GDP, and for much of the time it was substantially higher: 18.6 per cent in the early 1880s and 18 per cent in the late 1920s. Thus, while Australians sensibly borrowed from Britain to take advantage of lower British rates of interest and to increase their ability to develop their economy, most of their development costs were met from their own savings. It must be added that, by contrast with many modern Third World countries, much of the British investment was wisely used in durable and economically rewarding facilities such as railways, ports, improvements to pastoral holdings, and urban housing. It was almost never used to make good budgetary deficiencies, as was common in many Latin American countries before 1914 and in most Third World countries in the later twentieth century.[43]

Another area in which Australians provided most of their own financial needs was banking. At first sight there might be grounds for thinking that this was an area in which British finance was dominant: the presence of British-owned and run banks which held a large share of Australian banking and were accused of putting their own interests before those of Australia in moments of crisis, such as the early 1890s; close contacts between all banks in Australia and the London money market; the absence until 1924 of a central bank, the Commonwealth Bank; and the presence for a brief period after 1835 of chartered British 'Imperial' banks.

In fact, none of these things seriously affected Australia. The Imperial banks had no advantages over Australian chartered banks, and were mostly reconstructed after 1858 as normal joint stock companies. The important fact is that banking in Australia was Australian before any British-based banks operated there. The Bank of New South Wales was set up in 1817 on the basis of a local charter issued by the governor, and it remains the largest single Australian bank. Other local banks with local capital were established before any British banks were set up there. Australian banks provided all normal banking services, including the issue of notes, since there were no government-owned banks. There is no doubt that many of these locally owned banks relied heavily on the London banking system for credit, but this was entirely rational and in Australian interests: they could borrow in Britain at rates well below those current in Australia and make a profit from lending at higher local rates. Thus money could flow back and forth between Britain and Australia according to Australian needs. The only time before 1914 when it seemed that this mechanism might operate against Australian

---

[43] All statistics are based on N. G. Butlin, *Australian Domestic Product, Investment and Foreign Borrowing, 1861–1938/9* (Cambridge, 1962); N. G. Butlin, *Investment in Australian Economic Development 1861–1900* (Cambridge, 1964).

interests was in the depression of the early 1890s. It has been alleged that British banks withdrew considerable sums in and after 1893 for fear of bank failures and that this caused the bankruptcy of some Australian banks and deepened the depression. In fact, as S. J. Butlin has shown, this is false. British deposits in Australia continued to grow well into 1892/3, by which time the Australian depression was well advanced; and the fact that British-owned deposits in Australian banks declined by some £21 million between 1893 and 1897 was due not to withdrawals but to losses in failed banks and a variety of technical bank reconstructions. Indeed, a significant part of the remaining apparent British withdrawals represented Australian purchases of devalued deposit receipts, most of which were later redeemed at their higher face value.[44]

The key to the very satisfactory relationship between Australian banks, mortgage companies, etc. and the British banks and capital market lay in British confidence in Australian creditworthiness. Individual banks might fail, as in any country; but the greater part of British lending to Australia in the period before 1914 was to colonial or, after 1901, federal governments, and Australian public credit was impeccable. By marked contrast with some Latin American states, no Australian colony reneged on its overseas public debt. The dangers of such easy access to London credit were seen in the later 1920s, when very large Australian borrowing, much of it on overdraft or other forms of short-term credit other than long-term bonds, left Australia seriously exposed when the fall in commodity prices reduced Australia's favourable balance on visibles. Between 1925 and 1929 Australian borrowings accounted for more than two-fifths of all overseas flotations made in London. Overseas debt repayments rose from 17 to 28 per cent of export income between 1920 and 1929. Yet the crisis was averted by conservative Australian financial policies after 1930, including devaluation of the Australian pound against sterling, though these caused great hardship to many indebted farmers and businesses.[45] Australia was thus able to retain its excellent record of financial probity and to finance its development by tapping into the best and cheapest money market in the world.

The same confidence resulted during the twentieth century in a new flood of foreign investment, though now increasingly through foreign direct investment (FDI) rather than the earlier portfolio investment in government stocks. The larger issue of such FDI will be considered in chapter 9. Here it is necessary only to note that Australia proved as

[44] For analysis of the banking crisis, see S. J. Butlin, *Foundations of the Australian Monetary System* (Melbourne, 1953).
[45] For a summary of these problems, see P. J. Cain and A. G. Hopkins, *British Imperialism*, vol. 2: *Crisis and Deconstruction 1914–1990* (London, 1993), pp. 116–22.

popular a host for direct, mainly industrial, investment after about 1900 as it had previously been for other forms of foreign lending.

FDI in Australia was stimulated mainly by the benefits of a protected market with an expanding and increasingly affluent demand for consumer goods, and also for intermediate and capital goods for the growing domestic industries. Although such investment occurred as early as the 1890s, when, for example, William Lever decided to manufacture detergents there rather than export them from Britain,[46] the main influx came after 1945, and came from Britain and the United states.[47] It was encouraged by political stability, common language and law, political links with the Anglo-Saxon world, high levels of economic growth, a high investment ratio, population growth at around 2 per cent per annum, good labour relations, low inflation and a boom in the 1960s. But probably the greatest attraction was the relatively high tariff on manufactured imports: more than half the American firms that invested in Australia after 1945 gave this as their main incentive. Between 1947/8 and 1967/8 Australia received £A6,579 million in FDI, of which 47.6 per cent came from Britain and 39.1 per cent from the United States. This total was exceeded by foreign investment only in Canada, Britain, West Germany and the United States. The result was a high concentration of foreign ownership in some of the more technically advanced industries: by 1965 foreign companies owned 95 per cent of automobile manufacture, 55 per cent of automobile accessories, 83 per cent of telecommunications, 97 per cent of pharmaceuticals, 80 per cent of soap and detergents, and 95 per cent of oil refining. In that year 26–7 per cent of total post-tax company incomes in Australia were earned by foreign-based companies.[48]

The consequences of this huge inflow of foreign investment for the Australian economy are not the issue here: they were no different in principle from those in other host countries and will be considered in chapter 9. For the present the important point is that in the mid-twentieth century Australia remained as attractive to overseas corporate investors as it had been for individuals before 1945. Security was one continuing attraction; but equally important was the fact that the Australian government placed no restrictions on foreign investment, excluding only broadcasting and

[46] See Fieldhouse, *Unilever Overseas*, ch. 3, for an account of the growth of the Lever/Unilever business in Australia.
[47] This account leans heavily on the chapter by D. T. Brash, 'Australia as Host to the International Corporation', in C. P. Kindleberger (ed.), *The International Corporation* (Cambridge, Mass., 1970).
[48] For a critical analysis of the effects of FDI in the Australian mining industry, see K. Tsokhas, *Beyond Dependence: Companies, Labour Processes and Australian Mining* (Melbourne, 1986). For the significance of Australian protectionism after 1960, see L. Glezer, *Tariff Polices: Australian Policy-making 1960–80* (Carlton, 1982).

banking (apart from the two existing British banks), and did not limit repatriation of income and capital. Until 1965 foreign companies had unlimited access to the local capital market, though in fact most financed expansion from local profits. Thereafter the government required foreign companies to consult the Australian Reserve Bank before borrowing locally to prevent the outflow of Australian capital. By that time, in fact, some Australians were becoming concerned at the speed and extent of foreign takeovers. Alarm was raised in 1956 over the high level of dividend repatriation by General Motors, which had acquired the Australian company, Holdens to make what was publicized as the 'first all-Australian' car.[49] From the mid-1960s the government was stating that it was 'desirable' for foreign companies to sell shares in their local companies to Australians, and local participation was required for bauxite mining. In 1968 the populist prime minister Gorton was threatening to impose controls on FDI, as did also the Labor Party. But subsequent controls were too late to alter the fact that through FDI the Australian economy had been still more closely integrated into the international capitalist economy.

What light does the Australian experience throw on the general issue of development through trade and an open economy? Why has Australia been so relatively successful?

In examining the evidence, greater emphasis can be placed on either Australian dependence or Australian autonomy. Dependence flowed from the fact that the Australian economy evolved within and was conditioned by the international economy. The spheres of activity in which it was profitable for Australia to specialize were determined outside the continent, by the growth of demand for particular exports, by the willingness of capital and labour to flow to Australia, and by the levels of prices and costs in external markets.

On the other hand, emphasis must also be placed on the positive role of settlers and later native-born Australians in making the best use of these possibilities. Almost nothing came easily in Australia. In a drought-prone continent 12,000 miles from potential markets the settlers and ex-convicts might have degenerated into hill-billies. In fact they showed great energy and inventiveness in discovering by experiment what breed of sheep produced the most saleable wool, later developing a large export trade in meat and dairy products, in wine, wheat and minerals. Behind the

[49] For detailed accounts and analysis of this, see E. T. Penrose, 'Limits to the Size and Growth of the Firm', *American Economic History Review*, 45, 2 (1955), pp. 531–43, and 'Foreign Investment and the Growth of the Firm', *Economic Journal*, 66 (1956), pp. 64–99; H. W. Arndt, 'Overseas Borrowing – the New Model', *Economic Record* 33 (1957), pp. 247–61 For further reference to this episode, see ch. 9 below.

protection of distance and tariffs they established a number of industries, initially as import substitutes, eventually with considerable export potential. Equally important, from the start key areas of the commercial economy were in Australian hands, notably banking and internal marketing. Australians generated most of the savings required for investment. Australians owned their own economy and no one could dictate how they ran it.

But, in common with a number of other settler societies, Australia had peculiar advantages, particularly when compared with other non-settler developing countries. These settlers brought with them a basket of attitudes, experiences and expectations that reflected those of contemporary Europe. The mode of production, which determined also ownership of land and other forms of property, was instinctively capitalist. Though Denoon has defined the special result as a 'settler-capitalist' mode of production.[50] Whatever its specifics, settler capitalism in Australia benefited from the fact that a relatively small number of settlers were able to exploit the whole assets of their continent, ignoring the rights and interests of Aborigines, and unhampered by the weight of a preponderant pre-capitalist peasant population. They had no need to modernize or share their rewards with people who did not possess the same skills or attitudes.

Some of this was true of the Latin American societies surveyed earlier in this chapter. In the first decade of this century there seemed little to choose between, say, Australia and Argentina. Why, then, at the end of the century was Australia so much richer than these other settler societies?

There is no simple answer, but it is arguable that the most important differentiating factors were the quality of government and its effect on economic policy. Australia, in common with Canada and New Zealand, inherited the more beneficial features of British government as it evolved in the middle and later nineteenth century: a representative parliament, an autonomous legal system increasingly adapted to the needs of developing capitalism, and a professional civil service recruited on merit rather than by patronage. Australia experienced no political *coups* of the type common in most Latin American countries. Economic policies had to take account of a wide range of potentially conflicting interests, in particular to balance the needs of the exporting agricultural sector against those of the urban employers and working class, the first benefiting from free trade, the latter from industrial protection. Above all, perhaps, Australia never allowed monetary and fiscal policies to create the sort of hyperinflation experienced in Argentina and elsewhere in Latin America. These were the hallmarks of good government and a main reason for the country's economic success.

[50] Denoon, *Settler Capitalism*. See esp. pp. 221–30 for his definition of the term and his conclusions.

The New Zealand economy

A great deal of what has been said about Australia applies also to New Zealand, though there were obvious differences.[51] New Zealand was very much smaller but had a higher proportion of cultivatable land and few drought problems. Perhaps the most important contrast lay in the presence of the Maori people, who presented far more serious problems to land settlement than the Australian Aborigines, particularly in the North Island. It was not until after the end of the wars of the 1860s, when the relatively few settlers depended heavily on a large British regular army, that much of the North Island could be opened up.

That apart, settlers in New Zealand faced the same problems as those in Australia. Apart from early exploitation of indigenous resources, notably whales, flax and timber, there was no obvious export staple to pay for imports. In the propaganda of those who promoted organized colonization from the 1830s to the 1860s the standard projection was of traditional mixed farming, presumably mainly for local consumption, the publicized attraction being that immigrants could expect to own their own land rather than be tenants or farm labourers. Although in the 1850s farmers, including some Maoris, found a market for grain and vegetables in the newly developed Australian goldfields, where population growth had temporarily outrun local food production, this did not last for long. In the longer run growing food for the small local population could not have provided high living standards or paid for the imports the settlers wanted.

New Zealand, therefore, like Australia, was saved from rural mediocrity by developing export staples. Wool was again the mainstay. Sheep could be pastured on the grasslands of the east of both islands with minimal expenditure, since pastoral leases of large areas of Crown land could be obtained cheaply, and sheep, initially mainly merino, could be imported from Australia and were well adapted to the coarse tussock grasses of New Zealand. In its earliest days sheep farming attracted a number of relatively wealthy people from the British middle and upper classes, many of whom enjoyed the not-too-dangerous life of the pioneer and some of whom made money by reselling as land prices rose.[52] Over time the industry became far more sophisticated. Runs were

---

[51] This account is based primarily on G. R. Hawke, *The Making of New Zealand: An Economic History* (Cambridge, 1985). See also W. H. Oliver with B. R. William (eds), *The Oxford History of New Zealand* (Oxford, 1981), esp. chs 9, 14.
[52] The classic description of early station life in New Zealand is in the two books by Lady Barker, *Station Life in New Zealand* and *Station Amusements in New Zealand* (both Auckland, 1870). Other well-known early sheep farmers were Clifford and Weld, both of whom became leading politicians in the 1850s

fenced, tussock grass replaced by a variety of English grasses. The area available was extended by clearing forest, draining swamps, and acquiring more land from the Maoris. Merinos were largely replaced by the Lincoln breed and improved care improved the rate of increase. By 1911 there were 24 million sheep in New Zealand, by the 1980s over 65 million. The wool was marketed in much the same way as that in Australia, with the same benefits to the producer.

Wool thus provided the first basis of a viable New Zealand economy. It was joined, rather briefly, by gold in the 1860s. Gold was discovered in Central Otago and Westland in the South Island and in the Thames area of the North Island. In the 1860s it overtook wool as an export product, then fell away as the readily extracted ores declined and capital-intensive mining took over. Up to 1890 gold exports were worth £46 million, only about 13.5 per cent of the Australian total, but critically important to New Zealand at a time when the Maori wars were putting a great strain on its balance of payments. But perhaps the most significant long-term effect of gold was that it greatly increased the settler population, possibly by as much as 65 per cent. As the gold rush subsided, a considerable number of these immigrants remained. They provided an additional labour force for agriculture and urban employments. Together with the large number of immigrants attracted in the 1870s and 1880s by assisted immigration policies, they made it possible to build the railways and other infrastructural improvements that were associated with Julius Vogel's strategy of borrowing for development. In the longer term both groups of immigrants created problems of employment that stimulated protectionist tariff policies to assist the infant industries in which many urban workers were employed. It was from that time that the question of what might be the optimal population for New Zealand, given its factor endowment and dependence on commodity exports, became an issue.

The third main economic foundation of the New Zealand economy was the export of meat and dairy products, the product of the refrigeration revolution of the 1880s. As in Australia, the possibility of freezing sheep meat (rather than boiling down what could not be consumed locally for tallow) greatly increased the profitability of sheep farming and made dairying for export feasible. By 1914 the total value of meat, butter and cheese exports, almost all to Britain, was roughly equivalent to that of wool exports.

This huge expansion did not, however, happen easily or inevitably. Dairy and meat products required far more effort than wool. To break into the British market the quality of sheep meat – which soon came

---

and 1860s. For Weld, who went on to become governor of the Straits Settlements, see J. Graham, *Frederick Weld* (Auckland, 1983).

to be called 'Canterbury lamb' to please the British consumer (though in fact not all from the province of Canterbury) – had to be improved by breeding new strains. The meat needed to be frozen before shipment: by 1891 there were twenty-one large freezing works, pioneered by leading sheep farmers, though British and American firms moved in later. Dairy products required new breeds of cattle to provide larger milk yields. They needed far more complex arrangements for milking, preserving, transporting and processing the milk. The common answer was the farmers' cooperative, copied from Denmark and Wisconsin: by 1914 90 per cent of dairy factories were cooperatives, owned and run by the farmers. Finally, frozen products required efficient internal and maritime transport. New Zealand railways provided refrigerated vans to transport products to the main ports, and a range of specialized ships was built. Despite some complaints about the rates and quality of service, New Zealand enterprise was not handicapped by transport problems.

It is, therefore, clear that the international demand for quality wool and the specifically British market for meat and dairy products provided New Zealand with an economic base which, by 1914, had made it one of the richest countries per capita in the world.

But it would be misleading to assume that New Zealand was no more than a farm for Britain, or that it was entirely dependent on Britain for investment. Apart from government borrowing to pay for the almost exclusively publicly owned railways and other transport facilities, and some bursts of private borrowing for a variety of developments, most capital investment came from local savings. As for diversification of the economy, the population was for long too small to justify large-scale factory industry. But New Zealand soon developed a wide range of small-scale industries. As early as 1891 11.0 per cent of the workforce were employed in factories (rising to 15 per cent by 1921), plus 6.9 per cent in other manufacturing, presumably including homeworkers and handicraftsmen. An increasing proportion of imports can be described as intermediate inputs to various forms of local economic activity. Hawke describes this as a 'fabricating economy'. Such fabrication was helped by protective tariffs, which were applied fairly haphazardly on demand from the 1880s, but it did not depend on them. Local manufacture was the outcome of entrepreneurs calculating the relative costs of particular items when imported complete or partially manufactured. That is, there was no grand strategy of import substitution in New Zealand but a pragmatic cost-effective substitution of parts of the manufacturing process where this proved worthwhile.

The golden age of the New Zealand economy was the period before 1914, when the international economy was most helpful. The First World War was a boon, since Britain bought all the main export products on bulk purchase at satisfactory prices, as it did also from Australia.

The 1920s were less stable, yet in the decade's later years confidence within New Zealand resulted in a large borrowing and investment spree. Then came the depression of the post-1929 period, which provided the real test of the long-term viability of an export-oriented economy of the New Zealand variety.

In dependency theory recessions are commonly taken to demonstrate how vulnerable primary-producing countries are to the international market. Commodity prices fall more than prices of manufactures, resulting in deterioration in the terms of trade. This is taken to show that the commodity exporter would do better to be more or less self-sufficient, with a 'balanced' economy. How does the New Zealand experience of the depression fit this model?

There is no doubt that the depression that started in 1929 hit New Zealand very hard. Between 1929 and 1932 the value of exports fell from $108.9 million to a low of $58.7 million and of imports from $97.5 million to $49.3 million. Between 1929 and 1933 the terms of trade (1977 = 100) deteriorated from 138 to 84.[53] The GDP fell by some 30 per cent, prices by about 20 per cent, implying an average fall in real incomes of 10 per cent. Serious though these effects were, they were not as dramatic as in some other countries. New Zealand had about 80,000 registered unemployed at the depth of the depression, 12 per cent of the labour force, compared with 44 per cent in Germany, 25–30 per cent in the United States and Australia, and 20–5 per cent in Britain. In fact for New Zealand the depression was mediated by Britain, which took 80–8 per cent of its exports, so that the price received for New Zealand exports was determined mainly by British prices. New Zealand increased the volume of its exports from index 100 (1929) to 133 in 1933. She was helped in this by the quota system set up at the Ottawa Conference of 1932, which safeguarded empire shares of the British market against competitors such as Denmark and Argentina, so that the share of the British market held by New Zealand and Australian meat rose considerably in the early 1930s. This was a classic example of 'cooperation' within an imperial economic system, the sharing of limited economic opportunities between members of the same club. New Zealand exports were further helped by the devaluation of the pound in 1933 to £NZ1.25 = £1, which followed the earlier British devaluation.

In fact the long-term effects of the depression on New Zealand proved psychological rather than economic, and stemmed mainly from its effects on the confidence of its farmers. The country had an adverse balance

[53] Hawke, *The Making of New Zealand*, table 7.1, p. 128. Hawke does not specify which dollars these were: they probably relate to post-1967 New Zealand dollars rather than current US dollars.

of payments in only the two years 1929/30 and 1930/1, in each case including a small adverse balance on visibles, which was exceptional in New Zealand history.[54] The worst effects of the depression were on farm incomes, which were negative in 1931/2 and very low in both 1929/30 and 1932/3, after which they recovered rapidly. This carried over to other parts of the economy. Factory production declined, owing both to reduced local buying power and also to reduction in imported intermediates. Building dropped by 70 per cent and investment generally may have declined until 1942/3.

In about 1932, therefore, a New Zealander might well have concluded that all this indicated the ultimate failure of an economic system based on export specialization, and that an alternative strategy would have to be adopted. This, indeed, was the conclusion drawn by some historians and analysts both of New Zealand[55] and in relation to tropical economies. In fact, they would have been wrong on both counts. First, the depression proved quite short lived and by the later 1930s the New Zealand economy was virtually back to where it had been in 1929. Secondly, there was, in fact, no practical alternative short of immiserating autarky, and none of the New Zealand governments, even though Labour took over in 1935, attempted to go for self-sufficiency. Governments maintained orthodox fiscal strategies, rejecting deficit financing. Levels of tariff protection were increased in line with the Ottawa decisions on imperial preference, which benefited local manufactures. New Zealand struggled out of the depression as it lifted in most other parts of the world with its economic and fiscal structures intact.

In retrospect, therefore, the depression can best be seen as a short-run blip in New Zealand economic history. In fact, the most significant innovation of the 1930s, and possibly in New Zealand economic history before 1984, came in 1938, when the Labour government suddenly imposed both import licensing and exchange controls. These were not the outcome of the depression but were introduced as a temporary crisis measure to counter a projected shortage of foreign exchange caused by the US depression of 1937–8. The alternatives were devaluation and internal retrenchment, neither acceptable to the Labour government. The resulting regulated economic system might not have lasted indefinitely had not the outbreak of war in 1939 led to a much wider range of economic controls, including a prices and incomes policy.

---

[54] Ibid., table 7.2, p. 133.
[55] The classic statement of the dependency aspect of the New Zealand experience was by C. G. F. Simkin, *The Instability of a Dependent Economy* (Oxford, 1951), and his *The Sugarbag Years* (Wellington, 1974). See also W. B. Sutch, *The Quest for Security in New Zealand 1840–1966* (Wellington, 1942), and his *Poverty and Progress in New Zealand: A Reassessment* (Wellington, 1941).

Such economic and social regulation was no more severe in New Zealand than in Britain. The difference was that in western Europe import and export licensing, wage and price controls, and much of the paraphernalia of state control of the economy were gradually dismantled in the 1950s, culminating, for Britain, in the convertibility of sterling in 1958. No such liberalization occurred in New Zealand. Total control of the economy had become the norm, accepted by both main political parties as necessary to insulate the country from the vagaries of the international economy as experienced in 1929–33. Moreover, it seemed for long to provide results: Hawke argues that the growth in real per capita incomes from the 1950s to the 1970s was of the order of 2 per cent a year.[56]

It is clear, however, that this relative prosperity was due not to official management but to the generally beneficial effects of the international economy before the OPEC oil-price increase of 1973. New Zealand maintained a ratio between exports and national income of 22–3 per cent at constant prices. The terms of trade were largely neutral over the longer period. The main change lay in the alteration of markets for exports and sources of imports. After about 1960 New Zealand finally emancipated itself from dependence on the British economy. In 1960 it sent 52.9 per cent of exports to Britain and took 43.4 per cent of imports from there. By 1970, even before Britain joined the EC, the figures were 35.5 and 29.5 per cent respectively. In 1980 they were down to 14.4 per cent for both exports and imports. No other single country emerged as the successor to Britain as New Zealand's economic metropolis. In 1980 exports were spread more evenly over a far wider range of countries, while the largest single source of imports was Australia, with 19.1 per cent of the New Zealand market.[57]

But even before the oil crisis of the mid-1970s there were signs of strain in this highly managed New Zealand economy, mainly because of the pressure of demand for imports, held back only by import licensing and currency controls. The foreign exchange constraint became continuous, with devaluation (and decimalization) in 1967, followed by further devaluations.

This was the hallmark of an overstretched managed economy, and was found in more extreme forms in many Third World countries. It was closely related to the differential rate of development in the domestic economy. Agriculture continued, as the farmers constantly reiterated, to be the backbone of the economy and by far the largest earner of foreign exchange. Yet it provided a declining share of the national income: from about 30 per cent in 1938–9 it had dropped to about 13 per cent

[56] Hawke, *The Making of New Zealand*, pp. 177–9 and fig. 9.4, p. 177.
[57] Ibid., fig. 11.8, p. 220; fig. 11.9, p. 221.

in the mid-1970s and its share of the male labour force declined from 24 per cent in 1952 to 16.5 per cent in 1970. Its leading sectoral position was taken not by manufacturing, whose share of both the labour force and GDP remained fairly constant from the mid-1950s to the mid-1970s, but by services, few of which contributed directly to earning foreign exchange. Thus New Zealand was becoming less of an export-oriented economy and more akin to the urban economies of the industrialized West. The question was whether the continued earnings of agriculture, along with the still small but growing export of manufactures, would be sufficient to maintain New Zealand's relatively very high standard of living for a growing and increasingly urban population.

The argument, then, is that, with the exception of the early 1930s, the international economy did not let New Zealand down. The country's growing economic problems after about 1960 were due largely to the rigidities of the economic and social systems developed since 1938, though intensified by the increase in oil prices and subsequent inflation of the mid-1970s. Clinging to the 1930s concept of 'insulation', New Zealand policies 'bore an increasingly old-fashioned and antediluvian look'.[58]

There followed, with the election in 1984 of a Labour government, a revolution in New Zealand social and economic policy as significant as the one that had resulted from the adoption of import licensing in 1938. The reforms began as a crisis measure to combat a serious foreign-exchange problem. They developed during the next dozen years into the virtual dismemberment of the managed economy of the previous half century. Trade, capital flows and investment were freed. Corporatism, nationalization and regulation of industries were ended. Taxation was reformed. Public expenditure peaked at 50 per cent of GDP in 1990, then dropped to under 40 per cent. The Employment Contracts Act of 1991 was as radical in its effects on trade unions as parallel British legislation of the 1980s. The result was that by the mid-1990s New Zealand was by some measures the most liberal economy in the OECD, able at last to compete as an exporter of manufactures in the international market.

The general argument of this chapter has been that the history of this group of 'settler' societies in Latin America and the South Pacific suggests that these 'new countries' were able to prosper by specializing in commodity exports. For all, the golden age was before 1914, or perhaps 1929, when all the elements that had created this international division of labour

[58] D. Henderson, *New Zealand in an International Perspective* (Wellington, 1996), p. 6. The following account of liberalization since 1985 owes much to this pamphlet.

were operating at their best. All suffered from the depression of the early 1930s, though some at least recovered well. None became leading industrial countries, though all developed substantial manufacturing sectors. Their later development and the fact that wide contrasts emerged between the more successful (notably Australia, along with Canada and New Zealand) and the less, mainly the Latin American countries, owed more to the way in which their governments used or abused the benefits of an export-oriented economy than to failings in the international economy.

How can their relative success be explained? First, all grew as extensions of the rapidly expanding European and North American economies. Their economies were complementary with those of the more developed West: they precisely conformed, at least initially, with Wakefield's concept. In the case of the British Dominions this complementarity was accentuated by the protective quotas provided by the Ottawa agreements of 1932 as a form of imperial cooperation.

Secondly, all developed ISI on the back of their exporting. For some this proved a partial dead end because their manufacturing industries did not become competitive at international prices: this demonstrated the potential weakness of the 'infant-industry' argument. For others, however, including Canada, Australia, and New Zealand, some at least of these industries became fully competitive by the later twentieth century, and this demonstrated that commodity exporting might be combined with and lead to efficient manufacturing.

Ultimately, however, the main reason for the success of all these economies may have been that they had very favourable population – resource ratios. Whether their main assets were land or minerals, a small population able to exploit extensive factor endowment was far better placed than a large population dependent on the same limited range of resources. As Ian Little has written, in the specific context of modern South-east Asia, 'Small size, in numbers, may be reckoned an advantage if the country discovers or can develop some natural wealth or asset whose proceeds are then shared among few people.'[59] It was this advantage, coupled with the fact that they had no large pre-capitalist indigenous population with whom to share the fruits of their economic success, that largely explains the prosperity of these 'settler' economies.

Another factor that may help to explain their affluence is the accident that many of their exports were those also produced in the developed world, and whose price was therefore conditioned by that current in the affluent West, a point emphasized by those supporting 'unequal-exchange'

[59] I. M. D. Little, 'An Economic Reconnaissance', in W. Galenson (ed.), *Economic Growth and Structural Change in Taiwan: The Postwar Experience of the Republic of China* (Ithaca, NY, and London, 1979). p. 451.

theories. In this sense, the 'settler' societies of the temperate regions were more fortunate than some tropical economies, whose products were more vulnerable to market fluctuation and technical change. This suggests that there may have been special factors that resulted in the success of these temperate settler economies. In the following chapters it is proposed to examine whether this was so, whether the same international trading environment and the principle of complementarity provided equivalent benefits for non-settler communities, particularly European dependencies, and, if not, why they did not do so.

6

The Concept of a
Colonial Economy

Colonialism may be described as a particular form taken by the process of creating an integrated world economy and the development of an international division of labour. The obvious and main difference from the same process in the settler societies was that in colonies this incorporation was not voluntary. Colonies were conscripts. Clearly this might make a fundamental difference to the effect that incorporation had on its peripheral members. The conventional view has been that the effects were almost universally bad, largely neutralizing any incidental benefits of trade. Yet this should not be taken for granted. It is equally possible to argue that, despite the predictable disadvantages of being conscripted and then coerced, there may have been residual benefits for the indigenous inhabitants of these colonies. That is, they may have experienced greater growth, and possibly also development, in a colonial situation than they might have done had they remained both independent and outside the international division of labour. In short, in the post-colonial era, when analysis of colonialism no longer has any polemical function, the proper question to ask about the economic consequences of colonialism is not whether they were optimal but how closely they resembled the effects of voluntary membership of the international capitalist community by states such as the settler societies. This approach will be adopted here.

It is proper to start with a synopsis of the standard list of the alleged economic disadvantages of colonialism for dependent societies. This will be followed by an analysis of the way in which imposed capitalism actually affected pre-capitalist societies, taking the evidence of British colonies in Africa as a model. Thereafter, while it would be impossible to provide potted histories of any proportion of the modern colonial territories, the experience of two contrasting colonies as components of the international trading economy will be examined briefly in chapter 7, and one of them will be compared with that of a settler society.

1 The General Economic Case against Colonialism

Colonialism in the twentieth century has had a generally very bad press. On the far left, among neo-Marxists, it has been axiomatic that colonialism existed to enable the capitalist states to exploit the resources of their dependencies. For example, Walter Rodney's widely influential book *How Europe Underdeveloped Africa* argued that European colonialism destroyed the native viability of African societies and their capacity for sustained development, leaving them marginalized helots on the periphery of the western capitalist world. He encapsulated this argument in the aphorism that most Africans 'went into colonialism with a hoe and came out with a hoe'.[1] Among many other Marxist critics of colonialism Samir Amin has argued that the type of development imposed on French West African territories, notably concentration on commodities for export, could lead only to a dead end because this was based on mere extension of land use without technological improvements, and because monoculture left such an economy dangerously vulnerable to fluctuations in the market and deterioration of the terms of trade.[2]

A similar argument is developed in Jean Suret-Canale's *Afrique noire*.[3] Particularly in French West Africa, economic strategy was dominated by the big, mainly French, trading companies which expected and received full governmental support. These companies had no interest in real economic development: they merely wanted to export commodities and sell imported consumer goods. This could be achieved simply by making alliances with dominant indigenous groups who ensured that production was extended and who benefited as middlemen or landowners. Production could be expanded without technical improvement merely by extending the area under cultivation, leading to the danger of serious

[1] W. Rodney, *How Europe Underdeveloped Africa* (London, 1973), p. 239. John Iliffe, in quoting this remark, added 'although it was often a better hoe' (J. Iliffe, *Africans: The History of a Continent* (Cambridge, 1995), p. 216.
[2] See, in particular, S. Amin, *L'Afrique de l'ouest bloquée: L'Économie politique de la colonisation, 1880–1970* (Paris, 1971).
[3] J. Suret-Canale, *Afrique noire: L'Ère coloniale* (2 vols, Paris, 1964; Eng. edn, *French Colonialism in Tropical Africa* (New York, 1971)).

soil exhaustion on marginal land. The state cooperated by providing infrastructure and forcing Africans to produce or take paid work by imposing taxes or by physical compulsion. These foreign companies had no interest in industrialization, because this would have reduced the demand for their imports. Nor did they need to make substantial capital investments. They employed only working capital to finance the trade from producer to ultimate markets in Europe or America. Such companies could make 'super-profits' because they had a *de facto* trade monopoly, could pay low prices for the commodities they bought, thus exploiting 'cheap' labour, and could charge high prices for the consumer goods they imported as monopolists. Thus colonialism was mainly exploitative, extracting value from Africa and making no significant contribution to economic development.

Examples of such denunciations of the economic effects of colonialism could be multiplied indefinitely. To move out of Africa, Tapan Raychaudhuri, not a Marxist like these other writers, has summed up the effects of nearly two centuries of British rule in India as follows.

> Thus, when power was transferred [in 1947], South Asia was a typically underdeveloped region, with a vast and growing population, stagnant agricultural output, a small industrial sector, and inadequate infrastructure. In per capita terms India was nearly at the bottom of the international ladder both in commerce and in modern industry. Very low per capita income, low saving, and hence low investment completed the vicious circle. This was not the logical outcome of the buoyant pre-industrial economy of the sixteenth and seventeenth centuries, but a reflection of the workings of the colonial economic relationship.[4]

These and many other hostile critics of colonialism were specialists in regional developments and in some cases ideologically hostile to capitalism as well as colonialism. Let us now consider the views of other writers who appear to be doctrinally uncommitted but who have studied colonialism in a broad context.

First, Lloyd Reynolds, whose *Economic Growth in the Third World* has been quoted frequently above. Since his general argument is that export trade and incorporation into the international division of labour have generally been the 'turning point' for peripheral economies, he has to consider whether colonialism was a special case and to what extent it invalidated this general argument. His starting point is that no generalizations are possible: different imperial powers followed different strategies and no two colonies had the same experience. Colonialism was no necessary bar to reaching his 'turning point': he lists seventeen countries

---

[4] In P. J. Marshall (ed.), *The Cambridge Illustrated History of the British Empire* (Cambridge, 1996), p. 364.

that did so while they were colonies before 1947. Colonies could probably have grown faster had development been the primary imperial objective, which it very seldom was before the later 1940s and the rush to buy the loyalty of colonial subjects by providing rapid development. Conversely there is no certainty that any of these colonial economies would have done much better had they remained independent: the record of the few non-colonial Third World countries outside Latin America during the modern period was unimpressive.

Reynolds then draws up a conventional balance sheet. On the credit side colonialism clarified territorial boundaries and provided internal peace. It stimulated new and old export crops, thus encouraging the pursuit of comparative advantage. It provided the beginnings of a modern infrastructure, particularly communications, however limited. It took steps to prevent famine evolving out of scarcity.

But there were commonly negative aspects. Reynolds lists seven. There was typically a drain of profits from colonies to the metropolis via investors, trading companies, etc. Export production tended to generate enclaves, particularly when in plantations or mines. Retained profits from the modern sector were likely to generate income inequalities. Colonial governments did not protect domestic handicrafts from foreign competition, nor did they foster modern industry, partly because government revenues depended heavily on import duties. Educational provision was very limited, particularly at the secondary and tertiary levels. Colonial authorities often encouraged immigration to fill intermediate roles between the top echelon of Europeans and the mass of the indigenous workers – for example, of Indians to East Africa, Natal, Mauritius, Burma, Fiji and the West Indies – thus creating a three-tier division of labour.

Attempting to construct a balance sheet, Reynolds points to the fact that independence coincided with the greatest boom in modern history, which makes comparisons difficult. Nevertheless he concludes that, out of twenty ex-colonies in his sample, eleven experienced more rapid growth after independence than seems to have occurred under colonial rule (granted the lack of reliable statistics before the 1950s), three had much the same rate of growth, and six did worse. He concludes that the legacy of colonialism was worse in Africa than elsewhere, reflected in the racialist stratification of occupations, limited education, and the poor economic performance of many Black African countries since independence.[5]

This would imply that the main economic contrast between colonies and the Latin American republics and the Dominions stemmed from

[5] L. G. Reynolds, *Economic Growth in the Third World, 1850–1980* (New Haven and London, 1985), pp. 41–3.

the amount of help governments in the second group provided for economic and social development. They were much more ready to borrow abroad to provide infrastructure and utilities. They were ready to help indigenous manufacture with protective duties and subsidies. Generally their educational provision was better. In addition, though Reynolds does not mention this, there was relatively little state pressure on the mass of the people to work in mines, plantations, etc. which will be seen to have been a major factor in many parts of colonial Africa.

Reynolds's conclusions are replicated by many other non-dogmatic commentators. For example, M. Havinden and D. Meredith examined the developmental record of the British in their tropical colonies – excluding India, Ceylon and Burma – from 1850 to 1960.[6] Their conclusion was that British colonialism did not prevent all growth, but had serious limitations. The 'major economic failing was structural imbalance which created colonial economies which were excessively dependent on the export of a narrow range of unprocessed primary commodities and which experienced deteriorating terms of trade as a result'. Britain did little to stimulate secondary industries. Colonial boundaries had little relevance to ethnic or economic realities and resulted in non-viable small independent states. Living standards rose very slowly, as did provision of social and welfare services. Above all Britain was not prepared to invest sufficiently to generate real growth. It 'always wanted quick results from colonial economic expansion and expected to obtain these from unrealistically small financial outlays': this was particularly true after 1945, when Britain attempted to exploit Africa's economic potential to alleviate its own serious shortage of hard currencies.

Finally, we may quote a Swiss, and therefore possibly neutral, historian, R. von Albertini.[7] At the end of a book based on exhaustive examination of the literature on most parts of the colonial world to 1940, von Albertini reached a measured conclusion. Concepts such as 'plunder economics and exploitation' were unhelpful. There was economic growth in these colonies, but it was 'export-oriented growth, primarily profiting the metropolises, and was one-sided in character'. Colonial governments helped development by building communications systems, 'though these were primarily intended to open up the hinterland and thus to serve foreign trade'. The most serious lack was a 'Development policy in the modern sense … implying a careful

[6] M. Havinden and D. Meredith, *Colonialism and Development: Britain and its Tropical Colonies, 1850–1960* (London, 1993). This summary can be found on pp. 316–18.
[7] R. von Albertini, *European Colonial Rule, 1880–1940: The Impact of the West on India. Southeast Asia, and Africa* (Oxford, 1982), esp. pp. 507–8.

orientation to the specific needs of a given area and having as first priority the raising of agricultural productivity', because such planning was only in its infancy before about 1940. Metropolitan governments were 'unwilling to budget moneys for [colonial] development'. Colonies could borrow, but only at the cost of servicing the debts out of their own very limited revenues. In short, 'the economic development of the colonies until World War II and after thus remained subordinated to metropolitan interests, which were one-sidedly committed to exports and dualistic in structure'.

The main common denominator of these various critiques of modern colonialism is belief that colonial economies were restructured to serve the interests of the parent states through expansion of commodity exports. All accept that such specialization was deliberately imposed, and that it primarily benefited the metropolitan capitalists who conducted it and the imperial economy; though precisely how a reserved colonial commodity trade would be an advantage to a European state except in times of acute shortage or to save foreign currency, which was really only true during and after the two world wars, is seldom addressed. Adopting the structuralist arguments of the post–1945 period, critics of all sorts assume that specialization in commodity production for export could not be in the long-term interest of the exporting country: development could come only through industrialization. It was because there was so little manufacturing in these colonies that this exporting strategy was to be condemned.

This raises important questions. First, if, as was shown in chapter 5, Latin American economic historians accept that the expansion of commodity exports proved the starting point of growth and development in Latin America, including the first stages of industrialization, why was it not so in the contemporary colonial world? Secondly, and consequentially, were there special factors operating in the colonies which inhibited the benefits to be expected from export production as predicted by the classical economists?

These problems will be considered below. But, before leaving these general and broadly hostile critiques of colonialism, it is necessary to consider the arguments of Bill Warren, one of the very few Marxists who have argued to the contrary: that colonialism was in fact necessary for the genesis of Third World development.[8]

Warren's starting point in assessing the impact of colonialism on economic development in the Third World was, rightly, the fact emphasized above: that the key difference between colonialism and the general

---

[8] The argument that follows is based on Bill Warren, *Imperialism: Pioneer of Capitalism*, ed. J. Sender (London, 1980), ch. 6, 'Colonialism: Dr Jekyll and Mr Hyde'.

impact of the West on Third World societies was the ability to use force. Colonialism as a means of opening LDCs to the international economy was denounced as immoral by both colonial nationalists and western liberals because it was undemocratic and involuntary. There was assumed to have been a better alternative way in which these countries could have progressed: Warren quotes Thomas Hodgkin as writing that imperialism (which in his terminology included colonialism) was 'essentially retrogressive, destructive of African Civilization (which did not require colonial conquest to develop in interesting and fruitful ways)' – a theme that has been carried on by, among others, Basil Davidson.[9] To Warren force is not necessarily bad: this depends on how and for what purpose it is used. All societies use force when they regard it as unavoidable. Its use by colonial governments was not different in kind: it appeared so only because used by an alien power.

Warren then turned to the general effects of colonialism. Economic development could not be examined in isolation from other aspects of the effects of colonialism; and Warren argued that colonial government provided at least three major benefits. First, health improved very considerably – 'the most dramatic, significant and conclusive proof of the advantages of Western colonization' – resulting in a great reduction in disease and suffering and the prolongation of life. Greater longevity in turn increased the size of the market, and therefore consumption, assuming per capita consumption remained constant. This improvement was due primarily to western medicine and medical facilities, but also to measures taken by colonial governments to prevent food shortages deteriorating into famines. Comparison between the records of the two independent African states – Liberia and Ethiopia – and other African countries under colonial rule, or of Thailand with colonial South and South-east Asia, demonstrated the special achievements of colonialism in this field.

Secondly, colonialism and foreign trade greatly increased the provision of incentive goods, which were critical to stimulate production in the poorer levels of society. Warren disputed the conventional argument that importation of such goods necessarily destroyed local handicrafts: there was a relative decline, but 'an *absolute* rise in the volume and number of items of traditional production, because the market underwent a massive expansion during this period'.[10] Thus between 1900 and 1950 buying power in Nigeria increased fourfold. While this was evident in

[9] Ibid., p. 127, n. 3, quoting from T. Hodgkin, 'Where the Paths Began' in C. Fyfe (ed.), *African Studies since 1945* (London, 1976). For Basil Davidson, see, in particular, his *The Black Man's Burden: Africa and the Curse of the Nation State* (London, 1992).

[10] Warren, *Imperialism*, p. 131.

most parts of Africa, it was less certain in India, over which the debate concerning handicrafts had begun; though it seems likely that even there the total availability of textiles increased substantially.

Finally there were the benefits of education. Although much of the education provided was irrelevant to local conditions, Warren maintained that colonial schools had a vital function 'in dissolving traditional outlooks in a manner which, however traumatic, could only facilitate individualism, rationality, and a democratic outlook'.[11] Such education was obviously 'one of the crucial elements in economic progress'. Warren, following Marx, clearly had no hesitation in proclaiming the superiority of western culture as a necessary prerequisite of economic and social change.

Warren then turned to the main arguments commonly put forward to demonstrate that colonialism had a destructive effect on dependent societies. As has been seen, the key to these arguments (Warren took A. G. Frank as his main exemplar) has been the assertion that the international division of labour imposed by western imperialism, and involving relative free trade, colonial rule and foreign capital investment, was deliberately intended by western capitalism to convert the Third World into a marginalized and proletarian source of cheap labour and resources. In particular, Warren considered the two accusations that colonialism drained the economic surplus from colonies and that the international division of labour was against the interests of Third World peoples.

Considering first the drain of real resources, which, if it existed, would have to be absolute and not relative, Warren argued that the repatriation of profits by western capitalists did not constitute a net drain because the transfers represented only a proportion of value added in the host country, leaving a substantial benefit. Thus repatriated profits were not a measure of wealth creation. Nor had Warren any time for the concept of 'unequal exchange', which could be true only if trade was regarded as a zero-sum game. Neither investment nor trade therefore necessarily reduced the wealth of a colony.

There remained the larger question of the effects of the international division of labour. Did it freeze sectors of the Third World economy in an 'unbalanced' state, thus creating and perpetuating 'underdevelopment'? On this Warren was more cautious. The effects of an export-dominated economic system and its relative advantages depended on two things: whether there was a viable alternative line of development to exporting; and whether concentration on exports blocked developments leading to industrialization. In the first instance, the development of commodity exports during the nineteenth century was largely a spontaneous reaction by producers throughout the Third World to the

[11] Ibid., p. 135.

expanding European market. In this they were only following in the footsteps of Britain and other European states that had evolved a modern economy on the basis of improved agriculture and primary exports. Latin America, the United State and the British settler colonies had clearly chosen freely to follow this path. Japan was initially compelled to do so, but, once pointed in this direction, seized on the possibilities and financed most of its industrialization from exports, initially of raw silk, later of cotton textiles. Nor was specialization on agricultural exports necessarily undesirable economically. 'There is no inherent tendency for agricultural productivity to be lower than productivity in manufacturing, nor is there any secular tendency for the terms of trade of primary commodities to decline as against manufactures.'[12] Agriculture could also make a good contribution to diversification. Thus in itself concentration on commodity exports might be a perfectly satisfactory basis for economic development.

This, however, assumed that such specialization was undertaken voluntarily. In fact in most colonial situations it was imposed by the colonial power; and the conditions set by foreign capital, European settlers and colonial governments might be very different from those in an independent state. Warren summarizes the standard list of alleged defects in colonial economic management: artificially low wages (due to compulsion, poll taxes, seizure of indigenous land, etc.), infrastructure skewed to benefit the export trade but not other forms of economic activity, the blocking of potential industrial development in the interests of foreign trading companies, and refusal to allow tariff protection, which had been critical for every western industrializing country except nineteenth-century Britain. Did such limitations on the potential value of export trades destroy their economic validity and condemn colonialism as an obstacle to progress?

On this Warren was not specific. But he appeared to believe that the transition to commodity production for the international market, along with the other benefits brought by colonialism, was likely to have better consequences than continuation of earlier pre-capitalist modes of production might have had. If colonialism was less favourable to development than it might have been, at least it paved the way for potentially better and faster development once colonialism ended.

Finally Warren considered the accusation that colonialism preserved 'archaic modes of production' as part of its exploitative system, so hindering economic modernization, simultaneously (and often as a necessary consequence) allying with 'feudal' classes in the colonies to bolster its political strength. Warren recognized that these things might have been common in the colonies, but denied that they significantly affected his general thesis that colonialism was progressive, not tending towards

[12] Ibid., p. 146.

underdevelopment. Marxists accepted that pre-capitalist classes and modes of production could coexist with capitalist forces: this was a transitory stage. Indeed, the temporary preservation of backward modes of production in some sectors might be necessary for capitalist development in others. Moreover, the very 'feudal' classes which seemed to obstruct modernization had historically often become modernizers when the time came, as in parts of Latin America. In addition, the rise of an indigenous middle class in the colonies, which was likely in the end to challenge the feudalists for power, was itself almost invariably the direct result of colonialism, often as a reaction to alien rule.

Warren, then, seems to argue that, on balance, colonialism, though intrinsically undesirable because based on force, not consent, and because the selfish interests of both metropolitan and settler capitalists reduced the advantages these countries might have obtained by joining the international economy, was a necessary stage in the development of some Third World countries which might not otherwise have been willing or able to become part of the international division of labour. In this, of course, he was following Marx, as was seen in chapter 2. Colonialism thus becomes an unpleasant but necessary stage in the evolution of worldwide capitalism, ultimately leading to the death of capitalism and the birth of socialism.

In all these contrasting approaches to colonialism the argument clearly turns on one central issue. Assuming, from the experience of some at least of the Latin American and anglophone settler societies, that specialization on commodity exports as part of an international economy may enable a country to pass from 'extensive' to 'intensive' growth, and then to further development and affluence, how seriously did the undesirable aspects of colonialism, summed up in the concept of force, weaken this case?

To approach this question it is proposed to look in some detail at precisely what colonial rule and its imposition of capitalism might mean in a newly colonized region, taking as a model arguments from recent work on British East Africa, which essentially takes off where Warren stopped.

2   'Articulation' and the Political Economy of Colonialism in East Africa

In its simplest form, as summarized by Berman and Lonsdale, the common approach by Marxists and structuralists to the purpose and methods of colonialism states that colonial rule existed in order to enable metropolitan capital to exploit the resources of an undeveloped Third World country.[13] Formal imperial rule was necessary because capital alone lacked

---

[13] This section is based mainly on B. Berman and J. Lonsdale, *Unhappy Valley: Conflict in Kenya and Africa* (2 vols, London, 1992), hereafter B&L.

the power adequately to penetrate such an economy: it required the support of a state apparatus to do so. Thus the primary function of the colonial state was to compel an indigenous society to accept its assigned position in the international division of labour. This involved Africans and others adopting at least in part a cash economy, producing for the market or working for those who did, and accepting rewards that did not fully represent the value created. Since the indigenous peoples commonly resented conscription into this economic and social system, it was the function of the colonial state to overcome their resistance.[14]

At the same time it was important for capital, if it was to obtain the greatest possible advantage from this system, that for as long as possible Africans and others should remain 'peasants' and that the 'peasant mode of production' should continue alongside the growing capitalist sector. This dualism has often been called 'articulation of modes of production'. Allegedly there were two main results. First, metropolitan capital gained what some neo-Marxists called 'super-profit': some have even argued that the existence of these pre-capitalist modes of production was essential to the continued expansion of capitalism in the metropolitan centres.[15] Secondly, these colonial societies were left in a hybrid state, neither fully converted to capitalism nor in their earlier pre-capitalist condition.

Articulation thus becomes the key concept in examining the interface between intruding capitalism and the indigenous society. But, as Berman points out, to talk of a 'peasant mode of production' as a concrete economic reality is misleading. It is more correct to say that it is 'a form of production that can exist and takes on its particular historical character within the dominant dynamic forces of different societies that determine the conditions of its reproduction or transformation'.[16] Neither capitalism nor the peasant mode of production is a 'pure' form, but each has a peculiar developmental dynamic. Yet, as Henry Bernstein has written, there is no doubt that the effect of colonialism was that the

---

[14] For a straightforward exposition of this argument as it relates to Kenya, which Berman and Lonsdale criticize, see R. D. Wolff, *The Economics of Colonialism: Britain and Kenya 1870–1930* (New Haven and London, 1974). Wolff assumes that virtually every aspect of Kenya's economic and social development was planned by the British authorities, in the interests of the British economy in general and of British settlers in Kenya in particular.

[15] See e.g. J. G. Taylor, *From Modernization to Modes of Production* (London, 1979), ch. 13, quoted in B&L, p. 130. Rosa Luxemburg, of course, had argued along the same lines in her *Accumulation of Capital* (1913). Marx himself suggested that a higher rate of return could be obtained from the labour of 'slaves, coolies, etc.' when arguing in vol. 3 of *Capital* that trade was one of the ways in which the declining tendency of the rate of profit might be offset.

[16] B&L, p. 130.

dominant capitalism

> subjects the elements of other modes of production to the needs and logic
> of its own functioning and integrates them, more or less, in the mechanism
> of its reproduction ... there is no question that the 'autonomy' of the
> pre-capitalist modes or relations of production are preserved, nor any doubt
> that the law of motion governing the articulation is determined by capital.[17]

The key moment in the victory of capitalism over pre-capitalist modes
of production came when the relative self-sufficiency of an indigenous
economy was disrupted. This disruption might be caused peacefully
through market incentives, typically by the activities of foreign merchants who persuaded Africans or others to produce for the market in
order to be able to buy imported goods. But in some parts of Africa the
process had gone a long way before the imposition of colonial rule during the last two decades of the nineteenth century. Alternatively, if this
economic stimulus was inadequate, the colonial state would be required
to help foreign capital by imposing head or hut taxes, which could be
earned only by taking paid work or producing for the market, by forced
labour, or by compulsory production of stated quantities of cash crops.

The key to 'articulation' lies in the fact that for most Africans the
wages they could earn or the cash they could obtain from selling produce
was insufficient for their needs. That is, the transition to capitalism was
incomplete. Peasants had therefore to maintain their pre-capitalist base.
They remained strung between two worlds.[18] The general result was

> the subjugation and exploitation of peasant labour on the basis of partial
> restructuring and partial preservation of pre-capitalist forms with a min-
> imum of capitalist investment. While pre-capitalist forms appear to persist
> at the surface of social relations, their significance and continued existence
> is actually transformed and determined by capital. Domestic production
> is no longer an autonomous mode of production but a form of the
> reproduction of labour power within capitalism.[19]

Berman and Lonsdale accept all this as a useful formal statement of
the economic impact of colonialism in Black Africa. Its weakness is that

---

[17] H. Bernstein, 'Capital and Peasantry in the Epoch of Imperialism' (Occasional Paper 7(2), Economic Research Bureau, University of Dar es Salaam,
1977), p. 35, quoted in B&L, p. 131.
[18] Goran Hyden's concept of an 'uncaptured peasantry', though relating primarily to post-independence Tanzania, suggests that there was another side to
this. Unlike the true proletarian, the peasant, so long as he retained his access
to land, could survive economic crises and government pressures and maintain
his partial independence of choice and action. See G. Hyden, *Beyond Ujamaa
in Tanzania: Underdevelopment and an Uncaptured Peasantry* (London, 1980).
[19] B&L p. 132.

it is too rigid and static. Above all it is too deterministic. It treats capital, the colonial state and the colonial peoples as abstractions. In particular it regards colonial officials as mere puppets of abstract capitalism and Africans and other colonial peoples as 'passive receptors of external forces'. It is, therefore, necessary to adopt a more historical approach to the economic impact of colonialism and capitalism.

First, articulation was not imposed overnight or easily: it was the product of a long process of 'struggle and uncertainty', with many variations and limitations as Africans resisted the impact on their ways of life. Secondly, articulation progressively weakened peasant forms of production. For some it led to impoverishment, but for many others, who used their assets to exploit the market, there was substantial accumulation, resulting in class differentiation. Finally, the role of the colonial state was in no sense simply to support capitalists against Africans. It had a double role: it had to acquire political legitimacy by seeming to act as arbiter between capital and indigenous society, even while performing its role as promoter of capital.[20]

These definitions lead Berman and Lonsdale to an examination of the actual workings of colonial rule in Africa and its many contradictions. Starting with the role and character of the colonial state, they argue that it had a double function: 'to secure the conditions for the extraction of commodities and accumulation of capital by metropolitan interests . . . second, to provide, as an essential precondition for accumulating, a framework of stable political order and effective control over the indigenous population.'[21] Since these functions were different and in some degree conflicting, they are examined separately.

First, the colonial state had to act as an agency to promote the interests of European capitalism. In both West and East Africa the main investment by metropolitan, as contrasted with settler, capitalism was in trade, 'based on state-protected monopolies and monopsonies, which made possible large and sustained profits, especially for merchant capital'.[22] Except in coastal West Africa, this foreign investment took place mostly after the imposition of imperial rule. The promotion of export-commodity production resulted in three broad patterns of African employment: as peasants growing crops

[20] Ibid., pp. 132–8.
[21] Ibid., p. 145.
[22] It is arguable that, particularly in West Africa, this is an exaggeration of the role of the state. The position of large foreign trading companies, such as the United Africa Company, which operated in both West and East Africa, did not depend on state protection: in fact the state was generally hostile to their position and tried to protect the interests of Africans against this 'big business'. Nor, for most periods, did these companies make 'large and sustained profits'. See D. K. Fieldhouse, *Merchant Capital and Economic Decolonization: The United Africa Company 1929–1987* (Oxford, 1994), for detailed evidence on this for one such company.

for export; as wage workers in plantations and mines; and as part of a 'deliberately preserved' labour reserve to provide workers for the mines and plantations. It was the main role of the colonial state to ensure that Africans either produced or provided labour within these categories. The question is why it was necessary for it to do so, where in most independent societies the state did not have this responsibility?

Berman and Lonsdale do not here directly address this crucial question: they simply point out that 'no colonial official had any faith either in the productivity or reliability of free peasantries', assuming that peasants required 'political supervision or the discipline of employment'.[23] But the literature on economic development suggests at least three possible explanations. First, pre-capitalist societies lacked the 'work ethic' of modern Europe: people did not feel any obligation to work beyond satisfying their conventional needs. Until and unless additional effort demonstrably resulted in worthwhile benefits, Africans would not produce more or take paid work. The availability of 'incentive goods' was one way of overcoming this reluctance, but only if the potential rewards were seen to justify the effort involved in acquiring them.

This leads to a second possible explanation. It was clear from the development of a number of export commodities in many parts of the Third World that peasant production would respond willingly to market incentives if these were seen as adequate: the classic case is cocoa in West Africa, undertaken on African initiative in the later nineteenth century when the rewards were regarded as good. But for some crops, and at times of international economic recession for virtually all commodities, the reward to the peasant cultivator was not seen as sufficient. The reasons might lie in factors such as high internal or international transport costs, the profits taken by middlemen or trading companies, or competition from other producers. Under such circumstances indigenous producers, provided they had an option, would tend not to concentrate on cash crops, reverting to subsistence production or exercising a leisure preference. An additional factor was limited market information, particularly in areas most remote from the market, and limited expectations.[24]

[23] B&L, p. 147. The argument is stated more fully in J. Lonsdale, 'The European Scramble and Conquest in African History', in R. Oliver and G. N. Sanderson (eds), *The Cambridge History of Africa*, vol. 6: *From 1870 to 1905* (Cambridge, 1985), ch. 11, esp. pp. 750–66.

[24] The concept of the 'backward bending labour supply curve', implying that unsophisticated workers would work only until they had satisfied restricted needs or desires, was widely quoted as a reason why Third World workers could not be induced to work longer, harder, or for longer contracted periods. While there may be some validity in this argument, it must be tested against other variables, such as the availability of incentive goods, rates of pay, etc. For analysis, see H. Myint, *The Economics of Developing Countries* (New York, 1965), p. 60.

Finally, so far as large-scale capitalist enterprises, such as plantations or mines, were concerned, there were serious deterrents to Africans taking paid employment. Such work commonly involved leaving home, travelling long distances, accepting poor or dangerous working conditions that often resulted in high mortality, but ultimately receiving relatively poor rewards.

Such problems were in no sense unique to Third World countries in the twentieth century. Elsewhere, in the past, they had normally been resolved by resorting to slavery or virtual slavery, such as villeinage or peonage (debt slavery), the last still common in some countries. In modern Europe the alternative solution had been provided by increasing populations that generated a surplus labour force beyond the needs of an increasingly mechanized agriculture. This created the proletariat, which had to look for paid work to survive, but whose employers had at least to pay sufficient for the labour force to reproduce itself – Marx's variable capital.

In early twentieth-century Africa this solution was not available. So long as population did not grow beyond the limits of potential agricultural land, and so long as the mass of Africans had access to sufficient land to provide for their basic needs – reproduction – they would produce for the market or take paid employment only if these options seemed sufficiently attractive.

These were rational economic choices: but they did not fit the interests of colonial governments, the metropolitan economy, or local European settlers. Colonial governments needed revenue, which came mainly from taxes on imports and exports. It was, therefore, vital to ensure maximum overseas trade. In addition, governments needed labour to build communications and utilities, but normally lacked the money needed to pay for it at market rates. From a metropolitan standpoint, particularly during the period between 1914 and the 1950s, it seemed important to maximize colonial production of important commodities either to support a war effort or to save on hard currencies – for example, raw cotton, which would otherwise be bought from the United States and paid for in dollars, expensive in peacetime, given the post-1931 exchange rate, scarce after 1939. Finally, for the European settlers or foreign owners of plantations or mines, cheap labour was often critical for the economic functioning of their enterprises in a highly competitive international market.

Thus the key factor which determined the economic role of the colonial state in Africa, and to a degree also in South and South-east Asian and the Pacific colonies during the twentieth century, was that the state had artificially to replicate the effects of advanced capitalism in the West. Since capitalism was not sufficiently advanced to create a genuine proletariat, the state had to provide the compulsion of the wage packet.

The ways it did so have often been described. The basic and virtually universal technique was to impose head or hut taxes, payable only in cash, which compelled Africans either to produce for a market or to work for wages.[25]

But taxation alone did not serve all needs. Colonial governments commonly used compulsion, usually through the agency of indigenous chiefs, to provide labour for public works: in French colonies before 1944 this included unpaid labour under the *indigenat*, the legal code for natives. Even private labour contracts were generally backed by criminal penalties for breach of contract, as under the eighteenth-century British masters and servants acts. Other devices used to increase production of desired cash crops included imposition of quotas of a particular product, use of local 'cooperatives', and agricultural extension services. To make these strategies more effective the colonial state adopted a far more positive role in the provision of social services than did most European states before the mid-twentieth century. It provided a variety of specialist technical departments to improve methods of production and built transport facilities to enable people and goods to move efficiently to and from the ports. In short, faced with initially major obstacles to the development of pre-capitalist societies, the colonial state became both authoritarian and, in a sense, socialist.

Assuming this analysis of the role of the colonial state to be correct, the fundamental issue is whether the economic and social strategies it adopted resulted, as the 'underdevelopment' theorists maintained, in colonial economies that were 'blocked' or 'arrested' within the capitalist international world system, or whether, as Warren and others have argued, they created the possibility of change and development. In their analysis Berman and Lonsdale appear to point successively to two alternative outcomes.

First, at least in the short term, colonialism resulted in articulation, which produced 'a situation in which African labour and commodities were appropriated below their value through the partial preservation of the pre-colonial domestic sphere of production'. Moreover, at least before 1945, there was virtually no improvement in the means of peasant

[25] To avoid the socially disruptive effect of forcing Fijians to take work on plantations to earn wages, Sir Arthur Gordon, the first governor of Fiji in the 1870s, adapted a technique, borrowed from the Dutch 'culture system' in Java, of allowing taxes to be paid in cash crops. But he found it necessary to import large numbers of indentured Indian labourers to work the sugar plantations and generate sufficient revenues to pay for government, with serious long-term social consequences. See, in particular, J. K. Chapman, *The Career of Sir Arthur Hamilton Gordon, First Lord Stanmore, 1829–1912* (Toronto, 1964); J. D. Legge, *Britain in Fiji, 1858–1880* (London, 1958).

production: greater output resulted from extension of land under cultivation, and cash crops invaded land previously used for food and pastoral pursuits. The result was soil depletion and reduced yields, which, coupled with population increase, led to malnutrition and rural pauperization. In addition, colonial governments, frightened of potential urban unemployment and political troubles, discouraged migration to the towns and the growth of urban industries.[26]

The article from which this chapter of *Unhappy Valley* derived was originally published in 1984.[27] By the time of publication of their book in 1992 Berman and Lonsdale appear to have modified their views on several aspects of this scenario and suggest a more constructive outcome. In chapter 8, 'Up from Structuralism', they point to a number of weaknesses in the argument summarized above.

First, the assumptions both that the prime mover of colonial economic development was external capitalism, and also that there was no differentiation between metropolitan and local (settler) capitalism, were illusions. In fact, 'capital' was in no sense a unity. There were great differences of aim and method between various foreign enterprises, and even greater conflicts of interest between overseas and local, mainly settler, capitalists. Nor was the colonial state simply the agent of these fractions of capital. It had an autonomous existence. On the one hand, it had to facilitate the process of articulation in order to serve the interests of capitalism. But, on the other hand, it had to govern with relatively small punitive resources. To do this it needed to acquire legitimacy in the eyes of Africans and also to rely extensively on African collaboration in all aspects of government. This forced the state to provide rewards for those Africans on whom it depended as administrators, etc., and this in turn made it possible for a minority of the more enterprising Africans to become capitalists, though often still 'straddlers' because still strung between capitalist and pre-capitalist economic spheres.

Secondly, it was equally false to treat Africans as lay figures unable to influence their fate. At every stage from the first European occupation Africans attempted to protect their interests and to benefit from opportunities. It proved very difficult to move them from their own land or to modify their social and economic processes. Conversely they were usually quick to spot and exploit new economic opportunities, provided these offered a satisfactory return. In West Africa this had resulted in the survival of a landed peasantry and autonomous adoption of cash crops. In Kenya Africans did the same, but were to some extent

---

[26] B&L, pp. 150–1.

[27] B. Berman, 'Structure and Process in the Bureaucratic State', B&L, ch. 7, pp. 140–76, was originally published, under the same title, in *Development and Change*, 15, 2 (1984).

prevented from growing the most profitable export crop, coffee, by the colonial state, under pressure from the settler farming interest.

Thus articulation was as much the product of African resistance to change and seizure of opportunity as of European strategy. The result of African entry into the commercial economy in most parts of Africa was the emergence of class differentiation. Large landowners, commercial middlemen, subordinate state officials, small merchants, artisans, were all to some extent products of the new orientation of the society. This petite bourgeoisie was proof of economic and social dynamism: articulation was not a static condition.

Moreover, the rise of the African bourgeoisie constituted a threat to the political permanence of the colonial state and the economic and social dominance of at least local, if not overseas, European capitalism. Economically, the African middle class was performing the same role as the European middle classes in their earlier struggle against the aristocracy. Politically, while for a time it found it necessary to ally with the colonial state, eventually it found it a constraint. Nationalism expressed the determination of the emergent African middle class to complete its conquest of the economy. Thus the inherent contradictions of the colonial situation were eventually resolved in political independence and indigenous conquest of the commanding heights of the economy.

3   The Wider Implications of Articulation

If this is an accurate model of the impact of colonialism, as the special agent of the international division of labour, in Africa, how greatly does it differ from the experience of politically independent developing societies and non-African dependencies in the same period? What light does it throw on the economic and social functions of modern colonialism?

The critical difference between colonies and independent states was, of course, the fact of self-government. Incorporation into the international division of labour was not imposed on the latter by a foreign power. Governments were responsible only to their own people and, where democratic, to the local electorate. The rulers, at least in principle, therefore had an identity of interest with the mass of their subjects.

These were fundamental contrasts. Yet there were many similarities. First, for all of them much of the capital needed to provide modern infrastructures and the technology for manufacturing came from abroad. In the important extractive and plantation sectors these foreign-owned firms constituted enclaves with limited linkages to the local economy. This, in turn, as most Latin American theorists have argued, resulted in dualistic economies, divided between the modern, capitalist and the pre-modern sectors, heavily dependent on the pre-modern sector for labour and many commodity inputs. This bears a close resemblance to articulation as described by analysts of African economic development, resulting in vast contrasts in affluence between those in the modern, largely urban, and the pre-modern rural areas. In both cases, also, the character of economic development was determined by the external market.

That leaves the question of compulsion. Was there a Latin American or British settler equivalent of the tropical African colonial state as the agent of capitalism to overcome resistance from those on whose labour capitalism depended and to ensure that capitalism could extract a surplus from the masses? Initially, during the sixteenth century, the Spanish had faced the same problems in America as Europeans were to face in Africa during and after the nineteenth century. Their solution had been various forms of conscripting indigenous labour for mines and agriculture, later importing slaves. By the twentieth century neither was needed. Four centuries of occupation had transformed Latin American societies so that conventional forces of capitalism could provide the compulsion to work that in early colonial Africa was provided by the colonial state.

Although conditions varied very widely from one Latin American society to another, the basic fact of their agriculture was the concentration of land ownership in the hands of a small minority of the population, holders of *latifundios*.[28] The great majority of the population were *minifundistas*, smallholders who might own their land, rent it, or be provided with it in return for services or sharing the crops with the land owner, *métayage*. Furtado estimates that in Latin America as a whole these *minifundistas* made up about half the agricultural labour force, the other half being full- or part-time wage earners. The key to the system was that the great majority of these small holders could not produce enough from their land for subsistence. They had, therefore, to take paid work, while remaining peasants. The effect was to provide a labour force for commercial agriculture that could be paid low wages, both because there was a large reserve army of labour and because their plots provided a part of their needs. As Furtado puts it, 'Control of land use in many parts of Latin America was a social technique used by a minority to impose a rigid discipline of work on populations living in extreme misery.'[29]

If this is compared with the African model of Berman and Lonsdale, it is clear that the main difference is in the length of time during which Europeans had controlled a territory. Putting it bluntly, in Latin America colonialism had done the job of converting a peasantry into a component of capitalist accumulation some three centuries before the European occupation of tropical Africa. The result in Latin America was what

[28] This paragraph is based mainly on C. Furtado, *Economic Development of Latin America*, (1970; 2nd edn, Cambridge, 1976), ch. 7.
[29] Ibid., p. 71.

European colonialism was, according to Berman and Lonsdale and others, aiming at in modern Black Africa: the establishment of articulation between modern and pre-modern sectors of the economy.

There were, of course, major contrasts between different parts of Latin America, other settler societies, different parts of Africa, and other underdeveloped countries. In the Third World as a whole the main exceptions to this pattern of articulation imposed by land expropriation are found in those parts of Africa, South and South-east Asia, and the Pacific, where there were relatively few European settlers or large-scale land transfers. The classic example is West and Equatorial Africa, where, apart from some largely unsuccessful French attempts to lease huge areas in the Congo for development at the end of the nineteenth century, there was very little land annexation by Europeans, nor were there many extractive enterprises and virtually no factories. Most West Africans were already converted to the benefits of commercial farming before colonization. If articulation is applicable in these places, it relates mainly to the division of largely family labour between commercial and subsistence activities. Much the same was true of Uganda, which, unlike Kenya and Tanganyika, had very few large foreign-owned farms or other enterprises, other than cotton-ginning factories.

The Belgian Congo was a special case. There the presence of large plantations – more accurately until the 1930s huge concessionary areas from which natural products such as palm oil could be collected – and of mines, particularly the copper mines of Katanga, created the need for a large African labour force. Since wages and conditions in both these were generally unattractive, the colonial state used the whole range of devices available, notably taxation, indentures and physical compulsion, to provide a wage labour force.

Finally, in most parts of colonial South and South-east Asia there was no need for the colonial state to adopt the techniques found convenient in parts of Africa to ensure either producing for the market or taking wage employment. Apart from the fact that these societies were already highly commercialized before European occupation, Indians, Javanese and others had their own devices for ensuring an adequate supply of labour. The two most common were land shortage or concentration, and debt peonage. In many parts of India a large proportion of the population controlled insufficient land for family subsistence. Thus a survey of 20,000 peasant families in Bengal made in 1938–9 showed that 40 per cent of them held land as sharecroppers (*bargadars*) or supplemented their incomes by working as day labourers.[30] This clearly represented a form of articulation. The other very common form of

---

[30] D. Kumar (ed.), *The Cambridge Economic History of India*, vol. 2: *c.1757–c.1970* (Cambridge, 1983), p. 164.

compulsion was debt peonage, widely found among landless labourers and also smallholders who had experienced poor harvests or other disasters. Thus in India the colonial state had no need to use state power, including extraction of revenue, to compel reluctant peasants to work: by the twentieth century land shortage in alliance with complex patterns of indigenous class and economic relationships ensured that virtually all Indians were engaged in an articulated commercial system.

Java provides a very clear example of articulation between traditional agriculture and modern industry that resulted primarily from economic and social conditions. A key stage in this was the so-called culture system of the period after 1830, whose essential feature was that Javanese communities had to render fixed quantities of cash crops to the government in lieu of taxes. Although this did not necessarily disturb the character of indigenous rural society, it established the principle of cash cropping and opened the way to capitalist production. After the abolition of the culture system by the agrarian law of 1870, alienation of land to foreigners was forbidden. Plantations were made possible by grants of leases for seventy-five years, but mainly in the outer islands, where unoccupied land was freely available, rather than in densely populated Java, where this was not feasible. There, in the irrigated regions that had been growing cash crops in lieu of taxes under the culture system since the 1830s, Europeans built sugar mills. Since they were not allowed to acquire land to grow sugar, they made contracts with local villages or individual peasants by which the mills acquired a short-term lease of the land. The Javanese remained in occupation, but were obliged to produce sugar for the mills. This they rotated with rice and other crops for their own consumption. Around 1930 180 sugar mills employed in this way some 800,000 Javanese. Since they were paid both rents for use of their land and wages for their labour, the effect was to monetize the economy and increase the market for both imported and locally produced consumer goods, which in turn was to generate light consumer industries in Java after 1914. On the other hand, continuation of peasant ownership and production meant that there was very little technical improvement in agriculture, while the increasing population tended to reduce per capita incomes and lead to land deterioration.[31]

From this limited evidence some tentative suggestions can be made concerning the predictable economic impact of colonialism.

Only in colonies where European settlers constituted the main labour force was western capitalism seen in its full form, because in these, once

---

[31] The standard work on the Javanese sugar economy is C. Geertz, *Agricultural Involution: The Process of Ecological Change in Indonesia* (Berkeley and Los Angeles, 1963). This pessimistic assessment contrasts with that of G. C. Allen and A. G. Donnithorne, *Indonesia and Malaya: A Study in Economic Development* (New York, 1954).

the indigenous population had been subordinated and marginalized, there was no obstacle to western relations of production. In all other colonies the development of a capitalist economy involved in some degree the transformation of the indigenous economy and society. This was almost never from mere 'subsistence' to 'commerce', because all pre-capitalist societies were to some degree commercialized. Rather, the need was to make the commercial element dominant and link the economy to that of the western world.

The easiest way of doing this was by persuasion, inducing non-Europeans to produce internationally needed commodities for the market through the attraction of the superior rewards this might offer. But, from a western standpoint, this strategy had limitations. It left control of both the commodities produced and their volume to non-Europeans. The expansion of production was likely to be held back by limiting factors such as transport, shortage of capital, limited indigenous understanding of the market, and in some places indigenous resistance to the attractions of cash cropping. The case for colonialism was that it could help to solve these problems.

The role of the modern colonial state was, therefore, to carry through rapidly transformations that in earlier colonies had taken several centuries. From a Marxist standpoint, its function was to transform the indigenous society into a source of labour for capitalist enterprises and a producer of commodities, in each case at wages or costs below those current in the developed world. From the standpoint of the classical economists, it was to liberate underutilized resources of land and labour and to enable the society to benefit from the principle of comparative advantage.

From either point of view, the critical feature of this process was that the transformation into capitalist societies proved very difficult and was not complete by the end of the colonial period, nor, in fact, by the end of the twentieth century. Some Marxists would argue that this was because the West did not wish the transformation to go beyond a certain point, that articulation best served the interests of western capital. Other Marxists have held that commercialization of Third World economies was incapable of leading to real development, again for some or all of the reasons put forward by the 'pessimists'. From a liberal standpoint, however, failure could be explained in other ways. Indigenous societies proved extremely resistant to fundamental change, and in many colonies their resistance was backed by colonial governments which idealized peasant forms of life and production and feared the political effects of change.[32] Another explanation is that the forces of capitalism were too weak to carry through a total transformation. Neither the colonial

[32] This has been forcefully argued in the case of the Gold Coast/Ghana in G. B. Kay, *The Political Economy of Colonialism in Ghana: A Collection of Documents and Statistics, 1900–1960* (Cambridge, 1972).

powers nor international capital was able or willing to invest sufficiently in these countries, and almost by definition a Third World country could not itself generate sufficient savings to overcome the structural obstacles to development. In the widely quoted aphorism, the trouble with the Third World was not that it was exploited by capital but that it was not sufficiently exploited.

Finally, therefore, the evidence suggests that, while colonialism (or something nearly equivalent) seems to have been a necessary condition for the initial stage of the incorporation of much of the Third World into the international division of labour, and thus potentially to the benefits of capitalism and ultimately to economic and social development, it was not a sufficient condition.[33] At the end of the twentieth century virtually all countries outside Europe, North America and parts of East and South-east Asia remain strung between their pre-capitalist pasts and the world of modern capitalism, or state capitalism of a socialist type: they were still in varying degrees underdeveloped. It remains in the next chapter to consider very briefly, in the light of two case studies, whether this was the necessary consequence of colonialism: whether, as the pessimists have argued, colonialism was itself an inevitable, possibly deliberate, bar to true development; or, alternatively, whether limited success was the result of the insufficient strength of the forces of international trade and investment.

[33] The most obvious exception to this was, of course, Japan, which was never a western dependency and which grew from being an apparently undeveloped country in the later nineteenth century to one of the economic giants of the late twentieth century. The reasons for this success have been very extensively examined, but the key elements in all explanations seem to be that even before the Meiji era Japan had many very advanced commercial, banking and industrial elements and a government which was anxious and able to promote industrialization and foreign trade. A standard account is in L. Klein and K. Ohkawa (eds), *Economic Growth: The Japanese Experience since the Meiji Era* (Homewood, Ill., 1968). By contrast, the development of China, the other major Third World state that escaped colonial rule, did not seriously take off until after 1945 nor gain great momentum until the 1970s.

7

The Colonial Economy in Practice: Trade and Development in India and Ghana

Even two swallows do not make a summer. The evidence of India and the Gold Coast/Ghana cannot prove or disprove any of the generalized hypotheses presented in chapter 6. These two countries do, however, represent two widely contrasting models in two continents: one very large, one small, one with relatively limited overseas trade, the other a typical export-oriented economy, and both very well documented. Moreover, they provide evidence on the basic question posed at the start of this book: how far incorporation of a Third World country into the international economy through trade and colonialism could promote growth and development.

1 India: An Overview

For many reasons India must be regarded as the most important single test of the effects of trade and colonialism on a Third World country. It was under effective British control for some two centuries. It was the largest colonial territory in terms of population. Marx, as was seen above, predicted that the building of railways from the 1850s would revolutionize the Indian economy, injecting capitalism, and leading ultimately, after political independence, to increasing affluence. Yet India remained at the time of independence one of the poorest countries in the world; and this was blamed by Indian nationalists from late in the nineteenth century on British policies. We have, therefore, to attempt to discover why Marx's prediction proved false, why India remained in 1947 predominantly a country of poor agriculturalists, with only 1 per cent of the labour force in manufacturing. Was this proof of the weakness of trade as an engine for transmitting growth, or of British rule, or of other factors? This very brief account will concentrate only on three aspects of development under colonial rule: trade, industrialization and investment.

Consider first trade. Indian nationalists and many western critics have complained that Britain treated India as primarily a source of cheap raw materials and a market for British exports. This might imply that overseas trade became the dominant factor in Indian economic life. But in fact it did not, at least by comparison with other developing countries.

Exports are a critical factor, since it has often been argued that British strategy was to 'de-industrialize' India, converting it into an agricultural economy providing raw materials such as cotton for British industry. There is no doubt that Indian exports increased substantially over the whole period from the 1830s to the Second World War. The average compound rate of growth of exports from 1834/5 to 1940/1 was 3.23 per cent, the fastest period of growth being between 1851/2 and 1860/1, when the rate was 6.3 per cent. Since the average growth rate of the population from 1871 to 1941 was 0.61 per cent, this suggests that exports were growing faster than population. Imports, though nearly always smaller than exports because of the need for a favourable balance to service overseas obligations, grew at roughly the same rate, though from a lower base. Their cumulative average rate of growth from 1834/5 to 1940/1 was 3.68 per cent.[1]

A more useful measure of the relative importance of trade to the Indian economy would be to calculate its export coefficients and to compare them with those of other 'colonial' economies. There are technical difficulties in doing this with confidence for any long period because of the lack of reliable statistics for national incomes.[2] For what they are worth, rough estimates are as follows.

---

[1] D. Kumar (ed.), *Cambridge Economic History of India* (*CEHI*), vol. 2: c.*1757–c.1970* (Cambridge, 1983), table 10.6, p. 832; table 5.8, p. 490.

[2] In the case of India the best estimates of national (or domestic) gross product are summarized in *CEHI*, vol. 2, table 4.3A–B, pp. 397–9, which is for the net domestic product (NDP). These might be compared with figures in ibid., vol. 2, tables 10.7A–D, pp. 833–9, for exports and imports. Unfortunately, while the latter are at current prices, the NDP statistics are at constant 1946/7 prices. To construct useful export or import coefficient figures involves deflating the NDP statistics. This can be done with some confidence for both the late 1930s and the mid-1940s, using the implicit deflator of Sivasubramonian: Rs85 in 1946/7 equals Rs32.5 in 1938/9. See *CEHI*, vol. 2, p. 403, n. 2. But earlier estimates using the same deflator are likely to be speculative and are omitted here.

In 1937 (the best year during the 1930s for commodity trade) India's export coefficient (exports as a percentage of net domestic product) was 8.1; in 1940, 7.6; in 1946/7, 3.6. The coefficient may have been higher before 1929: Angus Maddison put it at 10.7 per cent of GNP in 1913.[3]

By the standards of most tropical commodity-exporting countries these Indian export coefficients were very low indeed. It is difficult to calculate them for most tropical territories before the later 1950s because of lack of data on the domestic product. But for 1950–2 Reynolds provides, among others, the following average export coefficients: Thailand, 18.2; Malaysia, 52.0; Nigeria, 26.5; Indonesia, 18.4; Egypt, 19.2; Colombia, 12.0; Kenya, 18.5; Venezuela, 34.1; the Ivory Coast, 28.3; Ceylon, 33.9; Peru, 18.0; Northern Rhodesia, 74.6; the Belgian Congo, 38.6; Uganda, 27.9; Ghana, 32.2; Brazil, 9.0. For India the figure was then 6.7. It is significant that several countries which were to develop very rapidly in the next few years, and which in 1950–2 had low export coefficients, had high ratios by 1978–80: for example, South Korea rose from 1.2 to 28.1 and Taiwan from 9.2 to 53.6.[4] For comparison, two developed countries also had much higher export coefficients in the twentieth century. Canada, the great majority of whose exports consisted of agricultural, forest or extractive products, had an export coefficient of 14.3 per cent in 1913, rising to 21.2 per cent by 1937 and to 25.1 per cent in 1950.[5] In the same three years, Britain, the first fully industrialized country, had export coefficients of 36, 21 and 19.[6]

Such statistics strongly suggest that, by comparison with other modern colonial, ex-colonial and mature developed countries, exports were relatively very unimportant in the economy of India. Other aspects of the Indian export economy strengthen the argument that there colonialism did not play the role conventionally ascribed to it as the creator of an economy devoted to export of commodities intended primarily for the metropolitan market.

First, not only were exports small in proportion to the national product; they were minute in absolute terms and by international comparison. Thus in 1941 exports were Rs5.1 a head, or about £0.4.

Secondly, the range of export commodities was not only very narrow but was by no means all intended for the British market. To consider their distribution in 1930/1, raw cotton was by far the largest single

---

[3] Quoted in L. G. Reynolds, *Economic Growth in the Third World, 1850–1980* (New Haven and London, 1985), p. 299, from A. Maddison, *Class Structure and Economic Growth: India and Pakistan since the Moghuls* (New York, 1972).
[4] Reynolds, *Economic Growth*, table 8, p. 410.
[5] M. C. Urquhart (ed.), *Historical Statistics of Canada* (Cambridge, 1965), pp. 130, 141, 173.
[6] B. R. Mitchell, *British Historical Statistics* (Cambridge, 1994), pp. 453, 829–30.

export at 21.0 per cent of total export value. But much of this was in fact re-exported from Britain to continental Europe, where the short-stapled Indian cotton was more acceptable than it was in Britain; and after 1914 Japan became the largest single consumer of Indian cotton exports. In any case, by the 1930s the majority of Indian raw cotton was being consumed by Indian spinning mills. The second largest share of exports was manufactured jute goods, mainly bags, the greater part of which went to the United States, Australia and elsewhere, not to Britain. By that time raw jute, initially sent for manufacture in Dundee, was down to 5.8 per cent of export value. The third largest export was food grains at 13.5 per cent. The Indian element in this was mostly wheat, particularly from the irrigated areas of the Punjab, which took its chance on the international wheat market; but in fact much of the food-grain export was rice from Burma, still technically part of India at that date. Finally, tea provided 10.7 per cent of exports, and this was indeed mainly for the British market. Oilseeds, which had been the third largest Indian export before 1914, were becoming relatively less important, facing increased competition from West Africa, South-east Asia and the Pacific.[7] This does not look like an export economy structured to meet the needs of the British economy.

Another significant feature of these exports from India proper was that, of all these exports, only two were in any sense produced by expatriate capital. Tea was grown mainly on British-owned plantations. Jute manufacture was mainly in mills in Calcutta, originally owned by British firms, but by the 1930s increasingly being taken over by Indians. Conversely, cotton and wheat were produced by Indian farmers as a direct response to market forces.

The evidence, therefore, suggests that India had little or nothing in common either with the 'new' settler economies of the later nineteenth century, whose economic development was launched on the back of profitable commodity exports, or with the typical open economies of twentieth-century Black Africa and South-east Asia. There were times in the mid-nineteenth century, as the new railways opened up inland producing areas and European demand for food and raw materials was growing very fast, when India was expected to develop into a commodity-exporting economy: Marx certainly thought so in the 1850s. But India did not respond to the opportunity as efficiently as did others. Jute and tea were its only market leaders, once opium sales to China had tailed off after 1860. As a wheat producer, its sales were marginal on the international market, profitable only when a devalued currency enabled it to compete with North and South America and Australia. Moreover of the main commodity exports,

[7] *CEHI*, vol. 2, table 10.11, p. 844.

only two – cotton and jute – seem to have had valuable downstream effects on industrialization.

All this suggests that India was far from being a conceptual export-oriented economy, structured to meet the demands of the international division of labour and to produce commodities for the West. It was, in fact, as a market for British manufactures rather than as an exporter of commodities that India before 1947 came closest to matching the model of a dependent colonial economy. The pattern of its overseas trade in 1913/14 gives a clear picture. While manufactures provided only 22.4 per cent of its exports, they constituted 79.2 per cent of its imports. In 1910/11 31.2 per cent of total imports by value were cotton piece-goods, and in that year 62.2 per cent of its imports came from Britain. These proportions had been much higher in the later nineteenth century, but were to drop very fast after 1921. By 1933/4 cotton piece-goods provided only 13.1 per cent of total imports, with machinery for the then expanding industries up to 11.1 per cent; and by 1940/1 total imports from Britain were down to 22.9 per cent, whereas those from the United States had risen to 17.2 per cent and from Japan to 13.7 per cent.[8]

In this sense, then, the Indian economy was 'colonial' down to at least the 1920s, in that it depended heavily on manufactured imports and that until then most of these came from Britain. Yet there is another paradox here. Both absolutely and by comparison with other colonial Third World countries, India's imports were very small. In 1913 the import coefficient was in the region of 10.2 per cent, while the per capita value was around £0.5. This compared with average per capita imports at the same date of £10.3 for Argentina, £16.8 for Australia, £18.8 for Canada and £11.4 for Chile.[9] These, of course, were all much richer countries. But comparison with a range of colonies in Black Africa in the late 1950s also shows a huge contrast. The value of imports as a percentage of the value of their monetized domestic product[10] in 1959 was: Kenya, 37; Tanganyika, 32; Uganda, 28; Central African Federation, 35; Nigeria, 22; Ghana, 33; the Belgian Congo, 23. In 1960 the figure for Indonesia was 13, for Malaysia, 39. For India it was 8.0 per cent.[11]

The conclusion must be that, despite its long period under British rule, India was never converted into what one can describe as a conventional

---

[8] Ibid., vol. 2, pp. 856–64.
[9] D. Denoon, *Settler Capitalism: The Dynamics of Dependent Development in the Southern Hemisphere* (Oxford, 1983), table 1, p. 50.
[10] For Nigeria the domestic product includes estimates for the non-monetized sector.
[11] P. Duignan and L. Gann (eds), *Colonialism in Africa*, vol. 4: *The Economics of Colonialism* (Cambridge, 1975), table 106, p. 443; V. N. Balasubramanyam, *The Economy of India* (London, 1984), table 9.1, p. 182.

colonial trading economy. This may well have been a significant reason for limited economic growth.

This, of course, runs counter to the conventional argument that India's relative economic inertia stemmed, not from failure to follow an export-led route to development, but from the fact that it was prevented by the British from adopting an industrial strategy: that this was the real measure of colonialism in India. It is, therefore, necessary to consider briefly the development of industry in colonial India and the reasons for its limited growth.

The standard argument is that in the eighteenth century India had been the largest exporter of cotton textiles in the world and was in a sense an 'industrial' country, with a very large range of manufacturing products and enterprises. In order to ensure a market for its growing manufactured exports during the nineteenth century, the British treated India as an open economy, insisting on free trade, preventing the use of import duties for protective purposes until the 1920s, deluging the country with British factory-made consumer goods which could outsell indigenous products, compelling the Indian state to purchase capital equipment, as for the railways, in Britain rather than making them in India, and failing to invest in modern manufacturing which might lead to competition with British imports. In addition, from the 1890s the British insisted on a strong rupee, which reduced Indian export competitiveness, and they 'drained' real resources from India through the 'home charges', consisting of interest on the Indian debt and payments for a variety of services provided by Britain, including the cost of the India Office and the British troops stationed in India.[12] It has also been argued that, from the later nineteenth century, Britain positively discouraged British investment in Indian industry for fear that this might reduce the market for British exports. The combined outcome was that India was unable to develop a modern industrial economy from its initial industrial base and remained a poor agricultural economy, heavily dependent on imports of most manufactures.

Most elements of this scenario have been challenged. Thus Morris D. Morris argues that the technology of almost all Indian industry before the British occupation was 'quite simple' by the standards of contemporary Europe, and however skilful the handicrafts, these showed no signs of evolving into anything resembling contemporary western factory manufacturing.[13] Others have argued that the 'drain' was in fact small in relation to the Indian GNP and that the country would have had to

[12] This 'drain' approximates to the concept of 'economic surplus' as defined by Paul Baran, and described in ch. 2 above.
[13] Morris D. Morris, 'The Growth of Large-scale Industry', *CEHI*, vol. 2, pp. 558–63. Much of the present discussion is based on this chapter.

pay quite as much for the same foreign investments and services if independent. As regards free trade, the success of two major industries, cotton and jute textiles, without protection suggests that it was quite possible to exploit comparative advantages in this way; in any case, since the market for such products was initially partly overseas, protectionism would have been little help. In fact, cotton spinning and weaving were the great success story, and around the turn of the century India was a major exporter of cotton goods, both yarn and textiles. But, by the 1930s, it had been overtaken by others, notably Japan. With exports of jute then declining in the face of synthetic substitutes, India was already falling behind in the international race for markets for manufactures, though it had become almost entirely self-supporting in textiles and also iron and steel.

It is impossible here to debate the causes of such limited industrial development. Clearly the imposed open market was a major deterrent before the 1920s, though there is no evidence that British capital actively discouraged investment in Indian manufacturing. The results, however, are clear. At the end of the colonial period India was in no sense an industrial country. Although, in 1947, mining and manufacturing combined contributed some 17 per cent of total output, more than half of this came from small-scale, largely unmechanized industry. The proportion of the workforce employed in 'industry' (including mining, manufacturing, transport, storage and communications) remained roughly constant at 12 per cent between 1901 and 1951. In 1947 less than 2 per cent of the labour force was employed in large-scale factories. Industry was concentrated in two relatively small areas based on Bombay and Calcutta.[14]

Finally, there is the question of metropolitan investment in India. Was it, in line with Leninist theory, regarded as a valuable, because entirely secure, field for British capital investment? Did British capital flow in to stimulate production of commodity exports and transform India into a capitalist economy, as Marx had predicted? Above all, what contribution did British investment make to India's economic development?

By definition development requires investment, which can come either from domestic savings or from foreign loans or grants. In common with almost all Third World countries, India's capacity to save and invest was very limited. Tomlinson calculates that between 1860 and 1947 the average rate of domestic capital formation was between 1 and 1.5 per cent of GNP, which was above the rate of population increase until about 1920, but thereafter below it.[15] By any standards this was very low indeed and suggests that development would depend heavily on foreign investment.

[14] B. R. Tomlinson, *The Economy of Modern India, 1860–1970* (Cambridge, 1993), pp. 92–5.
[15] Ibid., p. 135; table 1.1, p. 4.

This is where one might, in accordance with conventional descriptions of the aims of colonialism, or alternatively by the standpoint of post-1945 western attitudes to Third World development, have expected the metropolis either to seize a profitable opportunity or to meet India's need.

Britain did not do so. In common with all imperial states before 1945, it did not expect to make grants to colonies, except in case of urgent fiscal crisis. Capital had to pay its way, which meant that it had either to be borrowed and serviced by the colonial state or to be invested by private enterprise in expectation of profit. Government borrowing was thus restricted by the cost of paying interest and amortization. By 1939 India's accumulated foreign public debt, almost all to British bondholders, stood only at around £313 million.[16] This compares with total government expenditure on economic overheads (railways, irrigation, roads and buildings, and others) between 1898/9 and 1937/8 of £1,036 million.[17] Thus government borrowing from Britain provided less than a third of public investment in Indian infrastructure in this forty years. Even so, the cost of servicing this debt in 1931/2 amounted to 12 per cent of total government expenditure: defence cost an additional 28 per cent.[18] Nor was the British private investor ready to fill the gap. Total accumulated private foreign investment in India in 1948 has been estimated at only about £170 million.[19]

Thus the total of public and private foreign investment in India before independence may have amounted to under £500 million. In the late 1930s, when the population of India was some 318 million, this represented only around £1.50 a head. To point to some contrasts, in 1913 British investments in Argentina represented £47.7 a head; in Australia and New Zealand, £73; in Chile £19.4; in South Africa, £55.2; and in Uruguay, £34.7.[20]

Clearly, then, for better or worse, colonialism had only a limited effect on the economic development of India before 1947. This is not the place to debate the relative significance of British policies, the structural problems of land, labour and capital markets that blocked the way to growth, nor the many other indigenous obstacles to development. But the limited role of the colonial state has been well summed up by B. R. Tomlinson:

> The colonial state operated by deliberate neglect of developmental considerations for most of its life between 1860 and 1947. It was concerned

[16] *CEHI*, vol. 2, p. 944. An alternative estimate of some £326m. is given in ibid., p. 876.
[17] Ibid., vol. 2, table 12.9, p. 936.
[18] Ibid., vol. 2, table 12.8, p. 931.
[19] Balasubramanyam, *The Economy of India*, table 7.1, p. 148.
[20] Denoon, *Settler Capitalism*, table 2, p. 51.

to follow its own narrow administrative interests – interests which did not always reflect the wants of its imperial masters in London, but certainly often ignored the needs of its subjects in India. For most of its life the colonial state was able to assert itself to achieve its ends, but was semi-detached from the life of its citizens, and did not see itself as capable of influencing their economic progress very much.[21]

In terms of the general argument of this book, then, the Indian case does not throw much light either on the benefits obtained by undeveloped countries from incorporation into the international division of labour through trade, or on the economic effects of colonialism. On the contrary, it suggests that neither trade nor colonial rule was likely to make much economic impact on a large continental country such as India, though it is arguable that a colonial government with a different set of priorities could have done more to break down internal barriers to trade and development. How far was this true of other, smaller Third World countries that also experienced colonial rule in the twentieth century?

2 West Africa: The Gold Coast/Ghana

West Africa in general and the Gold Coast (Ghana after independence in 1957) in particular stand at the opposite pole to India. Ghana's area was some $258,537 \text{ km}^2$ and its population in 1911 about 2 million, rising to over 4 million by 1948. Population density was 17.3 per km^2, compared with 112 in India. In 1950 its average per capita income was about £40, as compared with about £18 in India. More significant for the present argument, Gold Coast exports represented 39.5 per cent of gross national expenditure and cocoa exports alone represented about 30 per cent of GDP.[22] In short, the Gold Coast provides a much better example than India or other highly populated Asian countries of a tropical colony whose economy was highly geared to the international economy.

It also represents a different facet of the colonial impact from the East African colonies on which Berman and Lonsdale based their analysis of 'articulation'. The two key factors in their analysis, particularly of Kenya and Tanganyika, were that economic life was dominated by foreign capital – both metropolitan and settler – and that Africans had to be forced to contribute to the commercial economy by various governmental devices. Neither was substantially important in West Africa. Before the 1950s there was very little permanent foreign capital investment in any

[21] Tomlinson, *The Economy of Modern India*, p. 217.
[22] D. Rimmer, *Staying Poor: Ghana's Political Economy 1950–1990* (Oxford, 1992), pp. 30–2.

of the West African colonies, apart from the relatively small mining companies, and virtually no permanent settlers: under 7,000 non-Africans in Ghana, for example. Foreign capital consisted mainly of the working capital of the big trading companies and banks, which ebbed and flowed with the crop seasons. Before the 1950s there was virtually no fixed foreign investment in industry, apart from a Swiss-owned brewery, established in 1932. There were very few plantations.

For these reasons, and also because government could depend for its revenues mainly on export duties on cocoa and duties on imported consumer goods, the state did not, there or in most of British West Africa, use taxation or physical compulsion to force Africans to take paid work or to produce cash crops unwillingly.[23] There were direct taxes, but they were light, and they were never used, as in East Africa, as a means of compelling Africans to become involved in the commercial economy.[24] Thus, if articulation developed, it was largely due to the choice of Africans to straddle the commercial and 'traditional' economies.

Indeed, the key to Ghana's economic development in the early twentieth century, which is also true of much of coastal West Africa, was that there was no need for Europeans or colonial governments to instil commercial attitudes and practices. These were voluntary members of the international economy. As most modern economic historians of the area have made plain, this was a highly commercialized region long before Europeans started trading there.[25] The domestic production was extremely varied and much of it traded. From the sixteenth century Africans saw the possibility of expanding their only significant distant trade, across the Sahara, by tapping the need of Europeans for slaves and a wide range of commodities, receiving in return highly valued goods such as guns and spirits. These trades generated elaborate internal trading organizations and produced considerable wealth for those who controlled them. It was fortunate for the future of the West African economies that Europeans did not conduct their own slave hunts into the interior, as Arab slavers did in East and East-central Africa: they remained on the coast and conducted their business through African intermediaries. Although from the later nineteenth century Europeans

---

[23] The French, however, did use taxation and compulsion for both public and approved private ventures.
[24] The point is emphasized in G. B. Kay, *The Political Economy of Colonialism in Ghana: A Collection of Documents and Statistics, 1900–1960* (Cambridge, 1972), pp. 28–9. Since Kay was concerned to denounce colonial practice as a main reason for limited economic growth in Ghana, this is significant.
[25] A useful and compelling survey of the evidence for this is in A. G. Hopkins, *An Economic History of West Africa* (London, 1973), esp. chs 2, 3. Much more evidence has been published since then.

penetrated inland, in most places they still relied on Africans as middle-men between themselves, as buyers of produce and sellers of consumer goods, and the mass of Africans, as producers and consumers.

The point, then, is that in West Africa Europeans found enthusiastic associates in their drive to enlarge trade: Africans welcomed and responded to any foreign initiative. The modern economies of West Africa were based on this enthusiasm for innovation. Compelled by Europeans to wind up the slave trade in the sixty years after the British had abolished their own slave trade in 1807, they responded by developing 'legitimate' products to satisfy the new demands of industrializing Europe.[26] Two external developments made this possible: the rapidly increasing western demand for indigenous products, such as vegetable oils, and the dramatic growth in the number and size of European ships, which made bulk commodity trades commercially viable. The advent of colonial rule expedited this process, mainly by integrating larger territorial units, and so removing obstacles to free movement of goods (though this was at the expense of some monopolistic intermediaries), and eventually by building railways to make the export of bulk crops from the interior economically possible. But in almost every case the initiative in expanding existing or developing new export commodities lay with Africans. Their response to the market created the modern economies of West Africa, and their shape was becoming clear even before the full extension of colonial rule late in the nineteenth century.

This is the starting point for analysis of the development of the Gold Coast economy. Although the focal point of the country's economic development in the twentieth century was cocoa, the Gold Coast had a very long experience of trading with Europe as well as other parts of Africa; and until 1911 cocoa, whose production there did not start until 1892, was not the largest single export by value: in 1908, out of total exports of £2.2 million, more than half was gold. Wild rubber was worth £68,000, palm oil £129,000, palm kernels £78,000, logs £158,000 and cocoa £541,000. By the 1920s these were joined by other commodity exports, notably diamonds and manganese. Thus this was already a substantial export-oriented economy before cocoa became king, and it would no doubt have expanded these or other products if cocoa had not become the leading sector.

---

[26] On the 'crisis of adaptation' from the slave to 'legitimate' trades, see the useful collection of essays in R. Law (ed.), *From Slave Trade to 'Legitimate' Commerce: The Commercial Transition in Nineteenth Century West Africa* (Cambridge, 1995). For the Gold Coast, see, in particular, ch. 4, by Gareth Austin, 'Between Abolition and *Jihad*: The Asante Response to the Ending of the Atlantic Slave Trade, 1807–1896'. See also M. Lynn, *Commerce and Economic Change in West Africa, The Palm Oil Industry in the Nineteenth Century* (Cambridge, 1997).

Nevertheless the economic history of modern Ghana hinges on cocoa, and this account must concentrate on the economic consequences of specialization in this crop. The critical fact is that cocoa was entirely alien to the Gold Coast. Precisely when and by whom it was introduced remains conjectural. Cocoa originated in Central or South America and was spread widely by the Portuguese and Spanish and cultivated in the Caribbean. It reached São Tomé and Fernando Po early in the nineteenth century, and it is said that the Basel missionary society introduced it to the Gold Coast as early as the 1860s. But its special value was not recognized there until the early 1890s. Among the claimants to spreading its use was the Ga blacksmith Tettn Quashie, whose nursery in Mampong (Akwapim) may have been the source of pods or seedlings for local farmers. By 1892–3 the government's botanical garden at Aburi was also selling these. The first to take up the new crop were Akwapim Ridge farmers, whose incomes from sale of palm oil, their main cash crop, were reduced by lower prices in Europe. They also tried coffee, but this did not thrive. Thus cocoa emerged as a substitute cash crop in an area already tied to commodity exports.[27]

But cocoa was not merely an alien import. Its development was made possible by migration of the farmers from their Akwapim Ridge in the south-east of the Gold Coast north-east into the virtually unoccupied forest lands of the Akim people. They were joined by farmers from the Accra plains. The migrants were able to buy land and wait for the trees to grow and produce because they had accumulated savings from the palm-oil and kernels trade, and also because for the first few years food crops could be grown under the newly planted cocoa trees. The original capital was gradually increased by ploughing back the first payments for cocoa, and the scale of the operation and the area covered grew very rapidly: in the years before 1914 tens of millions of trees were planted on new land each year. By 1913 cocoa exports were worth £2.4 million. They rose to a first peak of £10 million in the boom of 1920, then, after the recession, recovered to over £11 million in 1927.

This was a staggering rate of growth, which bears comparison with the early growth of staples in settler societies.[28] The essence of staple

---

[27] Summarized in J. S. Hogendorn, 'Economic Initative and African Cash Farming', in Duignan and Gann (eds), *Colonialism in Africa*, vol. 4. There is a very useful analysis of the economic consequences of the cocoa industry for the Gold Coast by G. M. Meier, 'External Trade and Internal Development', in ibid. The classic account of the genesis of the industry is Polly Hill, *The Migrant Cocoa Farmers of Southern Ghana: A Study in Rural Capitalism* (Cambridge, 1963). See also her *The Gold Coast Cocoa Farmer* (London, 1957).

[28] The best-known and widely influential application of staple theory in a colonial context was H. A. Innis, *The Fur Trade in Canada: An Introduction to*

theory is that a new society uses whatever factor endowment is available to provide exports that in turn will pay for imports and so establish a domestic market. This provides a base from which a young economy can grow and diversify. How successfully it does so will depend on the nature of the staple, how it is produced, and the linkages between its production and export and the rest of the economy. In Innes's treatment, the Canadian economy had grown successively from fishing, to furs, to lumbering, all indigenous and needing only to be culled, but providing the basis for the establishment of communications, towns, primitive manufactures and services. The economy could then move on to wheat, minerals, manufacturing and all that belongs to a diversified European-style economy. A similar model could be applied to most colonies of settlement in the Americas and Australasia.

It has not, as a rule, been applied to tropical dependencies; but Hopkins argues convincingly that it is highly relevant to West Africa from the nineteenth century.[29] The key period was after the abolition of the slave trade. Slaving did not act as a satisfactory staple. It tended to concentrate economic power in the hands of a minority of the powerful who did not use the wealth it produced to develop the rest of the economy. Slaving was replaced by a variety of natural and later cultivated indigenous products, notably palm oil and groundnuts, which, since they could be produced by a large number of people, stimulated the economy as a whole and provided linkages to the land and labour markets, both of which were increasingly commercialized. These trades in turn generated the need and the funds for improved communications, while the export incomes they produced stimulated domestic demand for incentive goods. But how far this process would take an economy would depend on many variables, notably the accumulation of capital and increasing efficiency in the use of land and labour. If a society remained immobile at an early evolutionary stage of its staples, its growth would be limited. It was seen in chapter 5 that the key to the economic growth of Australia and New Zealand was that they moved progressively from early staples (whaling, sealing, timber, wool, gold) to a wide range of primary exports and also into processing and manufacture. The question here is whether African colonies, more particularly the Gold Coast, were able to do the same.

The case for treating cocoa in the Gold Coast from the standpoint of staple theory, and for comparing its fortunes with those of a settlement colony – here New Zealand – is twofold.

Canadian Economic History (New Haven, 1930; rev. edn, Toronto, 1956). For a later analysis, see M. H. Watkins, 'A Staple Theory of Economic Growth', *Canadian Journal of Economics and Political Science*, 29 (1963), pp. 141–58.

[29] See Hopkins, *An Economic History of West Africa*, pp. 125–75.

First, cocoa as it evolved from the 1890s was as much a result of earlier staple development as that of, say, dairy products in New Zealand. Cocoa emerged after a considerable period when the export economy was based on exploitation of long-established indigenous products such as palm oil, wild rubber, gold, timber and gum arabic. Cocoa came relatively late in the process. It was as much an alien import to the Gold Coast as sheep or cattle to New Zealand. Those who took it up were equally migrants in search of vacant and suitable land, though moving across land rather than oceans. They brought with them capital and skills deriving from their previous activities. Cocoa farmers were as much capitalists as New Zealand dairy producers. Their product was in great international demand and its market value was relatively high. It therefore offered a promising route towards African affluence.

The second reason for comparing the Gold Coast/Ghana with New Zealand is that, despite many points of initial similarity, the longer-term outcomes were very different. In size they were similar. The area of New Zealand is some $265,000\,\mathrm{km}^2$, that of the Gold Coast about $258,000\,\mathrm{km}^2$. In 1911 the population of New Zealand was around one million, giving a population of density of 3.7 per km^2, that of the Gold Coast 2.1 million, at 8.1 per km^2. For both, specialization in the production of commodity exports was the dominant fact of economic life, the means of earning exchange to pay for imports. Britain was the major trading partner of both until after the Second World War, though it remained the main export market for New Zealand much later than for the Gold Coast. Both depended heavily on Britain for capital investment and services.

But at that point the similarities end. While the population of New Zealand crept up to a mere 3.5 million by 1994, a 75 per cent increase, that of the Gold Coast had doubled to 16.6 million. In 1950 the per capita income of New Zealand was about £500; that of the Gold Coast was £40.8. The ratio between their per capita incomes was thus 12 : 1; by 1994 it was 32.4 : 1 – about £8,300 to £256. It is this increasing divergence of two commodity-exporting economies, equally dependent on the principles of comparative advantage and vent for surplus and on the efficiency of the international market, which has to be explained.

In approaching this problem it is important not to assume that it was inevitable that the fortunes of the Gold Coast and New Zealand should diverge to this extent. Rather we should expect that the Gold Coast, effectively starting its push for growth through specialized export production some half century after New Zealand, might move in step if not actually catch up in terms of per capita incomes. We should, therefore, be surprised that this did not take place and consider why it did not.

There are a number of possible explanations, but three of those most commonly put forward will be considered here.

First, that cocoa, or other export commodities developed by the Gold Coast, along with other comparable tropical economies, were not as profitable as those of New Zealand, possibly because of differential changes in the terms of trade.

Secondly, that there were social or other obstacles in the Gold Coast which did not exist in New Zealand to the efficient production of export commodities, which reduced their effectiveness as the leading sector and restricted their impact on the rest of the economy.

Thirdly, that the Gold Coast was a colonial dependency until 1957, and may have been disadvantaged by the rules of the British imperial economic system. Alternatively, that the policies adopted by the local colonial government may have been an obstacle to growth. Again, the presence of large expatriate trading companies, banks, etc. may have inhibited indigenous development, as they did not in New Zealand.

The first of these explanations bristles with technical difficulties. The standard argument, based on League of Nations and United Nations publications,[30] has for long been that, from a baseline in the 1870s, there was a secular decline in the terms of trade of Third World primary products. Thus the League of Nations stated that there was a 59 per cent decline between 1876–80 and 1931–5, and even of 7.1 per cent between the earlier years and 1911–13.[31] As was seen above, Bairoch challenged this argument on several grounds. In fact, taking India as his main example, he argued that between 1866–75 and 1926–9 there was a 31 per cent improvement in the barter terms of trade, based on twenty-eight export and eleven imported goods. There were also substantial improvements for other raw material exporting countries, though none of his other examples was in the Third World.[32] Again after 1945, following a substantial deterioration in the terms of trade in the 1930s, there was a considerable improvement to the end of the 1960s.[33]

This suggests that one should take all estimates of terms of trade with caution. The British Board of Trade statistics do not provide separate prices for individual commodities at most times. Nevertheless, in order to provide a tentative answer to the question of whether cocoa in Ghana proved less satisfactory as an export crop than the primary products of settler societies such as New Zealand, tables 7.1 and 7.2 set out some of the information.

For what they are worth, and although, according to Bairoch, the data on which the terms of trade are based exaggerate the cost of manufactured imports to West Africa and understate the price of commodity

---

[30] League of Nations, *Industrialization and Foreign Trade* (Geneva, 1945); UN, *Relative Prices of Exports and Imports of Under-developed Countries* (New York, 1949).

[31] Quoted in P. Bairoch, *The Economic Development of the Third World since 1900* (London, 1975), p. 114. The argument of this paragraph is based on ch. 6 of this book.

[32] Ibid., p. 122.

[33] Ibid., table 38, p. 127.

Table 7.1 Indices of import and export prices and the terms of trade of the Gold Coast/Ghana, 1900–1960 (1953 = 100)

Year	A Price of total imports to the Gold Coast	B Price of imports of clothing	C Price of Gold Coast cocoa exports	D Price of total Gold Coast exports	E Barter terms of trade of the Gold Coast (D/A%)	F Barter terms of cocoa and imported cloth (C/B%)	G Barter terms of cocoa and total imports (C/A%)
1900	11	9	21	32	291	233	191
1905	12	9	15	28	233	166	125
1910	14	10	16	25	178	160	114
1915	17	10	20	23	135	200	118
1920	43	43	34	35	81	79	79
1925	26	35	16	17	65	46	61
1930	23	30	15	18	78	50	65
1935	18	17	8	12	66	47	44
1940	28	26	8	19	67	31	28
1945	53	64	13	20	38	20	24
1950	80	90	86	86	107	95	107
1955	89	68	134	120	134	197	150
1960	82	71	92	101	123	129	112

Source: Based on G. B. Kay, The Political Economy of Colonialism in Ghana: A Collection of Documents and Statistics, 1900–1960 (Cambridge, 1972), table 20c, pp. 332–3 (imports) and table 21c, pp. 338–9 (exports).

There is a figure in A. G. Hopkins, An Economic History of West Africa (London, 1973), fig. 4, p. 180, for the net barter terms of trade for the Gold Coast/Ghana 1900–1960, based on Stephen Hymer's chapter in G. Ranis (ed.), Government and Economic Development (New Haven, 1971), pp. 136–7, which shows a slightly different profile. Since Kay based his statistics on work done with Hymer, this is surprising, but I can see no explanation.

Table 7.2 Indices of the wholesale price of meat and fish and of wool in Britain, 1913–1933 and 1930–1950

(*a*) Index of prices, 1913–1933 (1913 = 100)

Year	Meat and fish	Wool
1913	100	100
1920	262.5	n.a.
1921	218.5	158.3
1925	161.7	196.9
1929	146.2	165.6
1932	105.7	90.2
1933	107.1	99.9

n.a. = not available.

(*b*) Index of prices, 1930–1950 (1930 = 100)

Year	Meat and fish	Wool
1930	100	100
1934	81.2	95.0
1938	85.9	101.4
1942	116.7	172.9
1946	123.5	186.5
1950	173.6	505.6

Source: B. R. Mitchell, *British Historical Statistics* (Cambridge, 1994), table 5B–C, pp. 729–30. The data are taken from the *Board of Trade Journal*.

Michell's table 5A also provides an index of prices for 1871–1920, based on the *Board of Trade Journal*; but as this does not distinguish between meat and fish and dairy products, or between wool and other fibres, it is of little use here.

exports at their source, these tables suggest that the exports of a temperate country such as New Zealand suffered less from market fluctuations than those of the Gold Coast and were probably more rewarding in the long run.[34] This was obvious between 1920 and 1939, but still greater contrasts existed in the period between 1940 and 1945. Cocoa prices remained very low and the barter terms of trade of cocoa, against either imported cloth or all Gold Coast imports, plumbed the depths to 20 and 24 per cent respectively, while the price of both wool and meat rose very substantially to well above their 1930 level. This, however, was due not

[34] G. R. Hawke, *The Making of New Zealand: An Economic History* (Cambridge, 1985), table 7.1, p. 128. See also fig. 11.4, p. 212.

to economic factors, but to the very low price fixed arbitrarily by the British government as bulk buyer of tropical commodities from 1939; whereas the prices agreed with the Dominion government for bulk purchase of its exports were well above those of the depression years.[35]

The long decline of the terms of trade of the Gold Coast and its cocoa producers from the golden age before 1914 to the Second World War, which saw a drop in the barter terms of trade from 91 in 1900 to 38 in 1945, rising only to 123 in 1960, has commonly been taken to demonstrate that the strategy of specialization in cocoa was a failure. That remains to be discussed. But it is important to note that the market for cocoa was sufficiently price elastic before the end of the free market in 1939 for the cocoa producers to be able to offset reduced prices by increased production. Martin has shown that between 1910–14 and 1935–9 the index of the volume of Gold Coast cocoa production rose from 100 to 655. The result was that the income terms of trade increased from 100 to 166 in the same period. This was made possible by the maturing of the massive planting of cocoa trees before and after 1914. An even greater proportionate expansion of cocoa, though from a lower base, took place in Nigeria. Inevitably, as joint market leaders, with some 70 per cent of world output, the effect of increased output was to push down prices still further. Yet, although the farmers deeply resented the drop in the unit price of cocoa, and twice, (in 1930–1 and 1937–8) held up cocoa deliveries in protest, from the standpoint of the Gold Coast economy the effect was to cushion the impact of recession. The same thing happened less dramatically in New Zealand, where export volume increased from an index of 100 in 1929 to 136 in 1936.[36]

For both countries this suggests that, with no realistic alternative, the course they adopted in the recession years, probably by reflex, justified continued specialization in export commodities. Moreover, in the 1950s the barter terms of cocoa had more than regained their 1910 level, though, given the existence of the Gold Coast and Nigerian marketing

---

[35] For a detailed study of the imposition of these prices in British West Africa, see D. K. Fieldhouse, *Merchant Capital and Economic Decolonization: The United Africa Company 1929–1987* (Oxford, 1994), ch. 6. Low prices were set both to keep down price in Britain and also to damp inflation in the colonies. Although prices were gradually raised after 1945, it was not until the early 1950s that they were allowed to reach market levels. Even then the fact that the marketing boards determined the price paid to the producer reduced the incentive to plant new cocoa trees and expand other crops, and so kept down the volume of exports.

[36] S. M. Martin, 'The Long Depression: West African Export Producers and the World Economy, 1941–45', in I. Brown (ed.), *The Economies of Africa and Asia in the Inter-War Depression* (London, 1989), table 2, p. 89; Hawke, *The Making of New Zealand*, table 7.1, p. 128.

boards, this benefited the economy as a whole and its capacity to invest in development rather than the individual cocoa producer. In this sense the period 1920–45 appears more as an extended blip than a long-term trend, caused by the breakdown of the pre-1914 international economy and, after 1939, the effects of British policy. It also suggests that there was nothing intrinsically wrong with specialization in the production of cocoa, any more than with specialization in wool, meat or dairy products. On the other hand, the value of such an export commodity to the economy as a whole depended largely on the mode of production, on productivity in terms of land, capital and labour, and on the transfers from the exporting to other sectors of the economy.

Indeed, the second issue is whether limited economic development in the Gold Coast in the longer term was due not to specialization in cocoa but to other features of the Gold Coast economy. Three key facts to consider are, first, that by 1960 no large-scale export commodity had developed to parallel cocoa: the nearest competitor was gold, worth about one-sixth of cocoa in 1960, whereas New Zealand had at least three other export lines of comparable size and value to wool. Secondly, that, even in cocoa, productivity per worker and acre did not change significantly, and was very much lower than in New Zealand farming. Thirdly, that the cocoa had not generated the externalities which might have diffused its benefits and stimulated general economic development both up and downstream.

The continued dependence on cocoa as the Gold Coast's main export staple is emphasized by comparison with the wider spread of major primary exports from New Zealand. Table 7.3 shows this contrast for the years 1911, the first peak of the Gold Coast export economy, and 1956, on the eve of its independence, when cocoa prices were at a post-war peak.

Ignoring changing money values, which may be deemed to have affected both countries more or less equally, these figures suggest some important conclusions.

First, the value of total exports from the Gold Coast increased by a greater proportion than those of New Zealand, by a factor of 22.0 compared with 13.7, which suggests that, ignoring the intermediate recession and war period, the Gold Coast economy had more export potential still in hand in 1911 than the New Zealand economy, which was more mature by then.

Secondly, however, the main contrast lay in the relative diversification of the two economies. In the Gold Coast the largest single export commodity, cocoa, provided 41 per cent of exports in 1911 but 60.9 per cent in 1956, whereas wool remained remarkably constant at 32.5 and 32.7 per cent of the New Zealand total. In fact, cocoa exports had increased by a factor of 31.8 compared with 13.8 for New Zealand wool. Meanwhile, other New Zealand exports had grown faster than wool: meat by a factor

Table 7.3 Concentration of exports, Gold Coast and New Zealand, 1911 and 1956 (£m current prices)

(*a*) The Gold Coast

Year	Gold	Diamonds	Manganese	Cocoa	Palm oil and kernels	Timber, logs and sawn	Total exports
1911	1.0	n.a.	n.a.	1.6	0.3	0.2	3.9
1956	7.5	7.9	7.0	51.1	0.5	9.5	86.6

n.a. = not available.

Source: G. B. Kay, *The Political Economy of Colonialism in Ghana: A Collection of Documents and Statistics, 1900–1960* (Cambridge, 1972), table 18, pp. 325–6; table 21a, pp. 334–5.

(*b*) New Zealand

Year	Wool	Meat (mutton, lamb, beef)	Butter	Cheese	Wheat	Total exports
1911	6.5	3.5	1.6	1.2	0.2	20
1956	90.1	55.9	52.1	22.5	n.a.	275

n.a. = not available.

Source: 1911: C. G. F. Simkin, *The Instability of a Dependent Economy* (Oxford, 1951), table 11.1, p. 174; 1956: *Encyclopaedia Britannica* (1964 edn, vol. 16, p. 403A).

of 14.3, butter by 32.5, cheese by 18.7. Between them these three were worth £130.5 million and constituted 47.4 per cent of total New Zealand exports: in 1911 they had provided 31.5 per cent of total exports. In the Gold Coast the four main exports other than cocoa – gold, diamonds, manganese and timber – the second and third virtually new since 1911, provided £31.9 million or 38.0 per cent of total exports. This was a significant widening of the export base since 1911 but still well below that of New Zealand. Moreover, it is significant that all four of these additional exports were extractive and largely controlled by expatriate companies. Conversely, the agricultural basis of the export economy had contracted with the relative decline of oil-palm products. Whereas oil-palm products (oil and kernels) constituted 42 per cent of exports in 1900 and 5.1 per cent in 1911, they were only 0.57 per cent in 1956, and palm oil was no longer listed. Equally significant was the failure to generate new export crops.

The obvious implication of these figures is that New Zealand was already a far more diversified export economy than the Gold Coast in 1911 and that the contrast was still greater by 1956. The six Gold Coast products listed in 1956 provided 96.4 per cent of total exports by value.

Those listed for New Zealand provided only 80 per cent of exports: the balance consisted of a wide range of commodities, including sheep-skins and other hides and processed or manufactured derivatives of the primary industries. By 1955 a large-scale pulp and paper industry was being developed, based on unexploited timber reserves: the contrast with the export of logs and sawn timber from the Gold Coast reflects its failure to process its own natural products and the comparative development of manufacturing and industrial skills in New Zealand.

But there are more important contrasts between the character of these two export-oriented economies than diversification. The key lies in comparative ratios between land and labour and the value of the export crop.

It is uncertain how many people worked on cocoa production, since there was a large migrant labour force from the north during harvest. One estimate for 1938 puts the total number of farms at about 300,000 and the total acreage at between 1,250,000 and 1,500,000 acres.[37] The total value of cocoa exports in that year was only £4.5 million, because of a recession and the cocoa hold-up. Taking the 1937 figure of £9.9 million as more representative, that means that output was £6.6 per acre and £33 per farm. A later post-war estimate for the early 1960s puts the total acreage under cocoa at 4.2 million and the total workforce at over 500,000, of whom 312,000 were self-employed farmers, 90,000 family workers, 50,000 sharecropping caretakers and 70,000 paid workers. In 1960 the total value of cocoa exports was £66.4 million. This suggests that the value of the crop was £132 per head of those engaged in it, £221 per farm, and around £15 per acre.[38] By contrast, in 1955 there were 92,395 farm holdings in New Zealand, though, since much of the agricultural land was pastoral, the area is not comparable with that under cocoa in the Gold Coast. Total farm income was then in the region of £200 million, giving an average farm income of £2,165. That was almost ten times that of the average Ghanaian cocoa farm. With a primary sector workforce of perhaps 180,000 in the later 1950s, this implied an income of around £1,100 per worker.

These figures are extremely crude owing to the limitations of the data. But they suggest one obvious conclusion. Irrespective of the relative international price of the product, there was almost no relationship between the modes of production of cocoa and the range of New Zealand agricultural commodities. Although early New Zealand wool production was as extensive as one could imagine, after the refrigeration revolution of the 1880s all other sectors of the industry became increasingly intensive, with a steadily decreasing labour force. This was made

[37] Meier, 'External Trade', p. 448.
[38] H. W. Ord and I. Livingstone, *An Introduction to West African Economics* (London, 1971), p. 127, n. 1.

possible by the application of modern technology, particularly in the meat and dairying industries, in which New Zealand became a world leader, able to undersell virtually all other producers of sheep meat, butter and cheese, and by a system of cooperative processing plants, so that the final product left New Zealand with considerable value added, ready for the consumer. By contrast, production methods in cocoa farming scarcely changed between the 1890s and the 1960s, or indeed later. As Meier has remarked, it remained 'a pure labour–axe–cutlass activity', most of whose final product (bar that made into cocoa butter) left the country unprocessed with no value added.[39]

Such simple facts show quite clearly why specialization on cocoa production in Ghana did not generate the level of incomes that farming did in New Zealand. Whether it could have done so is another question. Higher productivity would have depended on a great reduction in the labour force, conditional on mechanization of production, and probably development of new strains of disease-resistant cocoa trees to make this possible. No sufficient research work of this kind was ever done, either during or after the colonial period. Cocoa therefore remained an extensive, relatively inefficient crop.

Cocoa, moreover, had a limited long-term developmental impact on the economy as a whole. This was not always so. In the first two decades before 1914 it resulted in a huge increase in downstream activities, particularly carriers, middlemen, dock-workers, etc. It increased the capacity to import nearly fourfold between 1900 and 1914, which implied an advantage to the consumer of cheaper imported than domestic goods and, in so far as imports were investment goods, a potential stimulus to growth. Imported consumption goods consisted primarily of textiles and 'provisions', which stimulated new wants and therefore the urge to produce. Moreover, there is no evidence that this flood of goods had an adverse effect on domestic handicrafts, though their relative share of the market declined. Investment goods, consisting mainly of transport equipment and tools, increased as a proportion of imports from 24 to 34 per cent between 1891 and 1911. Taxes on cocoa exports and imports made it possible to finance the elements of a modern economy, notably railways, roads, port facilities and public buildings. In short, during these early years cocoa gave the Gold Coast economy a dynamic comparable to that provided by other export staples in the settler societies.

But this was not sustained. In the context of a non–settler society, cocoa (or any other comparable new export commodity) would, if it

---

[39] Meier, 'External Trade', p. 451. It must be said, however, that there were overwhelming climatic reasons why cocoa could not profitably be transformed into chocolate or other consumer products in West Africa. Conversely, milk in New Zealand could be exported only after conversion into cheese or butter.

was to lead to sustained development of the economy as a whole, need gradually to affect and transform the rest of the economy. This was less necessary in, say, New Zealand or Australia, whose European inhabitants brought or acquired the skills and assumptions of contemporary capitalism in Europe and North America. In the Gold Coast cocoa was a relatively small employer of labour: in 1911 about 185,000 of a total population of about 2.1 million or about 8.8 per cent; in 1960 around 500,000 out of a population of 6.7 million or about 7.5 per cent. Thus, as Meier put it, 'In terms of size, the cocoa-export sector was quite marginal compared with the amount of surplus labour-time that could be absorbed from the traditional sector.'[40] Again, because it did not require processing, cocoa did not stimulate downstream industries. Nor did those Africans who could accumulate capital as middlemen or large-scale producers invest in any form of industry.

Here the role of expatriate trading companies and banks was critical. Although it was open to Africans to consign cocoa direct to Europe or America on commission, as did the wool producers of Australasia, and though some attempted this, they found it almost impossible to compete with the large expatriate firms such as the Niger Company and African and Eastern (combined as United Africa Company in 1929), the British chocolate manufacturers (who bought only for their own use), or John Holt. These firms had a great advantage in the capital they could tie up in the trade, their knowledge of international markets that enabled them to speculate on futures, and their ability to buy goods for import in the cheapest markets. These firms thus had a contradictory impact on the Gold Coast. On the one hand, they provided the facilities and much of the working capital which enabled the cocoa industry (along with other export industries in other African colonies) to expand rapidly in the first instance: without their services and those of the shipping companies it is doubtful whether the cocoa miracle could have occurred. On the other hand, they gained a stranglehold on the trade from middleman to foreign market, and so made it both unnecessary and almost impossible for African entrepreneurs to develop in competition.

Meier argues that the main blockages to transfer from the cocoa sector were domestic, and listed five: factor immobility into activities outside cocoa farming; narrow and relatively isolated domestic markets; ignorance of technical possibilities; limited infrastructure; and the slow rate of human-resource development. He concluded that 'As long as the domestic economy remained fragmented and compartmentalized, the transfer of resources to more productive employment was restricted, and the linkage of markets and their subsequent extension were limited.' Markets and the price system, in fact, were a critical weakness, since

[40] Meier, 'External Trade', p. 452.

they conditioned the allocation of resources as between sectors of the economy.

> But the functions of the price system were poorly articulated during the colonial period, when markets remained localized, subsistence production continued to account for a substantial proportion of national product and traditional rules and customary obligations prevailed. Under these conditions the price system was too rudimentary to operate on an economy-wide basis as an instrument for development – either through decentralized choice or through deliberate governmental policy....
>
> In the final analysis, trade may transmit growth, but only if there are also latent indigenous forces of development that can be released through trade. In the absence of receptivity elsewhere in the domestic economy, the stimulus from exports can initiate only a limited integrative process....
> There were favourable features of cocoa production that made the stimulus a strong one; but there was at the same time a neglect of some of the crucial development foundations and an insufficiently responsive domestic economic structure.[41]

P. T. Bauer, in his path-breaking *West African Trade*,[42] though it was based more on research in Nigeria than the Gold Coast, came to similar conclusions. In his view there were four main obstacles to the dissemination of growth from this export specialization.

First, these countries had difficulty in adjusting to a monetized economy. The family system, though it might enable resources to be pooled for a new venture, tended to spread gains rather than accumulate them as capital and may have discouraged the use of banks for fear that accounts might become known to others. The complexities of land tenure denied Africans credit for loans. Acquisition of wealth was commonly assumed to be a zero-sum game, success being at the cost of the rest.

Secondly, specialization was very imperfect. Except for a minority of rich cocoa farmers, who were in effect capitalists, few Africans concentrated on single activities, mainly because the market was too narrow to allow for specialization.

Thirdly, productive resources were very small in relation to the size of these economies. Investment in infrastructure was totally inadequate; too much capital was tied up in stocks of export commodities. Capital accumulation lagged behind production, so that there was no indigenous capitalist class to run the import–export economy, leaving these critical roles to expatriates. Even the African middlemen depended on foreign firms for the capital advanced to finance their trading activities.

Finally, there was a general lack of employment, owing to the shortage of educated and skilled Africans, caused variously by shortage of

---

[41] Ibid., pp. 452–3.
[42] Lord P. T. Bauer, *West African Trade* (Cambridge, 1954), ch. 1, pp. 7–21.

land, capital and skills, and the fragmentation of the West African economies.

Thus, from a strictly economic and social standpoint, the contrast between the Gold Coast and New Zealand may be summed up as follows. In New Zealand the effects of successive waves of export expansion were very quickly disseminated throughout the country. Increased income from wool and gold exports from the mid-nineteenth century was converted into investment in railways, roads, ports and other facilities. Capital was accumulated rapidly to pay for these, or borrowed in Britain when accumulation was inadequate. With the exception of some sections of the Maori population, virtually every part of the economy was capitalist, from the smallest dairy farmers, the 'cow-cockies', to the owners of large sheep runs. There was almost no subsistence production: small-scale horticulture served urban markets. The labour force was for the most part reasonably well educated. Enterprise in almost any field had little difficulty in raising capital from banks or mortgage companies. Although manufacturing was limited by the size of the market and the relative cheapness of imported goods, industry developed wherever there was some comparative advantage. In short, the gains from trade could be and were translated into increased production of all kinds because there were no significant domestic barriers to development. The only real limits were set by the international market and by the size of the population, the first out of New Zealand's control, the second determined by immigration policies.

Yet such a purely economic analysis ignores the third dimension mentioned above: the role of the state, both metropolitan and local. New Zealand was a self-governing colony from the 1850s, effectively independent in all domestic policies. It was highly democratic, so that governments were very sensitive to movements of public opinion. Economic policies were populist rather than dirigiste: despite the strict licensing of imports and currency from 1938, no government went in for development planning. The state existed to serve the interests of its citizens, and all politicians sought to please them and them only. Loyalty to Britain, very obvious from the later nineteenth century to the mid-twentieth century, was perfectly compatible with this self-interest. It did not prevent relatively high protective duties against British imports, though these were tempered by still higher duties against foreign goods under the post-1932 Ottawa system.

In the Gold Coast, by contrast, the government remained in the hands of the agents of the imperial government and its local agents until 1951. It was only in 1951 that a new constitution provided something approaching democratic and semi-responsible government, with an assembly two-thirds of whose members were directly elected by popular vote and one-third indirectly by the councils of chiefs. In 1953 this was replaced by a fully democratic assembly and a cabinet responsible to it. Ghana, as it was called from 1957, had reached full self-government.[43]

We have, therefore, to consider the role both of the imperial state and of its local subsidiary, the Gold Coast government. Taking first the imperial role, on the face of it Britain had a very limited direct effect on Gold Coast development, at least before 1939. For reasons outlined in chapter 4, the Gold Coast, along with Nigeria, remained free-trading throughout: there were no tariff preferences in favour of metropolitan exports, as there were in India and throughout French Africa. The only blemishes on this otherwise exemplary open-market system were short-lived export duties on palm kernels after 1918 and the imposition of import quotas on textiles from 1934, which deprived the Gold Coast consumer of cheaper Japanese goods. Conversely, Britain provided no special advantages for Gold Coast exports, as it did for the settler colonies through quotas in the 1930s, and the sugar-exporting colonies through both quotas and special prices. The main benefit the Gold Coast received was preferential access to the London money market for loans with gilt-edged status under the Colonial Loans Act. It did not significantly benefit from the Colonial Development Act of 1929, which came too late to help finance the big transport schemes of the 1920s: it received a total of £333,000 between 1930 and 1939, £185,000 of that in 1939, and very little thereafter until 1945.[44] The main function of the British government before 1939 was, therefore, to ensure that the colonial government kept to the rules, including those concerning the monetary system, and balanced its budgets. If ever there was a European colony that was left to pursue its own destiny, it was the Gold Coast.

After 1939 this changed totally. In common with all other dependencies, as seen in chapter 4, the Gold Coast economy was put on a war footing. All hard-currency earnings were converted into sterling and held in London. All the major exports were bought by Britain in bulk and, in contrast with arrangements made with the Dominions, at prices fixed arbitrarily and well below current world prices. Since British exports were limited, the colony had to accumulate a very large credit balance in London at low rates of interest. These constraints continued until after 1945 and were then gradually removed. But the most enduring

---

[43] Details of the pre-1951 constitutions are in A. F. Madden and J. Darwin (eds), *The Dependent Empire, 1900–1948* (Westport, Conn., and London, 1994), pp. 656–9, 664–6, 675–6.

[44] Kay, *Political Economy*, table 24a, pp. 352–3. Neither D. J. Morgan, *The Official History of Colonial Development*, vol. 1: *The Origins of British Aid Policy, 1924–1945* (London, 1980), nor S. Constantine, *The Making of British Colonial Development Policy 1914–1940* (London, 1984), provides details of individual grants under the CD Act.

THE COLONIAL ECONOMY IN PRACTICE

and in the long term economically critical innovation was the mechanism of the marketing board, introduced first for buying cocoa in 1939, and extended to other commodities from 1942. Seen initially as a device to ensure a market for cocoa under war conditions, then as a means of accumulating surpluses to even out market fluctuations by payments to farmers, the Cocoa Marketing Board (CMB) evolved into a mechanism for extracting surplus from the producer for use in other sectors of the economy. The Board was largely responsible for the dramatic decline during the war in the barter terms of trade of cocoa producers to their lowest point; and its later use under self-government ensured that the producer was heavily taxed and usually exploited by the government.

This transformation of the metropolitan role during and after the Second World War was to have a determining effect on the future economic development of the Gold Coast. Yet it is important, given the arguments of Berman and Lonsdale, Kay, and others, to discover whether and how far the metropolitan government acted in support of private expatriate capital in both Britain and the Gold Coast. Given the absence of manufacturing, such interests on the Coast were limited to British holders of Gold Coast bonds, used to raise loans, to the owners of the gold and later manganese and diamond mines, and above all to the big trading companies, such as United Africa and John Holt, who dominated the import–export trades. In fact, although Kay alleges that the pattern of railways and the siting of the first deep-water port at Takoradi rather than Accra were designed initially to help the mines rather than peasant producers of cocoa, this is dubious. More significantly, neither railways nor any other aspect of policy appeared intended to favour the interests of the trading companies. Indeed these were widely suspected in London and Accra of exploiting the African producer and consumer, as was very clear from the Colonial Office debate in the early 1940s over the future of the CMB.[45] Put simply, while London officials accepted the inevitability of such companies until the colonial state could take over their exporting and importing functions, and of their special utility during the war, 'big business' of this kind was believed to be incompatible with the sort of peasant society which was their ideal in West Africa. There is no reason to think that the metropolis regarded it as part of its functions to support metropolitan capital in the Gold Coast: on the contrary, its duty was to restrict its functions to a minimum.

Until 1951 government in the Gold Coast was typical of the type of colonial regime described above in chapter 3. That is, it bore no relationship

---

[45] For a detailed analysis of British official attitudes to UAC and other trading firms in the context of produce marketing, see Fieldhouse, *Merchant Capital*, ch. 6, and esp. p. 253.

to the nature of the local society ('the specificity of the colonial state') and was not subject to popular electoral control. On the other hand, as Berman and Lonsdale argue, in common with every colonial government, it had to serve the local constituency as well as the imperial metropolis in order to earn legitimacy in the eyes of the local population. The question here is how well government in the Gold Coast served these local interests and how far the limited economic effects of the export trade were due to governmental policies and limitations.

The Marxist case, as summarized by G. B. Kay, is briefly as follows.[46] The duty of the Gold Coast government was to maintain itself through sufficient taxation, to promote civilization, and to serve the interests of British capital. Conversely, it failed to take an active or well-conceived role in economic development. It did little to help the cocoa industry or to stimulate diversification. Its policy on ports and railways was designed to benefit the mines rather than agriculture. Development finance was raised abroad rather than locally. Education was geared to the limited practical needs of a rural society. Thus the main achievement of the British in the Gold Coast was 'to hold this situation stable for so long, and to prevent the structural contradictions that faced them from becoming absolute'.[47]

I find this analysis of limited value in explaining the restricted development of the Gold Coast. Kay's most valid criticism of government is that the Agricultural Department was totally inadequate in size and expertise to promote the efficiency of cocoa or to develop other export crops. The semi-official West Africa Commission of 1938–9 made devastating criticisms of the inadequacy of the research facilities and agricultural stations and of its lack of interest in increasing food production. The Watson Commission of 1948 made even stronger criticisms.[48] In short, the colonial government paid far too little attention to, and invested too little money in, the development of the agricultural base of the economy. If there was an inherent contradiction in the character of the colonial economy, it lay there.

Meier, by contrast, regards education as the main failure of the Gold Coast government, and sees this as a major cause of limited economic development. Until the 1930s primary education was left largely to missionary schools, which had inadequate resources. There were very few Africans with secondary education or the skills required in business.

> In consequence, the country's need for trained manpower was met mainly by importation, not only of university graduates, but also of secondary and technical personnel. It could be argued that the neglect of education

[46] See Kay, *Political Economy*, introduction, pp. 3–37.
[47] Ibid., p. 36.
[48] Extracts from these documents are printed in ibid., pp. 227–36.

was perhaps the greatest failure of the colonial government, because the cost of importing intermediate personnel and the shortage of this kind of manpower continued to be a brake on economic progress throughout the pre-independence period.

Although much improvement took place in primary education between 1935 and 1957, when government subsidies to missionary schools increased the number in primary schools from 63,000 to 456,000, the number of secondary-school pupils increased only from 919 to 7,711 between 1938 and 1955.[49]

The Gold Coast was, therefore, inadequately supplied with the indigenous human capital needed for the dissemination of the gains from trade into the economy as a whole. This weakness was reflected in the managerial structure of the United Africa Company. From the mid-1930s the company had recruited a few men from Achimota, the secondary school and college, as apprentices, and had trained them as managers. As a result, by 1939 there were 39 African managers on the trading side of the Gold Coast business compared with 435 Europeans. But there was not a single African technical specialist compared with 139 Europeans. While there was until the mid-1950s an unstated convention that Africans could not rise to the higher managerial ranks, the main obstacle, particularly in technical employment, was lack of education.[50] Thus the export industry was mainly run by expensive expatriates, as was mining. They constituted an employment enclave from which Africans were largely excluded, by lack of qualifications as well as racist assumptions. Such a situation was consistent with a governmental strategy based on preserving the integrity of an idealized traditional society, but it was totally inconsistent with development based on indigenous resources.

There remains the question of how far British metropolitan interests blocked or checked economic diversification in the Gold Coast. The main criterion is whether there, as in India before the 1920s, British manufacturers were able to oppose proposals for secondary industry because this might affect their export markets, above all those for cotton textile piece-goods.

Before 1939 this was not a significant issue, since there were no capitalists, African, expatriate or metropolitan, who showed any interest in local factory industry. Both the limited size of the market and the availability of cheap imports in a free-trade economy made virtually all factory industries uneconomic. After 1939, however, wartime shortages and the presence of large numbers of allied servicemen on the Coast generated a number of relatively small industrial ventures, and increasing incomes

---

[49] Meier, 'External Trade', p. 451.
[50] For details, see Fieldhouse, *Mechant Capital*, pp. 375–82.

made it conceivable that these and others might become established and lead to further industrial development.

For the first time, therefore, the British and West African governments had to consider the longer-term future of industry on the Coast.[51] Although there was considerable interest in and even enthusiasm for limited manufacture of consumer goods between 1942 and 1947, and although even the Board of Trade, conventionally the defender of British export industries, seemed temporarily to accept its inevitability, the debate in London, Accra and Lagos demonstrated much the same alliance of forces as had opposed protection for industry in India from the 1880s to the 1920s. Lancashire cotton manufacturers were anxious not to lose this market, as they had already lost the Indian market. The Board of Trade sympathized with them, and was also keen to maintain free-trade principles against proposals for moderate protection for infant industries. The Colonial Office was moderately keen, but was split between those who feared that wartime industries might not survive into the peace, and others who were keen on industrialization as the best route to greater affluence. On the Coast, both Lagos and Accra officials were doubtful about local factories, fearing that these might encourage the drift to the towns, threaten their idealized peasant societies, and reduce the import duties on which public revenues largely depended. The results were that by 1947 no positive strategy had been agreed; that the possibility was then put aside because the colonies were needed to provide export commodities to save dollars; and that it was not until the early 1950s and the onset of self-government that any active steps were taken by the colonial state to stimulate local industry.

It would be too much to say that this demonstrates that colonialism blocked industrialization in British West Africa, since before 1939 economic factors were a virtually absolute obstacle. But it is also clear that neither the imperial nor the colonial state took the positive steps necessary to encourage development of the type the New Zealand government had taken, piecemeal, from the 1880s. It also suggests that, had proposals for protection of West African manufacturing arisen before the 1950s, they would have met serious and probably overwhelming resistance from the imperial authorities. This in turn pinpoints one of the major potential contrasts between the role of the colonial state and that of the state in a self-governing Dominion such as New Zealand or Australia.

The post-1957 economic development of the Gold Coast/Ghana lies out side the scope of this chapter, and in any case has been too well documented

---

[51] The following account is based mainly on L. J. Butler, *Industrialisation and the British Colonial State: West Africa 1939–1951* (London, 1997).

to need detailed treatment here.[52] The only question now at issue is whether independent Ghana, adopting dramatically different economic strategies from those of the colonial period, and in particular going for industrialization rather than commodity specialization, was able to achieve greater and more balanced development. If so, what light does this throw on the argument concerning the retarding effects of colonialism and on export-led growth based on comparative advantage?

The short answer, notoriously, is that independence did not provide sustained economic growth: that, in fact, Ghana was substantially worse off in the 1980s and 1990s than it had been in the 1950s.

Between 1960 and 1980 the per capita income of Ghana (at 1975 constant international prices) declined from $1,009 to $739. The World Bank put the per capita income (at current prices) at $360 in 1982 and $410 in 1994. The average annual growth rate per capita from 1960 to 1982 was minus 1.3 per cent, recovering to plus 1.4 per cent for the period 1985–94 under the Rawlings regime. In 1955 total external assets were $532 million, or $83.1 a head, much of it the result of the accumulated savings of the CMB, plus the backing for the currency and blocked sterling credits. This compared with $87.1 a head for Australia and $1.5 for India. In 1955 Ghana's foreign assets were more than seven times its long-term debts: even in 1960 total foreign debts were only $40.8 million. In 1957 the debt-service ratio (interest and amortization as a percentage of the value of exports) was under 1 per cent. By 1967, a year after the fall of Nkrumah, the total outstanding foreign debt was $526.6 million, and the debt-service ratio 7.2. Foreign indebtedness then levelled out for a decade, mainly because foreign creditors refused to lend any more long term, and the debt-service ratio dropped to 3.6 in 1977. Foreign debts then rose to $1,398 million in 1980, with a debt-service ratio of 13.2, and to $5,389 million in 1994, with a debt-service ratio of 24.8.[53]

[52] The standard books include the following: D. E. Apter, *Ghana in Transition* (2nd rev. edn, Princeton, 1972); D. Austin, *Politics in Ghana 1946–1960* (London, 1964); R. H. Bates, *Markets and States in Tropical Africa* (Berkeley and Los Angeles, 1981); B. Beckman, *Organising the Farmers: Cocoa Politics and National Development in Ghana* (Uppsala, 1976); T. Killick, *Development Economics in Action: A Study of Economic Policies in Ghana* (London, 1978); D. Rimmer, *The Economies of West Africa* (London, 1984), and *Staying Poor: Ghana's Political Economy, 1950–1990* (Oxford, 1992).

[53] Sources for these figures are: Rimmer, *Staying Poor*, p. 195; D. K. Fieldhouse, *Black Africa 1945–1980: Economic Decolonization and Arrested Development* (London, 1986), table 2.4, p. 50; table 5.1, p. 148; table 5.2, p. 148; table 5.3, p. 149 (sources indicated); World Bank, *Toward Sustained Development in Sub-Sharan Africa* (Washington, 1984), table 1, p. 57; World Bank, *World Development Report 1996: From Plan to Market* (Oxford, 1996), table 1, p. 188; table 2, p. 190; table 17, p. 220.

These figures should not be taken too precisely. But their general implications are clear. Between 1957 and the mid-1990s Ghana had moved from economic and fiscal viability at a level that was high by the standard of tropical primary-producing countries to being eighteenth of the thirty-seven states of Black Africa in terms of per capita GNP in 1982; though by 1994, after a decade of recovery, it had climbed back to seventh position.

The question at issue here is not the larger one of why the Ghanaian economy ran down so dramatically after independence, which is discussed in the context of Black Africa as a whole in chapter 10, but rather how far this was due to failure to maintain and expand the export sector and so exploit comparative advantage. Conversely, does Ghana's failure support the Marxist and *dependencia* view that any economy based on commodity exports is bound to reach a point at which it can no longer expand, condemning that country to static or declining affluence?[54]

To consider Amin's explanation first, based on Marxist and dependency assumptions, the key assertions are as follows. Ghana's economic miracle, based on the 'spontaneous' growth of export agriculture, came very early on and had lost its dynamic by independence. Moreover, the increase of overseas competition and, during the 1960s (Amin published the French version in 1971, so had not seen later developments), the relative decline of cocoa prices meant that export earnings were reduced. Meantime, Nkrumah's industrializing strategy had resulted in a huge investment in local industries and subsidies to those that were uneconomic, most of which had to be paid for from foreign borrowing, much of it credits at medium term, since the long-term lenders had sheered off. Meantime the bureaucracy grew much faster than the national income and became a serious economic problem. By about 1967 Ghana was 'bankrupt'. This implied errors of strategy. But ultimately failure was due to 'the international system', which drained the country of its wealth and potential.[55]

Rimmer, representing the non-socialist consensus of the 1980s, takes a different view.[56] He pinpoints three main errors of policy or its implementation: failure to maintain comparative advantage in exports; abuse of money; and the ineffectiveness of government in executing its own strategies.

---

[54] See, in particular, S. Amin, *Neo-colonialism in West Africa* (New York and London, 1973).
[55] The material specifically on Ghana in Amin, *Neo-Colonialism*, is on pp. 41–8, 240–50.
[56] The following argument is based mainly on Rimmer, *Staying Poor*, ch. 9. The figures for cocoa exports are taken from table 7.3, p. 144, and table 8.2, p. 186; those for shares of cocoa proceeds from table 9.1, p. 201.

His primary explanation is that independent Ghana partially destroyed the economic base that had made it relatively affluent by the 1950s. The government, using the CMB, continued and intensified the late-colonial strategy of paying the farmers a small proportion of the export value of their crops. In only one year between 1949 and 1985 did the farmers receive more than the market value of that year's crop (a populist gesture by the Rawlings regime in 1981/2), and in only fourteen years did they receive more than half that value. In 1977/8 they received only 30 per cent. The low prices paid by the CMB discouraged new planting and efficiency: the export volume was down from 412,000 tons in 1972 to 189,000 tons in 1979 and 149,600 tons in 1984. Meantime, the CMB had ploughed very little of its profits back into cocoa. By the mid-1980s, from being by far the largest single cocoa producer in the world, Ghana had only one-tenth of the total market. Thus the post-independence Ghanaian governments had deliberately mulcted the most easily accessible source of quasi-taxation and in doing so had virtually killed the country's most efficient productive sector. Between 1970 and 1982 cocoa production and marketing fell from 14 to 1.1 per cent share of GDP.

This failure in the export economy was, in fact, only one aspect of the fundamental weakness of economic strategy. Other main policy defects included an overvalued currency, budget deficits, excessive central control, and artificially induced and overprotected industries that could not export because they were not competitive at international prices.

From either ideological standpoint, therefore, the Ghanaian experiment in rapid growth after 1957 proved a disaster. What light does this throw on the main problem with which this book is concerned – the effect of close relations between the West and the less developed world, and in particular the principle of comparative advantage? Was the Ghanaian failure the inevitable consequence of Ghana's conscription into the international division of labour, so that its attempt to diversify and industrialize was foredoomed to failure?

The evidence suggests otherwise. It is undeniable that the cocoa boom of the period before 1914, while it probably doubled the country's income and financed the basis of a modern infrastructure, had a limited long-term effect on the development of the economy as a whole. The Gold Coast remained in the 1940s a poor country, excessively dependent on a single export commodity, and apparently unable to carry through a fundamental economic transformation.

But after 1945 the Gold Coast/Ghana had a second chance, with the greatest international boom period offering the opportunity to exploit its comparative advantage in cocoa and at the same time to use cocoa profits and its overseas assets to transform the rest of the economy.

From about 1960 to the early 1980s perverse government policies wasted this opportunity. From being based on comparative advantage, the Ghanaian economy came to operate on comparative disadvantage.

This is not to suggest that, even in the 1960s, there was any chance that Ghana might suddenly have become one of the world's richer states. But why was Ghana's per capita income in 1994 only about one-seventh of that of, for example, Malaysia, which is considered in chapter 11, whose population was roughly the same, which had also been a commodity-exporting British colony, and which became independent only in the same year as Ghana? The answer must be that at root the relative economic failure of Ghana was not due to its having been a European dependency, nor that it was a commodity-exporting economy. The reasons for its poverty lie in the limited impact of the capitalist sector of the economy before independence and the failure of its government to make proper use of the advantages and opportunities it had in the quarter century after 1950. It was not the impact of the West that caused Ghana's backwardness but the fact that that impact was too limited in the early period and misapplied after 1960.

What, then, is the short answer to the question posed at the start of chapter 6? How closely did the economic development of countries forced into the international division of labour under colonialism resemble that of countries which entered that system voluntarily? No conclusive answer can be derived from the two colonies considered here. Yet, even on so limited a sample some general suggestions may be made.

First, the evidence suggests that, in so far as a colony was able to develop viable export products, it benefited proportionately as much as any independent state. Conversely, the general economic impact of such specialization was relative to the size of the export sector. In India it was very small; in the Gold Coast much larger. But in neither case was the exporting sector as large relatively as in the settler economies, particularly in their earlier period, nor could it compare in terms of technology and productivity with those. As a result, in neither India nor the Gold Coast was the export sector able to have a sufficiently transforming effect on the rest of the economy. The most that can be said is that exporting measurably increased the absolute wealth of these societies.

Secondly, the impact of colonialism as a recruiting sergeant for the international division of labour appears to have been limited. The broad trends of economic development seem to have been determined far more by the nature of these societies and by the vicissitudes of the international economy than by imperial policy. There does, however, appear to have been some correlation between the character of an imperial trade regime and economic development. Imperial free trade came closest to allowing colonial commodity exporting to operate freely on the principle of comparative advantage. British colonies benefited from the fact that until 1932 the British empire was free-trading, so that they were not compelled to pay artificially high prices for imports and could sell exports at world market prices. Some colonies, though not those in West Africa, were adversely affected by imperial preference after 1932. India may have suffered from an imposed strong rupee between 1926 and 1932, many others from the manipulation of markets and monetary controls between 1939 and the late 1940s. In some African colonies, notably in East Africa, fiscal regimes and official pressures may have compelled peasants to produce unprofitably for the market. Wherever there were European settlers, non-Europeans suffered loss of land and economic deprivation. Independent successor regimes were sometimes, notably in India, able to improve economic performance by adopting a more positive economic role for the state than the British colonial state was willing to do. But it is difficult to avoid the conclusion that, while British colonialism was not necessarily optimal for economic development, its effects on the colonies were comparatively limited. The main weakness lay not in what it did but in what it failed to do.

At the other end of the imperial spectrum lay France. As was suggested in chapters 3 and 4, the French made no pretence of leaving their empire to the operation of economic forces and were far more overtly determined to exploit their colonies than the British. Hence, by means of tariffs, trade and shipping controls, subsidies and monetary policy they attempted to insulate their empire from the international economy, to make it an extension of the French economy. Within colonies they were exceptionally active in compelling the production of desired crops, whether or not economically justifiable, and in using forced labour on both public and private enterprises. The general effect on their colonies was much as described by hostile critics such as Amin and Suret-Canale: an extreme degree of specialization in export commodities and excessive dependence on a partially protected French market, made necessary by high import prices inflated by protectionist tariffs. Although in the post-1945 period the French did more than any other colonial power to develop their colonial economies by providing financial and technical support, the end result, apart from those which (like Vietnam and Guinea) broke entirely from the French economic and political orbit, was to leave the ex-colonies very heavily dependent on France and the EU as markets for their primary commodities.

How, then, can one strike a balance on the extent to which the fact of colonial cooption into the world trading system determined the benefits received? Perhaps the closest approximation to a general rule might be that, while the introduction, more or less voluntarily, of commodity production for export was in no sense an optimal, and certainly not a sufficient, condition for sustained economic growth, neither was it an absolute obstacle. In some places it may even have been a necessary first step. Its success or failure seems to have been in direct proportion to the extent to which this forcible linking of peripheral countries with the West injected and nurtured the virus of capitalism, or 'modernization'. In the British settler colonies colonization did this very effectively: in most tropical dependencies the effects were limited. The relative poverty of many Third World countries reflects this partial failure. Yet the modern experience of a number of one-time colonies in South-east and East Asia also suggests that colonial rule and foreign trade may lay the foundations for much more dramatic economic development as part of the international division of labour, and this will be the theme of chapter 11.

Part IV

After Colonialism:
The New International System

8

Aid and Development

From the later 1940s the international political and economic environment changed profoundly, and with it the relationship between the West and the Third World. For the argument of this book this had two main dimensions: the dismantling of the colonial empires, leading to political freedom for the one-time colonies; and a new international economic order, of which the new ex-colonial states were full members, free to pursue their own development.

First, decolonization by the European states, which was virtually complete for all but the Portuguese possessions by the mid-1960s, meant the end of the whole system of political and economic regulations that was described in chapters 3 and 4. The ex-colonies were now free to adopt whatever systems of government and style of economic management they chose. Those that had been compelled to be free-trading were now able to protect local enterprise by tariffs or licensing; those that had been conscripted components of protectionist empires could adopt self-serving strategies. As for currency, the new states could, if they wished, leave the currency bloc of their former imperial states and use money supply as an element in their development strategies.

Secondly, the new states were now full and autonomous members of the international economic system, open to both its benefits and its hazards. Previously they had, in varying degrees, been insulated by their imperial masters. Thus, while there was never a total ban on investment from outside an imperial system, foreign capital tended to be discouraged by imperial governments: in any case, European investors normally preferred their own colonies to those of others because of the greater security of the flag and the relative simplicity of transactions within a common

monetary, linguistic and commercial system. Conversely, the one major
foreign investor which possessed few colonies – the United States – had
made disproportionately few investments in the colonial Third World
before the 1950s, and those mainly in extractive enterprises. Hence one
consequence of decolonization was that investment, and along with it
large-scale lending and that post-war novelty 'aid', became multinational
and multilateral. Or, to put it in perspective, the new states of Africa
and Asia were now in the same position as the one-time Spanish and
Portuguese colonies in the Americas had been since the 1820s.

There was, however, a third, new, and very important, though transient, influence on Third World economic development after about 1950:
the unprecedented world trade boom which lasted for most countries
into the 1970s. Fuelled, among other things, by post-war reconstruction, population growth, industrial expansion, technological innovation,
the reduction of obstacles to trade under GATT, and the expansion of credit
through the new international agencies, such as the International Bank
for Reconstruction and Development (IBRD, commonly known as the
World Bank) and the IMF, the opportunities for sustained growth resembled those of the golden age of development before 1914. The contrast
with the depressed, protectionist and pessimistic 1920s and 1930s was apparently total. This was the age of optimism, of belief that any economy, however underdeveloped, could achieve both growth of its national income
(its GNP) and development in its economic and social structure. This,
as was suggested in chapter 2, was also the age of development planning,
of belief in the all importance of the state as the primary agent of
development, of five- to ten-year plans, which were expected to overcome the 'structural' obstacles which many economists then saw as the
main reason why some countries remained underdeveloped. Only the
committed Marxists and their intellectual bedfellows continued to believe
that 'real' development was impossible within a capitalist framework.

Central to all post-1950 attitudes to Third World development was
belief that the primary need was capital investment. The defining feature
of underdevelopment was thought to be lack of sufficient capital to pay
the cost of overcoming the perceived 'structural' obstacles to development. A short shopping list of what were then believed to be the necessary
measures would include the following: first, the improvement of infrastructure – communications, power and water supplies, urban facilities
and hospitals; secondly, education to raise the general level of literacy
and to generate skilled workers at all levels, from the highest posts in
government and industry to labourers in factories and agriculture; thirdly,
manufacturing industry, which was believed to be the basis of western
affluence and must therefore become that of the Third World.

The problem, however, was how these essentials were to be paid for.
In the West the capital had been built up over a long period of slow

growth and accumulation, paid for by the slowly increasing productivity of agriculture and industry and the limited savings these provided. Thus in Britain, the pioneer of industrialization, the annual growth rate per capita during the nineteenth century had been relatively slow, perhaps 1 per cent. But for most of Africa and Asia such a prolonged developmental effort was thought to be unacceptable. In most countries the starting point in terms of incomes and technology was much lower in the 1950s than it had been in western Europe before modern industry developed. Hence the rate of possible local saving for investment was very small, particularly since population was increasing far more rapidly in most places under the influence of improved medical provision than it had done in nineteenth-century Europe. If the Third World was ever to 'catch up' on the West, it needed far more capital than it could possibly generate itself.

In addition, there was a political factor. During the period after about 1940, even during the war, expectations of rapid development – 'the development imperative' as it has been called – had been raised by the colonial powers in an attempt to buy continued acquiescence in alien rule. Necessarily the opponents of the imperialists, the first generation of Asian and African nationalist movements, had met this strategy by promising that independence would result in unprecedented affluence in the very near future, once the adverse effects of colonialism had been cut off. An additional fact was growing western sympathy for the Third World, fuelled by publicity put out by the wide range of new (or revived League of Nations) agencies in the United Nations: the International Labour Organization (ILO), the Food and Agriculture Organization (FAO), the United Nations Educational, Scientific and Cultural Organization (UNESCO), and others. All came under the influence of the United Nations General Assembly, with its inbuilt Third World majority, to support the interests of the poorer states. There was also the influence of the media, particularly the developing television, which brought home to the western audience the deprivations of the poorer countries and their recurrent crises, such as famines and wars. Economic and social development came to be seen as a moral obligation on the West, very much as the dissemination of Christianity had appeared a century earlier.

Thus the main theme of this and the following chapter is the unprecedented flow of resources from the developed to the underdeveloped countries during the second half of the twentieth century. It was unprecedented in three main ways: in sheer size; in the forms it took; and, above all, in the fact that a significant proportion came as a grant or on concessional conditions, rather than on commercial terms.

This flow of resources to the Third World was not, of course, a novelty. From the earlier nineteenth century to 1914 there had been an increasing flow of investment from Europe to the then less-developed world, much of it to North and South America, to India, the Middle East and the Australasian colonies. For the most part this took one of two forms.

First, there was portfolio investment. Europeans (during the nineteenth century predominantly the British) had lent money to these countries by buying government bonds, or by buying shares in foreign-based and owned enterprises such as railways, utility companies or banks. The European investor took no part in the actual running of these enterprises, whether public or privately owned, but received interest or dividends so long as governments or companies remained solvent. By far the largest proportion of European overseas investment before 1914 was of these types.

But there was also 'direct' European investment overseas, 'direct' in the special sense that the investors, probably in the form of a European-based company, retained a potentially controlling interest in the venture. Typically such an enterprise might be a plantation, a mine, a jute or cotton mill. It is important, in order to distinguish such ventures from the multinational corporation or enterprise discussed in chapter 9, that such enterprises and companies were usually specific to a particular venture and that the companies were set up with that operation in mind. Typically the initiative would come from a mineral prospector or would-be plantation or factory operator in the overseas country concerned, who would then form a company and float shares in the European stock markets to finance his project. Conversely, such ventures were not as a rule a by-product of existing industrial or other enterprises in Europe or the United States.

This fact distinguishes most pre-1914, and indeed pre-1939, direct overseas investment in the Third World from what came after about 1945. Portfolio and single-enterprise investment continued, but increasingly the main source of FDI was an established commercial enterprise in Europe or America which set up a subsidiary overseas. Such parent companies, variously known as multinational corporations or enterprises (MNCs) or, to use the preferred United Nations term, transnational enterprises (TNEs), might be of many kinds, ranging from mineral extractors and processors to manufacturers of consumer goods. Their common and definitive features were that they were capitalist enterprises, that they had their head office and usually their main productive and research and development (R&D) operations in a developed country, and that they owned (though not necessarily 100 per cent) and controlled related enterprises in other countries.

The MNC was in no sense a novelty after 1945: as will be seen in chapter 9, enterprises that conform to these general specifications can be traced back to the later nineteenth century. But most of these earlier overseas investments took place in North and South America, in Europe, the Middle East, and in the settler societies of South Africa and Australasia.

There were a few MNC subsidiaries in Asia and Africa before 1939. Hence the real novelty after about 1945 was the huge and rapid expansion of the MNC in these two continents.

FDI on a large scale in the Third World was one great novelty of the post-independence era. The second was the availability, initially at least, of almost infinite quantities of money and goods, either on loan at commercial rates of interest and repayment, or on 'concessional' conditions as 'aid'. Why had this revolutionary change taken place?

There is no difficulty in explaining the flow of commercial loans and credit after independence. From the standpoint of western banks and exporters, most new states, initially at least, were very good risks. The anglophone British territories all became independent with substantial dowries, much of it built up from blocked earnings during the Second World War, from the cover required for their currencies, and from the profits of their commodity marketing boards. Their overseas debts were small. Although India had small external assets in relation to its population – $670 million or $1.5 a head in 1961, after it had spent much of the credits it held in 1947 – the interest on its public debt was still only 1 per cent of GNP. The francophone colonies had relatively very small credits and debts, because the French system, as described in chapter 4, did not allow either large credit balances or indebtedness.[1]

Thus most of the new states of the post-war period appeared to provide attractive investment opportunities and safe lending risks. Their evident prosperity during the period of high commodity prices from the early 1950s to the early 1970s further encouraged the lenders, including manufacturers and exporters, who offered easy short-term credits. From 1973, moreover, the western banks had an additional motive for lending to LDCs. The oil-exporting countries had huge receipts from the oil they sold at four times the previous price after the OPEC oil-price increase. They deposited much of this in western banks, which in turn had to find borrowers and offered low rates of interest. By that time also there were large quantities of Eurodollars in European banks, which represented the persistent US deficits on foreign trade and other transactions. These also were available for lending. Because there was so much credit available, the terms offered before about 1980 were relatively favourable to borrowers, with low rates of interest (in the 1970s often below the rate of inflation), and generous amortization conditions.

The result was an unprecedented flow of capital to virtually all Third World countries. It made a huge contribution to investment and development. But by the early 1980s, when economic conditions and the

[1] Based on D. K. Fieldhouse, *Black Africa 1945–1980: Economic Decolonization and Arrested Development* (London, 1986), table 2.4, p. 50; table 2.5, p. 52; table 2.6, p. 53; which give sources.

terms of trade turned against commodity exporters, these debts were to create very serious problems, which will be considered in chapters 10 and 11.

By no means all of these debts were, however, to commercial banks or private firms, nor were they all at commercial rates of interest. From the 1940s an increasing proportion of foreign money and goods came from western governments and international organizations such as the World Bank and the IMF. Their common feature was that the terms were, in varying degrees, 'soft'. Such loans and grants fall under the generic head of 'aid', bilateral from individual governments to particular recipient countries, multilateral from the international organizations. Their only common feature was that the terms were, in varying degrees, non-commercial. Aid has become a highly controversial institution and is the main subject of this chapter.

1   The Genesis of Aid

As was seen in chapter 3, the origins of modern aid lie in the late-colonial period. To recapitulate, before about 1930 all the colonial powers expected that colonies would meet their own current public expenditure from taxation and that investment in development would be financed either from government surplus on current account or from borrowing. The change began around 1929. Relatively depressed conditions during the 1920s, followed by the major world recession of 1929–33, created serious economic problems for both imperial and colonial societies. Colonies could not afford to borrow in order to finance major public works, and this had adverse effects on European manufacturers, typically of iron and steel, and the engineering products for railways, docks, etc., in the colonies. Some colonies could no longer cover even their basic costs, however many economies they made, let alone invest in development projects. The result was a tentative movement towards subsidizing the colonies. Brussels made substantial grants to balance the accounts of the Congo in the early 1930s. Britain and France also made grants in aid of current expenditure. But far more significant for the future was the establishment of imperial funds to encourage capital investment in the colonies: the British Colonial Development Act of 1929, the Colonial Development and Welfare Act of 1940, and the French *Fonds d'investissement pour le Développement Économique et Social*, which were described in chapter 3.

The Second World War effectively blocked the operation of these projects, but the war had a dramatic effect on the attitude of all the colonial powers to the future of their colonies. During the 1940s many of the colonies, far from being a liability, became economically critical for their imperial master because of their dollar-earning and saving exports. Their development, and investment in them, thus became a matter of self-interest for the imperial states, and this was clearly set out at the Brazzaville Conference held by the Free French in 1944. It was from this time also that serious attempts were first made to draw up plans for colonial economic development, which in turn implied imperial commitment to help to finance them. Equally significant, Britain and France came to accept an obligation to subsidize the day-to-day running costs of the poorest colonies, notably those in the West Indies.

But in this same period a new factor came into play which, under different conditions, was to become a main motive for the continuation of aid during the rest of the century: the assumed need to buy political support in the overseas world. After 1945 the imperial powers had to face up to the reality of colonial nationalist movements. By 1948 Britain had lost control of India/Pakistan, Ceylon (Sri Lanka) and Burma. In 1949 the Netherlands had to withdraw from Indonesia in the face of Javanese nationalism and US disapproval of attempts to suppress it. The French were fighting in Indo-China against the Chinese-backed North Vietnamese and had lost the struggle by 1954. By that time they were facing a growing nationalist movement in Algeria. In Black Africa there were nascent nationalist movements in most territories.

The conclusion seemed obvious. If they were to hold onto their remaining possessions, at least for the short to medium term, the imperial states must offer something substantial to counter the nationalist claim that colonialism was necessarily exploitative: they had to promise rapid economic development coupled, at least in the British case, with phased introduction of self-government. The problem was that in the critical period between 1945 and the early 1950s, when the colonial nationalist movements were gathering force, the European states were unable to provide either the capital investment or the consumer goods the colonies wanted and of which they had been starved since 1939. As a strategy to save colonialism, aid had therefore clearly failed by the middle of the 1950s, even if it had ever had any chance of success. Colonial nationalist movements were too deeply entrenched and decolonization had become inevitable, though the Portuguese refused to accept this until after their domestic revolution in the early 1970s.

From the late 1950s, therefore, European imperial strategy changed. Once colonial independence was accepted as inevitable, the aim was to buy the continued friendship and political and economic collaboration of the prospective successor regimes. In the first instance this had economic objectives: to hold the new states as far as possible within the commercial, and possibly also the monetary, systems of the metropolis, and so retain the supposed economic benefits of empire. The British empire would become a cooperative Commonwealth, the French empire a franc zone tied by the accords signed with colonies on independence. This was the crucial link between aid to colonies in the late colonial period and aid after independence.

It was not, however, certain that aid designed to hold the British empire together would continue after independence, since the costs were escalating in the mid-1950s and putting a strain on the fragile British balance of payments and the pound sterling. In 1957 Harold Macmillan, newly translated from Chancellor of the Exchequer to Prime Minister of Britain, and concerned at the cost of British development funds, asked his senior officials what might be the costs and benefits to Britain of early decolonization of the remaining colonies – the assumption presumably being that this would reduce both aid and defence expenditure. Predictably he received a neutral and unhelpful bureaucratic reply; but at least the fact that he asked the question suggests that it was by no means certain that aid would continue after empire: decolonization might relieve the metropolis of this incubus.[2]

That it did not do so, but that in fact it increased in size, was largely the result of international conditions after the coming of the cold war in 1948–9. Thereafter polarization of the world system between the Soviet–Chinese bloc and that dominated by the United States affected all relationships. Every state now had a market for its favours and aid became the main currency. The key initiative was that of the United States in 1948, when Congress passed the Economic Cooperation Act, as suggested previously by General Marshall. Its aim was to provide western European countries with very large dollar credits to pay for the essential imports from dollar sources to rehabilitate their economies after the war and to keep them out of the clutches of the Soviets. The effects on western Europe were decisive: by the early 1950s rehabilitation was far advanced and the dollar famine virtually over. Equally significant, the momentum of communism in Europe had been checked: after 1950 no European state became part of the Soviet bloc by its own choice.

That was merely the start of international aid. What had threatened western Europe was by then seen as a threat to the newly independent Third World, then still mainly in South and South-east Asia. India, Pakistan, Burma and Indonesia, all independent by 1950, seemed vulnerable to Soviet influence. The United States therefore built up a system of economic aid and, where possible, political alliances in that region, supported France financially in Indo-China, and took over the burden of attempting to prevent its total control by North Vietnam after 1954. By 1960 the United Nations had latched onto the idea of international

[2] The details are in D. J. Morgan, *The Official History of Colonial Development*, vol. 5, *Guidance towards Self-government in the Colonies, 1941–71* (London, 1980), pp. 96–102.

aid: Resolution 1522 of the General Assembly, dominated numerically by Third World states, declared the 1960s to be a 'development decade', and asserted that the developed countries should devote 1 per cent of their national product to Third World aid. The following year the Organization for European Economic Cooperation (OEEC), set up in 1948 to organize the distribution of American aid, was joined by the United States and Canada and renamed Organization for Economic Cooperation and Development (OECD). It then set up a Development Assistance Committee (DAC) to organize its aid contributions.

In this way the system of imperial subsidies to colonies was integrated into a new international pattern of patron–client relations. The transition was symbolized in Britain by the passage in 1966 of the Overseas Aid Act to replace the CD&W Act. French aid to francophone states was integrated into aid from the EEC, established in 1958, under the various Yaoundé and later Lomé conventions, which reduced the pressure of aid on the French economy by spreading it among all members of the Community. Other countries, including those that had not been colonial powers, also set up their aid organizations – for example, the United States Agency for International Development (AID). The Soviet Union and its East European dependencies also provided aid, most of it to their political affiliates, Cuba, Mongolia and Vietnam.

This type of aid, from one country (or group of countries) direct to a recipient, is called bilateral aid. It may relate to a specific project and may have strings attached: for example, that the money must be used to buy from the donor state or for specified purposes. Meantime, however, new sources of aid had developed which, in principle, had no such political affiliations and provided 'multilateral' or 'programme' aid. The hub of the system was the World Bank. The Bank itself lends money, but this is raised in the money markets and is lent on nearly commercial terms. But the Bank has a soft loans agency, the International Development Association (IDA), which makes loans on concessionary terms, using funds subscribed by the richer states. Other agencies that grew up in the 1960s include the Regional Banks, and the wide range of UN organizations mentioned above. Their common denominator is that all make loans or provide goods free or on concessional terms, and that the donor countries have no individual control over who receives aid or how it is spent. But such multilateral or programme aid was always much smaller than bilateral aid: in 1988, for example, ODA was three–quarters bilateral, only a quarter multilateral.

Thus, during the early 1960s, aid became part of the accepted international economic order. Aid was based on a new general consensus that the developed countries had moral, material and political interests in subsidizing the less-developed world: moral on broad humanitarian grounds; material because it was thought essential for the West to stimulate the economies of customers and sources of raw materials; political to preserve a perceived global balance of power. Once these principles had been conceded (or not denounced) by the West, the rest of the world began to claim aid as a right rather than a benefaction, often on the ground that current poverty was the creation of colonialism. The United Nations Conference on Trade and Development (UNCTAD), set up in 1964, was dominated by Third World countries and became a forum for pressure for more aid, and also for economic strategies to benefit poorer countries.

In 1969 the Report of the Pearson Commission, set up in 1968 by the World Bank, defined the currently accepted imperatives. Aid was primarily essential on moral grounds – the rich must help the poor – but also to preserve international security by eliminating extremes of wealth and poverty. Pearson provided a formal definition: aid consisted of 'funds made available by governments on concessional terms primarily to promote development and the welfare of developing countries'. Aid thus excluded finance for defence. It also excluded private investment: aid was for things the private sector could or would not provide. Pearson was against tied bilateral aid (which had constituted some 90 per cent of all aid in 1967) and proposed that, of the 1 per cent of GNP proposed by the United Nations in 1960 for aid contributions, 70 per cent should be concessional. Underlying these recommendations and the whole concept of aid in the 1960s was the assumption that aid was not to be perpetual but to be once for all. Its function was to bridge the relatively small margin between the investment capital a Third World country needed and what it could generate by it own savings. This was in line with much contemporary thinking on development, as represented by W. W. Rostow's then influential book *Stages of Economic Growth*.[3] Since Pearson claimed that on average the Third World already provided some 85 per cent of its own investment capital, the gap seemed easily bridgeable.

This last assumption is critical for any assessment of the value of aid, and will be discussed in section 2 of this chapter. But the general effect of these developments was that by the 1980s and 1990s the transfer of resources from the West to the Third World under the broad heading of aid had become highly institutionalized and integral with the economic life of most Third World countries. To take a snapshot view in 1989, the net receipts of ODA for all countries were $54 billion, of which $16 billion went to Asia and $18 billion to sub-Saharan Africa, whose share of total aid had risen from 31 per cent in 1980 to 39 per cent in 1989. In that year ten African countries received more than $500 million each, Egypt ($1.58 billion) and Kenya ($967 million) getting the most.[4] Officially all this was 'development aid', intended to raise

[3] W. W. Rostow, *The Stages of Economic Growth* (Cambridge, 1960).
[4] R. Cassen and Associates, *Does Aid Work? Report to an Intergovernmental Task Force* (2nd edn, Oxford, 1994), table 1.1, p. 4; pp. 5–6.

the economic level of these countries through investment. In practice, for many countries, aid had become an essential means of helping to balance the national accounts, partly at least because of the deterioration in the terms of trade of many commodity-exporting countries from the early 1980s. Thus, to take a small sample of some 'low-income' economies in rising order of per capita GNP, ODA constituted the following percentages of their GNP in 1994: Rwanda, 123.4; Haiti, 37.8; Nicaragua, 41.6; Ghana, 11.1; the Ivory Coast, 36.2; Congo, 31.2. In all these, except for Ghana, gross domestic investment was significantly smaller than aid as a percentage of GDP, which suggests that a substantial proportion of aid was used to finance a current shortfall in national resources and the deficit on current foreign account.[5]

It is, therefore, clear that, during the half century after 1945, aid had changed its character twice. Initially seen as a weapon in the competition for the loyalty of colonies and uncommitted Third World states, aid then became a device to enable underdeveloped countries to overcome the assumed structural obstacles to sustained development by increasing capital investment, and ended up, at least in part, as a form of international subsidy to the living costs of the poorer countries. In the terms of the British act of 1940, the emphasis had thus shifted from development to welfare.

This evolution partly explains why aid became a matter of controversy. It points to the main question to be considered in section 2 of this chapter. To what extent has aid had the beneficial effects predicted, and so justified its existence?

2   Aid and Development

It was suggested above that in its inception aid had three main purposes or expressed three impulses. The first was moral: the rich always have an obligation to help the poor. The second was political: to keep or recruit Third World states within imperial or later western or Soviet power blocs. The final purpose was to make a significant contribution to the economic development of underdeveloped countries in the hope and expectation that sufficient injections of capital would enable them, once and for all, to overcome the obstacles in the way of growth and so put them on the road to sustained development.

The first of these is not a matter of debate. Some would extend this moral duty to redistribution of income, though many would reject the proposition that the obligation stems from the alleged evils of colonialism. Nor is there any doubt that there has been a strong political element

[5] World Bank, *World Development Report, 1996: From Plan to Market* (Oxford, 1996), table 3, p. 192; table 13, p. 212.

in the choice of who should receive bilateral aid, though this became less significant after the end of the bipolar global political system at the end of the 1980s.

Thus the really significant issue raised by aid is whether it fulfils its stated purpose of enabling Third World countries to make greater progress towards affluence and sustained development than they might otherwise have been able to do. That is, does aid work? This, of course, contains an implicit counter-factual: success must be measured against what might not have been possible without it. Hence there can be no conclusive answer to the question. The useful approach is rather to ask whether the evidence suggests that aid has been at least positive in its effects, or whether it has had neutral or even negative consequences.

It is important to define precisely what aid can do and how it might aid growth and development. From the early 1960s the main economic rationalization of and argument for aid has been based on the so-called two-gap model.[6] Development in any country may be held back by two main shortages: of domestic savings for investment and of foreign exchange to pay for the necessary capital imports. In a developing country with ambitious investment schemes the shortage of foreign exchange is almost inevitable, since investment not only requires foreign inputs but will take time before it pays its way. In addition, in a poor country the accumulation of domestic savings is likely to be very slow. Hence the basic economic argument for modern aid is that it may enable poor countries to increase the flow of foreign resources, both capital and foreign exchange, beyond what they might have been able to afford on the open market. Aid has, therefore, to be seen in relation to the total flow of resources, measured in proportion to other sources of overseas funds; and the question to be asked is how much more development was made possible by aid than might have been possible without it.

These principles, of course, conceal an unstated assumption: that the economic effects of aid will be proportionate to the amount of aid provided. This, in turn, assumes that the forms in which aid is given match the needs of the recipient country. This may well not be true. Aid, typically bilateral, which is arranged to suit the economic interests of the donor, may come in an indigestible form: for example, machinery, for non-existent factories requiring maintenance by non-available technicians, or a steel mill for a country with no ferrous metals or refining plants, or even wheat for a country whose staple diet is rice. Such aid will certainly make little or no contribution to development and merely inflates the published statistics.

[6] See D. Colman and F. Nixson, *Economics of Change in Less Developed Countries* (New York, 1994), ch. 2, for a useful exposition of this concept.

Aid theory has also tended to assume that the receiving country will make the best possible use of what it is given. For long it was a polite assumption in the West that Third World governments were both well intentioned and competent, so that all aid would be put to good use. By the 1970s this assumption had been shown to be unsound: aid was only as good as the government and administration of the receiving country, and this gave rise to what may be called an alternative view of aid, which will be considered below.

First, however, it is necessary to examine some evidence on the quantity of aid provided, and how much it added to the general flow of resources to Third World countries. Table 8.1 gives some indication of the volume of different types of resources flowing into developing countries between 1970 and 1988.

There are two key features of this table. First, apart from 1982, when they were almost exactly the same, official flows were larger than private flows. On the other hand, concessional flows were significantly less than total official flows. In two of these years (1978, 1982) they were less than private flows and in the other years not very different from them. If one is considering the relative increase in foreign resources made by this concessional aid, it was 41.1 per cent in 1970, 29.1 per cent in 1982, and 47.8 per cent in 1988. Thus, the remainder of aid under all

Table 8.1 Total resource flows to developing countries, 1970–1988 ($bn, at constant 1981 prices and exchange rates)

Source	1970	1974	1978	1982	1986	1988
A. *Official flows*						
Concessional	21.3	29.1	33.5	34.5	37.0	34.3
Non-concessional	10.2	13.5	22.9	24.5	9.3	8.0
Total official	31.5	42.6	56.4	59.0	46.3	42.3
B. *Private flows*	20.3	23.6	48.2	59.5	22.2	29.2
Total Flow (A+B=C+D)	51.8	66.2	104.6	118.5	68.5	71.5
C. *Bilateral flows*						
Total official	18.5	24.1	26.3	44.6	31.9	30.4
Private grant	2.2	2.2	2.0	2.4	2.8	2.8
Direct investment	9.5	3.3	13.8	13.1	9.4	16.9
Export credit, etc.	16.9	28.4	51.6	44.0	10.0	9.5
D. *Multilateral*	4.7	8.2	10.9	14.4	14.4	11.9

Source: D. Colman and F. Nixson, *Economics of Change in Less Developed Countries* (New York, 1994), table 6.1, p. 185; based on OECD, *Financing and External Debt of Developing Countries*, various issues.

heads was on more or less standard commercial terms, so that the net benefit of aid was represented by the reduction in the costs of borrowing on concessional terms for those proportions of the total flow of resources. This, in turn, suggests that the benefits of aid may have been rather less than the gross figures might suggest.

Secondly, it is clear that 1982 was a watershed in the flow of resources. In real terms total resource flows increased nearly 300 per cent between 1970 and 1982, with a dip in 1980. In this trend the main variables were non-concessional official payments, export credits and other lending, presumably mainly by banks. The first of these peaked in 1982, the second in 1978, at the top of the Third World borrowing spree to take advantage of low interest rates and the banks' enthusiasm for lending. FDI also was at its peak between 1978 and 1982, declined in the mid-1980s, then rose towards the end of the decade. The crisis came after 1982, with the rise in variable interest rates as the major western states grappled with inflation: for example, the six-month Eurodollar rate payable on variable debt rose from an average of 8.3 per cent in 1972–8 to a peak of 17.2 per cent in 1981, before falling. Simultaneously, the terms of trade turned against most Third World commodity exporters, resulting in consistently adverse balances on visible trade.

In such circumstances capital flows into LDCs could not match their deficits, let alone provide a margin for investment. As table 8.1 shows, total resource transfers declined very sharply in real terms between 1982 and 1986. Bilateral official aid rose from 58.7 per cent of total official flows in 1970 to 71.9 per cent in 1988, reflecting the determination of major donors to insist on more control over the use of their funds; and export credits and other forms of lending fell away dramatically. Mexico suspended payment on its huge foreign debt in 1982 and this and many other Third World countries had to ask for their debts to be rescheduled.

The combined result of reduced aid, higher interest rates and adverse terms of trade was that, just when the needs of the Third World became most acute, aid failed even to balance the Third World's current accounts, let alone provide a surplus for development expenditure. Between 1983 and 1989 there was a deficit on the overall balance of LDC capital-importing countries, after taking account of the outflow on account of net dividends and other income, interest on long-term private borrowing, and the flow of official aid, net of repayments and interest. That is, for these LDCs aid was unable to match the outgoings on account of previous foreign investment and LDC borrowing.[7]

This suggests that aid, at least at the level the western countries were prepared to pay it, which was very much less than the 1 per cent of GNP

---

[7] Based on ibid., table 6.2, p. 187.

set up as a target by the UN, could not meet the needs of the Third
World under the conditions of the last years of the twentieth century.
Aid as provided was no miracle worker. But this does not necessarily mean that aid was useless. We must therefore now turn to consider the argument concerning the basic economic value of aid: does
it work?

The question has been debated ever since the early 1970s, once the
system had become firmly institutionalized. Broadly, two positions have
been adopted by different writers. First, aid is denounced as either unhelpful or positively harmful to LDCS. This may be from either an open-
market or a socialist standpoint. Secondly, aid is accepted as necessary,
potentially beneficial and generally successful, but either the mode of
giving or the use to which it is put may be criticized. These positions
will be described briefly in turn.

The first important critic of aid, from an open-market standpoint,
was (Lord) P. T. Bauer, for whom aid was merely part of a generally
unacceptable dirigiste approach to the economics of development. Bauer
had earlier studied the rubber trade in Malaya and the system of trade
in West Africa, and his published work on both subjects criticized all
forms of monopoly, monopsony and restrictive agreements.[8] In 1959,
in the context of US aid to India, he argued that the size of the flow
should be reduced and its level should depend on the economic and
social strategies adopted by the government of India.[9] Then, in 1971,
he published the first of a series of books which attacked the whole strategy adopted by many LDCs, often on the recommendation of western
development economists, and aid and its uses became integral with this
analysis.[10] The following summary of his mature views on aid is taken
from his later collection of essays, *The Development Frontier.*[11]

His starting point is that aid is a misnomer. Aid implies moral purpose
and benefits to the recipient population. In fact it is merely a govern-
ment-to-government transfer of resources, even if mediated via some
international organization. It is assumed that it is virtually costless to the
donors and that it cannot harm the recipients. It is given indiscriminately
to governments, irrespective of their policies, however economically

[8] See P. T. Bauer, 'Malayan Rubber Policies', *Economica*, NS 14 (1947); *West African Trade* (Cambridge, 1954).
[9] P.T. Bauer, *United States Aid and Indian Economic Development* (Washington, 1959).
[10] P. T. Bauer, *Dissent on Development* (London, 1971); *Equality, the Third World and Economic Delusion* (London, 1981); *Reality and Rhetoric: Studies in the Economics of Development* (London, 1984).
[11] P. T. Bauer, *The Development Frontier* (Cambridge, 1991), ch. 4, 'Foreign Aid: Central Component of World Development?'

perverse. The probability of it actually causing benefit to the mass of the recipient state's people is, therefore, slight.

In fact, Bauer argues, aid is both unnecessary and potentially harmful to LDCs. It is unnecessary because external help has never been necessary for any developing society. The idea that aid is necessary for capital formation in LDCs is itself fallacious: capital is the result, not the precondition, of economic achievement, and is acquired through effort and saving. Moreover, much capital is not productively invested. If developing countries need more capital, then they can save. Moreover, they have other possible sources: FDI, which had served very well since the early nineteenth century in other countries; commercial government borrowing; and domestic sources of capital, including foreign firms operating in a country. So all that aid can do is to reduce the cost of servicing normal debts, and this saving is small for most larger LDCs: for India in the 1980s, for example, aid might have been worth between 0.25 and 0.5 per cent of GNP.

If aid is unnecessary, it is certainly harmful to its recipients. The main reason is that most aid is paid to governments, and, in Bauer's view, most Third World governments are either incompetent or dishonest. Aid, therefore, helps governments and elites to pursue perverse economic policies which they would not otherwise have been able to afford, including overvalued currencies, and inflationary strategies; to block or limit FDI, which would have more beneficial effects, on pseudo-nationalistic grounds; and to reward select groups of political supporters, and so block democratic influence on government. Even aid that does not provide cash to governments has bad effects. Food aid, for example, depresses local prices and discourages farmers: it can also be used as part of government policies. Ironically, since the quantity of aid is broadly related to per capita incomes, the most incompetent and perverse governments get the most, and are merely encouraged to continue as before. Moreover, although the amount of aid received may be too small to have any significant effect on a country's development, it may be large in relation to government revenues and the balance of payments. Thus in 1980 aid to India was only 1.6 per cent of recorded GNP, but 16.8 per cent of tax receipts and 31.2 per cent of export earnings. In Tanzania in the same year the proportions were 18.1 per cent, 106.8 per cent and 152.8 per cent. Hence the main benefit was to governments, not the country as a whole.

Bauer then goes on to argue that evidence that countries receiving aid had developed proved nothing. 'The contribution of aid can never exceed the avoided cost of borrowing the investible funds as percentage of GNP.'[12] The success of individual aid projects, often provided by

[12] Ibid., p. 51.

bilateral aid, merely shows that they were intrinsically viable and could have been paid for by government or private enterprise: indeed, they would then have been even more likely to succeed because based on market considerations. The analogy of Marshall Aid for Europe was false. That had been needed to revive, not create, developed economies, and had indeed played only a minor role in the revival of Western Germany.

Reversing the standpoint, Bauer considers the assumption that aid benefits the West, either politically or economically. Despite standard arguments that aid is politically related, in fact much of it is multilateral, so could have no political consequences; and even bilateral aid is seldom closely geared to the political interests of donor states. In fact, many recipients are hostile to the donors. Nor does the West gain economically by improving the markets for its products. Aid merely gives assets, even though these, under bilateral aid, come from the donor country. Spending the same sums at home would be more effective in reducing unemployment, and any asset created would then remain at home. 'In sum, the idea that aid helps the economies of the donors simply ignores the cost of the resources given away.'[13]

Bauer's root-and-branch denunciation of aid stems from two main basic beliefs: that the market economy is the only true route to development; and that governments in most LDCs are either incapable or corrupt, so that aid has no appreciably beneficial effects on the population as a whole. At the other end of the political spectrum, many critics of aid reject the first of these propositions, believing that highly regulated and probably socialist economic systems are desirable; but they broadly agree with the second, mainly on the ground that LDC governments as at present constituted are helped to avoid socialist strategies by aid from capitalist donors.

One of the first such critics was Teresa Hayter, whose *French Aid* claimed that the apparently very large sums spent by France on aid to its colonies and ex-colonies were to some extent fictitious, since, among other factors, a considerable proportion of the money never left France because it represented payments made to French 'technical advisers'.[14] Then, in 1971, Hayter published her *Aid as Imperialism*.[15] Assuming that aid came from the capitalist West, she held that aid was 'a complicated edifice of deception' and that it could be explained only as 'an attempt to preserve the capitalist system in the Third World'. Since capitalism necessarily implied exploitation and dependence, it was clearly against the interest of the Third World peoples that it should continue. But on

[13] Ibid., p. 55.
[14] T. Hayter, *French Aid* (London, 1966).
[15] T. Hayter, *Aid as Imperialism* (Harmondsworth, 1971).

one matter Hayter agreed with Bauer: the poor quality of most Third World governments and the uses to which they put aid. Given the nature of their regimes, aid merely helped to preserve the dominance of the indigenous privileged classes. It could be used for projects that made the masses worse rather than better off; and, because mostly used unprofitably, it merely added to a country's indebtedness, and therefore its 'dependence' on the capitalist West. On the other hand, however, Hayter, in common with most critics of capitalism in the 1970s, assumed that aid could be and was used by donors to enforce acceptance of western political alignments and the capitalist domestic policies favoured by the donors.[16]

Right and Left, free marketeers and socialists, could thus meet in condemning aid. But the great majority of commentators fall into the second category: aid is necessary and potentially a significant contribution to development, though the means of giving and the use to which it is put may be criticized. The following is merely a small sample of this category of analysis.

Judith Tendler expressed moderate support for aid in a book published in 1975, but doubted how much of it was usefully disbursed.[17] Though professional aid practitioners – the agents of the international organizations and national aid agencies – complained that the quantity of aid was totally insufficient, they often wasted resources on unsuitable projects. Large-scale and often prestige projects with high capital intensity suited them well, both because they looked good in annual reports and because they could be supervised relatively easily. Conversely, smaller projects involving less foreign aid but more local expenditure were less prestigious and more difficult to monitor. Tendler argued that aid should be concentrated on proposals that were both practicable and economic, and would make a maximum contribution to the welfare of a society at large. This pointed towards what became known as the 'basic-needs' approach.

Another supporter of aid, though with reservations on its actual use in the mid-1970s, was John White.[18] While aid was intrinsically desirable, there were conditions under which it might actually harm the recipients. Tying aid to the exports of the donor was one of these. Because the equipment for a project had to be taken from the donor country at prices it set, the net cost of carrying it out and subsequently servicing the debt, even on concessional terms, might be greater than it would have been had it been financed by commercial borrowing and the inputs bought on the open market. It was simply not true that any aid was better than no aid: its conditions determined its utility. On the much-debated

---

[16] Quoted from J. E. Goldthorpe, *The Sociology of Post-colonial Societies* (Cambridge, 1996), pp. 234–5.

[17] J. Tendler, *Inside Foreign Aid* (Baltimore, Md, 1975).

[18] J. White, *The Politics of Foreign Aid* (London, 1974).

issue of whether aid tended to discourage domestic savings and capital accumulation, which Keith Griffin alleged in 1970 had occurred in Latin America,[19] White maintained that, even if this was true, it did not invalidate the utility of aid as a supplement to local savings; but he held that Griffin's case had not, in fact, been proved. On the other hand, as Hayter had argued, aid inevitably made recipients in some degree clients of the donors and therefore created dependence. Donors might insist on conditions involving painful changes of policy for the recipient, which might involve high domestic political costs. In short, aid had its price, a view increasingly expressed in the 1980s as major multilateral donors, such as the World Bank and the IMF, began to make aid conditional on domestic reform, which the IMF was to call 'structural adjustment'.

Although aid continued to be generally regarded during the later 1970s as economically essential and desirable on moral grounds, evidence of its limited economic benefits and dubious social and political effects was increasingly undermining confidence in it, at least as it was then operated. By the early 1980s what John Toye has labelled 'the development counter-revolution' was under way.[20] As he describes it, this involved rejection by many of the leading development economists of the previous two decades of the conventional assumptions about Third World development in general and the functions and value of aid in particular.

The underlying assumption of these alleged counter-revolutionaries against Keynesianism was that, while aid was necessary and could be beneficial, it would be so only under the right conditions. The evidence in fact suggested that aid could do little if the recipient countries rejected the price mechanism and the case for free trade and export-led growth, and continued to believe that government controls on virtually all economic and social matters were essential to relieve poverty. To be effective, aid must be linked to liberalization of LDC economies along lines to be defined by the donor institutions. Thus Deepak Lal wrote in 1983:

> The major benefit the developing countries derive from ... the multilateral aid institutions ... is the technical assistance built into the process of transferring the aid money to the recipient countries. Though often sound on general economic grounds, their advice is nevertheless resented for political or emotional reasons.... When heeded, the advice has done some good ... in some instances it may have had an appreciable effect in making public policies more economically rational.[21]

---

[19] K. Griffin, 'Foreign Capital, Domestic Savings and Economic Development', *Bulletin of Oxford Institute of Economics and Statistics*, 32, 2 (1970).

[20] The following account attempts to summarize the relevant parts of J. Toye, *Dilemmas of Development* (2nd edn, Oxford, 1993), chs 3, 4, 7.

[21] D. Lal, *The Poverty of 'Development Economics'* (London, 1983), pp. 56–7, quoted in Toye, *Dilemmas*, p. 94.

Lal, of course, was expressing only what by then had become a widely held, though by no means universal, reaction against the whole trend of western attitudes to Third World development since the 1950s and the so-called development economics in particular. Similar views were published by Ian Little, a leading specialist in development planning, in 1982.[22] By that time, moreover, the main aid agencies, particularly the IMF and the World Bank and its offshoots, had decided that aid should no longer be given indiscriminately to Third World governments, trusting in their efficiency and honesty to ensure that proper use was made of it. Many forms of aid would continue as before; but in 1980 the World Bank introduced a new form of aid called 'Structural Adjustment Lending' (SAL), whose main feature was that aid was to be made conditional on the recipient agreeing to certain prescribed conditions.[23]

Strictly speaking 'conditionality' in aid was not new. From the start the IMF had been obliged to prescribe conditions for loans it made to governments when they applied for loans to tide them over crises in their balance of payments. From 1974, moreover, the IMF had moved from this limited function to provide medium-term credit to countries for development purposes, using a surplus in its accounts: in 1976 this had been called the Extended Fund Facility (EFF), which was followed in 1986 by the Structural Adjustment Facility (SAF) and in 1987 by the still more generous Enhanced Structural Adjustment Facility (ESAF).[24] All involved conditions, mainly relating to exchange policy.

Thus from 1976 the World Bank was competing for business with the IMF. Moreover, the Bank itself had previously dabbled in conditionality in programme aid – conditions were, of course, always present in project aid. In 1965–6 the Bank made large loans to India at a moment of crisis for the Indian economy, and insisted as a condition on devaluation of the admittedly grossly overvalued rupee in 1966. The results of this devaluation were unsatisfactory, and this had discouraged the Bank from conditionality, even as it moved towards programme aid. But the serious economic effects of the OPEC oil-price increase of 1973 and of deteriorating macroeconomic conditions, especially in Black Africa in the mid-1970s, made project aid largely ineffective. Such aid was,

---

[22] I. M. D. Little, *Economic Development: Theory, Policy and International Relations* (New York, 1982).

[23] Much of the material on Structural Adjustment Loans (SALs) that follows is based on P. Mosely, J. Harrigan and J. Toye, *Aid and Power: The World Bank and Policy-based Lending* (2 vols; 2nd edn, London, 1991), vol. 1, esp. chs 1–5, 9.

[24] For a critique of IMF and World Bank lending strategies, see G. Bird, *IMF Lending to Developing Countries* (London, 1995); R. van der Hoeven and F. van der Kraaj (eds), *Structural Adjustment and Beyond in Sub-Saharan Africa* (The Hague, 1994).

moreover, very slow to have any impact on critical problems of debt servicing and public finance.

The result was that the World Bank, with considerable hesitation, came to the conclusion that, in these circumstances, programme aid would be more effective than project aid, but that it would work only if it was tied to major reforms of LDC economic strategy. In 1973–5 Zambia, Tanzania and Kenya were all given programme aid with strings attached; but it was only in 1979 that Robert McNamara, as president of the Bank, announced the new approach to an UNCTAD meeting as a general strategy, and not until 1980 that the Executive Board of the Bank agreed to implement conditionality as a main Bank strategy. Even so, the Board pointed to what became a major ambivalence in the concept: was a loan to be used as a lever to induce governments to undertake measures which the Bank thought essential, possibly against their will, or was it to be the result of prior agreement between the Bank and a government on the intrinsic desirability of policy changes?

Despite these uncertainties, Structural Adjustment Loans (SALs) began in 1980. Between then and 1986 thirty-seven SALs were made (though some to the same country in different years) with a total value of $5,259 million. Of this, 35 per cent went to Turkey, whose progress appeared to demonstrate the virtues of the system. In addition, from 1984, there were Sectoral Adjustment Loans (SECALs), targeted on specific parts of an LDC's economy.

The general purpose of SALs and SECALs was to help with the acute current balance-of-payments problems of many LDCs without seriously affecting their growth, but at the same time to persuade them to undertake a bundle of economic reforms which the Bank, following current neoclassical thinking, deemed essential to their success. Broadly this involved unravelling the complex of dirigiste strategies adopted since the 1950s by most LDCs. Exchange rates should not be overvalued, since this encouraged imports and penalized indigenous producers. Rates of interest should reflect market forces. The public sector should be reduced because of the evident inefficiency of many state enterprises, and much of it handed over to private enterprise. Markets, such as the prices paid to producers of commodities, should be freed and made properly remunerative. Direct controls over trade and investment, including the almost universal import licensing, should be reduced, along with protectionist import duties. In general, domestic prices should be nearer to international prices.

In the World Bank's terminology this meant 'liberalization', and the assumptions that lay behind these strategies are reflected in a large number of the Bank's publications on Third World development. One of its clearest early statements of the case for liberalization was the publication in 1981 of its *Accelerated Development in Sub-Saharan*

Africa: An Agenda for Action (commonly known as the Berg Report),
which analysed most of what the Bank regarded as the major defects in
African economic policies since the 1950s and set out its proposed
strategy for recovery.[25] Chapter 4 provided a general critique of what
the authors regarded as the main defects in post-independence African
governmental policies, which were broadly along the lines summarized
above, and subsequent chapters spelt out in more detail what needed
to be done in particular fields. Chapter 9 then dealt with 'External
Assistance in the 1980s'. Its central message was that, while it was
essential that more aid be provided, it would be effective only with the
cooperation of the recipient states. But it was conditionally optimistic.
'Policy reforms supported by substantially increased aid flows promise
substantially improved growth prospects for Africa in the 1980s.'[26]

This was the standpoint of the World Bank at the start of its new
reforming crusade. The Bank, at least publicly, maintained its optimism
and faith in its remedial prescriptions into the 1990s. Thus its *Adjustment
in Africa: Reforms, Results, and the Road Ahead* had the following sub-heads
for chapter 1: 'Overview', 'policies are getting better', 'better policies
pay off', 'policies are not good – yet' and 'the road ahead for adjustment'.[27] By then, however, the Bank seems to have learnt from hard
experience that the success of an SAL depended largely on the degree
of cooperation provided by the recipient.

> Only with strong government commitment and widespread public back-
> ing will policy reforms be sustained.... When an adjustment programme
> is launched there must be a solid consensus on the need for change, as
> well as an increase in the power of the interest groups that will benefit
> from reforms in the course of adjustment. If government commitment
> is weak, opposition forces strong, or short-run costs high, the likelihood
> of stalls or reversals in policy reform is great....
>
> When commitment is strong, it may be advantageous to design adjust-
> ment programs to minimize their vulnerability to derailment by those who
> stand to lose from the reforms, particularly in the initial phase of the
> program.[28]

If experience made the World Bank rather more cautious in claiming success for conditionality, others have been far more critical. Those,
both in the West and in LDCs, who remained wedded to the

[25] World Bank, *Accelerated Development in Sub-Saharan Africa: An Agenda for
Action* (Washington, 1981).
[26] Ibid., p. 121.
[27] World Bank, *Adjustment in Africa: Reforms, Results, and the Road Ahead*
(Oxford, 1994).
[28] Ibid., pp. 217–18.

developmental approach of the 1960s, with its emphasis on state planning and direction, public ownership, welfare expenditure to help the
poorer sections of society, and autarkic industrial development, have
throughout resented the fact that the Bank's emphasis has been on a
return to free-market strategies. This was to be expected.[29] A more useful
approach,however, may be to consider how far the SAL experiment has
succeeded on its own assumptions: that is, did it manage to combine
effective financial relief with agreed reform of underlying economic
strategies in the recipient countries?

A balanced answer is given by Mosely, Harrigan and Toye in their
study of the World Bank's 'policy-based lending'. Essentially SALs failed
to kill the two birds with the same stone. In their view, Structural
Adjustment Lending was 'a leap in the dark'. Economic theory offered
the Bank little help on what solutions would be best for the highly
distorted economies of the poorest LDCs. The Bank saw their main
target as the 'protective walls designed to shelter special interest groups
("rent seekers") from the pursuit of efficiency through competition in
the market'. With limited information of the precise conditions in particular countries, the Bank often prescribed reforms without proper analysis
or consultation with the recipient government, which might be too
anxious to obtain a loan to fight over the conditions imposed. The inevitable result was considerable resistance within the LDCs: a 40 per cent
'slippage' on the conditions set out was found in the country studies
made by these authors. The result was that SALs had limited effect.
When implemented, their conditions almost always improved export
growth and external account balances. Their effect on aggregate investment was almost always negative. Their influence on GNP, financial
flows and distribution of wealth within LDCs was, on balance, neutral;
but where income levels of particular groups fell, this was commonly
due to the effect of Bank pressure to pay more to farmers, to cut food
and other subsidies, and to make prices more competitive.

The implication of these findings for Mosely, Harrigan and Toye is
that it is quite unclear whether there was a net return to GNP growth
from the $35 billion invested in policy-based lending to about 1990,
whereas between 1960 and 1980 the Bank's project-based lending had
provided an average *ex post* return of 17 per cent.[30] In their view, the
key weakness of the whole conditionality approach was that the package offered was more relevant to middle-income states which had relatively advanced economies and strong governments, such as Turkey and
Thailand, than to very poor and underdeveloped countries, such as
Guyana and Malawi, which had not. Thus trade liberalization worked

[29] Such doubts, for example, are clearly stated in Toye, *Dilemmas*, esp. ch. 7.
[30] Mosely et al., *Aid and Power*, p. 308.

much better if the LDC's industry was already more or less competitive internationally. Offering price incentives to underpaid farmers would only induce them to increase production if they had access to adequate credit, fertilizers and transport. Privatization of public enterprises worked well only if there were sufficient private entrepreneurs with the ability to run them better. Thus:

> The point is that structural adjustment policies of the Bank's chosen variety constitute in very poor countries a gratuitous obstruction, just as in NICs they constitute a welcome acceleration, of the policy evolution above described. [Although the Bank later recognized that uniform packages of reforms were impracticable], it still has to grasp the point that in very poor countries, privatisation and removal of infant–industry protective structures are at best an irrelevance. True structural adjustment requires the building up of the country's export sectors and associated infrastructure, which in the short term may require more rather than less state intervention.[31]

It is now necessary to return to the question posed at the start of this section: does or did aid work? The answer must, of course, depend on how one defines 'work'. This could mean one of two things. First, has aid achieved the stated objectives of the 1960s, as rationalized by the two–gap theory of development: that is, has aid enabled LDCs as a whole to destroy the 'structural' obstacles perceived to lie in the path of their development and become self-sustaining, no longer dependent on aid, even though they may, like most developed countries, welcome conventional foreign capital flows? Secondly, however, 'work' may be interpreted in a more limited sense, as being 'effective' in the development process. Robert Cassen and Associates define 'effectiveness' in terms of the following tests.

> Does aid contribute macroeconomically or otherwise to growth? Does it reach the poor? Is the policy dialogue which accompanies aid successful and valuable? How have specific types of financial and commodity aid performed? What is the contribution of technical cooperation? What are the effects of having many donors working in a single country? Does aid help or hinder an appropriate functioning of market forces?[32]

Cassen's Report was the result of a research commission in the mid-1980s by a number of governments which contributed to the World Bank and the IMF, and was entirely independent of the views of both these governments and the two institutions. It was based on detailed research into the experience of seven developing countries as well as general information, and the wide range of the collaborators suggests a

[31] Ibid., p. 310.
[32] Cassen et al., *Does Aid Work?*, p. 6.

balanced, non-dogmatic approach. My answer to the second of these questions will, therefore, be strongly influenced by their findings.

First, however, has aid worked: has it enabled LDCs to move into what the development economists of the 1960s saw as sustained growth from their own resources? The answer must surely be that it worked for only a very few and that it is quite possible that these would have been successful even without aid. There is, of course, no firm measure of what 'developed' might mean, but statistics (in so far as they are reliable) are probably a reasonable indication of self-reliance: the degree of dependence on Official Development Assistance (ODA); the relationship between gross domestic saving and the GDP; and the resource balance after consumption, investment and exports.[33]

In 1994 the ODA contributions received by almost all the fifty-one countries listed as 'low-income economies' was 10 per cent or more of their GNP: the exceptions were Vietnam, Bangladesh, Nigeria, India, nine ex-Soviet states, Albania, Pakistan, China, Honduras, Sri Lanka, Egypt and Lesotho. In addition, in the middle-income group, Bolivia received 10.3 per cent of its GNP in ODA. For some, particularly those recently affected by civil war, ODA represented a very large proportion of GNP: for Rwanda, 123.4 per cent; Mozambique, 100.1; Guinea-Bissau, 74.2 per cent; Nicaragua, 41.6 per cent. The weighted average figure for sub-Saharan Africa was 12.4 per cent. Such figures, of course, do not indicate levels of poverty, since the giving and taking of ODA depend on many non-economic factors. But the fact that so many states still depended so heavily on aid suggests continuing serious underdevelopment and dependence.

Secondly, only seventeen of these fifty-one states had gross domestic savings of 10 per cent or more of GDP, which the development economists of the 1960s had regarded as a minimum for sustained growth or 'take-off'. On the other hand, the large majority reported gross domestic investment rates of 10 per cent or more: only seven states did not. That points to the likelihood of a substantial negative resource balance, since this investment had to come from somewhere; and in fact all but twenty-one of these low-income states had negative resource balances of 10 per cent or more of their GDP. Conversely, only four had positive resource balances. Of course, negative resource balances are not necessarily an indication of lack of development or growth: the United States, Canada and Britain all had negative balances of 1 per cent in 1994. But, coupled with the other indicators mentioned here, they strengthen the impression that aid had not, by 1994, succeeded in overcoming the alleged structural obstacles to self-sustaining growth. It must, however, be said that some countries to which earlier

---

[33] These statistics are taken from World Bank, *World Development Report 1996*, table 3, p. 192; table 13, p. 212.

World Bank aid had been given, notably Turkey and Thailand, had made very respectable progress up the ladder of comparative affluence, with relatively high domestic saving rates and positive or low negative resource balances.

If aid has not 'worked' in this specific, and indeed highly problematic and conceptual way, how 'effective' has it been. Cassen provides a general answer and supports it with analysis of the effect of aid under different headings. His broad conclusion is that 'most aid does indeed work. It succeeds in achieving its developmental objectives (where these are primary), contributing positively to the recipient countries' economic performance, and not substituting for activities which would have occurred anyway.' The World Bank estimated that 80 per cent of IDA projects (as distinct from programme aid) provided a minimum 10 per cent return. The rate of failure of aid as a whole is not known: it might be a quarter or more. But Cassen argues that this must be accepted as part of the risk element in all economic ventures, and that aid is no different from many private investment schemes. Thus 'the answer to the question "Does aid work?" is "Most of it, yes; however ..."'.[34]

Cassen then examines the operation of aid under eight headings in chapters 2–9. Chapter 2 considers 'the macroeconomic contribution of aid'. Accepting the point made by Bauer, that capital investment is not the only or main cause of economic growth, as compared with labour, skills, etc., Cassen argues that the effectiveness of aid in stimulating growth depends on its relationship with other factors in the recipient country. Moreover, the value of aid in relation to a country's GNP has varied immensely: in 1988 aid represented about 20 per cent of GNP in the least developed countries but only 0.6 per cent for China and 0.8 per cent for India. But aid typically represented a far higher proportion of a country's investment and foreign exchange. For the poorer Black African countries aid in 1988 represented 56 per cent of gross domestic investment (GDI), 42 per cent for the middle-income oil importers. It also financed very high proportions of public expenditure: about 80 per cent in Malawi in the early 1980s, 53 per cent in Tanzania. A rough calculation suggests that, if aid adds 20 per cent to the level of investment, it will raise the income investment ratio by 3–5 per cent, while a 1 per cent rise in that ratio will raise the growth rate of output by between 0.3 and 0.2 per cent.

But does aid in fact increase savings and therefore investment and growth? Cassen rejects Bauer's claim that aid reduces the savings effort, though he admits that the evidence is uncertain. A World Bank estimate suggests that 'most development assistance *is* saved (and invested)'.[35]

[34] Cassen et al. *Does Aid Work?*, pp. 7–9.
[35] Ibid., p. 25.

Evidence of some countries, such as India, South Korea and Colombia, also suggests that aid has enabled some countries to become more self-reliant in capital accumulation, and in any case to move from dependence on soft loans to normal commercial borrowing. Finally, aid can help countries to increase their exports by helping in the transition from restrictive import-substituting strategies to open markets. In short, while the evidence does not demonstrate conclusively that aid does or does not promote economic growth, the anecdotal evidence of individual countries suggests that, under the right conditions, it may do so.

Chapter 3 tackles the question of whether aid can reduce Third World poverty or whether, as Bauer and others maintain, it helps only elites. The evidence suggests that aid may not in fact help the poor significantly, mainly because there is not enough of it to do so, though they may benefit from better provision of public services and from the provision of food aid, which helps the consumer, though not the local farmer. Chapter 4 then considers the way in which aid is negotiated with recipient states, 'the policy dialogue'. This is clearly critical for the success of aid projects, and the evidence suggests that in the past there was too much dictation by donors, whether individual states or multilateral organizations such as the IMF and the World Bank. Chapter 5 analyses the performance and value of project, programme and food aid. All had their advantages and disadvantages, and the effectiveness of all depended largely on how well they were planned in relation to the needs and potential of the recipient country. Chapter 6 analyses aid in the form of technical cooperation, which covered some 25 per cent of all DAC aid in about 1990. Again, estimate of its long-term value is conceptually difficult. Cassen calculates that perhaps a half to two-thirds of such aid of those projects that have been examined were in some sense successful, of which a third were judged fully satisfactory, while outright failures were reported in 10–15 per cent of projects. Technical aid was least successful in Africa (though some 20 per cent of French aid in sub-Saharan francophone Africa was 'technical', mostly the supply of teachers), largely because of government incompetence and corruption, which had driven a large proportion of indigenous experts abroad. Subsequent chapters examine the role of coordination of various aid agencies and projects, the effect of aid on market forces, and the relative weight of multilateral and bilateral aid.

The final conclusion (chapter 10) repeats and expands the broad finding of the book, already outlined in chapter 1.

> Its basic finding is that *the majority of aid is successful in terms of its own objectives*. Over a wide range of countries and sectors aid has made positive and valuable contributions. The report also refutes some of the common criticisms of aid – that it cannot reach the poor, or that it conflicts with development of the private sector.

> This does not mean that all is well with aid. A significant proportion does not succeed. The question is, how this should be judged? ... Considering the difficult circumstances in which aid operates, one might conclude that the record compared well with the average for complex human endeavours.[36]

Cassen thus joins the general consensus that aid is necessary and probably beneficial. But neither he nor any of the other studies I have read really deals with the basic problems posed by Bauer. What would have happened, or might now happen, if there was no aid? Is it really essential for economic development? What effects does aid have on the nature of the political regimes of the recipient countries: does it enable and encourage them to persist in political autocracy and economic perversity? None of these questions is, in fact, answerable. The first is a counter-factual, the second theoretical, the third depends on one's assessment of alternatives. But on the evidence surveyed above at least two things seem clear.

First, aid has not, for most states, been a sufficient means of overcoming the perceived structural obstacles to sustained development on the two-gap theory. Aid has been given to some – notably the NICs of East Asia – with spectacular economic success, at least until 1997–8; but it is arguable that the reasons for this (which will be surveyed in chapter 11) lay more in their domestic arrangements and strategies than in the provision of foreign resources below their commercial cost. Supporters of aid could, of course, answer that the main reason for this limited success lies in the inadequacy of the aid provided: that the rich states have consistently failed to provide the specified proportion of their national incomes: that, given sufficient aid, the whole Third World could be brought to the point of self-sustaining growth. This is arguable but improbable. It assumes a capacity on the part of the recipients, particularly in many states of Black Africa, to make far better use of aid than they have so far shown themselves capable of doing. It also assumes the validity of the developmental approach of the 1960s: that sufficient capital can transform any economy. Few would now regard that as defensible. In short, the case that aid can transform the Third World seems not to have been made.

Secondly, however, there is no doubt that aid has become necessary for the foreseeable future. The reasons for this lie in the position of many Third World countries, particularly those in Black Africa, at the end of the twentieth century. Aid for many of them has long since ceased to perform a primarily developmental function. Ignoring humanitarian aid, which lies outside the present argument, programme aid has

---

[36] Ibid., p. 225. Emphasis in original.

been essential, particularly since the early 1980s, for the economic, and possibly the political, survival of a considerable proportion of the Third World. Although theoretically still given for investment, in practice aid, in addition to commercial borrowing, now enables the poorer states to maintain and sustain at least minimal levels of economic and social activity. It makes it possible for them to limit their huge deficits on both overseas current-account and internal government revenues, and to continue to service the overwhelming burden of their foreign debt. Without aid the whole structure of international credit might collapse, with wholesale default of the poorest states, despite the substantial 'rescheduling' of much of this debt.

Thus aid is no longer charity. It has become intrinsic to the maintenance of the international capitalist economy, a system by which western governments, directly or through multilateral agencies, subsidize debtors so that they can continue to meet their obligations to both public and private creditors. This, of course, is precisely the situation that the colonial powers feared when refusing before the 1930s to subsidize colonial expenditure. It is a direct result of the way in which aid was conceived and expanded after the Second World War.

The argument, then, is that after about 1945 the unprecedented availability of both commercial lending and subsidized intergovernmental aid may have helped some Third World states to increase the rate of their growth, but that for many of them the result has been limited development and heavy indebtedness. Yet aid has, in general, not received the strong criticism often directed at the other important and to some degree novel source of foreign finance – the MNC. Chapter 9 examines the debate over the MNC and in particular considers whether it is beneficial or harmful to the Third World.

9

The Multinational Corporation and Development

Along with aid, FDI was the most important new feature of economic relations between the West and the Third World after about 1945; and the dominant agent of this investment was the multinational corporation (alias multinational or transnational enterprise (TNE), or transnational corporation (TNC), but hereafter MNC).[1] Some idea of the relative importance of this FDI can be derived from the statistics in table 8.1. Taking four years in that table, in 1970 FDI represented 18.3 per cent of total resource flows to developing countries and 45.8 per cent of total private flows. In 1978 the proportions were 13.2 and 26.5 per cent; in 1982 11 and 20.3 per cent; and in 1988 23.6 and 57.8 per cent. Since all these are constant dollars, the variations reflect changing economic circumstances in both the West and the Third World.

It is, however, important to keep this in proportion. The share of the total global FDI inflow of resources that went to the developing countries was always relatively small. Thus in the 1970s developing countries took on average only 24 per cent; in 1980–5 25 per cent;

---

[1] Some of the argument and material in this chapter, and much that had to be excluded, can be found in two essays I have published previously: D. K. Fieldhouse, 'A New Imperial System? The Role of the Multinational Reconsidered', in W. J. Mommsen and J. Osterhammel (eds), *Imperialism and After: Continuities and Discontinuities* (London, 1986), ch. 15; 'The Multinational: A Critique of a Concept', in A. M. Teichova, Levy-Leboyer and H. Nussbaum (eds), *Multilateral Enterprise in Historical Perspective* (Cambridge, 1986), ch. 1.

in 1986–90 17 per cent: the rest of the flow was between developed countries, always both the main providers and the main recipients of FDI. Moreover, the flows to the Third World were largely concentrated in two areas, Latin America and East, South and South-east Asia: Africa never received more than 3 per cent of these flows.[2] Nevertheless, FDI in the form of MNC investment had become an important component of the general flow of resources to the Third World.

If the MNC was thus a conduit for the transfer of resources to the Third World, it may seem surprising that it had, by the 1960s, become a focus of controversy and, for many, a serious threat to both the economic development and the political sovereignty of developing countries. Earlier forms of private investment had almost never been denounced, except where nationalist movements made a foreign-owned public utility or extractive enterprise a target for xenophobic accusations and strategies. Moreover, FDI had existed long before 1945, yet was never then a serious issue in the theory of economic development. This chapter is, therefore, concerned with two main questions.

First, when, and why, did the MNC become a matter of serious debate over its consequences? Secondly, should the MNC be regarded as beneficial or damaging to Third World economic and social development?

1   The Growth of the MNC as a Concept and an Issue

The short answer to the first of these questions is that FDI, and with it the MNC, became an issue between 1938 and the early 1970s because in that period the volume of FDI worldwide, at constant prices, more or less doubled, increasing over six times in current prices, and also because in that period the main investor ceased to be Britain and became the United States, the greatest and feared superpower (see tables 9.1 and 9.2).

FDI and the MNC were not, of course, new in this period. As Mira Wilkins has shown, American firms were setting up manufacturing subsidiaries overseas from the 1860s, perhaps starting with Singer Sewing Machines, which began manufacturing in Scotland in 1867. It was followed before the 1880s by a number of other American firms, particularly in the electrical, chemical and petroleum lines of business. Their common motive was not to export capital but to use their skills more profitably overseas, then exclusively in developed countries that could provide both the local managerial and workbench skills needed and an affluent market.[3]

---

[2] Based on D. Colman and F. Nixson, *Economics of Change in less Developed Countries* (New York, 1994), table 10.7, p. 356.

[3] For the early history of US MNCs, see M. Wilkins, *The Emergence of Multinational Enterprise: American Business Abroad from the Colonial Era to 1914* (Cambridge, Mass., 1970). For post-1914 developments see her *The Maturing of Multinational Enterprise: American Business Abroad from 1914 to 1970* (Cambridge, Mass., 1976).

Britain, the world's largest overseas investor before 1914, was also the largest
direct investor, though it is unclear how much of the 'direct investment'
recorded in tables 9.1 and 9.2 was strictly by MNCs, as contrasted with
traditional forms of portfolio or single enterprise investment. Large firms
such as Lever Brothers had followed the same logic as the Americans of
setting up manufacturing subsidiaries in the more affluent parts of the world,
primarily in order to jump protective import duties and to meet the specific
needs of local markets.[4] Other European countries also set up overseas
subsidiaries, again mostly by companies to exploit their special advantages
more effectively than they could do by exporting their finished product.
In addition to manufacturing, western firms set up subsidiaries for extracting
raw materials, or growing commodities in plantations. It is significant, as is
clear from table 9.2, that Latin America and Asia were major recipients of
FDI in this early period, much of it in extractive industries.

Between the two world wars the flow of FDI slowed up markedly,
owing to depressed international economic conditions and the serious
financial state of most of western Europe. Only the United States, and
surprisingly Italy (though on a much smaller scale), significantly increased
their FDI in constant prices. Thus the great leap forwards came after 1945
and was made by the United States. Wilkins suggests that the main reasons
for this were as follows. Politically, the US government was anxious to
support its anti-communist strategy by investment in other countries, and
provided very favourable tax and other conditions to encourage American
companies to invest overseas. Financially, the huge provision of dollars
through Marshall Aid and the OEEC (later OECD) provided the funds
to finance overseas investment and expanded markets for American products. The overseas dollar surplus provided funds for foreign investment.
Above all, the expansion of world demand stimulated production, and
in no field more than in extraction and refining of minerals, including
petroleum. Conversely, as Europe recovered from the war, American companies were anxious not to lose export markets and saw the opportunity
to preserve these by operating within the protectionist systems of individual
countries and, from 1958, the EEC.[5]

It was primarily this torrent of post-war American FDI that made the
MNC a controversial and conceptual issue. There had been much earlier
analysis of the special features of the MNC, but most writers concentrated on the motives behind FDI and on its effects on developed

---

[4] See e.g. D. K. Fieldhouse, *Unilever Overseas: The Anatomy of a Multinational*
(London, 1978), ch. 2, for detailed studies of pre-1914 Lever manufacturing
enterprises in Australia and South Africa, and also of plantations in the Pacific
and the Belgian Congo.
[5] For detailed analysis of these developments, see Wilkins, *The Maturing of
Multinational Enterprise*, esp. chs 12–14.

Table 9.1 Estimated stock of accumulated foreign direct investment, by country of origin, 1914–1978 ($bn at constant 1972 prices)

Country of origin	1914		1938		1960		1978	
	$bn	%	$bn	%	$bn	%	$bn	%
Developed countries	72.6	100	91.9	100	90.8	98.9	249.0	96.8
North America								
USA	13.5	18.5	25.5	27.7	47.7	52.0	112.1	43.5
Canada	0.7	1.0	2.4	2.7	3.6	4.0	9.1	3.5
West Europe								
UK	32.9	45.5	36.6	39.8	15.7	17.1	30.6	11.9
Germany	7.6	10.5	1.2	1.3	1.2	1.3	21.2	8.2
France	8.8	12.2	8.9	9.5	5.9	6.5	9.9	3.9
Belgium	n.a.	n.a.	n.a.	n.a.	n.a.	n.a.	3.1	1.2
Italy					2.9	3.2	2.2	0.9
Netherlands	6.9	8.7	12.2	13.3	7.3	7.9	15.8	6.1
Switzerland					2.9	3.2	18.5	7.2
Sweden					0.6	0.6	4.0	1.6
Other developed countries								
Russia	1.5	2.1	1.6	1.7	neg.		neg.	
Japan	0.1	0.1	2.6	2.8	0.7	0.8	17.8	6.9
Others	0.9	1.3	1.0	1.1	2.2	2.4	4.7	1.8
LDCs	neg.		neg.		1.0	1.1	12.5	3.2
TOTAL	72.6	100	91.9	100	91.8	100	257.4	100

The investments of Italy, the Netherlands, Switzerland and Sweden are combined for 1914 and 1938.

n.a. = not available.

neg. = negligible.

Source: based on J. H. Dunning, 'Changes in the Level and Structure of International Production: The Last One hundred Years', in M. Casson (ed.), *The Growth of International Business* (London, 1983), table 5.1, p. 87. Current prices in the original have been adjusted by the implicit price deflator for US GNP, US department of Commerce, *National Statistical Income and Product Accounts of the US, 1929–82* (Washington, 1986).

countries, rather than on its significance for the Third World. Criticism tended to focus on the balance-of-payments effects, rather than on economic or social consequences.[6] The common and central feature of

---

[6] Some of this literature is summarized in my paper 'The Multinational: A Critique of a Concept'. Among leading earlier theoretical analyses are the following: A. Plummer, *International Combines in Modern History* (London, 1934); R. W. Liefmann, *International Cartels, Combines and Trusts* (London, 1927), and *Cartels, Concerns and Trusts* (London, 1932); E. T. Penrose, 'Limits to the Size

most of this early analysis of FDI was that, in principle, the presence of an MNC was thought likely to be beneficial to the host country. The main 'direct' benefits would be an increase in the production, tax capacity and wealth of the host country, while the 'indirect' benefits would include the importation of technology and the demonstration effect of more efficient foreign firms.

For none of these early writers, except for Byé, did the MNC, therefore, seem a serious threat. The root of most later debate over the role of the MNC in the Third World therefore lies in the genesis of a quite different approach to the MNC, one which sees it as essentially a threat rather than a potential benefit to the host country and may concentrate on its social, nationalistic and ideological, rather than purely economic, effects. This in turn was to stem from an analysis of the special nature of the MNC and its propensities, and can be dated back to the later 1950s and early 1960s.

The germ of such an approach can be found in three publications by Edith Penrose – two articles in 1955 and 1956, and a book in 1959.[7] Penrose was not overtly hostile to the MNC but argued that it was innate in any large corporation to expand to the limit of its managerial capacity, first at home, then possibly abroad. Moreover, once established abroad, the subsidiary was likely to develop life and logic of its own: 'growth will continue in response to the development of its own internal resources and the opportunities presented in its new environment.'[8] Thus the MNC could be seen as a self-creating and permanently expanding octopus.

While Penrose was developing this concept of the international firm, the French economist Maurice Byé was evolving the idea that the key

---

and Growth of the Firm', *American Economic History Review*, 45, 2 (1955), pp. 531–43, 'Foreign Investment and the Growth of the Firm', *Economic Journal*, 66 (1956), pp. 64–99, and *Theory of the Growth of the Firm* (Oxford, 1959); A. D. Chandler, *Strategy and Structure* (Cambridge, Mass., 1962); H. W. Arndt, 'Overseas Borrowing – the New Model', *Economic Record*, 33 (1957), pp. 247–61; (Sir) D. MacDougall, 'The Benefits and Costs of Private Foreign Investment from Abroad', *Economic Record*, 36 (1960), pp. 13–35; M. Byé, 'Self-financed Multiterritorial Units and their Time Horizon', *International Economic Papers*, 8 (London, 1958), pp. 147–78; J. H. Dunning, *American Investment in British Manufacturing Industry* (London, 1958). Two standard textbooks on the MNC which have good bibliographies to the later 1970s are N. Hood and S. Young, *The Economics of the Multinational Enterprise* (London, 1979), and R. E. Caves, *Multinational Enterprise and Economic Analysis* (Cambridge, 1982). Colman and Nixson, *Economics of Change*, also has a good bibliography to the late 1980s on pp. 389–94.
[7] See n. 6.
[8] Penrose, 'Foreign Investment and the Growth of the Firm', p. 70.

Table 9.2 Estimated stock of accumulated foreign direct investment, by recipient country or area, 1914–1978 ($bn at constant 1972 prices)

Recipient country	1914		1938		1960		1978	
	$bn	%	$bn	%	$bn	%	$bn	%
Developed countries	26.6	37.2	29.1	34.3	53.4	67.3	167.7	69.6
North America								
USA	7.4	10.3	6.3	7.4	11.1	13.9	28.2	11.7
Canada	4.1	5.7	8.0	9.4	18.7	23.7	28.8	11.9
Europe								
West Europe	5.6	7.8	6.3	7.4	18.2	22.9	90.8	37.7
(UK)	1.0	1.4	2.4	2.9	7.3	9.2	21.6	9.0
Other European	7.1	9.9	1.4	1.6	neg.		neg.	
Australasia and South Africa	2.3	3.2	6.8	8.0	5.2	6.6	15.9	6.6
Japan	0.2	0.2	0.3	0.4	0.1	0.2	4.0	1.7
Developing countries of which:	44.9	62.8	55.7	65.7	25.6	32.3	66.9	27.8
Latin America	23.3	32.7	26.1	30.8	8.5	15.6	34.9	14.5
Africa	4.6	6.4	6.3	7.4	4.4	5.5	7.4	3.1
Asia	14.9	20.9	21.2	25.0	5.9	7.5	16.8	7.0
(China)	5.6	7.8	4.9	5.8	neg.		neg.	
(India and Ceylon)	2.3	3.2	4.7	5.6	1.6	2.0	1.6	0.7
Middle East	2.0	2.8	2.2	2.6	2.2	2.8	5.5	2.3
International and unallocated	neg.		n.a.	n.a.			6.3	2.6
TOTAL	71.5	100	84.3	100	79.3	100	240.9	100

n.a. = not available.
neg. = negligible.

Source: Dunning, 'Changes in the Level and Structure of International Production', table 5.2, p. 88.

feature of such firms was their ability to transcend the limitations inherent in geographical boundaries and normal economic and political constraints. In his 'Self-financed Multi-territorial Units and their Time Horizon', originally published in French in 1957, he defined his 'large unit' as 'an organized set of resources depending on a single decision centre capable of autonomous activities in the market'.[9] Its special feature was its ability to control many factors internally that would be exogenous

[9] Byés, 'Self-financed Multiterritorial Units', p. 146.

to smaller firms: for example, capital formation and planning rates of output. His evidence was drawn mainly from the big American petroleum companies, which, he said, planned their international operations so that they could maximize profits over the long term, which they did by using both high-cost American and low-cost Middle Eastern sources. On this example he based a critique of the general effects of large international companies on host, and particularly less-developed, countries under three heads.

First, in relation to the host countries' balance of payments, the MNC (assumed to be an extractive or export-oriented enterprise) arguably determined the rate of exports and the use of export earnings, since it controlled their main source of foreign exchange. Nor did the MNC compensate by importing significant amounts of capital: most expansion was financed out of reinvested local earnings. All investment decisions of this kind were autonomous to the MNC: 'it operates like a world distribution centre of capital funds for its subsidiaries.'[10]

Secondly, the MNC generated a 'dual economy' in host countries. It did not invest significant proportions of its savings there, nor buy many of its inputs locally. This pointed to the concept of the enclave and lack of linkages with the local economy.

Finally, Byé held that the MNC had adverse non-economic effects on its host. In its defence against the MNC the host government would have to use state power to create local investment and development, which would give the state an excessive hold over the society and economy.

The year 1960 may be regarded as a turning point in perceptions of the MNC: coincidentally it was in that year that the name itself was coined. Minting it was claimed by the one-time head of the Tennessee Valley Authority, by then head of an investment bank, David E. Lilienthal.[11] Within a year or two the term had slipped into general use. The important point, however, is that the very popularity of the term reflected a now general belief that this type of large corporation had unique features and presented special practical and theoretical problems distinct from those associated with the traditional export of capital through loans and portfolio investment. The great debate over the MNC was under way.

[10] Ibid., p. 171.
[11] See Fieldhouse, 'The Multinational: A Critique of a Concept', pp. 9–11, for the evidence on Lilienthal's claim to paternity. There is a disparity between Lilienthal's published journal, *The Harvest Years 1959–63* (New York, 1971), where he states on p. 86 that 'my talk at the Carnegie Tech. in [April] 1960 ... was the first time the word had been used; I rather think I coined it ...', and a claim by Howe Martyn that the term had previously been used by Lilienthal in 1958. See H. Martyn, 'Development of the Multinational Corporation', in A. A. Said and L. R. Simons (eds), *The New Sovereigns: Multinational Corporations as World Powers* (Englewood Cliffs, NJ, 1975), pp. 33–4. I owe this recondite piece of information to Mira Wilkins.

Possibly the most important single conceptual contribution to the later debate over the impact on LDCs of the MNC (though he did not then use the term) and to its demonization was made by Stephen Hymer. His Ph.D. thesis, 'The International Operations of National Firms: A Study of Direct Foreign Investment', was completed at the Massachusetts Institute of Technology under the supervision of Charles Kindleberger in 1960. It was published, under the same title, only in 1976, though it was widely read in typescript and had considerable influence before then.[12] Hymer, a Canadian, was not originally a radical, but a conventional North American liberal who believed in an anti-trust approach to large enterprises of all types in order to counter monopoly and promote competition within a market economy. The really original element in the study was the argument that the primary function of FDI was not to obtain higher returns by investing overseas (as was normal in portfolio investment) but to exploit fully control of investment and technology outside the home country of a large firm in order to obtain a monopoly rent.

There was little in this that was not acceptable to conventional neoclassical economists. But by the later 1960s Hymer had become a Marxist; and it was from this standpoint that he developed a more radical and very influential critique of the MNC in a series of articles which were subsequently collected and published after his accidental death (in 1974) in 1978.[13]

Hymer's later central message was that, although MNCs might increase wealth throughout the world by their efficient use of resources, the benefits would go mainly to the home countries of these firms, while the rest of the world paid the price of their monopoly profits. This was, of course, a version of the 'core–periphery' concept, then being developed by others in relation to trade, but now applied to production and the extraction of minerals. The result would be a hierarchical world order, as big corporations developed a complex division of functions within individual firms and throughout the international economy. Thus:

A regime of multinational corporations would tend to produce a hierarchical division of labor between geographical regions corresponding to the vertical division of labor within the firm. It would tend to centralize high-level decision-making occupations in a few key cities in the advanced countries, surrounded by a number of regional sub-capitals, and confine the rest of the world to lower levels of activity and income, that is, to the

---

[12] By MIT Press: S. Hymer, *The International Operations of National Firms: A study of Direct Foreign Investment* (Cambridge, Mass., 1976). Ironically, in view of its later influence, it is said that the Press originally turned the book down on the grounds that it was not sufficiently original.

[13] In R. B. Cohen et al. (eds), *The Multinational: A Radical Approach* (Cambridge, 1979).

status of towns and villages in a New Imperial System. Income, status, authority, and consumption patterns would radiate out from these centers along a declining curve, and the existing pattern would be complex, just as the structure of the corporation is complex, but the basic relationship between different countries would be one of superior and subordinate, head office and branch plant.[14]

Nevertheless, possibly because of his Marxist views on the nature of capitalism, Hymer came to believe that, despite its apparent strength, the MNC's foundations were weak and could not be sustained indefinitely. This led him to suggest (in 1971) that 'one could easily argue that the age of the Multinational Corporation is at its end rather than at its beginning'.[15]

By the time these later ideas were published, the MNC had long since ceased to be treated with the dispassion it had received from writers in the 1950s, and had become an intellectual and emotional battlefield. It would be impossible and inappropriate here to survey the vast literature that emerged, but it is necessary briefly to show how the MNC came to be regarded by many as a threat rather than a potential contribution to international well-being, yet by others as a necessary contemporary means of transferring wealth and skills.

Broadly the literature falls into four main categories: theoretical studies of the growth of the firm; popular, often journalistic, alarmist material; ideological anti-capitalist interpretations; and serious analysis by development economists and others concerned with the impact of the MNC on the Third World. The first of these will be ignored here: it is highly technical and relates to the economics of large corporations rather than to the effects of FDI on developing countries. The second and third will be summarized very briefly to indicate how the MNC gained its once almost universally bad reputation. The real issues will be tackled under the final head.

First, the popular alarmists and publicists. Inevitably, once a new and potentially emotive concept has been born, an instant literature is generated. It is said that the first widely noticed debunker of the MNC was the French journalist J.-J. Servan Schreiber, who published *Le Défi américain* in 1967.[16] His argument picked up the then common anti-Americanism of Gaullist France. Pointing to the rapid growth of US corporate investment in Europe after 1950, which he wrongly ascribed to the creation of the EEC in 1958, he argued that this gave the Americans a dangerous dominance in the critical field of high technology, which they kept at home. To compete, Europe must collaborate to match this technical innovation.

---

[14] Ibid., pp. 157–8.
[15] Ibid., p. 72.
[16] J.-J. Servan Schreiber, *Le Défi américain* (Paris, 1967; Eng. edn, *The American Challenge* (New York, 1968)).

The book, though basically misleading, stimulated a rash of similar attacks. Moreover, it encouraged the idea, later widely applied to LDCs, that the MNC might cauterize indigenous innovative development, leaving the host countries dependent on an alien source of modern technology. Among the better-known and sometimes respectable attempts to follow this lead were Louis Turner's *Invisible Empires*;[17] K. Levitt's *Silent Surrender: The Multinationals and Canada*;[18] (Lord) C. Tungendhat's *The Multinationals*;[19] Anthony Sampson's *The Sovereign State of I.T.&T.*;[20] and R. J. Barnet and R. E. Muller's *Global Reach*.[21]

These popular writers took much of their argument from the third of these groups, ideologues of the Left, who, once the concept of the MNC had been publicized, quickly adopted it into the mainstream of Marxism as a modern development of Lenin's 'monopoly capitalism'. Probably the first of any significance was Baran and Sweezy's *Monopoly Capitalism*.[22] Their lead was followed by many other Marxists, notably F. Mandel, R. Murray, Bill Warren, R. E. Rowthorn and H. Magdoff;[23] though it was probably Hymer, more than any other Marxist of this period, who established a coherent Marxist critique of the MNC in a series of essays published between 1970 and his death in 1974.[24]

But there was also, by 1984, a quite different and, to many of the orthodox, heretical Marxist position on the MNC and its effects on Third World countries. Bill Warren, in his posthumously published *Imperialism: Pioneer of Capitalism*, whose argument on colonialism was summarized in chapter 6, and Arghiri Emmanuel in *Appropriate or Underdeveloped Technology?* both criticized the conventional Marxist assumption that the MNC, as the agent of western capitalism, was bound to cause immiseration in the Third World.[25] Both, from different standpoints, held that MNCs were part of a historically inevitable and

[17] L. Turner, *Invisible Empires* (London, 1970).
[18] K. Levitt, *Silent Surrender: The Multinationals and Canada* (Toronto, 1970).
[19] (Lord) C. Tugendhat, *The Multinationals* (London, 1973).
[20] A. Sampson, *The Sovereign State of I.T. & T.* (London, 1973).
[21] R. J. Barnet and R. E. Muller, *Global Reach* (New York, 1974).
[22] P. Baran and P. Sweezy, *Monopoly Capitalism* (New York, 1966).
[23] e.g. F. Mandel, 'International Capitalism and "Supra-Nationality"' in R. Miliband and J. Savile (eds), *The Socialist Reporter* (London, 1967), and his *Late Capitalism* (1972; Eng. edn, London, 1975); and the collection of essays by Murray, Warren and others in H. Radice (ed.), *International Firms and Modern Imperialism* (Harmondsworth, 1975).
[24] See, in particular, R. E. Rowthorn and S. Hymer, *International Big Business: A Study of Comparative Growth* (Cambridge, 1971).
[25] B. Warren, *Imperialism: Pioneer of Capitalism*, ed. J. Sender (London, 1980); A. Emmanuel, *Appropriate or Underdeveloped Technology?* (Paris, 1981; Eng. edn, Chichester, 1982).

economically essential process of establishing capitalism in LDCs. While admittedly producing class stratification, MNCs also generated wealth; and ultimately true socialism and affluence could come only as the end product of this process. Emmanuel in particular argued that technology was the key to all economic development and that anything short of the latest technology was inadequate. The MNC was the best means by which an LDC could acquire the best modern technology. There were risks, owing to the size and efficiency of the MNC; but there were equal risks in alternative strategies; and in any case the MNC was by far the best means of transferring the practical skill and know-how modern manufacturing demanded through its demonstration effect. Third World governments should, therefore, use the MNC, but aim to harness and control it, minimizing its potentially bad effects while making full use of its ability to introduce modern technology and efficient business management.

The influence of the more conventional Marxist critics of the MNC on Latin American 'dependency' theorists, who had previously shown very little interest in this phenomenon in their analysis of the causes of poverty, was striking. The concept of a new international division of labour and global hierarchy being established by the MNC provided these dependency theorists with at least a partial explanation of the genesis of what they had called 'underdevelopment'. A. G. Frank, for example, incorporated the MNC into his general synthesis, *Dependent Accumulation and Underdevelopment*.[26] As early as 1972 O. Sunkel had adopted Hymer's concept of an international hierarchy, and argued that MNCs 'contribute significantly to shaping the nature of the economy, society and polity, a kind of "fifth column", as it were'.[27] From the late 1960s especially MNCs had moved from exporting commodities to controlling key sectors of the domestic economy. They tended to monopolize rather than diffuse their skills and technology. They blocked opportunities for indigenous enterprise. Their 'complete package' of capital, skills, etc. was likely to be 'inappropriate' and to have weak linkages with a local economy. They had undesirable ability to influence consumption patterns.

[26] A. G. Frank, *Dependent Accumulation and Underdevelopment* (London and New York, 1978).
[27] O. Sunkel, 'Big Business and *dependencia*: A Latin American View', *Foreign Affairs*, 50, 3 (1972), p. 519. Other influential publications by Latin American dependency theorists on the MNC include: T. dos Santos, 'The Crisis of Development Theory and the Problem of Dependence in Latin America', in H. Bernstein (ed.), *Underdevelopment and Development* (London, 1973); F. H. Cardoso, 'Dependent Capitalist Development in Latin America', *New Left Review*, 74 (1972), pp. 83–95; C. V. Vaitsos, 'Bargaining and the Distribution of Returns in the Purchase of Technology by Developing Countries', *Institute of Development Studies Bulletin*, 3, 1 (1970), pp. 16–23.

They could use monopoly power to extract excessive profits, much of them hidden and protected from local taxation by transfer pricing. Such accusations were part of the common currency of radical criticism of the MNC in the 1970s.

But not all Latin Americans agreed that the MNC was all loss to its hosts, or that there was a simple alternative. Celso Furtado, for instance, took a much less deterministic view. Posing the question 'would the Latin American countries have registered the high rates of growth characterising their manufacturing sectors in the post-war period if they had not been able to count on the effective cooperation of international groups, primarily North American, with considerable industrial experience and easy access to the sources of financing', he suggested that the answer must be 'no'.[28]

This points to an important division within the ranks not only of Latin American theorists but more generally among critics of the MNC by the later 1970s. While the extreme and hard Left had, from the later 1960s, welcomed the concept of the MNC as a reinforcement of their general critique of capitalism and the export of capital, others, who can broadly be described as 'reformist' rather than 'dogmatic', while accepting some of the criticisms made, also argued that, if tamed, the MNC could be a useful agent of technological transfer. This, indeed, was the position adopted by most serious students of the MNC, particularly development economists, during the 1970s and early 1980s. They constitute the fourth and last of the groups to be examined here.

Largely because of the growth of that brand of 'development economics' from the 1950s that concentrated on the assumed special 'structural' problems of LDCs, it was inevitable that its practitioners should build the MNC, once it had been conceptualized, into their models. It was around 1969 that the first serious studies of the role of the MNC in the Third World began to be published, with J. N. Behrman's *Some Patterns in the Rise of the Multinational Enterprise*,[29] C. P. Kindleberger's *American Business Abroad*[30] and R. E. Rolfe's *The International*

---

[28] C. Furtado, *Economic Development of Latin America* (1970; rev. edn, Cambridge, 1976), pp. 202, 209. But Furtado expressed substantial reservations about Emmanuel's arguments in favour of the MNC as the best or only vector for the transfer of technology and know-how. In his 'Comments by Celso Furtado', made at the conference on 10 Oct. 1980 when Emmanuel's theory was launched, he criticized many of Emmanuel's arguments, emphasizing particularly the vital role of the host country in making imported technology work. See Emmanuel, *Appropriate or Underdeveloped Technology?*, pp. 119–25.

[29] J. N. Behrman, *Some Patterns in the Rise of the Multinational Enterprise* (Chapel Hill, NC, 1968).

[30] C. P. Kindleberger, *American Business Abroad* (New Haven, 1969).

Corporation;[31] and only from 1971 that the main and continuing debate really got going. It is not proposed to list even the main participants in this debate, but to use the sensitive survey of the intellectual issues in S. Lall and R. Streeten's *Foreign Investment, Transnationals and Developing Countries* as a guide to how the main issues had come to be seen by the later 1970s.[32]

Their starting point was the proposition that, in assessing the impact of MNCs on LDCs, both the normal profit-and-loss measurements of the corporate accountant and the neo-Paretian welfare paradigm (the maximization of the economic welfare of the community) were inappropriate. The weakness of what Lall elsewhere[33] called 'the business–school approach' lay in the weakness of the following assumptions: that FDI must increase the host country's growth; that patterns of growth characteristic of an open-market economy are desirable in LDCs; that international economic integration is good for all parties; and that the 'externalities' resulting from MNC activity, such as the dissemination of skills in management, marketing, finance and technology, were good, but that other externalities, which may be less desirable, were economically unimportant. Equally inapplicable were conventional welfare assumptions, derived from developed western societies: that there was a basic harmony of interests in a society; that individual preferences were beyond question; and that the state was neutral as between social groups, benevolently pursuing the 'national interest'. In short, what might be good and true in well-run developed countries might not be true in the Third World. Along these lines they, in company with many other development economists, therefore argued that one must approach the impact of the MNC on LDCs with initial suspicion. Even if its activities raised the national income, 'it would not necessarily follow that economic welfare ... is increased, unless a number of other conditions are also satisfied'.[34]

Not all development economists agreed with this cautious approach, or with the underlying assumption that most LDC governments lack the will or ability to assess the pros and cons of FDI. In particular, I. M. D. Little, a pioneer of welfare theory and the cost–benefit approach

---

[31] R. E. Rolfe, *The International Corporation* (Paris, 1969).

[32] S. Lall and R. Streeten, *Foreign Investment, Transnationals and Developing Countries* (London, 1977). There are, of course, many other somewhat similar analyses of the radical or national case against the MNC. See e.g. V. N. Balasubramanyam, *Multinational Enterprises in the Third World* (London, 1980), and Caves, *Multinational Enterprise and Economic Analysis*, which adopt a very similar approach.

[33] S. Lall, *Developing Countries and the International Economy* (London, 1981).

[34] Lall and Streeten, *Foreign Investment*, p. 53.

to Third World economic development, provided a different critique of the MNC in Third World countries in 1982 as part of his general survey of the theory and practice of economic development since 1945.[35]

Little made two central points. First, any adverse effects MNCs may have in modern, post-colonial Third World countries are likely to be the responsibility of host governments, since it is normally their incompetence, anxiety for prestigious industrialization or 'autonomy', and the ill-advised macroeconomic policies they adopt as a consequence, that create conditions under which foreign firms can operate in ways that might be regarded as 'undesirable'. Secondly, there is in many cases very little difference between the way in which subsidiaries of MNCs and locally owned enterprises operate: that is, the mere fact of an MNC being foreign is not in itself a reliable guide to its economic effects. Little, therefore, dismisses as intrinsically unimportant many of the adverse 'external' effects pointed to by other development economists and radicals. Thus the threat of the MNC to 'national sovereignty' is merely popular alarmism. This does not, however, mean that MNCs are necessarily beneficial: merely that states must carefully test particular investment proposals, as Little himself did in his seminal study of the social costs and benefits of the Kulai Palm Estate in Malaysia.[36]

Little's critique, using the same basic tools as many other development economists, effectively deflates the more emotive arguments of hostile critics of the MNC. Its main effect is to reduce the whole question of FDI to a straightforward and entirely open cost–benefit calculation. In relation to the argument of this chapter, this implies that a main trend in the analysis of the MNC since the early 1960s has been in a wrong direction. The MNC should not be assumed to be unique simply because its activities transcend national frontiers. Its effects can properly be assessed in terms applicable to any form of productive investment, essentially as was done by economists before the concept was invented or taken up.

It is now possible to turn from the evolving concept of the MNC to its measurable economic effects on the Third World.

2 Costs and Benefits of the MNC for the Third World

By the later 1970s the character of the MNC had been widely debated and most of the arguments still in play two decades later had been ventilated. It will, therefore, be convenient to take as a starting point one of the many generally similar published formulations of the contrasting

[35] I. M. D. Little, *Economic Development: Theory, Policy, and International Relations* (New York, 1982), chs 10, 12.
[36] I. M. D. Little and D. G. Tipping, *Social Cost Benefit Analysis of the Kulai Oil Palm Estate* (Paris, 1972).

positions: that by T. J. Biersteker, who is primarily a specialist in the economic development of Nigeria, but who based his analysis of the impact of FDI and foreign enterprise there on a broad overview of the arguments as they had evolved in the previous two decades.[37] These can be summarized briefly, since they have already been noted in the work of others.

Biersteker divided approaches to the economic effects of MNC in the Third World into three broad groups: the 'conventional' economic approach (what Lall called 'the business-school approach'); the critical or radical approach; and a 'neo-conventional perspective'. He summarized each of these as follows.

The 'conventional' approach emphasizes the benefits the MNC may bring to an LDC. These are divided into direct and indirect benefits. Among the direct benefits are a package, which includes capital, technology and skills that would not otherwise be available or would have to be bought separately by the host country, possibly at greater cost. The MNC creates new jobs and makes a better or wider range of consumer products, so broadening the host market and stimulating production. There are also beneficial indirect effects. The MNC may energize local factors of production and have a multiplier effect. Its exporting activities may damp down prices and inflation. It will break local indigenous monopolies by increasing competition in the host market. More broadly, it will generate more taxes for the host government: foreign firms tend to be more honest fiscally because more vulnerable. They act as agents of change in lethargic economies. They counter rampant nationalism.[38] Thus, in principle, the MNC should increase the wealth of the host country, though a cost–benefit analysis is necessary to determine whether gains outweigh losses.

In the opposite corner the critics argue that whatever benefits the MNC may bring are normally outweighed by the consequential disadvantages. Biersteker lists these under two main heads, first- and second-order limitations, each with a number of subdivisions.

The main 'first-order' limitation concerns the alleged value of capital imports. This is exaggerated. MNCs in fact bring in little capital, raising much of it from local sources. Once established, the outflow of dividends, royalties, etc. outweighs the inflow. The potential benefit in terms of foreign exchange is small because most industrial MNCs restrict

[37] See T. J. Biersteker, *Distortion or Development? Contending Perspectives on the Multinational Corporation* (Cambridge, Mass., 1978). See also his later *Multinationals, the State, and Control of the Nigerian Economy* (Princeton, 1987), which concentrates on the reaction of foreign firms to the two Nigerian Enterprise Promotion Decrees of the 1970s and the extent to which they attempted to evade them.

[38] G. L. Reuber and Associates, *Private Foreign Investment in Development* (Oxford, 1973), provides a similar 'conventional' analysis.

their sales to the host market rather than exporting. They evade local taxation and facilitate repatriation of profits through abuse of royalties, licences and patents, and they use the technique of 'transfer pricing' to reduce taxes, either at home or in the host country.[39] Companies may use 'tie-in' clauses in their deal with the host to ensure that imported components come from the parent company. Importation of components, etc., reduces and may eliminate links with the host economy, making the subsidiary an insulated enclave.

Biersteker then lists a number of alleged adverse 'second-order' effects of the MNC. Local enterprises are displaced, taken over, or discouraged: MNCs often establish themselves by buying out local enterprises (between 1958 and 1967 42 per cent of US MNCs did this in Latin America), and may do so by using blocked local profits. Once there, MNCs may destroy local competition through their superior efficiency or their ability to manipulate the market. They tend to pre-empt the limited local supply of skilled labour by paying higher wages and so force up labour costs. MNCs may have a higher propensity to export profits than indigenous entrepreneurs. Overall their dominance of the host market will tend to increase its dependence on the West.

Another second-order problem relates to the value and nature of the technology imported by the MNC. In fact there is a limited transfer of technology and little increase in local technological capacity, since MNCs do virtually all the research and development work at home. Moreover, much of the imported technology is 'inappropriate'. It comes 'packaged' (so the host takes it or leaves it), is based on calculation of labour costs in the home country, and is therefore commonly capital intensive. This is quite unsuitable in countries with severe unemployment or under-employment problems, which would prefer more labour-intensive strategies. Such capital intensity in turn discourages backward linkages into the host economy. A related problem is taste transfer. Because the MNC makes and promotes goods designed for western consumers, they will create an artificial demand in the LDC for 'inappropriate' consumer goods: the classic highly publicized example was promotion of milk powder for babies in countries where mothers could not sterilize bottles and other utensils.

Another alleged secondary effect of the MNC is its impact on social structures. The company depends heavily on alliance with local elites, 'compradors' in the term borrowed from earlier European dealings with

---

[39] In its simplest form transfer pricing may involve marking up the invoices for goods brought into the host country so as to increase the accounting costs of production and so reduce local profits and taxes. Conversely, if company taxation is higher in the home than the host country, the MNC can artifically increase its taxable profits in the host so as to minimize the sums transferred home. There is a good exposition of the wider issue in Hood and Young, *The Economics of Multinational Enterprise*, pp. 107–10.

China. These can bias the policies of host governments through their political influence. Moreover, indigenous employees can be 'displaced' by high wages and new loyalties and become indoctrinated to the ethos of the foreign firm. These higher wages in turn affect local income distribution. They exacerbate the divisions between the rich and the poor, and also between town and country. They may result in an upward wage spiral and inflation.

The obvious contrast between these two approaches to the MNC is that the first is concerned almost entirely with its economic effects, while the second not only minimizes the economic benefits but concentrates on a wide range of allegedly adverse secondary, often social or cultural, effects. It is important to recognize that these defects are based on overtly normative assumptions. They all derive from the general consensus of the 1960s concerning the appropriate pattern of development in an LDC, which was considered in chapter 2. This should include industrialization, but it should be carried out as far as possible by the government or indigenous entrepreneurs of the country concerned. It should adopt techniques and technology, and make goods 'appropriate' to that society. The modern sector should pull the rest of the economy upward through its backward linkages, using local, not imported, inputs. Since the long-term aim was maximum autonomy, it was critical that the country should be able to develop its own technical and managerial skills, and not rely on those imported from the West. Since there was assumed to be a surplus of labour, industry must be labour intensive, and not capital intensive. In short, the character and speed of economic development must be determined by these partly non-economic criteria. Therefore, the MNC, interested only in economic efficiency and profits, was a threat to the development economists' blueprint.

There might, therefore, appear to be no middle ground between the 'business-school' and the 'radical' or 'nationalist' position. Biersteker, however, suggests that a compromise position had been worked out by the Harvard Multinational Enterprise Project, led by Raymond Vernon, originator of the 'product-cycle' theory of FDI and author of much published material on the MNC.[40] Their general approach, which Biersteker labels 'the neo-conventional perspective', was based on the

---

[40] See, in particular, R. Vernon, *Sovereignty at Bay: The Multinational Spread of US Enterprises* (New York, 1971); *Restrictive Business Practices* (New York, 1972); *Storm over the Multinationals: The Real Issues* (London, 1977). Vernon's product-cycle theory, in brief, suggested that a new invention will initially be exploited at high cost in a rich country, but that over time it will be produced more widely and cheaply and ultimately, as it loses its originality, in many countries, selling on price. This may result in the originating firm setting up production facilities overeseas, and so becoming an MNC.

assumptions that, in purely economic terms, MNCs do make a large contribution to global welfare by increasing production and wealth; that much of the radical critique was based on theory rather than fact; but that not all parties to transactions between MNCs and host countries benefit equally or indeed at all. The greatest problems were political and psychological, a composite of fear and jealousy of such alien and powerful organizations. The radical critique was, moreover, based on a counterfactual, that LDCs could do just as well without FDI. This was unproven and intrinsically improbable.

These three approaches, as defined by Biersteker, broadly cover the range of attitudes that had evolved towards the MNC by the later 1970s, and few radically new arguments have emerged since then. The main problem was and remains to decide which, if any, of them fits the facts. Is the MNC the modern equivalent of trade in the nineteenth century, a means of enabling less-developed economies to exploit the benefits of comparative costs and 'vent for surplus', a conduit for the transmission of wealth and the means of transferring wealth from the West to the Third World? Or is it the contemporary device by which the West exploits LDCs, consigning them to a subordinate role in the international hierarchy of capitalism?

It is as impossible to provide a firm answer to these questions as it is to determine whether aid is a means of promoting development or of creating pauperized dependence. Once again the question presupposes an unprovable counter-factual: that Third World countries would be better or worse off if the MNC did not exist. To attack the problem one can approach it either from the standpoint of particular industries and individual companies, or from that of one or more LDCs. Neither approach will provide a decisive general answer. One cannot generalize from individual examples of companies or countries; and in any case the form in which the questions are put will always influence the result.[41]

It is, therefore, proposed to adopt a different approach. Let us assume, in common with Arndt and most non–Marxist economists and analysts since the later 1950s, that FDI and its main agent, the MNC, must, in principle, provide 'direct' benefits to the host country. This is because

[41] There are a large number of detailed studies of the operation of individual MNCS in particular countries. For two examples of how difficult it is to decide what effects an MNC may have in a host country see the careful study by R. Montavon, *The Role of Multinational Companies in Latin America: A Case Study in Mexico* (Farnborough, 1979), which studies the activities and economic effects of a French food manufacturer, the Danone Mexico Corporation, there in the 1960 and 1970s; and also M. Aruda, H. de Souza and C. Alfonso, *Multinationals in Brazil* (Toronto, 1975), which examines a number of foreign ventures in some detail.

they bring in capital, technology and technical skills that would not otherwise be available in the host country. The result must be an increase in production, productivity and the national income. Hence the MNC must be accepted as a contribution by the West to the development of the Third World.

The main reason, as has been seen, why radicals have challenged this general conclusion is that they claim that the 'indirect' or 'secondary' effects of FDI may neutralize or submerge these 'direct' benefits. They may grant an overall increase in wealth but still claim that other consequences are so unfavourable that they outweigh this benefit. Let us, therefore, approach the problem by asking whether these alleged undesirable by-products of FDI outweigh its demonstrable benefits, and if so whether it is possible to arrive at a crude cost–benefit assessment.

In doing so it will be convenient to divide the MNCs into two broad categories. First, there are manufacturing firms, which have provided the great majority of new FDI since the Second World War and with which most of the critical literature is concerned. Manufacturing MNCs in turn divide into two categories: those which are export oriented ('offshore' subsidiaries) and those, the great majority, which are engaged in production for the domestic market of the host country, that is ISI. The following discussion will concentrate mainly on the latter.

Secondly, there are firms engaged in extraction of raw materials, or the production of agricultural commodities, commonly through plantations. Although probably a majority of western FDI was in these activities as late as the 1950s, thereafter they formed a rapidly diminishing proportion. Extraction will, therefore, be dealt with after manufacturing and more briefly. Plantations, which were always a very small proportion of western FDI and were mostly in decline or taken over by host governments or nationals by the 1950s, will have to be ignored for reasons of space.[42]

---

[42] There is, however, a considerable literature on the foreign-owned plantations, particularly those of American companies in Latin America. The most influential radical study is probably G. L. Beckford, *Persistent Poverty: Underdevelopment in Plantation Economies of the Third Word* (New York, 1972). Its antithesis is G. E. Graham with I. Floering, *The Modern Plantation in the Third World* (London, 1984). Other more specific country or crop studies include: J. Martinnez-Acier, *Haciendas, Plantations, and Collective Farms* (London, 1977) (on Cuba); J. H. Drabble, *Rubber in Malaya, 1876–1922* (Oxford, 1973); C. Barlow, *The Natural Rubber Industry: Its Development, Technology and Economy in Malaysia* (Kuala Lumpur, 1978); C. Geertz, *Agricultural Involution: The Process of Ecological Change in Indonesia* (Berkeley and Los Angeles, 1963); G. C. Allen and A. G. Donnithorne, *Western Enterprise in Indonesia and Malaya* (London, 1957); Fieldhouse, *Unilever Overseas*, chs 8, 9, and *Merchant Capital and Economic Decolonization: The United Africa Company 1929–1987* (Oxford, 1994), ch. 5.

The manufacturing MNC

One of the most useful surveys of the validity of the radical critique of the manufacturing MNC was made by Lall and Streeten, who claim to write from a moderate nationalist position.[43] Their findings were based on a survey undertaken for UNCTAD between 1970 and 1973 and were based on evidence from six host countries, not from the foreign firms. The countries covered and the number of foreign firms investigated in each were as follows: Jamaica, 11; Kenya, 8; India, 53; Iran, 16; Colombia, 56; Malaysia, 15. While these covered a wide range of different regions and types of host economy, it is important to note that only one was in Black Africa, and that virtually all were import substituting, not export oriented. All these countries were then generally favourable to FDI, though in different degrees. None provided a special fiscal incentive (tax holidays and the like) to foreign firms. The taxes they imposed on the profits of foreign firms ranged down from those in India, at over 50 per cent, to between 35 and 45 per cent in the others. There were varying limitations on the proportion of the equity a foreign firm might hold: in India the maximum was 40 per cent, in Iran and Malaysia 49 per cent. There was no ceiling in Colombia to 1967 – thereafter progressive indigenization was demanded – and none in Jamaica and Kenya. India was the only state that severely restricted the sectors in which FDI might operate. All provided varying forms of protection, export subsidies, etc. Only three controlled transfers: Colombia limited transfers to 14 per cent of a firm's net worth, while India and Malaysia regulated only payments in the form of royalties. Serious attempts to check on transfer pricing were made by India, Colombia and Kenya. Only India and Colombia had local control over patents. All these states had rules concerning localization of management. India and Colombia were, therefore, the two states best organized to regulate the MNC, though all attempted to do so to some degree.

How well did they succeed? In all these matters a critical question faced by Lall and Streeten was how MNCs compared with indigenous firms in the same industry. Taking Colombia and India as the best test cases for the first three issues, was there a significant difference?

First, the use of capital. Contrary to much radical assumption, MNCs had lower capital–output ratios than indigenous companies, probably owing to their greater efficiency. MNCs also had lower capital–labour ratios. There was no significant difference in the productivity of capital or labour between MNCs and local firms. Nor was there any perceptible difference between levels of product promotion, though MNC sales might benefit from international taste transfer.

---

[43] Lall and Streeten, *Foreign Investment*, chs 5–7.

Secondly, the pattern of financing local enterprises. There was no evidence that MNCs were using internal interest rates as a means of transferring profits. They got more of their capital from abroad than local firms did, but they did not have higher gearing between loan and equity capital. Hence, 'The origin of control or ownership does not exercise significant influence on financial patterns.'[44]

Thirdly, profitability was not significantly affected by the source or nationality of the investor, but promotional expenditure did have positive causal relationships with profits. Thus, the evidence suggested that, at least in India and Colombia, MNCs did not behave very differently from their indigenous competitors.

But, in the fourth place, the effects of FDI on the balance of payments was strongly negative for all the six countries except for Kenya, which then benefited from the East African Common Market for exports. This was because most of these MNC enterprises were import substituting, imported many of their capital and intermediate inputs, and had few exports, except for Kenya. This, in turn, was because MNCs were attracted to these countries mainly by protectionist or other devices: they were 'market oriented', not 'export oriented': the statistics would have been very different for countries such as South Korea or Taiwan, where FDI was largely for export industries.

There were other reasons for the negative balance-of-payment effects of the MNC. Two-thirds of the firms in this sample took out as profits, etc., more foreign exchange than they brought in as new capital. MNCs had heavy dependence on imported inputs in all but India, owing to the inability of these other countries to produce components or capital equipment for their production. But, significantly, this was common to most firms in the same categories in these countries: there was no real difference between foreign and indigenous firms. Another element in the outflow of foreign exchange was technical payments for patents, royalties, and so on. These were small in relation to total sales by these firms, but quite high as a proportion of post-tax dividends transferred: 12 per cent in Kenya, 16 per cent in Jamaica, 32 per cent in India (16 per cent for firms with foreign majority equity holdings, but 135 per cent for foreign minority-holding companies, which used such devices as a means of compensating for their limited share of the profits), 65 per cent in Colombia, 56 per cent in Malaysia.

Finally, the question of transfer pricing. The 'burden' of post-tax foreign profits and interest on loans was mostly under 10 per cent, though over 20 per cent in Colombia. How much of this was due to transfer pricing was very difficult to assess, because of the uncertainty of what might be a 'market' price for imported or exported intermediates.

---

[44] Ibid., p. 120.

Nor was there any evident difference between the activities of foreign and domestic firms. Transfer pricing was caused by high profits and high corporate taxes in some LDCs, though Lall and Streeten saw no reason why these countries should not adopt this strategy. In any case, the only firm data available were for Colombia, based on a comparison between prices charged locally, in other Latin American countries, and on the international market. In the later 1960s pharmaceuticals were by far the worst offenders, overcharging by amounts calculated by different Colombian departments at between 87 and 155 per cent.

Pharmaceutical MNCs, in fact, have been widely regarded as among the most serious offenders against the interests of host Third World countries; and the difficulty of dealing with them is worth more detailed consideration because it encapsulates the wider problem of the MNC and imported technology in an extreme form. According to Lall, who published a study of their special characteristics in another book,[45] this industry had unique features. It was highly oligopolistic, based almost entirely in the United States, western Europe, and Japan. It obtained no economies of scale in manufacture. Its profitability depended almost entirely on innovative and very expensive R&D expenditure, coupled with still more expensive promotional advertising.

These characteristics, excluding the R&D element, were transferred intact to Third World countries when the big western firms set up subsidiaries there, with the added inconvenience that the owners of the patents, etc., were foreign. Since the main value of the product lay in its underlying research and unique qualities, reflected in patent and royalty agreements, imported inputs were impossible to value in market terms and particularly subject to transfer pricing. The results were that the more advanced drugs were relatively very expensive in poor countries and that the pharmaceutical companies made and could transfer very large profits, largely through royalty and patent agreements.

Lall, in common with other 'nationalist' critics of the MNC, was, therefore, particularly critical of foreign pharmaceutical firms. On the other hand, one of his many other studies of the MNC, on food manufacturers, was far less critical.[46] Based on a study of leading food-processing MNCs in the United States and Britain, it concentrated mainly on the performance of the Anglo-Dutch firm Unilever, as the

[45] S. Lall, *The Multinational Corporation: Nine Essays* (London, 1980), ch. 7.
[46] S. Lall, 'Food Transnationals and Developing Countries', ch. 4 in Lall, *Developing Countries and the International Economy*, previously published as 'Private Foreign Investment and the Transfer of Technology in Food Processing', in C. Bacon (ed.), *Technology, Employment, and Basic Needs in Food Processing* (Oxford, 1979), ch. 9.

largest, oldest and most international of all in this field. Lall argued that the key elements in this type of MNC were that it spent relatively little on R&D, since its products were not high technology; that expansion in the Third World was a response to growing urbanization and higher incomes, with a consequential demand for processed foods; and that sales and profitability depended very heavily on the presentation and promotion of products by advertising. Taking the example of India, where Hindustan Lever, a Unilever subsidiary, was the largest single manufacturer of vegetable ghee as well as of soap, Lall was impressed by the extent of local R&D expenditure. Unilever subsidiaries chose relevant technology for local manufacture and were prepared to use any local raw materials that were available, thus creating linkages with the host economy. There was a low capital–labour ratio, and considerable freedom to adapt techniques to local conditions. Products were carefully designed to meet local demand, though Lall was unable to decide whether they were 'appropriate' or whether they were substituting more for less expensive indigenous alternatives. There was no clear indication of whether marketing strategies were 'unsuitable'. Overall Lall's conclusions on this type of MNC were agnostic. The entry of foreign firms offered both benefits and potential dangers to LDCs. It was up to their governments to consider carefully the balance of advantage.[47]

Pharmaceuticals and food products represent two technical extremes of MNCs in Third World countries and show very different characteristics. Towards the lower end of that scale of technology Biersteker examined the case of four types of industry in Nigeria: sawmilling, textiles, sugar refining and cement, using the criteria set out in his theoretical discussion summarized above.[48]

His argument cannot be detailed here. Broadly his evidence seemed to point in the same direction as that of Lall and Streeten: there was little difference between the strategies of MNCs and competing local firms and their economic consequences. Yet he drew from the fact that between 1967 and 1970 the breakaway state of Biafra was able to improvise remarkably effectively, using local technical resources and inventiveness, the counter-factual conclusion that Nigeria – and by extension

---

[47] There are very detailed studies of the main Unilever subsidiaries, most of them partly food manufacturers, in my *Unilever Overseas*, which Lall seems not to have seen when writing on the Indian subsidiary. Chapter 4 deals at length with Unilever in India and Pakistan and fully supports Lall's tentative conclusions on the adaptation to local conditions, use of local inputs, and the importance of the local R&D. Hindustan Lever was also exceptional in Third World LDCs in the extent of its early indigenization of management and the fact that it had an Indian chairman as early as 1961.
[48] See Biersteker, *Distortion or Development?*, chs 4–9.

most other LDCs – did not need the inputs of the MNC. This suggested the general conclusion 'that extensive multinational investments can create obstacles to the achievement of development objectives in underdeveloped countries and that the assessments made by writers critical of multinational corporations should be given serious attention'.[49]

Two points of general importance for the analysis of the effects of manufacturing MNCs stand out from these conclusions. First, Biersteker's conclusions do not fit with his own evidence, which for the most part was ambivalent. It was only on the counter-factual assumption that Nigeria could have done all the things the MNC did just as well without FDI that these conclusions stand up, and that is at least uncertain. Secondly, seen in the wider context of 'nationalist' studies of the MNC, Biersteker's analysis demonstrates how difficult it is to provide firm answers to the questions posed by the methodology which he, along with many critics of the MNC, have adopted. Most of these questions stem from radical assumptions concerning the economic consequences of capitalist enterprises such as MNCs. Even if they appeared to create wealth, they were bound to have undesirable side effects or 'externalities'. The difficulty comes when one attempts to quantify such externalities. Lall and Streeten, though adopting much the same approach, honestly admitted that no clear answers were possible: there was no possibility of 'objective judgement on the welfare implications of TNCs for developing countries'. The reasons were intrinsic to the problem. There was very limited accurate information on key factors such as pricing and transfers. There were many unmeasurable 'externalities' such as the effects on local cultures and domestic entrepreneurs. One's approach was conditioned by the choice of a theory of development, so that there were many potential alternatives to FDI.[50] It was for such reasons that, in this and other studies, Lall and Streeten tend to reach agnostic conclusions, even though their sympathies appear to lie with host LDC countries.

This may well be the best approach to that majority of MNCs in the Third World that are engaged in manufacture for a domestic market. There are different arguments relating to export-oriented firms, found mainly in the West and in South and South-east Asia, which cannot be examined here. But the case may be different for the other main category of MNC, the firm engaged in the extraction of minerals and other indigenous assets, or the production of agricultural commodities in plantations, though this also cannot be considered. It is, therefore, proprosed, before suggesting any general conclusions, to examine some limited evidence on the extractive MNC.

---

[49] Ibid., p. 162.
[50] Lall and Streeten, *Foreign Investment*, pp. 47–8.

The extractive MNC

In general terms the MNC which extracts and possibly processes minerals or other indigenous products has three features that distinguish it from the manufacturing MNC and which have tended to make it the butt of strong criticism from both Third World nationalists and western radicals.

First, the extractive company deals in a finite asset. In principle at least it would be possible for such a company to exhaust the whole exploitable deposit of the mineral, move out, and leave the host country deprived of a major asset.

Secondly, because most of the material extracted is destined to be processed and consumed abroad, a mining enterprise is likely to have very limited linkages with the host economy.

Thirdly, there is the fact of scale. The technology used in most modern extractive industries requires very big investment and huge organizations. Except for petroleum, many of the large modern extractive industries began with small-scale indigenous mining, or, in the case of certain goldfields, with individual prospectors. This was true, for example, of the Malaysian tin-mining industry and the Australasian, South African and Ghanaian gold industries: the large-scale firm moved in when demand exceeded supply and the limited technology of the small man. In other circumstances, particularly for petroleum, foreign firms might start operations on the basis of unproven geological or other evidence. In this case they commonly gained a monopoly concession from the local ruler, usually for a period of years and with a specified division of the highly speculative return. Such concessions might cover very large areas and constitute virtual baronies, which in time were likely to be seen as inconsistent with the authority of a sovereign host state.

In all these respects extractive industries and the role of the foreign companies/MNCs that ran them were fundamentally different from the modern Third World manufacturing enterprise. Historically, western MNCs were engaged in extraction and plantations before they invested in manufacture in the Third World, for the obvious reason that expanding industrial economies needed commodities that were only or most economically available in LDCs before it became profitable to establish industries there. Thus British companies were heavily involved in mining, among other things, for copper and phosphates in Latin America and elsewhere, long before 1900.[51] The Americans, with supplies of most raw materials available at home, seem not to have invested heavily in

---

[51] For detailed studies of early British investments in Latin America, see, in particular, C. Platt, (ed.), *Business Imperialism 1840–1930; An Inquiry Based on British Experience in Latin America* (Oxford, 1977).

extractive enterprises overseas before the 1920s: the big petroleum companies, for example, initially concentrated on refining domestic or imported crude at home and overseas. From about 1920, however, they invested very heavily in a wide range of foreign mineral sources, mainly because of the shortages during the First World War, which made it seem important to secure access. Chile attracted the largest US investment, in copper and nitrates: by 1929 US firms controlled some 45 per cent of nitrate and 40 per cent of copper exports. By that year the bulk of Latin American mineral concessions were US owned, often acquired from British firms. US extractive companies were also very active in Canada (nickel), in Malaya (tin) and in Central and South Africa (gold, diamonds, copper).

This was also the period when the Americans became leading players in Third World petroleum. After the nationalization of the largely US–owned Mexican oil fields in 1917, followed by long–delayed and totally inadequate compensation, the big firms such as Jersey Standard began to look for safer and potentially cheaper sources. They found them in Venezuela, in Indonesia and above all in the Middle East, hitherto dominated by Anglo–Dutch and French companies.[52] Looking forward, extractive industries remained a very important, though declining, element in western FDI in the later twentieth century Thus in 1971 extractive industries still constituted 30.6 per cent of the stock of US FDI, 33.9 per cent of that of Britain, 22.5 per cent of that of Japan.[53]

What were the motives of these and other foreign investments in extractive industries in the Third World? For US investment in the 1920s Wilkins suggested three main aims: for some firms, notably copper and petroleum, it was to achieve vertical integration; to obtain cheaper sources of the same materials than at home; and to have certain access to them.[54] Others have expanded these aims into more complex explanations of MNC behaviour. The most common is that floated by Byé in 1957.[55] As was seen above, the key feature of his *grande unité* or big firm was that its size enabled it to act largely independently of the market. In particular, it could choose the length of its 'planning period'. Taking the seven large oil companies (five of them American) which then still dominated the industry, Byé argued that their long-term strategy was to control both high- and low-cost sources. This enabled them to fix prices in relation to the high-cost (Caribbean) wells, but to extract largely from the low-cost wells in the Middle East and elsewhere. By forming a cartel with the other big producers, the large firms could fix

[52] Based on Wilkins, *The Maturing of Multinational Enterprise*, pp. 102–28.
[53] Hood and Young, *The Economics of Multinational Enterprise*, table 1.13, p. 33.
[54] Wilkins, *The Maturing of Multinational Enterprise*, p. 127.
[55] Byé, 'Self-financed Multiterritorial Units', pp. 148–67.

the 'posted' price of crude so that it provided a satisfactory return to the smaller American producers, and also offer large profit margins to the big firms. By these devices the big seven could both maximize their profits and ensure adequate supplies for the indefinite future.

These concepts of the long planning period and the need for oligopolistic control of the international market became central to all analysis of the extractive activities of MNCs.[56] From the standpoint of the investing MNC such devices were rational and possibly essential. The development of mineral extraction involved very large investments. To make these worthwhile the company needed a substantial concessionary period, freedom to operate efficiently without intervention by the local authorities, and financial arrangements that provided adequate returns. Until perhaps the 1920s in Latin America, and after 1945 in most other parts of the Third World, these conditions were usually accepted. Governments of poor independent states and the rulers of colonial territories were normally too anxious to obtain the benefits of such investments to bargain hard, however one-sided the conditions. From their standpoint the MNC promised to convert inert potential assets into marketable commodities, which would bring in capital and probably improvements in the infrastructure (roads, railways, power supplies, etc.), provide employment, and increase trade. Moreover, the host could arrange for royalties on the product and possibly taxes on MNC profits. In short, few Third World states or their colonial predecessors could afford to refuse to allow foreign firms to exploit their mineral resources.

The key questions, however, have always been whether the terms of this original bargain were fair as between host and foreign firm, and whether the LDC received worthwhile rewards for what necessarily involved a partial loss of both its sovereignty and its assets. It would be impossible here to examine in detail the activities of any significant proportion of the extractive MNCs to judge whether they conformed to Byé's model and whether they posed serious economic and political problems. It is proposed instead to use the summary and conclusions to an important collection of studies of the performance of a range of extractive enterprises, mostly in Latin America, to test whether these MNCs had the limited or adverse effects postulated by Byé and others; then to consider how permanent these conditions and effects were.

In the conclusion to his edited studies of mineral and petroleum-extracting firms R. F. Miksell used the evidence of the wide range of country studies in this book on the effects and limitations of past and

---

[56] For example, in Hymer's work. An excellent analysis of the complex pricing strategies of petroleum companies is in E. T. Penrose, *The Large International Firm in Developing Countries: The International Petroleum Industry* (London, 1968). The issues are summarized in Vernon, *Sovereignty at Bay*, pp. 27–36.

recent practice to pose two questions. How great a contribution did these foreign extractive firms make to the economic development of their host countries? How could they be forced to make a greater contribution to LDC as well as to global welfare?[57]

First, their effects on economic and social development. In recent years host countries had retained some 50–70 per cent of the export value of minerals. Of these retained profits, 50–75 per cent consisted of government revenues, wages and salaries. Local purchases of their inputs by the MNCs were usually small – perhaps 10 per cent in Venezuela, 5 per cent in Saudi Arabia, but over 20 per cent in Chile. Thus, while the host retained a large proportion of the export value, the direct effect on the host economies was indeed small. There were very few backward linkages, largely because these LDCs could not provide the equipment and other needs of technically advanced enterprises. Moreover, the inflated currencies of many Latin American countries made local inputs relatively very expensive. Forward linkages were probably stronger. There was a substantial petrochemical industry in some Latin American countries and more processing was being undertaken in producing countries – for example, of copper, bauxite and iron ore. Reduced transport costs for these processed commodities helped to offset the higher import duties normally charged in the United States and elsewhere. But employment effects were generally small and becoming smaller as capital intensity increased with higher levels of technology. MNCs normally paid higher wages than were common locally to their managers and skilled labour. This had a beneficial demonstration effect on wage rates and skills, and provided some stimulus to downstream consumption; but it also tended to increase demand for imported consumer goods. Thus the major contribution extractive industries had been making to local economic development was through governments channelling their rent into the host economy. Unfortunately, most LDC governments tended to use this rent to pay for public consumption rather than for investment. In general, therefore Miksell and his contributors saw no serious danger to the economy of an LDC from the fact that extractive export industries constituted the leading sector; but whether they provided large positive economic benefits depended on what proportion of the profits the host government could obtain and how wisely it used this rent.

These conclusions were reflected in Miksell's policy recommendations. The most important was that there should be no more of the traditional concessions to foreign firms; they should be replaced by joint ventures between the host state or its entrepreneurs and the foreign firm, or by contracts to operate a locally owned enterprise. Those that

[57] R. F. Miksell (ed.), *Foreign Investment in Petroleum and Mineral Industries: Case Studies of Investor–Host Relations* (Baltimore, 1971).

remained in private foreign hands should be regulated by specific laws, not left to operate under the general legal system. Secondly, it was important that as far as possible minerals and petroleum should be refined and processed in the host country, rather than be shipped out as ores or crude oil. Thirdly, taxes on foreign firms should be increased, subject to the danger of deterring new foreign investment, as had become evident in Chile and Brazil since about 1950. Fourthly, LDCs must attempt to control the prices fixed by international cartels, particularly the posted price for crude oil. Fifthly, governments must be able to control the volume of production and export so that foreign firms could not determine the foreign-exchange position and supplies could be conserved. They should also have far greater control over the down-stream aspects of these industries, such as shipping and marketing.

In short, the main defects of extractive enterprises were not that they were extractive or even foreign owned, but that they had been too powerful and too exempt from public control. By the time these studies were made, however, the great age of the autonomous and dominant extractive MNC was virtually over, and many of Miksell's proposals had been adopted in a number of LDCs. Western FDI was flowing into industry and a range of other activities rather than into extraction. Between 1967 and 1980, to take two examples, the proportion of total US FDI that was in extraction had dropped from 49.6 to 26.4 per cent, that of Japan from 44.4 to 24 per cent.[58] The experience of other western states, such as Britain and France, was much the same. The basic explanation is that most host countries had been able to break the oligopolistic control of the big extractive companies, either taking over mines, oil wells, refineries etc., or imposing new partnership agreements, a process that has been called 'the obsolescing bargain'.[59]

Thus, by the later 1970s the reign of the MNC over the extractive world in its earlier form had ended. It was by then clear that any government, including even those of richer states such as Canada and Australia, would renege on earlier contracts if this seemed desirable and profitable; and it has proved almost invariably impossible, short of an induced political revolution, to prevent their doing so.[60] In the last resort

---

[58] Colman and Nixson, *Economics of change*, table 10.11, p. 359.

[59] The following summary is based mainly on C. F. Bergsten, T. Horst and T. H. Moran, *American Multinationals and American Interests* (Washington, 1978), ch. 5.

[60] The best general study of this issue is C. Lipson, *Standing Guard: Protecting Foreign Capital in the Nineteenth and Twentieth Centuries* (Berkeley and Los Angeles, and London, 1985). Although it does not relate exclusively to extractive companies, there is a considerable literature on the alleged manipulation by MNCs of political forces leading to a change of government in LDCs. The classic case was the alleged activities of the American communications company IT&T

the only constraint on the LDC in its dealings with the extractive multinational is that it may still need its capital, skills and marketing ability. If the state pushes too hard a bargain, it may find itself unable to obtain any of the benefits of its mineral endowment. That is why nationalization or partial nationalization has commonly led to new contracts with the same firms to do the same work, though often under less favourable conditions.

Is it, then, possible to draw up a meaningful balance sheet for the MNC, to decide whether it is an aid or a threat to Third World development? Before this question is examined, it is significant to note that few of the standard textbooks on the MNC or its synonyms seem prepared to do so. Two quotations will demonstrate this reluctance. The first is from Hood and Young's, *The Economics of Multinational Enterprise*, which provides one of the best and most balanced theoretical and empirical surveys of the activities of the MNC. After surveying a wide range of both radical and conservative hypotheses and much empirical evidence, they concluded their chapter 5 on 'Multinationals and Economic Development in Host Countries' as follows:

> Overall, no clear generalisations are possible either in regard to the impact of MNEs on *national income* in developing host countries or in respect of the effects on *other development goals*. In turn this conclusion indicates serious limitations in existing knowledge concerning the impact of direct foreign investment on economic development.[61]

A comparable conclusion was reached by Richard Caves after a similarly methodical survey of the theoretical literature:

> Some researchers have tried to identify the overall effects of MNE's presence in developing countries on the LDCs' subsequent rates of economic growth. The possible causal connections are numerous but speculative and ill-defined in terms of economic models. Empirical investigations, whether by those disposed to think good or ill of the MNE, have employed inadequate research procedures and have yielded no trustworthy conclusions.[62]

---

in bringing down the socialist Allende government of Chile, which as threatening nationalization of this and other industries, including copper. On this see A. Sampson, *The Sovereign State of I.T.&T.* (London, 1973); C. V. Vaitsos, 'The Changing Policies of Latin American Governments towards Economic Development and Direct Foreign Investment', in R. B. Williams, W. P. Glade and K. M. Schmitt (eds), *Latin-American–US Economic Interactions* (Washington, 1974); H. Radice, *International Firms and Modern Imperialism* (Harmondsworth, 1975).
[61] Hood and Young, *The Economics of Multinational Enterprise*, p. 222.
[62] R. E. Caves, *Multinational Enterprise and Economic Analysis* (Cambridge, 1982), p. 278.

Fair though these summaries are, they are too agnostic for the present purpose. What we need is a balanced general conclusion on what determines whether an MNC is or is not helpful to a Third World country and what differentiates the good from the bad. A valuable lead comes from the argument of I. M. D. Little that was quoted above from his book *Economic Development*. First, the impact of the MNC will depend primarily on how it is dealt with by the host government and the conditions it faces. Secondly, there may, in fact be very little to distinguish the way in which MNCs operate and their economic effects from those of indigenous enterprises.

This is also the line adopted by Colman and Nixson, whose conclusions to their chapter on 'The Transnational Corporation and LDCs' may roughly be summarized as follows.

First, there is an inevitable potential for conflict between the MNC and a host country, because the former is pursuing a global strategy, the latter its own, possibly conflicting, objectives. These conflicts of interest are likely to centre, among other things, on balance-of-payments issues, employment creation and technology transfer.

Secondly, the impact of the MNC on a particular country will depend on three sets of variables: the global environment; the national environment; and the sectoral distribution of the MNC investment. The last of these is critically important. 'Other things being equal DFI in ISI (and ISI industries which eventually turn to exporting) is likely to offer important possibilities for the effective regulation of the TNC and the maximization of its developmental impact.' Export-oriented investment, however, is less likely to be helpful because it 'is likely to be highly mobile between different LDCs, involve a limited transfer of technology and create few linkages with the local economy ...'.[63]

Thirdly, the effects of even the most potentially useful MNC will depend ultimately on the nature of the host state, and on the interplay between different political and class groups within the host state and between these and the MNC. The MNC may well benefit from income inequality, urban–rural inequality and other factors, all of which have been denounced by development economists, but it does not create or control these. Moreover, any conflict of interest is not between the MNC and whole host country but between it, the state and various domestic sectoral interests.

> From the point of view of longer-run development ... the crucial issue is not the presence or absence of foreign capital or the existing weakness or subservience of domestic to foreign capital, but rather it is the strength of the state and the policies that it may be pursuing to overcome the weakness and eliminate subservience that is important. Over time, a

[63] The potential value of export-oriented FDI will be examined in ch. 11.

combination of controls on foreign capital, active participation by the
state in productive enterprises and the positive promotion of indigenous
enterprise may well prove sufficient to create an environment within
which indigenous enterprise can flourish and compete on an equal footing
with TNCs in at least key sectors of the LDC economy.... the presence
or absence of foreign capital does not in itself determine the outcome of
the development process.[64]

It was fashionable, they add, to state that the main contribution of the
MNC to development in the Third World was technology, foreign
markets and managerial and technical skills, and this might well be true,
given the need of LDCs for these things and the fact that they might
only, or most effectively, be obtained through an MNC.

But it is the structure of the arrangement with the TNC that is important,
the way in which the vital factors are acquired, the use to which they
are put, and the price that is paid for them. The LDC must first put its
own house in order ... before it can hope to approach the TNC and
strike a just bargain. This ... is essentially a matter of political change
within the LDC itself. Without this political change, new institutional
forms (joint ventures) or more effective bargaining procedures will not
fundamentally affect the economic position of the majority of the population of LDCs nor eradicate the conditions of poverty and inequality.[65]

In short, the MNC will be only as useful or as dangerous as the host
country allows it to be. In the late twentieth century the governments
of Third World states are no longer helpless in the face of the MNC.
They have destroyed the baronies of the extractive companies with their
apparently impregnable concessions, and they can destroy a manufacturing MNC by starving it of inputs, refusing to allow it to repatriate
dividends, forcing it to sell its equity, imposing very high taxes, or
preventing it from using its own expatriate managers. In the last resort
all that the MNC can do in retaliation is to fold its tents and leave.
Nationalization of manufacturing subsidiaries has proved a rare last
resort, mainly because even very large MNCs will normally accept these
constraints, even from very small and weak states, rather than sacrifice
their whole investment.

Thus it is arguable that, as Hymer predicted, the great age of the MNC
in the Third World was already passing by the 1970s, when host states
were learning to use their strength. His concept of 'a new imperial system'
was already becoming unreal. Hence, paradoxically, the remaining danger
of the modern MNC to a Third World society may lie not in its power

[64] Colman and Nixson, *Economics of Change*, p. 387.
[65] Ibid.

but in two much less dramatic qualities: its cleverness and its apparent harmlessness, both of which make it look very attractive to a prospective host. It was the second of these, coupled with the obvious gifts' an MNC could offer, that persuaded so many LDCs to invite these foreign companies in the 1960s and 1970s. The results may be good or they may be bad. This will depend, as Colman and Nixson suggest, primarily on how the host state treats its guests. Sovereignty may be proof against the power of the MNC but it carries no guarantee against lack of wisdom.

Thus the essential message of the radical and nationalist critics of the MNC may be *caveat emptor*. FDI carries the same warning as other forms of foreign investment, including aid. All may expedite development but any of them may lead to heavy liabilities and diminution of sovereignty. The point may be summed up in two quotations, one modern, one ancient. Edith Penrose gave this warning a quarter of a century ago against the attraction of FDI for a state anxious to industrialize quickly and cheaply:

> One suspects that for some countries there may be a basic incompatibility between the economic objectives of fostering very rapid industrial development and at the same time promoting domestic full employment at all times regardless of the state of foreign balance, and the acceptance of an unlimited, unknown and uncontrollable foreign liability.[66]

Virgil put the same point more simply into the mouth of Laocoön, the Trojan priest, during the siege of Troy: 'I fear the Greeks even when they come bearing gifts.'[67]

---

[66] Penrose, *The Theory of the Growth of the Firms*, p. 79.
[67] Virgil, *Aeneid*, 2, 49: 'Timeo Danaos et dona ferentes.'

10

Trade and Development after 1950: Black Africa and India

There is a paradox in the history of economic development in the Third World after the Second World War. The previous two chapters have argued that during the quarter century after 1950 conditions were more favourable for developing countries than ever before. The end of colonialism enabled the new states to adopt development strategies that were in their own interests, free from restrictions imposed by their former masters. International trade became more free than at any time since 1914, so that markets for their exports could be expected to grow in much the same way as they had done in that golden age of Third World commodity exporting after the 1870s. Post-war shortages, briefly intensified by the Korean War of 1950–2, ensured high prices and high demand for Third World exports. The growth of aid, the easy availability of commercial loans, and the expansion of the activities of multinational corporations provided both the finance and the technical skills needed for rapid industrialization. In short, it would have been surprising if this had not been a period of unprecedented economic and social development in the Third World, in which trade would once again play the leading role it had played before 1914.

Nevertheless as early as the 1950s there were influential voices which rejected this optimistic scenario. Two may be taken as representative. The first was Ragnar Nurkse, whose very influential Wicksell Lectures were published in 1959.[1] Nurkse argued that before 1914 trade had indeed been an engine of growth for developing countries, because the industrial countries of Europe needed raw materials and food and were prepared to invest capital overseas to make expansion of production and its transportation possible. This had been the basis for economic growth through comparative advantage for the settler societies and also for parts of Asia and Africa. But in the post-1945 world this system of growth through trade was no longer viable. Since 1928 the volume of world trade had not kept pace with production, and for this Nurkse suggested several reasons. The United States had replaced Britain as the main potential market for exports and source of capital; but the United States was a low importer in relation to its production. The industrialized countries now exchanged far more between themselves than with developing countries. These developed countries no longer had the same incentive to invest in a high rate of growth in the Third World, because, among other factors, modern industry required less raw materials. Third World commodities had a low-income elasticity, and home agriculture demanded protection. The main exception to this was petroleum, in which the West was prepared to invest heavily, much as it had done in the wheatlands of the nineteenth century.

From all this Nurkse's policy conclusions were that official transfers from western states would have to take the place of pre-1914 private investment; that Third World countries would have to concentrate on industrialization rather than commodities; that developed countries would have to shift their production to higher technical levels and accept manufactured consumer goods from the Third World; and that, in addition, or failing such liberalization, developing countries must increase their trade with each other in relatively simple consumer goods.

This amounted to 'export pessimism'; and the same conclusions, though based on other assumptions, were drawn by economists on the Left. What became known as the Prebisch–Singer thesis was developed by H. W. Singer in an article published in 1950[2] and R. Prebisch in an article in 1959.[3] Their starting point was the evidence provided by the UN publication of 1949, *Relative Prices of Exports and Imports of Underdeveloped Countries*, which suggested that there had been a significant

[1] R. Nurkse, *Patterns of Trade and Development* (Wicksell Lectures; Stockholm, 1959), reproduced in Nurske, *Equilibrium and Growth in the World Economy* (Cambridge, Mass., 1961).
[2] H. Singer, 'The Distribution of Gains between Investing and Borrowing Countries', *American Economic Review*, 40 (1950), pp. 473–85.
[3] R. Prebisch, 'The Role of Commercial Policies in Underdeveloped Countries', *American Economic Review*, 49 (1958), pp. 251–73, and *Towards a New Trade Policy for Development* (New York, 1964).

secular deterioration in the terms of trade of Third World countries. The argument was that exporters of primary materials were faced with low income and price elasticities for their exports because of changing patterns of demand in the industrialized countries. Increased production to maintain their income terms of trade merely resulted in further depression of prices relative to those of manufactured goods imported from the West. The obvious conclusion, which was widely accepted at the time, was that the doctrine of comparative advantage no longer operated in its classical form. Third World countries must, therefore, concentrate on rapid industrialization, initially mainly for domestic consumption, behind protective walls.

There were, therefore, two strongly contrasting predictions concerning the economic future of Third World countries. One suggested that developing countries should prosper as never before on the back of the great world commodity boom and unprecedented flows of resources. The other painted a gloomy picture of declining demand for commodity exports and for trade of all sorts between the Third World and the West, so that an export-oriented development strategy could no longer work. The purpose of this and the following chapter is to examine the evidence of the period between about 1950 and the 1980s to see which approach more nearly fits the facts. The specific questions that will be considered are as follows.

First, how far was this a period of substantial growth in Third World countries? Secondly, how far was economic growth promoted by exporting, either of commodities or manufactured goods? Thirdly, is it possible to define those factors that distinguished the successful from the less successful economies?

In attempting to answer these questions the frame of reference will be much narrower than the Third World as a whole. In order to emphasize the effects of decolonization, detailed analysis will be restricted to countries that were colonial dependencies until after 1945; and to provide contrasting models the focus will be on Black Africa, India, and a group of countries in South-east and East Asia. Each of these will be considered separately, leading to some general conclusions.

1   Black Africa

There can be no doubt that the two decades after 1950, and for most countries down to the OPEC oil-price increase of 1973, saw the most rapid economic development in the history of Africa: the only qualification is that calculations of the size and growth of gross domestic product (GDP) for most of these countries only began in the 1950s and 1960s, so that it is impossible to know how fast the growth rate was in earlier periods, particularly before 1914.[4] According to the World Bank, the weighted average growth of GDP for all Black Africa between 1960 and 1970 was 3.8 per cent.[5] Even during the troubled 1970s GDP grew at an average rate of 3.0 per cent between 1970 and 1982, though this was buoyed up by the high growth of the three main oil-exporting countries, Nigeria, Cameroon and the People's Republic of the Congo. Other indicators were favourable, at least for the 1960s. The value of exports grew at an average of 6.2 per cent between 1960 and 1970, imports at 6.0 per cent. The share of the labour force in agriculture declined from 82 to 72 per cent between 1960 and 1980, while that in industry grew from 7 to 12 per cent. In the 1970s (there are no comparable figures for the 1960s) the average rate of increase of manufacturing was 3.4 per cent. The proportions of the relevant age groups enrolled in primary education increased from an average of 36 to 78 per cent, and in secondary education from 3 to 15 per cent.

To this point it would seem that African countries were benefiting to the full from the favourable conditions of the 1960s and early 1970s. But other indicators tell a different story. One critical fact is that population growth was accelerating, from an average of 2.4 per cent in the 1960s to 2.8 per cent in the 1970s. In the earlier period this left a margin of 1.4 per cent in per capita growth, in the second only 0.2 per cent. Moreover, this minute margin had by the 1980s been obliterated by the effects of Black Africa's debt burden. Africa had, indeed, taken full advantage of the resources on offer after 1950. By 1970 African countries had collectively received over $2.37 billion of aid, $324 million of official export credits, $842 million in multilateral loans, $1.87 billion in publicly guaranteed private loans, and $331 million in private nonguaranteed loans, making a total of $5.7 billion. By 1982 this total had risen to $51.3 billion. By then the annual debt service (interest plus repayments) amounted to $5.46 billion, which represented 12.6 per cent of exports of goods and services. For some big borrowers that had been hit by declining export prices, this debt service was substantially higher: for the Ivory Coast, 36.9 per cent; for a clutch of other countries, over 20 per cent. Since Black Africa as a whole was by then running a substantial deficit on its merchandise trade of nearly $5 billion, this could mean only that Africa was falling further into debt all the time.

It also meant that the average weighted per capita growth of GNP for the period 1960–82 was a mere 1.5 per cent. From 1985 to 1995 the weighted per capita GNP of Black Africa actually declined at an

---

[4] It must be said that many of the statistics provided by African and other Third World states for international orgnanizations such as the World Bank, on which most estimates are based, are highly suspect. Calculations based on them must, therefore, be taken to indicate very rough orders of magnitude.
[5] This and all other statistics in this section are taken from the World Bank, *Toward Sustained Development in Sub-Saharan Africa* (Washington, 1984).

average of 1.2 per cent a year.[6] The result was to undo most of the progress made since the 1960s. In constant (1987) dollars the per capita GDP of Black Africa in 1991 was about what it had been in 1965.[7] In short, Black Africa was no better off than it had been in the mid-1960s and was now laden with debts.

Does this mean that the pessimists of the 1950s were right, that in the post-decolonization world it was no longer possible for developing countries to become absolutely or relatively better off through incorporation into the international economy? The question has been and continues to be very extensively debated, and it is impossible here to analyse the arguments in detail.[8] Broadly, the explanations of relative failure fall into two main categories. The first blames factors beyond the control of African governments – the 'non-policy' explanation; the second, the macroeconomic and political strategies adopted by those who governed post-colonial Africa – the 'policy' explanation.

The 'non-policy' type of explanation normally starts with the colonial inheritance. To recapitulate, Africans had been forcefully incorporated into the international economy to serve the needs of the industrialized countries for markets for their consumer goods and for controlled sources of raw materials and food. Thus Africans were compelled to grow or harvest crops that were needed in the metropolis, whether or not it was in their best interests to do so: that is, even if, on the principle of comparative advantage, they might have done better to concentrate on other commodities or on the domestic market. The general result was that many African economies emerged into independence tied to the production and export of one or more staple crops, which in turn were vulnerable to the vicissitudes of the international commodity market. Moreover, much of the exploitable natural endowment had been taken over by Europeans. Mining was owned and controlled by big international corporations, whose profits were largely exported and which provided very few links with the host economy. In certain countries, though not in West Africa, large parts of the most useful land had been taken over by white settlers and plantation owners. In addition, the colonialists had spent far too little on education, on investment or on infrastructure. Thus African states started their development drive as 'dependent' economies, very ill equipped in every way and positively handicapped by the patterns of production imposed upon them.

[6] World Bank, *World Development Report 1966: From Plan to Market* (Oxford, 1996), table 1, p. 189.
[7] World Bank, *Adjustment in Africa: Reforms, Results, and the Road Ahead* (Oxford, 1994), fig. 1.2, p. 19.
[8] There is an extensive bibliography down to the mid-1980s in D. K. Fieldhouse, *Black Africa 1945–1980: Economic Decolonization and Arrested Development* (London, 1986), from which much of the following argument is taken.

This leads back to the arguments of Nurkse, Singer, Prebisch and the many others who denied that commodity exports could, in the modern world, lead to sustained economic growth. The crux of their argument was that the terms of trade between developing and industrial countries had deteriorated over time and would continue to do so, making commodity exporting unprofitable.

This remains a highly debated and uncertain question, answers depending largely on the nature of the statistics used. In fact, and ignoring the controversial period before about 1945, World Bank statistics suggest that there was no significant secular trend in the barter terms of trade of Black Africa between 1950 and about 1979. Thereafter, however, these declined sharply: the index fell from 100 in 1977 to 60 in 1991. This represented a very serious worsening of some 40 per cent in the terms of trade, and might well suggest that the export pessimists were right in the long, if not the short run. But the World Bank made two qualifying points about this. First, the terms of trade of twenty-four undefined non-African developing countries after 1970 followed almost precisely the same track as those of non-oil-exporting Black Africa. On the other hand, most other developing countries offset falls in the barter terms of trade by increasing their volume of exports. The value of exports from East Asia and the Pacific countries never grew at less than 8 per cent throughout this recessionary period, and were expanding at over 10 per cent after 1987, while thirty-six other developing countries kept increasing their exports at around 6 per cent. Secondly, while the deterioration in Africa's terms of trade implied a drop in external income of roughly 5.4 per cent between 1971–3 and 1981–6, net external capital transfers to Africa, excluding Nigeria, increased from 3.7 to 6.4 per cent of GDP. Taking both factors into account, it is argued that in those fifteen years the net effect of adverse terms of trade on the GDP of Africa, excluding Nigeria, was only minus 2.7 per cent, or 0.3 per cent a year. That was far less than the contemporary decline in Black Africa's growth rate.[9]

It is, therefore, less than certain that inherited commitment to commodity production for export or the evolution of the terms of trade thereafter was the main reason for Africa's limited economic growth after independence. The critical fact is that broadly, though not invariably, African countries did not increase production or exports of agricultural goods in line with the rest of the Third World. Between 1955 and 1980 the volume of world trade in agricultural products rose from an index (1963 = 100) of 64 to 203, while their value rose from 33 to 299.[10] Between 1965 and 1980 African agriculture grew at an average of

[9] World Bank, *Adjustment in Africa*, fig. 1.3, p.20; fig. 1.7, p. 27; pp. 26–29.
[10] Based on L. Moore, *The Growth and Structure of International Trade since the Second World War* (Bringhton, 1985), table 8.1.

1.3 per cent a year as compared with East Asia at 3.2 per cent and South
Asia at 2.5 per cent. The figures for 1980–8 were Africa, 1.8 per cent;
East Asia, 5.7 per cent; South Asia, 2.5 per cent.[11] This pattern was
reflected in African exports. While exports of most food and beverages grew reasonably well in the 1960s (the exceptions being cocoa,
owing to Ghana's decline, palm oil, mainly from Nigeria, and bananas),
between 1970 and 1982 there was a significant decline in the growth
of exports of all but sugar and tea. Yet world exports of these commodities generally continued to grow. In some instances African countries
lost a previously dominant market position in this period. Ghana is perhaps
the extreme example. From being the world's largest single exporter of
cocoa, its exports had fallen from an average of 383,000 tons in 1960–2
to 202,000 tons between 1979 and 1981, the shortfall being made good
by the Ivory Coast, Malaysia, Brazil and others. Parallel to this was the
decline in Nigerian exports of commodities. Groundnut exports fell from
an average of 576,000 tons in 1960–2 to zero in 1979–81, palm kernels
from 399,000 tons to 53,000 tons, and palm oil from 155,000 to 1,000
tons in the same period. In both cases the underlying reasons were the
same: disproportionately low payments to producers through the marketing boards, coupled with lack of governmental support and overpriced
currencies that seriously damaged the terms of trade of producers.

Such decadence was not, however, universal. The Ivory Coast demonstrated the potential of commodity exporting by increasing exports
of coffee beans from 149,000 to 232,000 tons and of cocoa beans from
84,000 to 298,000 tons between 1960–2 and 1979–81. This so-called
Ivory Coast miracle was made possible by relatively high payments to
farmers, a stable currency linked to the franc, and the fact that the
country had ample land and labour resources for extension of farming.
Senegal, however, also part of the franc zone, did less well. Its groundnut
exports declined from 557,000 to 265,000 tons, mainly because of the
operations of the state marketing board.[12]

The argument, therefore, is that the post-colonial commitment to commodity exporting in tropical Africa was not necessarily fatal to economic
development. Although there may have been limits to how far such a strategy could take these states (and Samir Amin in particular has argued that
in countries such as Senegal and the Ivory Coast that limit was set by the
availability of new land),[13] few African countries seriously attempted to push

---

[11] World Bank, *World Development Report 1990*, table 2, p. 180.
[12] D. Rimmer, *The Economies of West Africa* (London, 1984), table 28, p. 242;
pp. 242–6.
[13] See S. Amin, *Neo-Colonialism in West Africa* (New York and London, 1973),
chs 1 and 2 in particular. This was originally published in Paris in 1971 as
L'Afrique de L'ouest bloquée.

their exports to the limit of either land or market. While competing primary producers such as Malaysia and Indonesia were expanding production and exports, most of those in Africa were not. The only commodities in which Africa's share of world exports increased between 1960 and the later 1970s were iron ore, bauxite and phosphate. Africa's share of other mineral and metal exports declined, notably of copper and tin.

As a result Africa's share of world non-fuel exports declined steadily: from 3.1 per cent in 1960 to 2.4 per cent in 1970 and 1.2 per cent in 1978, while its share of developing-country non-fuel exports halved, from 18.0 to 9.2 per cent.[14] In short, most parts of independent Africa rejected, deliberately or by neglect, the traditional path of growth through commodity exporting, leading to industrialization. This strategy might have worked, as in fact it did in other parts of the world, leading to competitive industrial development, as will be seen in chapter 11 on East and Southeast Asia. In Africa it might not have been so successful, because of a number of obstacles, such as limitations of the market or of productive potential. But the important point is that in Africa it was not tried seriously and continuously; and that leads to the second possible explanation of Africa's relative decline after independence, the weakness of the development strategies adopted by most African states, the 'policy explanation'.

The arguments that lay behind these almost universal development strategies were summarized in chapter 2. Briefly, the way to overcome poverty and backwardness was through very large capital investment to overcome the 'structural' obstacles to growth, leading to intensive industrialization. This strategy was in no sense specific to the new African states. Generated in the then blooming world of development economics, it was already the staple of many Latin American states, India, Pakistan and much of South-east and East Asia. It was not necessarily misguided and had varying success, as will be seen later in studies of Asian development. But it was undoubtedly high risk. It required a high level of administrative skill to handle complex schemes and to tackle the problems of money supply and exchange rates. It assumed honesty on the part of governments, which took very large responsibilities for huge projects and vast sums of money. It depended on finding the right balance between each of the various sectors, particularly between agriculture and industry, countryside and town. Above all, perhaps, success would be determined by the ability of a new industrial system, once it had conquered and reached the limits of the protected domestic market, to reach out and start competing in the international markets. If this did not happen, the new states might be left with relatively inefficient import-substituting industries which could not provide a return on the capital invested in them, nor earn foreign exchange to service the debts incurred in setting them up.

[14] World Bank, *Accelerated Development in Sub-Saharan Africa: An Agenda for Action* (Washington, 1981), table 3.4, p. 19; table 3.5, p. 21.

The central fact of development in most Black African states after about 1960 was that very few of them proved able to meet any or most of these conditions. Much can be made of the special problems they faced. It was increasingly understood that the African environment, which included infrastructure, climate, soils and human capital, was not as propitious for economic development as had been predicted. Infrastructure, particularly transport, water and power supplies, was inadequate and absorbed large amounts of capital. Climate was very unpredictable, with many periods of drought in the 1970s. Soils were, for the most part, less fertile and more vulnerable to overcropping than those of Asia, Europe or America. As to human capital, while most Africans were highly commercial in outlook and perfectly capable of developing all the skills needed in a developed industrialized society, initially very few had the training or experience needed, itself a comment on the inadequacy of colonial educational and employment policies. Moreover, as was seen above, international conditions for exports and borrowing, which remained exceptionally favourable until various points in the 1970s, then ceased to be so. In short, it was always likely that the tropical African road to sustained growth and industrialization would be more difficult than the development economists had predicted. Many in fact blame these factors, particularly the influence of the international capitalist economy, as the root cause of African economic failure.

All such explanations of failure have one common feature. They treat Africans as lay figures, as victims rather than as the source of many of their own problems. But there is an alternative explanation, which evolved in the early 1980s. While making full allowances for the special obstacles facing Africa, this explanation placed the main emphasis on the policies adopted by the new rulers of Africa, on the way these were carried out, and, above all, on the political systems evolved to support the ruling elites.[15] In other words, Africans were now treated as masters of their own fates.

[15] Some of the pioneers of this approach, in order of publication, were: B. Beckman, *Organizing the Farmers: Cocoa Politics and National Development in Ghana* (Uppsala, 1976); T. Killick, *Development Economics in Action: A study of Economic Policies in Ghana* (London, 1978); R. H. Bates, *Markets and States in Tropical Africa* (Berkeley and Los Angeles, 1981), and *Essays on the Political Economy of Rural Africa* (Cambridge, 1983); D. Rimmer, *The Economies of West Africa* (London, 1984). On the economic policies of African governments, a key publication was World Bank, *Accelerated Development in Sub-Saharan Africa*, usually known as the Berg Report after Elliot Berg, leader of the Group that prepared it, which set out what was already the Bank's standard critique of African economic failure and caused a considerable debate. It is significant, however, that, presumably for political reasons, since most of these states were members of the World Bank, there was no specific reference to the incompetence or corruption of African regimes, which was to become a staple of later assessments.

The starting point of this approach is the fact that, while African states have mostly faced the same sorts of post-colonial and contemporary problems as other new Third World states, and have adopted much the same development strategies, they have done worse than most others. The question is why. An explanation that evolved in the 1980s can be summarized as follows.

At independence, African leaders in most of the new states (with exceptions such as Houphouet-Boigny of the Ivory Coast and Nkrumah in Ghana) were almost completely inexperienced in both politics and administration. In addition, the new African leaders, who had established their position by their ability to organize public demand for independence, faced a serious political problem: how could they maintain their position, and that of their associates, once the momentum of the demand for freedom had been lost? The root cause of the problem was that these societies consisted mainly of regions with different languages, religions and histories. There was no natural basis for class- or interest-based political parties covering the whole territory. In their absence the dominant factors were locality, kinship and ethnicity, what John Iliffe has described in terms of localism.[16] Such problems had been relatively unimportant during the campaign for independence, since most Africans could collaborate behind leaders offering freedom. But once that was achieved, politics became shapeless and fragmented. How then could the new political leaders maintain their power and run the country? What implications had their solutions for the economic policies they adopted?

The common answer, discovered by experience, was to construct a political and also an economic system based on patronage: that is, buying the support of those who mattered in all sections of the community, ignoring the interests of those who represented no threat to those in power. Briefly, this involved three closely related strategies.

First, it was necessary to use all that the state could offer – jobs, contracts, money – to reward supporters of the ruling party. In America this was called 'pork-barrel politics'. In Africa it is commonly called 'clientage' or 'patrimonialism' – that is, work or benefits for political supporters, personal friends or ethnic relations. J.-F. Bayart has accurately described this as 'the politics of the belly'.[17]

Secondly, it was usually found necessary or convenient to destroy the democratic systems set up late in the day before decolonization by all the imperial powers.[18] These were replaced by one-party or military regimes,

---

[16] J. Iliffe, *Africans: The History of a Continent* (Cambridge, 1995), p. 256. There is an excellent survey of the main features of African politics on pp. 257–62.
[17] J.-F. Bayart, *The State in Africa: The Politics of the Belly* (Paris, 1989; Eng. edn, London, 1993).

commonly on the ground that western-style democracy was unsuited to African conditions and that party politics would necessarily be based on divisive regional or ethnic groupings.

Thirdly, and most relevant to the present argument, the economic strategies of the new states were contrived to provide rewards and security for those in power and their supporters. Their good fortune (though not that of the people they ruled) was that the prescriptions of the development economists of the 1950s and 1960s were for a highly centralized economic management based on planning. This placed a huge amount of economic power in the hands of the elite. But the value of economic dirigisme as political patronage depended on its being specific rather than general. For example, licensing of all kinds was desirable, because licences could be targeted as rewards or threats. Price controls were preferable to rational monetary policies, because they could be used selectively, to favour particular interests: food subsidies or price controls, for example, to benefit urban workers at the expense of the politically unimportant farming community. High protectionism, nominally to promote industrial growth, was used selectively to help particular private manufacturing ventures along with state firms and parastatals. In short, economic policy was distorted by subordination to political need.

The point has been well summarized by Roland Oliver in his magisterial survey of African history, *The African Experience*.[19]

> Perhaps the greatest misfortune of the modern African nations was that their approach to independence coincided with a period when it was generally believed that the way to a better future lay through more and longer term state planning, with its implementation led by a large and ever-expanding public sector.... The run-up to independence took place amid a flurry of development planning, which ramified far beyond the mere provision of infrastructure, into grand schemes of industrialization, with the colonial state as chief entrepreneur.... On paper these projects looked very attractive. In practice, they all proved vastly more costly than had been anticipated. When taken over by newly independent

---

[18] Britain invariably established a democratic system and held elections before trasferring power, in the case of Southern Rhodesia (Zimbabwe) even going through the charade of reimposing imperial rule in 1980 after fifteen years of *de facto* independence. The sole exception was Hong Kong, handed over to China in 1997 with only very limited and short-lived democratic institutions. France followed the same path where possible, notably in West and Equatorial Africa, though not in the North African protectorates, Algeria or Indo-China (Vietnam). The Belgians left the Congo as a recently born democracy. The Dutch had no opportunity to do so in Indonesia, nor did Portugal in Africa, handing over to militarily dominant parties.

[19] R. Oliver, *The African Experience* (London, 1991), p. 241.

governments, they overstretched their technical and administrative resources, and led to borrowing and indebtedness. Above all, because they were government enterprises, economic systems were tilted in their favour at the expense of farmers who formed the main body of private enterprise producers.

The crunch came in the later 1970s (in some cases, such as that of Ghana, earlier), when conditions deteriorated and it was no longer possible to conceal economic failure behind a façade of borrowing. The World Bank, admittedly attempting to justify its 'Adjustment' strategies, provided a similar analysis of the situation in the early 1990s.

> There is no single explanation for Africa's poor performance before the adjustment period. The main factors behind the stagnation and decline were poor policies – both macroeconomic and sectoral – emanating from a development paradigm that gave the state a prominent role in production and regulating economic activity. Overvalued exchange rates and large and prolonged budget deficits undermined the macroeconomic stability needed for long-term growth. Protectionist trade policies and government monopolies reduced the competition so vital for increasing productivity. In addition, the state increased its presence in the 1970s, nationalizing enterprises and financial institutions and introducing a web of regulations and licenses for most economic activities. More important, the development strategy had a clear bias against exports, heavily taxing agricultural exports, one of the largest suppliers of foreign exchange.[20]

Many have criticized the World Bank's and the IMF's prescriptions to remedy these problems. But on one thing most people now agree. The main cause of Africa's economic problems lay in the inability of its governments to establish and sustain viable development policies. Above all, by rejecting the export option, whether of commodities or manufactures, and putting their faith in import-substituting industries at whatever cost, they condemned their countries to economic stagnation. That this was not inevitable as a consequence of their colonial inheritance, or the malevolence of the international economy, still less of the mere fact of governments taking a controlling role, is made clear by looking at the parallel experience of other ex-colonial economies in South, South-east and East Asia.

2   India after Independence

In the hierarchy of post-Second World War development among Third World countries, India stands somewhere between Black Africa and the more dynamic states of East Asia. In terms of population, India was larger

---

[20] World Bank, *Adjustment in Africa*, p. 20.

than the whole of Black Africa, with over 900 million in 1994 as compared with about 572 million in sub–Saharan Africa. India's per capita
income was then estimated at $320, as against a weighted average of
$460 for Black Africa. On the other hand, India had a higher propor-
tion of the labour force in 'industry' than the weighted average for
Black Africa: 16 per cent as against 9 per cent in 1990; and the share of
'manufacturing' in production in 1994 was 18 per cent as compared
with 15 per cent. Adult illiteracy was much the same at 35 per cent of
males, though female illiteracy was higher in India than in Africa.

In fact, however, the biggest contrast between India and Black Africa lay
in the relative importance of foreign trade. While Africa exported 21.3
per cent and imported 22.8 per cent of the value of its GDP in 1994,
India exported only 8.5 per cent and imported 9.1 per cent. Clearly
Africa, despite the efforts of most states to reduce their dependence on
trade and the decline of many export staples, remained a far more open
economy than India, which was still in the 1990s, as it had been half a
century earlier, essentially a continental economy. This fact is of considerable importance for analysis of Indian economic policy and growth
after independence.[21]

The main focus of almost all accounts of India's economic performance since independence has been why it did not do better during this
half century, why, late in the century, it remained low in the list of what
the World Bank defines as 'low-income economies'.[22]

The question is normally posed this way, rather than in terms of its
undoubtedly impressive achievements, because at independence India
appeared to have substantial advantages as compared with many other
post-colonial developing countries, particularly those in Africa.

To start with, India had a system of government and administration
that was more akin to those of the West than other Third World countries.

---

[21] All statistics are from World Bank, *World Development Report 1996*.
[22] There is, of course, a vast literature on this question, and I do not claim to
have studied any large proportion of it. My sources are mainly secondary studies
that provide summaries of more detailed analyses and provide particular points
of view. Among those I have found most useful are the following: V. N.
Balasubramanyam, *The Economy of India* (London, 1984); P. S. Jha, *India:
A Political Economy of Stagnation* (Bombay, 1980); S. Swamy, 'The Economic
Distance between China and India, 1955–73', *China Quarterly*, 70 (June 1977),
pp. 371–82; S. L. Shetty, *Structural Retrogression in the Indian Economy since the
Mid-Sixties* (Bombay, 1979); B. R. Tomlinson, *The Economy of Modern India
1860–1970* (Cambridge, 1993); J. N. Bhagwati and P. Desai, *India: Planning
for Industrialization: Industrialization and Trade Policies since 1951* (Oxford, 1970);
J. N. Bhagwati and T. N. Srinivasan, *Foreign Trade Regimes and Economic Development: India* (Delhi, 1976); F. Frankel, *India's Political Economy, 1947–1977: The
Gradual Revolution* (Princeton, 1978); M. Wolf, *India's Exports* (London, 1982).

It was a 'strong state', particularly when compared with the 'soft states' of much of Black Africa. India also inherited two other institutions and traditions of great potential value.

The first was the army, whose officer corps was imbued with the British assumption that the army should not interfere in politics. This was of critical importance after 1947: India experienced no military takeovers. Equally important was the long Indian experience in representative government, which dated from the 1870s. By 1947 Indian elites, both national and provincial, had a very long experience of and great expertise in elective politics. When the new fully democratic and quasi-federal Indian constitution came into force in 1949, Indians had no difficulty in operating it. In short, despite the problems caused by the partition of British India in 1947, the new Indian government was endowed with exceptional power to govern the whole of its territory both democratically and effectively. No new African state and few in other parts of Asia were as well equipped.

In other respects, however, the inheritance of the new India was a mixed bag. In terms of human resources there was a paradox. India possessed a minority of very highly educated people who were fully competent to run both government and the economy: on the other hand, the literacy rate in 1941 was only 15.1 per cent.[23] India had the largest rail network in Asia, which was critical for economic development. A major asset in 1947 was the fact that, during the war, India had earned enough credit from Britain for its contribution to the war effort to wipe out its overseas debts and to leave it with some £1.2 billion of foreign-exchange credits, which were available to pay for imported capital goods for its development strategy. It also had some large and internationally competitive manufacturing industries, particularly cotton and jute textiles, an iron and steel industry that made the country virtually autonomous by the later 1930s, and a number of consumer industries which, though largely import substituting and dependent on protection since the early 1930s, pointed to the potential for substantial industrial growth. In 1946/7 there were 2.6 million factory employees.[24] This gave India the largest industrial base of any Asian country except Japan.

Yet, despite this expansion, India could not be called an industrial country, at most an industrializing one. In 1947, although mining and manufacturing combined were said to contribute 17 per cent of GDP, more than half of this was provided by small, non-mechanized producers, and employment in large-scale factories was under 2 per cent

[23] Tomlinson, *The Economy of Modern India*, table 1.1, p. 4.
[24] Morris D. Morris, 'The Growth of Large-scale Industry to 1947', in D. Kumar, (ed.), *The Cambridge Economic History of India*, vol. 2: c.1757–c.1970 (Cambridge, 1983), tables 7.21, 7.22, p. 641; table 7.23, p. 643.

of the total labour force. In fact, the proportion of the workforce employed in the 'modern sector' (including mining, manufacturing, transport, storage and communications) had remained roughly constant at about 12 per cent for half a century between 1901 and 1951.[25] Moreover, factory industry was still dominated by cotton and jute textiles, and the bulk of the nation's industrial production came from two relatively small areas based on Bombay and Calcutta.

The main obstacle to growth, however, lay in the agricultural sector. It employed some 80 per cent of the workforce but produced only about 59 per cent of GDP in 1951. The critical fact was that output per acre had risen very slowly during the first half of the twentieth century. Since output grew more slowly than population, availability of food gains fell by an average of 1 per cent per year between 1911 and 1947. There were, admittedly, pockets of growth, particularly of wheat in the Punjab and in non-food-grain crops such as cotton and sugar. But overall agriculture was unable to perform its three historic functions in aid of growth. It could not provide enough food, a substantial surplus for investment in modernization, or an expanding market for manufactures.

In sum, India at independence presents a paradox. It was better equipped than virtually all African and many other Third World countries to initiate and carry out a successful development strategy. On the other hand, it was weighed down by an agricultural sector that was as low in productivity as that in many other parts of the developing world. In addition, in contrast with most African states, it faced the problem of limited supplies of uncultivated land. It remained to be seen whether the new Indian government, dominated for the first three decades of independence by Congress, and for most of the time by Jawaharlal Nehru and his daughter, Indira Gandhi, would adopt a 'continental' or an export-oriented approach.

There was, in fact, no doubt which strategy Nehru would adopt. He had long been impressed, as were many British observers in the later 1920s and early 1930s after visiting the USSR, by the twin agents of Stalinist development, five-year plans and concentration on heavy industry. The First Five Year Plan of 1951 was fairly conventional, constrained by acute economic problems. But the Second Five Year Plan of 1956–61, influenced by Professor P. C. Mahalanobis, was overtly socialist and dirigiste and set the pattern of Indian economic development for the next twenty years and more.

The central assumption of this Plan was what was later described as the need for a 'big push' to overcome structural obstacles to sustained growth. The key to growth lay in an 'industry-first' strategy dominated by the public sector. The main emphasis would be on investment in

[25] Tomlinson, *The Economy of Modern India*, p. 95.

capital goods and steel, on the assumption that, while in the short term
this would reduce the resources available for private consumption of
scarce commodities (including foreign exchange), in the longer term
these new industries would both generate savings for further investment
and lay the foundations for a modern manufacturing economy. As adopted
in 1956, the Plan referred explicitly to 'the socialist pattern of society
as the objective of social and economic policy'.[26] Industries were divided
into three categories. The state would monopolize seventeen 'strategic'
industries. Twelve were open to both public and private enterprise, while
others were left to private capital, subject to the needs of the Plan and
the regulation of imports and industrial capacity.

So ambitious a scheme in a poor and largely underdeveloped country
depended for its success on very strict regulation of the economy as a
whole, and in particular of foreign trade, since foreign exchange was
critical for capital investment. Regulation of imports, either by conventional tariffs or by quantity restrictions (QRs) through licences, had two
main functions. First, it had to ration foreign exchange so that this was
available for planned capital investment. Secondly, it had to provide protection for both public and private producers against international competition. Bhagwati and Desai, after exhaustive investigation of a wide
range of Indian industries in 1961 and 1962, concluded that 'the net
protective effect of the foreign trade regime might have been in the range
of levels as high as 80–100 per cent ... measured as the ratio of
incremental value-added to value added at domestic prices, and higher
still when measured as the ratio of incremental value-added at international prices ...'.[27]

This system of protection dictated the nature of Indian economic
development until the 1980s and beyond. India became in many respects
a closed economy, though after 1971 there was some liberalization of
the 'licence raj'.

Restriction of imports was not entirely dictated by development strategy. A major influence was shortage of foreign exchange, caused partly
by the very poor export performance. Exports were given no encouragement; and, because of the overvalued rupee, relatively high domestic
costs, and the effects of controls and export duties, India's share of the
world market for its traditional exports declined sharply in the 1950s.
Tea, for example, fell from 50 to 30 per cent of world sales, jute manufactures from 86 to 73 per cent, and cotton textiles from 18 to 11 per cent.[28]
In the early 1960s the serious shortage of foreign exchange persuaded

[26] Quoted in ibid., p. 177.
[27] Bhagwati and Desai, *India*, ch. 17; table 17.1, p. 354; table 17.2, p. 358;
table 17.3, p. 362; pp. 362–3.
[28] Ibid., p. 189.

the government in the Third Plan of 1961 to attempt to stimulate exports by a complex system of subsidies, tax rebates and import licences which had a market value. This amounted to an effective devaluation of the rupee for these exporters, and was followed in 1966 by formal devaluation (under severe IMF pressure) by 57.5 per cent, which led to gradually rising export volumes into the 1990s.[29]

But this did not imply that India had turned seriously to a strategy of export-led growth. At the end of the 1970s India's exports and imports constituted a very small proportion of its GDP. In most manufactures Indian growth was significantly below that of other Asian countries, notably the East Asian 'Tigers', and the value of Indian exports was disproportionately small as late as 1994. In that year Indian exports were $25 billion, as compared with $121 billion for China, $40 billion for Indonesia, $58.7 billion for Malaysia, $45 billion for Thailand, $151 billion for Hong Kong, and $98.8 billion for Singapore.[30]

There have been many attempts to explain this very poor export performance, apart from the official commitment to a 'continental' development strategy. The most persuasive is that exporters were handicapped by the economic consequences of a strategy based on import substitution and high protectionism. This generated relatively high domestic costs for inputs, a shortage of imported intermediates, and low-quality products, since most were for the protected home market. It also encouraged capital intensity, which prevented India from exploiting the main comparative advantage it, along with most other Asian countries, possessed, which was an almost limitless supply of relatively cheap and often well-educated labour. The export subsidies and other incentives adopted after 1965 were symptoms of this condition and could do little to cure it. Despite all the liberation of the following decades, the licence, regime continued almost unchanged. Although attacked by some of India's leading economists, it was defended by many other economists who remained committed to the original development strategy, and it was buttressed by vested interests, including civil servants, politicians and businessmen, all of whom stood to lose by a liberal trade system.

Nevertheless, it is important not to undervalue the success of India's development effort. Despite rapid population growth, per capita incomes consistently increased after 1947: by 1.6, 1.8 and 0.4 per cent during the first three planning periods to 1966, and by 1.8 and 2.9 per cent in the periods 1965–88 and 1985–94.[31] These rates of increase were not

[29] World Bank, *World Development Report 1996*, table 15, p. 216.
[30] Ibid.
[31] Tomlinson, *The Economy of Modern India*, table 1.1, p. 4; table 1.2, p. 5; Bhagwati and Desai, *India*, table 4.2, p. 62; World Bank, *World Development Reports, 1990*, table 1, p. 178 and *World Development Report 1996*, table 1. p. 188.

staggeringly high, at least by the standard of the fastest growing economies. Yet, compared with its speculative pre-independence performance, the Indian economy at least had a reasonably sustained rate of overall growth, often described as 'the Hindu rate of growth', which, apart from the crisis period of 1965–6, seemed relatively immune to the shocks of the international economy. We are, therefore, left with two parallel questions. How was this improvement achieved in the early years of independence down to 1965? Why did India not do better thereafter, perhaps as well as China or the East Asian 'Tigers'?

The answer commonly given to the first of these questions by most Indians and by many anti-colonialists elsewhere was, of course, that rapid development was inevitable once the shackles of colonialism had been removed. Certainly evidence of the period from 1947 to the mid-1960s seemed to support this assumption. Agriculture achieved a compound growth rate of 3 per cent, achieved not only by extending the area under cultivation but also by an increase in yield per acre, from an index of 100 in 1950/1 to 121 in 1964/5, before the drought of 1965 slightly reduced yields. Domestic savings rose dramatically from 5.5 per cent of national income in 1950/1 to 10.5 per cent in 1965/6. Investments, however, rose far more, from 5.5 to about 14 per cent of national income in 1965/6. This gap between savings and investment was significant, and will be considered later. Tax revenues also rose, from 6.6 per cent of net national income in 1951–6 to about 14 per cent in 1961–5. Moreover, there was relative price stability until 1963/4, with an average price increase of only 2 per cent; though this rose to about 12 per cent in the following three years.[32]

Higher savings, including government savings from taxation, translated into an impressive jump in industrial production. The index of production (1956 = 100) for all manufactures rose from 72.8 in 1951 to 186.0 in 1966. Significantly, the four largest proportionate increases were in state-dominated industries: basic metals from 83.1 to 318; manufacture of machinery (excluding electrical machinery) from 45.2 to 530.1; manufacture of electrical machinery from 43.6 to 340.6; and electricity and gas generation from 60.9 to 355.3.[33] These and other increases in production of basic and intermediate products laid the foundations for India to develop an autonomous industrial system. To this extent there had been a successful 'big push' in the two decades after independence.

Why was this possible? The key lay in the increased availability of factor supplies of all kinds. Private large-scale industry seized the opportunity provided by an expanded market and generous government protection to increase production: by contrast with many African countries, there was

[32] Bhagwati and Desai, *India*, pp. 64–75.
[33] Ibid., table 5.1.

no entrepreneurial bottleneck. For its part, the government established a range of institutions to provide capital for private industry. In a typical year these distributed some Rs100 million, representing 13–20 per cent of external (i.e. in addition to a firm's own savings) sources of finance for private industry. This, in turn, enabled these firms to double their institutional finance for expansion.[34]

In this way the state filled the gap between private and corporate savings and the need for investment. The question is how it was financed without the normal inflationary effects of credit creation by the state. The evidence suggests that aid and foreign investment may have been important in providing these resources, and therefore making possible the great industrial leap of the first two decades of independence.[35]

Of these, aid was the more important makeweight for India's limited savings and foreign earnings. There is a paradox here. On the one hand, India was one of the largest recipients of aid, receiving nearly 14 per cent of total world aid in the early 1960s. On the other hand, in relation to India's population, aid was very small: an average of only $1.80 a head in 1962 and 1963. Aid came in many forms and had many disadvantages, both political and economic. Yet aid, despite its limitations, bridged a critical gap in public finance, avoiding the need for deficit financing of development. As a proportion of the national income, aid rose from 0.86 per cent in 1951/2 to 3.04 per cent in 1966/7, after peaking at 3.80 the previous year. In 1966/7 taxation was about 12.5 per cent of the national product; so aid represented a 25 per cent addition to government income and the state's ability to finance investment.

Consider next the relative importance of FDI among resource flows. Kidron estimated that between 1948 and 1961 the ratio between aid and FDI was 4.6 : 1; net of servicing costs, it was 6 : 1. This is supported by official statistics. According to the Reserve Bank of India, accumulated FDI rose from Rs crores 255.9 (about £200 million) in 1948 to Rs crores 528.4 (around £397 million) in 1961, an increase of Rs crores 272.5 (£204.8 million). For comparison, Bhagwati and Desai put the figure for aid actually utilized between 1951 and 1961 at Rs crores 1,430 (some £1.2 billion), which supports Kidron's estimated 6 : 1 ratio between aid and FDI.[36]

It is, therefore, clear that at least a partial answer to the question of why Indian development could accelerate after independence is that the

---

[34] Ibid., pp. 76–9.
[35] The following argument is based mainly on ibid., chs 10, 11.
[36] M. Kidron, *Foreign Investments in India* (London, 1965), quoted in Bhagwati and Desai, *India*, p. 216; Balasubramanyam, *The Economy of India*, table 7.1, p.148, based on *The Reserve Bank of India Bulletin*, various issues; Bhagwati and Desai, *India*, table 10.2, p. 173, based on the Government of India, *Economic Survey, 1967–8* (New Delhi, 1968).

resources available for investment were far greater than ever before. While most of these were domestic, foreign aid and FDI added significantly to investment capacity, bridging the resource gap.

There were other favourable factors before the mid-1960s. The war had left a large pent-up domestic demand for consumer goods, which provided a market for expanded production. Because there were so relatively few manufacturing industries, there was huge opportunity for ISI development, stimulated by the intensified system of protection. There was considerable scope for increased food production, particularly in the wheat areas, despite the loss of the western Punjab, through expanding the area under cultivation, by adopting improved strains of food grains, and by the application of artificial fertilizers, improvement in irrigation and so on. Moreover, climatic conditions were unusually favourable until 1965.

In short, India after about 1951 had a unique opportunity to move the economy towards sustained growth. The consequential questions are how successful this 'big push' proved in the longer term, and why India did not do better, particularly by comparison with other East and Southeast Asian countries. To answer these questions it is proposed to examine briefly in turn the fortunes of government planning and the public sector, agriculture and food supplies, and manufacturing.[37]

The public sector

It was clear from the mid-1950s that the long-term success of the Indian economic development strategy depended very heavily on the results of the Mahalanobis model of the mid-1950s – that is, on the assumption that in a developing country the state must be the prime mover and that it must control the 'commanding heights' of the economy. How well did this dirigiste model work in India?

First, there is no doubt that India achieved an impressive increase in savings and investment: both net domestic savings and net capital formation rose from about 6 per cent of the national product in 1950/1 to over 19 per cent in the late 1970s and thereafter.[38] This fully met the criteria of some development economists of the 1950s and 1960s as a precondition for 'take-off'. On the other hand, whereas these economists normally postulated that government should take the lead in making savings, in India the state played a relatively small role. In the 1970s the household sector provided more than 70 per cent of domestic savings in all but one year; and the majority of this appears to have been invested in physical

[37] In what follows I am following the pattern and much of the argument of Balasubramanyam in *The Economy of India.*
[38] Ibid., table 4.1, p. 57.

assets, plus payments into insurance and other funds. Conversely, the government sector never provided more than 25.4 per cent of total domestic savings, and the corporate sector provided relatively very small amounts.

This poor government performance was due partly to a weak and regressive tax structure, still heavily dependent on indirect taxes, but also on the inability of the public-sector industries to produce the investible profits that had been assumed in the early plans. As a result, although budgetary and public enterprise surpluses provided some 40 per cent of development expenditure in the early 1980s, development depended on domestic borrowing as much as on government savings. In addition, the government had regularly to resort to deficit financing, with its inflationary implications, and on external aid: in 1981/2 deficits and aid provided 8.8 and 7.9 per cent respectively of five-year-plan outlays.[39]

Nevertheless, while this suggests that the Indian government failed to provide the savings needed for investment out of taxation or the profits of public enterprises, Balasubramanyam argues that limited economic growth was due not to inadequate savings – since the private sector provided a high level of savings – but to inefficient investment of capital. The critical fact is that capital–output ratios rose considerably during the thirty years after 1950. The net incremental capital–output ratio rose from 2.04 to 5.63; the net incremental fixed capital-output ratio from 1.72 to 4.19; and the average capital-output ratio from 2.03 to 2.38.[40] These figures suggest a low absorptive capacity in the Indian economy, the growth of idle capacity in manufacturing, especially in the state-owned basic industries, and limited demand for the products of industry, possibly because of the inability of the poor to buy the relatively expensive (because protected) consumer goods. They also suggest that India's chosen, state-directed development strategy succeeded in providing adequate savings for development investment, but that much of this was wasted because of the combination of high protection for relatively inefficient ISIs, and of huge investment in economically inefficient state-run basic industries, for whose products there was insufficient domestic demand, and which could not compete in international markets.

The agricultural sector

In a developing country in which over 80 per cent of the population lived in the country in the 1960s and where more than half the net domestic product came from agriculture in the early 1950s, the efficiency of farming was crucial for Indian development. How well did agriculture perform?

[39] Ibid., table 4.2, p. 58; table 4.7, p. 69.
[40] Ibid., table 4.8, p. 73.

First, food production. There is some disagreement over the rate of growth, but all agree that it was positive.[41] Moreover, the agricultural workers declined from 80 to 64 per cent of the labour force by 1990.[42] This expansion was made possible partly by the extension of land under cultivation, partly by increased yields helped by the 'green revolution'.

This was in many ways an impressive achievement, particularly in view of the virtual standstill of production before 1949. But food output did not keep pace with population growth, since nearly a third of the output was in non-food grains. India therefore had to import food grains. The most intensive period of imports was in the later 1950s and 1960s, when 'commodity aid', mostly wheat under the American PL480 pro-gramme, constituted nearly a third of all forms of aid by value. In 1974 India imported over 5 million tons of cereals, over a quarter as aid. In 1988 it imported nearly 3 million tons, but very little of it as aid.[43]

It is impossible to quantify agriculture's contribution in other direc-tions. It is probable that a considerable proportion of the household savings was made by farmers, particularly the minority of those with larger holdings, though they paid very little in direct taxation. But it seems clear that the great majority of farmers were too poor to provide an adequate market for the industrial sector. It is also certain that the rate of growth of agriculture slowed down after the mid-1960s. The critical issue is why this was so and why, as a result, the great majority of Indian farmers remained very poor.

In the literature on Third World agricultural development two main factors are commonly said to dictate the efficiency and growth of agri-culture: the price offered to farmers in relation to the price they have to pay for other goods – their barter terms of trade – and the size and degree of technical efficiency of their farms.

In the Indian case, farmers never faced the depredations of the market-ing boards of Black Africa. After independence, however, there were residual wartime price controls on food, and these were reimposed in the later 1950s on wholesale prices. In the 1950s and early 1960s the government deliberately used imports and food aid to keep down the price to consumers. The result was that between 1951/2 and 1963/4 the index of the net barter terms of trade between agriculture and manu-facturing (1960/1 = 100) remained more or less constant, while the income terms of trade crept up gradually from 67.07, and touched 100 only briefly in 1956/7. From the mid-1960s, however, government recognized the importance of the price mechanism. A system of state

---

[41] Tomlinson, *The Economy of Modern India*, table 4.2, p. 176; table 4.5, p. 180; Balasubramanyam, *The Economy of India*, table 5.2, p. 84.
[42] World Bank, *World Development Report 1996*, table 11, p. 208; table 4, p. 194.
[43] Ibid., table 4, p. 184.

procurement and price support was introduced, based on official assessment of the costs of production and the minimum profit margins farmers
needed. Although these official prices were below market prices, they
had the effect of levering the market up. The result was that between
the mid-1960s and the mid-1970s the barter terms of trade of food
grains improved by almost 50 per cent and the income terms of trade
doubled. It was even argued after this that food prices had become too
high.[44]

Farmers, therefore, had increasing incentives to produce for the market,
and this may have stimulated interest in the adoption of new improved
strains and other technical aspects of the so-called green revolution. But
the feasibility of adopting these innovations depended to a large extent
on the size of farms and the conditions on which they were held. This
in turn raised the issue of land reform. How far was this carried through
in post-independence India?

The central economic issue here was whether, under Indian conditions, small farms intensively worked had a higher yield than larger
farms. In addition, there was the ethical issue of landownership and
tenures: in 1960/1 it was estimated that 63 per cent of farming families
owned only 19 per cent of the cultivated area, on holdings ranging from
one to five acres. Fifteen years later 70 per cent owned 24 per cent.
In addition a large proportion of the land, perhaps 25 per cent, was
cultivated by tenants under a variety of tenures, many of them as sharecroppers, whose conditions were subject to arbitrary action by the landowners. Thus the Indian government had to take two decisions: whether
to impose a limit on the size of landholdings in order to redistribute
land to those with very small holdings; and whether to provide legal
security to tenant farmers.

Early Indian central governments passed laws on both matters, setting
limits to the size of individual holdings. These were widely evaded
through a variety of devices. By 1970 only 0.3 per cent of the agricultural
area had been redistributed, and legislation giving security of tenure to
tenants usually resulted in their eviction. The most solid achievement was
the abolition of the zamindari system in eastern India, providing greater
security for tenant farmers. Only in Kerala was land reform rigorously
carried out, and this had the effect of making Kerala one of the states
most dependent on imported food.[45] The Kerala evidence, in fact, suggests
that division into very small farms may not increase production per
acre and that the input-output ratio may decline with size of the farm.

[44] Balasubramanyam, *The Economy of India*, table 5.3, p. 98; pp. 95–100.
[45] A good study of this is in R. J. Herring, *Land to the Tiller* (New Haven and
London, 1983), chs 6, 7. It also provides a useful analysis of land reform in
principle and its implementation in Pakistan and Sri Lanka.

The main economic advantage of redistribution into small farming units was that it used less foreign exchange than larger farms, because small farmers could not afford chemical fertilizers, pesticides and so on.[46]

The conclusion must be that, while India's agricultural performance after 1947 was good by previous standards, and although the green revolution and the financial stimuli offered after the mid-1960s made it possible to sustain a reasonable rate of growth once the option of extending land under cultivation had disappeared, agriculture did not make a substantial contribution to Indian economic growth. Put another way, the basic problem was that there were too many people dependent on farming in relation to the land available, and that their productivity was too low either to provide the vast majority with a reasonable living or to generate substantial savings. Nor was India a significant exporter of any agricultural commodity other than tea, of which it had a declining world share. Indian growth had, therefore, to depend mainly on the industrial sector, and this, as has been seen, was the main plank in the development strategy from the early 1950s. How successful was it?

The manufacturing sector

There is a paradox at the heart of any study of industrialization in modern India. On the one hand, India became a major industrial country, tenth in the world in terms of value added in manufacturing in 1987.[47] Some parts of the sector were very advanced technically and India had considerable R&D facilities: it was increasingly independent of imports of foreign technology, reflected in the decreasing number of technical collaboration agreements with foreign firms over time. On the other hand, as a proportion of total production and employment, industry, both broadly defined and manufacturing, remained relatively small and increased very slowly over time. Industry provided 22 per cent of GDP in 1965, 26 per cent in 1980, 28 per cent in 1994; manufacturing 16, 18 and again 18 per cent in these years.[48] Industry employed under 12 per cent of the total labour force until the later 1970s, 13 per cent in 1980, 16 per cent in 1990.[49] By international standards this implies that, after forty years of independence, India remained at most a semi-industrialized country.

The profile of Indian industrial development followed a pattern common in LDCs. Starting with a relatively small industrial sector

[46] Ibid., pp. 248–252.
[47] World Bank, *World Development Report 1990*, table 6, pp. 188–9.
[48] Ibid., table 3, p. 182; World Bank, *World Development Report 1996*, table 12, p. 210.
[49] World Bank, *World Development Report 1996*, table 4, p. 194; Balasubramanyam, *The Economy of India*, p. 111.

dominated by low-technology industries such as cotton textiles and processed foods, India moved fairly rapidly to relatively high-technology production, which, by the later 1970s, was dominated by chemicals and engineering, and to a broadly diversified range of durable consumer industries. This was standard import substitution behind the barrage of protectionism. The question was, and remains, how far this form of development could take India, and whether it would come up against the normal limits of ISI that did not lead on to competitive export-oriented manufacturing.

The two key influences on industrial development were state planning and the public sector. As was seen above, from the Second Plan it was assumed that the state would virtually monopolize the capital-goods sector, on the assumption that private capital would not or could not provide sufficient investment or face the time lags involved. As a result, state enterprises took over 50 per cent of planned investment between 1956 and the 1970s and in 1977/8 had a 31 per cent share in total gross domestic capital formation in the manufacturing sector. It is a critical fact that there was no correlation between public manufacturing invest-ment, the share of the state enterprises in GDP, and public-sector employ-ment in manufacturing. In 1977/8 the public sector provided 31.4 per cent of gross domestic capital formation, employed 24.4 per cent of the manufacturing sector, but generated only 15.9 per cent of GDP. This suggests that public industrial enterprises were capital intensive and that their productivity was low, with high capital–output ratios.

It is arguable that this fact had a significant influence on the slowing down of Indian industrial growth after the mid-1960s. Over the fifteen years 1951–65 total industrial output grew at an average rate of 7.4 per cent. Some of the highest growth figures were for the state sector, led by basic and capital-goods industries. But after 1965 the rate of expansion slowed down: from 1965 to 1980 industry grew at an average of 4.2 per cent, manufacturing at 4.4 per cent.[50] The crucial elements in this slowing down appear to have been the state–owned basic and capital-goods indus-tries, whose growth rates respectively were 9.3 and 5.5, and 14.5 and 3.2 for the two periods. A parallel, but less drastic decline in the rate of growth occurred in the largely private consumer-goods industries, from 4.7 per cent in 1951–65 to 3.5 per cent in 1965–80. How are this relative decline and this inability to sustain the earlier rate of growth to be explained?

There is a very wide range of suggested explanations, probably as many as there are critics, and none is more than a hypothesis, often based on *a priori* assumptions. These range from Prem Jha's *India: A Political Economy*

---

[50] World Bank, *World Development Report 1990*, table 2, p. 180. Balasubramanyam (*The Economy of India*, p. 118), gives a lower figure of 3.8% for the sector, reduced to 2.5% if 1976 is excluded.

of Stagnation, which blamed the Stalinist principles adopted in 1956, to S. L. Shetty's *Structural Retrogression in the Indian Economy since the Mid-Sixties*, which blamed the partial liberalization of this strategy after Nehru's death in 1964. Balasubramanyam quotes several other interpretations of relative decline. Deepak Nayyar, for example, blamed limited private-sector investment in consumer-goods production, which in turn was caused by a shrinking home market. This resulted from increasing inequalities in income distribution, which limited the consumer capacity of the poorest half of the population. Thus the economy had reached the limits of import substituting industrialization.[51] An alternative view was that of Ashok Desai. As summarized by Balasubramanyam,[52] he thought the problem was essentially supply oriented. High rates of industrial investment combined with low industrial growth indicated high capital–output ratios, particularly in the public sector. This was because their capacity-utilization rates were low, in turn mainly because of over manning. Thus the large public investment was being partly wasted, and the low levels of public-sector saving meant that the government had to resort to money creation.

These are only a sample. My own preference is for an explanation based on the work of Bhagwati and Desai and Bhagwati and Srinivasan. The root cause of the slowing down in the rate of development after about 1965 was the inefficiency, at least in the longer term, of the rigid planning and control system inaugurated in the mid-1950s, which, despite liberalization in the mid-1960s, lingered on into the 1980s and beyond. The complex of controls imposed by the bureaucracy put a brake on human enterprise, particularly in the private sector. Efficient firms were held back, because the government wanted to disperse production and help the smaller firms: that was particularly true of the larger foreign firms.[53] Immense amounts of corporate and official time and money were spent on processing the paperwork, and projects might be held up for years while approval was awaited. At the same time the high level of effective protection enabled inefficient firms to make good profits, at the cost of the consumer, while the more efficient could make

---

[51] Balasubramanyam, *The Economy of India*, pp. 137–8, based on D. Nayyar, 'Industrial Development in India; Growth or Stagnation' in A. Baggchi and N. Banerjee (eds), *Change and Choice in Indian Industry* (Calcutta, 1981), pp. 91–117.

[52] Balasubramanyam, *The Economy of India*, pp. 139–41, from A. V. Desai, 'Factors Underlying the Slow Growth of Indian Industry', *Economic and Political Weekly* (Mar. 1981), pp. 381–92.

[53] For a detailed analysis of how such a foreign firm was affected by the licence regime and restrictions on expansion and diversification, see D. K. Fieldhouse, *Unilever Overseas: The Anatomy of a Multinational* (London, 1978), ch. 4, esp. pp. 187–91, 205–29.

very large profits. This gave the Indian industrial economy a strong bias towards producing only for the profitable home market and made it non-competitive overseas. The policy of granting import licences on the basis of existing capacity provided an incentive to overexpand capacity, which in turn resulted in large amounts of wasted productive resources. In short, regulation was throttling what might have been a highly expansionary period of Indian industry.

This is not, however, to argue that in the Indian context state planning was necessarily undesirable or the main cause of disappointing industrial growth. Given the backwardness of the economy in about 1950, a strong lead from the centre was probably essential. The argument is rather that this central direction had two main defects.

First, the planning of the mid-1950s was too close to the Stalinist model and committed India to overexpansion of basic and capital industries, and this resulted in an excessively capital-intensive structure of production with long time-lags between investment (and borrowing to pay for it) and production.

Secondly, most of the administrative regulations designed to carry through these plans were economically irrational, generated by *ad hoc* bureaucratic decision-making, with little serious consideration for their economic consequences. As will be seen in chapter 11, other Asian states adopted similarly strict state planning, but used it much more efficiently and, above all, flexibly. Conversely, comparison with mainland China suggests that to be successful a dirigiste strategy of development may require far more central dictation and authoritarianism than was possible in a democratic society and a mixed economy such as that of India.

It is, however, important not to paint too bleak a picture of Indian economic development after independence. Unlike most of Black Africa by the 1980s and 1990s, it was in no sense a disaster area. Relatively insulated from the rest of the world economy by its size and inward-looking economic structures, it proved almost immune to the major international shocks of the 1970s and 1980s.[54] India emerged with relatively small overseas debts, a low debt-service ratio, and an average inflation rate for 1984–94 of 9.7 per cent.

Moreover, at the end of the period, there were signs of further economic and trade liberalization. In 1991–2 the import licensing was made

[54] For a comparative treatment of Indian and other developing countries' experiences and reactions in this period, see I. M. D. Little, R. N. Cooper, W. M. Corden and S. Rajapatirana, *Boom, Crisis, and Adjustment: The Macroeconomic Experience of Developing Countries* (Oxford, 1993), *passim*. See also the related study by V. Joshi and I. M. D. Little, *India: Macroeconomics and Political Economy, 1964–1991* (Delhi, 1994).

less stringent, the list of banned imports reduced and simplified, import tariffs were lowered, though remaining very high on consumer goods, export subsidies were eliminated, though tradable import entitlements to exporters were retained. To make these changes possible, a floating exchange rate was introduced for 60 per cent of all foreign exchange transactions. Meantime, and eventually helped by these measures, the growth rate of exports rose from 5.9 per cent in the 1980s to 13.6 per cent between 1990 and 1994.

This might point towards a belated recognition of the importance of moving from a somewhat constipated import substitution to export-led growth. But there was a long way to go before Indian exports formed anything approaching the proportion they formed of the GDP in other developing countries. This would not be easy. The problem of developing competitive export manufactures in the later twentieth century was well summarized in 1985 by Professor S. Chakravarty, one-time member of the Indian Planning Commission, in a rhetorical question: what was India's comparative advantage in the electronic age?[55] This was the same problem that had been faced by the group of East and Southeast Asian countries after independence. Chapter 11 attempts to explain how they tried to solve it.

[55] In response to a question on Indian trading policies after a lecture given at the South Asian Studies Centre, Cambridge, in March 1985.

11

Trade and Development after 1950: East and South-east Asia

All the new states of East and South-east Asia, with the exception of Thailand, had been colonial dependencies until varying times between 1945 and 1963. Taiwan (Formosa) and Korea had been Japanese colonies from 1895 and 1910 respectively until 1945. Malaya became independent in 1957, then expanded in 1963 as Malaysia to include Singapore (for two years only), Sabah and Sarawak. Indonesia emerged from Netherlands control in 1949, when the United States prevented the Dutch from full reoccupation after the Japanese occupation of 1942–5 and the Indonesian declaration of sovereignty of 1945. Hong Kong remained a British colony until handed back to China in 1997. Thailand alone had never been a formal dependency, but had been under strong British economic influence from the mid-nineteenth century.

This almost universal colonial experience is important for the present argument because the post-colonial achievements of these East and South-east Asian states can be directly compared with those of other ex-colonies. Most of these countries had experienced alien rule for long periods. At independence they faced much the same problems as the new states of Black Africa and South Asia. Yet by the 1970s and 1980s several of them were among the most dynamic economies in the world, generating the concept of an East Asian 'miracle'. This fact immediately challenges the notion that it was impossible for new ex-colonial arrivals to join the ranks of the affluent industrial countries. More particularly, since their success was based to a large extent on manufactured exports, it demonstrated that it was possible for countries with predominantly agricultural economies to discover their comparative advantage in manufacturing and exploit it.[1]

These countries, however, divide into two groups. The first, consisting of Hong Kong, Taiwan, South Korea (after the Korean War of 1950–2) and Singapore, particularly after leaving Malaysia in 1965, were the pioneers in rapid manufacturing growth and exporting. The others followed in and after the 1970s. Of the first group, Hong Kong and Singapore were island city states, virtually unique in the Third World. Hence the main interest has centred on Taiwan and South Korea, and this account will concentrate initially on them, putting the main emphasis on Taiwan. How did these ex-Japanese colonies, which had been treated as extensions of the imperial economy even more completely than European colonies, emerge as leading actors in the international economy, so that by the early 1990s, measured by income per capita, they stood at the top of the World Bank's 'upper-middle-income' bracket?[2] What lessons did they provide for other developing countries? As a subsidiary question, how successfully have other Asian states followed their example?[3]

[1] This account was written before the banking and currency crisis in East and South-east Asia in late 1997 and early 1998. In the longer term the crisis may prove that the East Asian 'miracle' was a delusion, or it may turn out to be a short-term blip. I have left what I have written largely unchanged because what it says was, so far as I know, true until at least mid-1997.

[2] There is a problem in placing Taiwan in this type of comparison, since the World Bank, owing no doubt to the political problem of China's refusal to recognize Taiwan as a separate state, does not include it in any of its standard development publications. But in its publication *The East Asian Miracle* (Oxford, 1993) (hereafter *TEAM*), which will be used extensively for statistical material in this section, it is included, but always referred to as 'Taiwan, China'. This comparison of Taiwan's GDP in 1992 with that of Korea is in table 4.4, p. 177, which puts Taiwan above Korea in terms of international dollars per capita. World Bank, *World Development Report 1996: From Plan to Market* (Oxford, 1996), put Korea top of the upper-middle-income group in 1994, above Saudi Arabia, Greece and Argentina.

[3] There is, of course, a huge literature on each of these territories and on the wider issue, and I do not pretend to have read any large proportion of it. This account will be based mainly on information in the World Bank's *TEAM*, which has an extensive bibliography. On Taiwan my main sources are the wide range of essays in W. Galenson (ed.), *Economic Growth and Structural Change in Taiwan: The Postwar Experience of the Republic of China* (Ithaca, NY, and London, 1979), and T. Scitovsky 'Economic Development in Taiwan and South Korea: 1965–81', first published in 1985, repr. in his *Economic Theory and Reality* (Aldershot, 1995). On the colonial background I have relied mainly on R. H. Myers and M. R. Peattie (eds), *The Japanese Colonial Empire, 1895–1945* (Princeton, NJ, 1984), particularly part 3, 'The Economic Dynamics of

1   The East Asian 'Miracle': Taiwan and South Korea, Two 'Baby Tigers'

We may start with the colonial inheritance of Taiwan and Korea.[4] The Japanese had treated both as vital sources of food and raw materials for Japan: rice in both of them, sugar in Taiwan and mining in Korea. Particularly in the 1930s, when Japan was aiming at economic autarky, there was also an industrial drive. Whereas previously industry had consisted primarily of processing local commodities, it now expanded into the metallurgical and chemical industries, made possible by the increase in supplies of hydroelectric energy. Industry was not, however, broadly based. In both countries a very few, largely government- or Japanese-owned private companies dominated the manufacturing sector. Their output was largely for export to Japan as inputs to its industries, and they depended heavily for their viability on protection within the imperial system. Alongside the very large firms were a very large number of smaller, mostly Chinese or Korean, firms, which produced for the domestic market. There were few linkages between them, and the main contribution large-scale industry made to the economy was using local minerals and energy and employing Chinese or Korean labour.

Yet the Japanese did make a considerable contribution to Taiwanese and Korean development. To maximize agricultural production and exports they made great improvements in communications and power supplies. They introduced the elements of a green revolution long before this was adopted in South Asia. Between 1911 and 1940 agricultural output and productivity in Taiwan increased respectively at an average of 4.5 and 3.0 per cent annually, far better than that of India in the same period. Little suggests that by the 1930s Taiwan was far ahead of China and most of Asia in agricultural techniques, but added that it was probably already as advanced in 1895 as most Asian countries were as late as 1960. Korea, which was less favoured for agriculture than Taiwan, received less attention and had lower growth rates. Substantial contributions were also made to indigenous welfare. There was a considerable increase in life expectancy in both colonies owing to better medical services. Education was improved, though there was a two-track system that differentiated Japanese settlers from others. By 1945, however,

---

the Empire'. On Indonesia I found H. Hill, *Foreign Investment and Industrialization in Indonesia* (Singapore, Oxford and New York, 1988), very useful on a wider range of issues than the title might suggest. It also has a useful bibliography on the region as a whole.
[4] See I. M. D. Little, 'An Economic Reconnaissance' in Galenson (ed.), *Economic Growth*, and S. Pao-San Ho, 'Colonialism and Development: Korea, Taiwan, and Kwantung', in Myers and Peattie, *The Japanese Colonial Empire*.

perhaps 75 per cent of Taiwanese children of primary-school age were enrolled in schools, though 40 per cent of males and 75 per cent of women were still illiterate. This was comparable to many other Third World countries fifty years later.

The Second World War had adverse effects on both Taiwan and Korea. Most of the Taiwan industrial sector was destroyed by bombing and infrastructure was severely damaged. By 1945 agriculture, which suffered from shortage of fertilizer and lack of maintenance of irrigation, was possibly back to the level of 1910. On the other hand, perhaps 1.5 million Kuomintang supporters arrived in Taiwan from the mainland after 1945, bringing not only a very large army but many highly educated and technically expert Chinese, who were able to fill the gap left by the disappearing Japanese. Korea did not suffer as seriously from the World War but was devastated during the Korean War.

Thus, in about 1953, there was little reason to think that either of these ex-colonies would surprise the world by the rapidity of its growth or its success in manufacturing for a world market. Little estimated that, in terms of 1973 US dollars, the per capita income of Taiwan may then have been about $222, that of South Korea $145. This would have put Korea on a par with Thailand, South Vietnam and the Philippines; Taiwan above that, but below Malaya, which on the same count might have had a per capita income of $360.[5] What initial assets did these countries then possess?

Scitovsky lists five. First, both Taiwan and Korea possessed the tradition of Confucian philosophy, which included a high respect for learning, which later resulted in a relatively high literacy rate. Secondly, the Chinese possessed a high work ethic and willingness to work for very long hours, though how far this was due to the weakness of labour unions is unclear. Thirdly, they were accustomed to wage flexibility and employment stability. This was connected with the Chinese tradition of periodic bonuses, which may have contributed to high savings rates. Then, fourthly, there was the aftermath of Japanese rule and its end. As has been seen, the Japanese had raised productivity in agriculture, and, once the ravages of war had been repaired, this led to an impressive agricultural achievement. Moreover, the departure of the Japanese released a very large amount of land (some 21 per cent of arable land in Taiwan) that they, and in particular farming companies, had owned. This was confiscated and distributed as part of a fundamental programme of land reform, which also had the effect of releasing surplus labour, providing a substantial impetus to industrialization. In addition to one-time Japanese properties, all Chinese-owned land in Taiwan over 3 hectares was sold to tenants at low prices. This had an important effect

[5] Little, 'An Economic Reconnaissance', p. 452.

on the character of both farming and the society in both countries, producing a far more egalitarian structure. In Taiwan, though not Korea, industry moved out of the towns into the countryside, offering factory work for the poorer farmers. By the end of the 1970s over 72 per cent of farm family incomes came from 'straddling' of this sort, which in turn checked the drift to towns. In Korea there was no comparable pattern, but farm incomes were kept up by farm-support prices and food subsidies.

These were all part of the post-colonial inheritance. The new factor after about 1953, which played a major role in both Taiwanese and Korean development, was the exceptional amount of foreign aid they received. Between 1951 and 1967; Taiwan received some $1.5 billion, mostly in grants or very soft loans, an average of $90 million a year and $6 a head, though about $10 a head at its peak in the 1950s. Over the whole period this represented about 5.1 per cent of GNP. On the other hand, because of Chinese irredentism, a large amount of this aid was spent on defence, leaving little for development. Thus the main function of aid between 1951 and 1962 was to bridge a foreign exchange deficit of $1.3 billion. The great period of Taiwanese economic growth began in the early 1960s, just when the aid contribution was slowing down.

For Korea the position was different. It received even more US aid than Taiwan, a total of $1.9 billion between 1953 and 1960, or some $10 a head. Korea also received very large military aid. The contrast was that Korea spent only about 5 per cent of GNP on defence, so that a larger proportion of economic aid was available for economic purposes. Moreover, whereas aid to Taiwan was phased out in the mid-1960s, aid to Korea continued, and financed on average 10.2 per cent of total investment between 1965 and 1981.

Nevertheless, a general conclusion on the post-colonial inheritance of Taiwan and Korea must be that these countries were not exceptionally advantaged when compared to many other LDCs of that period. Both remained essentially agricultural communities. In short, there was no good reason in the early 1950s to predict that either would become dynamic economies, rapidly emerging from the ruck of poor Third World countries. We are, therefore, left with the question of how this was achieved and what significance their success has for the general problem of Third World economic development. To attempt an answer it is proposed to examine separately the strategies and experience of Taiwan and Korea, then more briefly those of Malaysia and Indonesia.

Taiwan

It is critical that Taiwan started as a fairly typical Third World country that depended on exports of agricultural commodities and adopted a conventional import-substituting strategy. In the early 1950s 91 per cent of the value of its exports were from agriculture, only 6 per cent from manufactures: by 1973–5 agriculture provided only 16 per cent of exports, manufactures 82 per cent.[6] In the early years after 1950 agriculture therefore played a major role in Taiwan's development.[7] In the period between 1946 and 1951–3 agriculture grew at 9.1 per cent, compared with growth of the domestic product at 13.2 per cent. In the next period up to 1964–7 the growth rates were 5.7 and 7.7 per cent, and from then to 1971–3, 2.4 and 10.1 per cent. Overall Taiwan's agricultural growth rate in the period 1952–4 to 1966–8 was surpassed only by Thailand (5.5 per cent) and Korea (4.5 per cent). Clearly until the mid-1960s economic growth depended very heavily on increasing agricultural efficiency. Its main importance was that it generated foreign exchange, which could be used to pay for imports of capital, intermediate and consumer goods. The agricultural export surplus rose from $12 million in 1952 to $120 million in 1965. It then disappeared, as agricultural labour moved into manufacture and the stock of uncultivated land ran out.

Parallel with this conventional dependence on agricultural exports went an equally conventional resort to protectionism and ISI.[8] This stemmed from the very serious balance-of-payments situation after the war, since the United States cut the trade link with Japan and, after 1949, with mainland China, coupled with raging inflation, until US aid resumed in 1950. In 1951 Taiwan adopted standard Third World devices to deal with these problems. Multiple exchange rates were introduced. High tariffs were placed on most imports, and importers had to deposit the full cost until 1965. Import licensing raised the effective rate of protection (ERP) considerably: thus in 1953 the ERP premium on cotton piece-goods and poplin was about 150 per cent and woollen yarn 350 per cent. Industrial capacity was strictly controlled. This was virtually the same as the 'licence raj' of India and had the same results. It stimulated a range of consumer goods, some of which were available for export. It benefited those who could obtain licences. On the other hand, since intermediate imports were covered by licences, the manufacturer had to pay above international prices for his inputs. It therefore encouraged high-cost manufacturers, and it led to manufacturers forming cartels to keep up prices.

[6] M. FG. Scott, 'Foreign Trade' in Galenson (ed.), *Economic Growth*, table 5.12, p. 350.
[7] The following material on agriculture is based mainly on E. Thorbecke, 'Agricultural Development', in Galenson (ed.), *Economic Growth*, ch. 2.
[8] The following section is based mainly on M. FG. Scott, 'Foreign Trade', in Galenson (ed.), *Economic Growth*, ch. 5.

Taiwan might, therefore, have followed the same path to an inefficient, highly protected ISI industrial system as India and much of Black Africa. The fact that it did not is the key to later success. Taiwan's industry grew fast: between 1952 and 1962 the average was 12.7 per cent annually. But this had adverse features. Until about 1964 it created substantial deficits on current account, resulting in heavy dependence on US aid. Exports continued to consist mainly of rice and sugar, both of which had limited prospects, because few manufactures were internationally competitive. GDP growth slowed and investment became more sluggish, mainly because the domestic market for ISI products was reaching its limits.

It was from this point that the main Taiwanese export drive began. It was made possible by a delayed and drawn-out liberalizaton of the trade regime. From 1958 QRs were mostly abolished, making imports freely available at competitive prices to fuel industry, and the bureaucratic obstacles to exporting were trimmed. The multiple exchange rates were gradually collapsed into a single rate in 1960, and devalued. This was critical, since it reduced the relative costs of Taiwanese exports considerably. Liberalization was never complete in a free-trade sense: there were residual controls of various kinds and some oddly high import duties on some goods. But it was from about 1960 that Taiwan began to move decisively from its ISI stage to becoming a major competitor in international trade.

Yet it required more than trade liberalization to produce this result, and there has been much debate over the special factors that enabled Taiwan to break through the ISI barrier and become competitive. This was not a conventional economic response to the market. In Taiwan, as in Korea, government played a major role. Scitovsky has analysed the 'philosophy' that lay behind the new economic policies.[9] Development would result from a mixture of state planning and free enterprise. The state would guide development and provide the stimulus and much of the means for investment: it was the driving force behind expansion. The state would undertake most large-scale industries, such as shipbuilding, steel and petrochemicals, not, as in India, from dogma, but for the practical reason that private resources were insufficient. Conversely, most export-oriented industries would be private and remain relatively small. In the decade after 1966 the main expansion in manufacturing came from an increase in the number of firms rather than in their size. This also increased competition. The result was that the average workforce of all Taiwanese industrial firms was a mere twenty-seven. In 1981 the gross receipts of Hyundai, Korea's largest conglomerate, were

[9] Scitovsky, 'Economic Development in Taiwan and South Korea: 1965–81', pp. 143–8.

three times as big as the gross receipts of Taiwan's ten largest firms combined.

There were four probable reasons for this pattern of production. Much, perhaps 30 per cent, of the total inflow of foreign capital was brought by immigrant Chinese, who used it to found their own small enterprises. The much higher personal savings rate in Taiwan made it relatively easy to obtain capital to set up small businesses. The small size of the average firm made it easier for newcomers to enter the market. Finally, and possibly most important, help was given by the state to would-be entrepreneurs who lacked capital. By the 1980s Taiwan had established industrial parks where it was possible to rent factories or to borrow capital on favourable terms, and where there were technical experts to provide help. Conversely, the government did nothing to stimulate the growth of large firms.

Scitovsky argues that a key to Taiwan's success in competitive industrialization was monetary policy. Accidentally, Taiwan inherited a high-interest policy from the mainland, where it had been devised to cure hyperinflation, which was in stark contrast with the low-interest policies adopted by most developing countries. Its effect in Taiwan was to encourage private savings, in contrast to hoarding or consumption. These savings not only provided the banks with funds for investment, but also, in marked contrast with Korea, led to the foundation of small firms by families who pooled their resources. It also encouraged labour-intensive manufacture, since the cost of borrowing for capital-intensive manufacture was relatively high. This in turn absorbed the large amount of labour available, Taiwan's main asset, and ultimately resulted in virtually full employment, and therefore relatively high wages and a large share for labour in the national product. It also limited the size of profits and therefore the rate at which individual firms could grow.

By the early 1960s, then, Taiwan's development strategy had evolved from conventional Third World agricultural exporting coupled with intensive ISI to a relatively liberal trading regime which provided strong stimulus for manufacturing for export. As Little pointed out, however, this revolution did not take place suddenly: it was spread over perhaps a decade from the early 1960s. Nor did it imply a genuinely open economy. Exporters were able to operate in a virtually free-trade environment by the free-trade zones and bonded factories. There was a very complicated system of rebates whereby manufacturers of exports could claim back domestic taxes and buy local inputs at world prices, the Taiwanese producer of these then claiming back the equivalent of the import duty the exporting manufacturer would have paid if these things had been imported. This resulted in a dualistic economy, in which the domestic market remained protected but the export sector operated at international prices.

This was a very sophisticated system which has been attempted by many other developing countries, with very much less success. It was successful in Taiwan largely because of the exceptional competence of the government in running it. Very few other countries were able to maintain this balancing act.

There remains the question of how dependent Taiwan was on imported technology and capital. This falls into two parts: official aid and foreign direct investment (FDI). Aid seems to have been a very important factor before the later 1960s. It was essential in the fight against inflation in the early 1950s and helped political stability. Scott concludes that in that period aid was a necessary, but not a sufficient, condition for rapid economic growth.[10] Nor was FDI a critical factor. There was very little in the 1950s and only an average of $4 million a year between 1960 and 1966. FDI then increased as aid diminished: between 1967 and 1975 it averaged $47 million, including that by overseas Chinese. This represented 6.5 per cent of fixed capital investment in manufacture in that period. But it was highly concentrated: 43 per cent of the cumulative total of FDI was in electrical machinery and electronics, non-electrical machinery and chemicals. The MNC making components for its external activities was important only in electronics, to exploit relatively cheap labour, and this had spin-offs in the local electronics industry. But in 1976 only twenty-one of the 321 largest corporations were foreign owned. Nor were the costs of importing technology unduly high. For the most part, especially in the less technically advanced fields, the Taiwanese imported obsolete or second-hand machinery and used it intensively. The result was relatively very small overseas debts and current outgoings in respect of royalties, etc.[11]

The general conclusion must be that Taiwan largely created its own economic miracle, using most effectively its comparative advantage in cheap labour. Although it can be argued that the timing of its initial expansion in the 1960s was exceptionally favourable, in that it was one of the very first Asian countries to take advantage of a still infant international market for electronics and before western countries began to curb the impact of cheap Third World exports through various forms of formal or informal protectionism, it was clear from the Taiwanese reaction to the potentially crippling effects of the post-1973 oil price increases that government was capable of effective macroeconomic policies. By using tight money strategies, the early inflation rate of 40 per cent was reduced by 5 per cent and then stabilized, despite the second oil crisis of 1979. The average inflation rate from 1961 to 1991 was 6.2 per cent, above that for Malaysia, Singapore and Thailand, but

[10] Scott, 'Foreign Trade', pp. 369–78.
[11] Little, 'An Economic Reconnaissance', pp. 478–9.

well below the average for all low- and middle-income countries of 61.8 per cent.[12] This reflected good economic management and emphasized the basic fact that the Taiwanese economic miracle was crafted from unpromising materials by an intelligent and adaptive government using exceptionally plastic human resources.

Korea

Korea also is important because it was one of the four main founders of the East Asian 'miracle'.[13] But, according to Scitovsky, Korea's underlying development 'philosophy' was substantially different from that of Taiwan. It was far more planned, controlled by the central government and its agencies, which were much more interventionist at the microeconomic level. It was also more corporatist, with close contacts between government and leaders in the economic sectors through consultative councils. This dirigisme may have been due partly to the very serious condition of Korea after 1952. During the 1950s, under the dictator Syngman Rhee, Korea depended very heavily on US aid. Although Rhee was deposed in 1960 and although, after three years of democracy followed by military rule, General Park nominally installed a democratic system, the central government remained essentially autocratic. It was thus capable of intensive economic direction.

The economic 'miracle' of Korea did not begin seriously until after 1961. During the previous eight years, however, important foundations had been laid. There was extensive land reform. Communications were rebuilt. A highly protectionist import-substituting strategy was adopted. But there was little sign of a dramatic take-off. In 1961 Korea's exports were worth only $9.4 million, compared with Taiwan's industrial exports of $71 million, and consisted mainly of plywood, silk yarn and cotton fabrics, the typical exports of an underdeveloped country. In 1963 exports were still worth only $43.6 million, but now included clothing, footwear and electrical goods. It was only from about 1963 and the new regime that the export strategy began, and then it followed much the same pattern as that of Taiwan, at least until 1973, after which there was a substantial difference.

In the decade after about 1960 the basic Korean strategy was to maintain very heavy protection for home production – standard ISI – but also to create favourable conditions for exporters. By 1965 a system very similar to that of Taiwan had evolved. Labour-intensive exports

[12] *TEAM*, table 3.2, p. 110.
[13] The following survey is based mainly on Scitovsky, 'Economic Development in Taiwan and South Korea, 1965–81'; Little, 'An Economic Reconnaissance'; *TEAM*.

were encouraged by exempting exporters from import duties on materials and components and from internal indirect taxes. Domestic suppliers of intermediates to exporters were also given tax and tariff relief, so that the whole export sector was effectively competitive. The methods adopted, however, were highly discretionary. The state used a wide range of instruments to stimulate or direct firms, including access to cheap credit, direct cash subsidies and permission to retain foreign-exchange earnings. This involved a great deal of administrative effort and was possible only because of the efficiency of the bureaucracy. In 1964 exchange rates, which had for most of the time been multiple, were unified and the won was devalued. Interest rates were raised to rates comparable with those of Taiwan. The result in terms of export growth was spectacular. Between 1963 and 1973 exports grew at an average of 52 per cent a year, reaching $2,879 million in 1973, within sight of Taiwan's $3,680 million.

The early 1970s were another watershed in Korea. The government then embarked on a programme of heavy and chemical industrial (HCI) development in steel, petrochemicals, non-ferrous metals, shipbuilding, electronics and machinery. The first three of these were chosen to provide self-sufficiency and for defence purposes, the other three for export. By contrast with the previous strategy of export expansion, this was possible only with massive government financial and technical backing. In particular, in 1977 the government accelerated the pro-gramme, with a huge investment in a complex for the manufacture of atomic, thermo- and hydroelectric power-generating equipment, equip-ped with the most up-to-date machinery and a capacity five times domestic requirements. To an extent exceptional in a Third World context, this strategy worked, at least up to 1979. Korea became a major player in world trade in ships, electronics and machinery, even auto-mobiles. Between 1960 and 1979 the proportion of 'heavy' exports rose from 30 to 55.3 per cent. The total value of exports continued to rise, though the rate was lower than before 1973.

The problem was that this huge push was made possible only by very large imports of capital and technology, including a limited amount of FDI. This was partly due to a lower domestic savings rate than in Taiwan. In Taiwan virtually the entire gross domestic capital formation from 1965 to 1981 was financed from domestic savings. In Korea these provided less than two-thirds. The rest came from aid and foreign borrowing. Internally one result was a very high ratio between corporate debts and their net worth – 488 per cent in Korea compared with under 200 per cent in Taiwan and under 100 per cent in the United States. Externally it resulted in very large indebtedness. In 1980 external debt represented 47.9 per cent of GNP and 134.5 per cent of the value of exports. The debt-service ratio was 20.3 per cent. Korea was running a current account

deficit of $5.4 billion.[14] In both 1974 and 1979 the inflation rate rose to
40 per cent. The exchange rate had appreciated, exports were faltering,
and capacity utilization in the new HCI sector was low.

This was a common situation in Third World countries at that time:
overambitious state-directed heavy industrial development with problematic markets; and in Africa in particular it led to very serious economic deterioration in the 1980s. It was precisely because countries
such as Korea in East Asia were capable of changing course rapidly
to deal with such problems that they were more successful. Following President Park's assassination, the new Korean government under
President Chun raised interest rates and industrial investment was
dramatically reduced. The currency was devalued. The immediate
effects were to reduce GNP by 6.2 per cent and to increase unemployment from 3.8 to 5.2 per cent. But the medicine worked: the
inflation rate came down to 5 per cent by 1982 and growth was
resumed: the industrial growth rate between 1980 and 1990 was 13.1
per cent, between 1990 and 1994 6.1 per cent.[15]

Government direction of the economy continued, but in new and
less dirigiste forms. There was greater reliance on market forces. Private
savings were encouraged by high real interest rates on personal bank
deposits. The margin between concessionary and ordinary loans (designed previously to stimulate selected industries) was reduced. Government plans became indicative rather than obligatory. In short, Korea
moved from a centrally directed economy comparable to that of India
to a centrally guided economy more similar to that of Taiwan. Two
residual problems were the huge internal debts of some of the HCI
enterprises of the 1970s, particularly non-performing bank loans, and
high external debts, the result of government preference for borrowing abroad rather than using FDI. The government gradually liquid-
ated internal industrial indebtedness, at large fiscal and economic cost.
External indebtedness was gradually reduced: from 47.9 per cent of
GNP in 1980 to 15.3 per cent in 1994, and the debt service ratio from
20.3 to 7.0 per cent.[16] Yet, as the crisis of 1997–8 demonstrated, Korea
remained dangerously vulnerable to international loss of confidence in
its ability to service this debt.

Taiwan and Korea stood with Japan and the two city states of Hong
Kong and Singapore as the most dynamic of the East and South-east
Asian economies during the three decades after 1950. With the unique
exception of Hong Kong, their success owed a great deal to the initiative

[14] World Bank, *World Development Report 1996*, table 16 p. 219; table 17,
p. 221.
[15] Ibid., table 11, p. 209.
[16] Ibid., table 17, p. 221.

and still more to the competence of their governments in making full use of their comparative advantages. None except for Hong Kong, was, in any real sense, a *laissez-faire* economy. Nor were the other two Asian countries that will be considered very briefly here: Malaysia and Indonesia. The question is whether their economic performance was comparable to that of Taiwan and Korea and how far their success was the result of similarly competent government initiatives.

2   South-east Asia and the Asian 'Miracle'

Malaysia

Until the 1970s Malaysia (formed in 1963 when Sarawak and Sabah were incorporated with mainland Malaya, along, briefly, with Singapore, but referred to as Malaysia throughout) was the quintessential commodity-exporting country with virtually no industry other than that required for processing commodity exports.[17] Thus in 1965 35 per cent of its exports consisted of fuels and metals (predominantly tin), 59 per cent 'other primary commodities' (mainly rubber with oil-palm products rising), 2 per cent machinery and transport goods and 4 per cent 'other manufactures'.[18] Moreover, Malaysia had very high proportions of the world market for these commodity exports. In 1950 it provided 35 per cent of tin production and 37 per cent of rubber. In 1980 the share had risen to 40 per cent of tin, 50 per cent of rubber and 60 per cent of palm oil, taking over from the now no longer exporting Nigeria and outperforming Sumatra.[19] The structure of production reflected this orientation. In 1965 agriculture accounted for 28 per cent, industry 25 per cent and manufacturing 9 per cent. In 1980 the comparable figures were 22, 38 and 21, and in 1994 14, 42 and 32.

These figures suggest a fairly conventional profile of Third World development, from agriculture and extraction towards manufacture in both production and exporting. But Malaysia had some special features, apart from its very high share of world trade in major commodities.

---

[17] Possibly the best general survey of Malaysian economic development, particularly in the 1970s and 1980s, is M. Ariff, *The Malaysian Economy: Pacific Connections* (Singapore, 1991).

[18] Unless otherwise stated, all statistics here are taken from World Bank, *World Development Report 1990: Poverty* (Oxford, 1990), and *World Development Report 1996*.

[19] J.-J. van Helten, and G. Jones 'British Business in Malaysia and Singapore since the 1870s', in R. P. T. Davenport-Hines, and G. Jones (eds), *British Business in Asia since 1860* (Cambridge, 1989) pp. 163, 179.

First, although the major growth in production and export from the 1970s was in manufactures, mining and agricultural exports also grew impressively. Thus in 1980 the value of non-manufactured exports was about $1.0 billion, some 81 per cent of total exports. Although their share had been reduced to 30 per cent by 1994, their absolute value had risen three times, to $3.2 billion. Thus, even while opting for rapid growth in manufacturing and the export of manufactures, Malaysia continued to benefit from its comparative advantage in primary production, and this made a major contribution to financing its industrialization.

Secondly, Malaysia was always relatively affluent by Third World standards. Little estimated that (in 1973 US dollars) per capita incomes there in 1953 may have been around $360,[20] far above both Taiwan and South Korea at the time, still more above most of Black Africa as late as 1982. By 1967–8 these may have risen to over $700 and by 1985 to around $2,000. In 1994 the World Bank put the figure at $3,480, having risen by the very high annual rate of 5.5 per cent in the previous decade.[21]

Thirdly, Malaysia was also exceptional in the large proportion of the productive economy initially owned by non-residents and foreign-controlled companies. As late as 1970, before the New Economic Policy (NEP) had been put into operation, the percentage of the share capital owned by these overseas interests in various sectors was as follows: rubber, 78; other agriculture, 67; tin mining, 71; other mining, 76; the wholesale trade, 70; retail trade, 45. Even in other fields in which the majority shareholding was by 'residents', the proportion owned by the non-indigenous group (that is, excluding Malays, Chinese, Indians and the government) might be high, as in transport, insurance and banking. Moreover, where there was a sizeable non-European 'resident' shareholding, this was likely to be in the hands of Chinese, particularly in banking, tin mining, manufacturing, insurance and domestic trade. The Malay proportion was very small in almost every department except landownership.[22] The origins of this situation lay in the evolution of the Malayan economy since the later nineteenth

---

[20] Little, 'An Economic Reconnaissance', p. 452.
[21] Since these figures are taken from different sources, they may not be strictly comparable. That for 1967–8 is calculated from D. N. Snodgrass, *Inequality and Economic Development in Malaysia* (Kuala Lumpur, 1980), table 4.2, p. 69, and is based on his estimate of 'personal income'. The 1985 figure is from D. Colman and F. Nixson, *Economics of Change in Less Developed Countries* (New York, 1994), table 1.1, p. 14.
[22] Snodgrass, *Inequality*, table 4.22, pp. 98–9.

century.[23] It had been largely British capital that had financed the development of the mechanized tin extraction and processing industry and had established rubber and later oil-palm plantations, together with the financial and commercial infrastructure, notably the managing agencies, transported from India, to make these industries commercially efficient.[24]

These three general features set Malaysia apart from the general run of Third World countries. It also had better education. In 1957 over 90 per cent of males and over 70 per cent of females in the age group 10–14 had primary education, while 23 per cent of Malays, 32 per cent of Chinese, and 34 per cent of Indian males in the age group 15–19 were in secondary education, though the proportion for females was substantially lower. By 1987 there was 100 per cent enrolment in primary, 59 per cent in secondary, and 7 per cent in tertiary education.[25]

But relative prosperity as a commodity-exporting economy, particularly when so much of the economy was controlled by foreigners, whether locally based or overseas, was not acceptable once Malaysia had become independent, though the drive for economic transformation did not really start until 1970. Then it was mainly the ethnic conflicts of 1969 that triggered the change, both of government and of strategy. Hitherto Malaya, and then Malaysia, under the rule of Tengku Abdul Rahman, had followed conventional ISI strategies, but with relatively very modest protection. After 1969 the government, led by his successor, Tun Razak, decided on what they called a New Economic Policy. This, however, was more than a mere change of economic direction. It was recognized that Malaysia faced two problems that neither Taiwan nor Korea had faced after 1950. First, while the Japanese ownership of both land and most of the industrial sector had been obliterated after 1945, in Malaysia foreign, especially British, domination of most of the modern

---

[23] The classical account is in G. C. Allen and A. G. Donnithorne, *Western Enterprise in Indonesia and Malaya* (London, 1957).

[24] The standard work on the Malaysian rubber industry to 1940 is J. H. Drabble, *Rubber in Malaya 1876–1922* (Kuala Lumpur, 1973). See also C. Barlow, *The Natural Rubber Industry: Its Development Technology and Economy in Malaysia* (Kuala Lumpur, 1978); and (Lord) P. T. Bauer, *The Rubber Industry: A Study in Competition and Monopoly* (London, 1948). On the tin-mining industry, see Yip Yat Hoong, *The Development of the Tin Mining Industry in Malaya* (Kuala Lumpur, 1969); Wong Lin Ken, *The Malayan Tin Industry to 1914* (Tucson, Ariz., 1965). For a general overview of the various British organizations and the extent of expatriate control, see van Helten and Jones, 'British Business'.

[25] Snodgrass, *Inequality*, pp. 242–3; World Bank, *World Development Report 1990*, table 1, p. 179.

sector continued. Secondly, the Chinese dominated most parts of the economy that were not controlled by expatriates, and their average incomes were more than twice those of Malays, with Indians, (though not important as owners of enterprises) coming second.[26] Hence the NEP had three closely integrated objectives. To reduce foreign owner-ship of existing economic assets; to generate new industries with a high export potential; and to use both policies to provide work and wealth for the Malay population, the *Bumiputra*. To a remarkable extent Malaysia was successful in all three strategies.

The diminution of foreign control of existing companies proved relatively simple and did not involve the costly compulsory national-ization common in other LDCs.[27] As in India during the 1930s, control of many companies had begun to slip out of British hands before 1970, though the managing agencies cooperated with a number of British industrialists to start manufacturing enterprises. During the 1970s very skilful (though highly politicized and corruption-prone) use of the stock exchange enabled the Malaysian government or indigenous corpor-ations to gain control of most of the managing agencies, plantations and tin mines. One result was the Malaysianization of the company boards and senior management. Thus the old export economy was brought under indigenous control and *Bumiputras* were able to take over its commanding heights.

The new strategy, however, required rapid expansion of industrial production, both to earn foreign exchange and to provide employment for Malays. The techniques were adopted from the other successful East Asian countries. During the first phase, in the 1970s, the govern-ment promoted exports of the traditional commodities, joined now by petroleum, but also a range of light, labour-intensive manufactures, such as textiles, garments and footwear. To do this it used tax deduc-tions linked to exports and domestic content, accelerated depreciation allowances for firms which exported more than 20 per cent of pro-duction, concessional credit, export-processing zones, free-trade zones and duty-free entry for inputs to manufacture. Attracted by these concessions and by the large supply of low-wage labour from the countryside, foreign investment flowed in. Between 1970 and 1979 the annual inflow of FDI was $300 million. Between 1980 and 1990 it rose to $1.1 billion. Increasingly this came from the NICs of East Asia, notably Singapore and Japan: between 1983 and 1986 19 per cent of total inflows came from this source, between 1987 and 1990 41 per cent. Initially foreign firms were limited to a maximum of

[26] Snodgrass, *Inequality*, table 4.13, p. 84; table 4.22, p. 98.
[27] The following section is based mainly on van Helten and Jones, 'British Business', pp. 179–86, and Colman and Nixson, *Economics of Change*, ch. 10.

30 per cent shareholding in new Malaysian-registered companies. This was increased for firms exporting at least 20 per cent of production in the mid-1980s; but in fact foreign shareholding was well below this by the later 1980s.

The special feature of Malaysian development after 1970 was, therefore, that, helped by strong commodity prices in the 1970s, it was based mainly on foreign capital and technology, though Malays, helped immensely by a variety of governmental agencies, now held a large and increasing share of both management and shares.[28] This marked Malaysia off clearly from both Taiwan and South Korea. In the later 1980s new FDI constituted between 5 and 10 per cent of gross domestic capital formation. A large proportion of this foreign investment was export oriented. In 1986 FDI firms were responsible for 51.2 per cent of manufactured exports and in 1988 employed 215,000 people. Of these 134,000 were in manufacturing, representing 27 per cent of paid employment, including many poor Malay women in the countryside. By the mid-1980s, moreover, the range of products in the FDI field had expanded, though predominantly in electronics. Malaysia became the world's third largest producer of semiconductors. The German firm Siemens built its fourth plant there to manufacture megachips. There were many other enterprises, mostly in the electronics field, but also in electrical consumer goods and even automobiles, notably Proton, which proved a costly mistake. Between 1980 and 1994 the share of manufactures in Malaysian exports rose from 19 to 70 per cent and the value of exports from \$13 billion to \$58.7 billion, above that for Brazil and only just below the Mexican figure. In 1994 export of goods and services was equivalent to 90 per cent of the GNP, a proportion lower only than that for Hong Kong (139 per cent) and Singapore (177 per cent).

From the mid-1980s, moreover, the share of the state in this development, vital at the start, diminished as private local capital expanded. Much of the industrial growth of the early 1980s had been pioneered by the Heavy and Industrial Corporation of Malaysia, which established nine subsidiaries in major capital-intensive areas such as steel, cement, paper and automobiles. But 1984–6 were crisis years for the economy, with negative growth in 1985/6. This resulted in a change of direction. Many of the 800 state-owned enterprises proved non-economic: in 1984 the total deficit of state firms had risen to 3.7 per cent of GNP. The state began to privatize its enterprises in 1983. The process was slow, but, even in companies still controlled by the state, direct governmental interference was reduced and efficiency increased. In fact from the

[28] For detail on these governmental agencies and their role in providing capital for private Malay businessmen and in controlling companies, see Snodgrass, *Inequality*, ch. 8.

mid-1980s the Malaysian government began to liberalize the economy as a whole. Private investment was stimulated by the conventional range of concessions. Tax incentives for exporters were increased and imports liberalized. The average effective protection for industry was reduced from an estimated 31 per cent in 1979/80 (still far below the Indian level) to 17 per cent in 1987, though this varied widely across sectors according to the government's strategy.

Malaysia, therefore, stands along with Taiwan and Korea as an example of the beneficial effects of adopting an export-oriented industrial policy in the post-war period. There was excellent macroeconomic management, with low inflation. Apart from 1979–85, protection was low. The state was the prime mover and controller. Malaysia differed from the others mainly in three respects: it began its industrializing drive a decade and more after them; it depended far more on imported technology and capital; and it was able to maintain a very substantial commodity-exporting sector of the economy, so buttressing itself against fluctuations in the international economy. It must, however, be said that the Malaysian strategy contained high risks. Many of the new industrial enterprises were offshore exporting firms, which manufactured components for final assembly elsewhere, and assembled imported components either for export or for domestic consumption. It was, therefore, very vulnerable to shifts in international prices and markets, as was demonstrated in the Asian economic crisis of the late 1990s. Its main asset and comparative advantage remained its supply of cheap labour, which had been greatly expanded by a massive influx of workers, who provided some 15–20 per cent of the labour force in the early 1990s; and in an increasingly competitive international environment that might prove a wasting asset.

Indonesia

Indonesia provides yet another contrasting pattern of South-east Asian economic development. In some respects it falls between Malaysia and India.[29] The population in 1994 at 190.4 million was about ten times that of Malaysia, but less than a quarter that of India.[30] The average per capita income, which had been a mere $73 in 1960, the same as that of India, had by 1994 risen to $880, well above that of India at $320

---

[29] The most useful general account of Indonesian economic development from the 1960s is H. Hill, *The Indonesian Economy since 1966: Southeast Asia's Emerging Giant* (Cambridge, 1996).

[30] All statistics in this paragraph are from World Bank, *World Development Report 1990*, and *World Development Report 1996*, and Colman and Nixson, *Economics of Change*.

but far below Malaysia's $3,480. Yet Indonesia was a fast-developing country after 1965. The growth rate of GDP in 1965–80 was 8.1 per cent, from 1980 to 1988 5.1 per cent, and the per capita growth rate in 1965–88 was 4.3 per cent. The structure of production showed a very marked trend from agriculture to industry. In 1965 agriculture provided 56 per cent of GDP, falling to 24 per cent in 1980 and 17 per cent in 1994. In these years industry rose from 13 to 41 per cent, manufacturing from 8 to 24 per cent, and services from 31 to 42 per cent of GDP. Exports showed a similar trend. In 1965 Indonesian recorded exports were only 5 per cent of GDP, though there was much smuggling. Their average growth rate between then and 1980 was 9.6 per cent, from 1980 to 1990 5.3 per cent, and in the early 1990s some 21.3 per cent. As a proportion of GDP, exports were 33 per cent in 1980 but then, as a result of falling oil prices, fell to 25 per cent in 1994. In 1965 43 per cent of exports consisted of fuels and minerals, 53 per cent of other primary commodities, and only 4 per cent of manufactures. By 1988 the proportions were 49 per cent, 22 per cent and 29 per cent; and in 1993 manufactures had risen to 53 per cent of exports.

The impression given by these figures is that Indonesia in about 1950 was a very poor country with very limited exports and hardly any modern manufacturing. While this was roughly true before 1965, it had not been so before 1941. Indonesia (then the Netherlands East Indies) had previously been one of the world's largest commodity-exporting regions. At the post-First World War peak of 1930 it had exported 2.8 million tons of sugar, 375,000 tons of copra, 296,000 tons of rubber, 4 million tons of petroleum, and large amounts of palm products, tin, tobacco and coffee.[31] Moreover, unusually in Third World colonies, Indonesia had a substantial industrial sector before 1941. A few industries were established under free trade during and after the First World War, but it was from 1932, under conditions of severe depression in the commodity export market and Japanese invasion of the consumer-goods import market, that the Dutch, following the British example in India and Ceylon, instituted a protectionist regime. They established import quotas, and protective import tariffs, which were rebated on raw materials and machine tools, provided easier credit and official participation for factory construction, spread technical information and licensed industrial capacity. These measures had dramatic effects. Between 1930 and 1941 hand looms rose from 500 to 49,000, power looms from 40 to 9,800. A wide range of previously imported consumer goods was manufactured locally, some by foreign multinationals such as Unilever, Bata and Goodyear, though a large proportion were indigenous. By 1940 there

---

[31] Allen and Donnithorne, *Western Enterprise*, p. 292.

were 5,500 factories employing over twenty workers and there were 324,000 employees. The entire secondary industrial sector, including artisans, employed 2.8 million by 1939. In short, by the time of the Japanese invasion of 1942 it looked as though Indonesia, though still a colony, was embarked on the first stages of transition from commodity exporting to ISI.[32]

The Second World War and its aftermath was a watershed. The Japanese milked, though did not lay waste, the Indonesian economy, and much of the nascent industry was destroyed or starved by lack of imported inputs.[33] There was the prospect of a revival after 1945 but this was short lived, owing first to the failed attempt at Dutch reconquest, ending in 1949, then to the financial and economic incompetence of the Sukarno regime.[34] To understand its strategies, however, it is necessary to take account of the extremely turbulent struggle for independence and the deep ethnic divisions. These generated intense anti-capitalist and anti-liberal feelings that went much deeper than in Malaysia. From about 1951 the government adopted a conventional import-substituting strategy with additional emphasis on indigenous ownership and the promotion of small-scale firms. From 1955, and still more from 1957 when Sukarno took personal control under the umbrella concept of 'guided democracy', the emphasis shifted to heavy, including capital, industry. Foreign investment was allowed under stringent restrictions; but after the nationalization of all Dutch properties in 1957 as part of the crisis over the future of Western New Guinea (Irian), foreign capital showed little interest. The informal takeover of British properties in 1963 during the Confrontation with Malaysia acted as a

[32] The standard accounts are P. W. H. Sitsen, *Industrial Development of the Netherlands Indies* (New York, 1944); J. H. Boeke, *The Evolution of the Netherlands Indian Economy*, (New York, 1942); H. G. Callis, *Foreign Capital in South East Asia* (New York, 1942); Allen and Donnithorne, *Western Enterprise*, ch. 15. For a detailed account of the Unilever factory at Batavia (Jakarta) and its subsequent history, see D. K. Fieldhouse, *Unilever Overseas: The Anatomy of a Multinational* (London, 1978), ch. 5.

[33] For example, the Unilever factory, kept going by its non-European management, was unable to import tubes for its toothpaste, and resorted to using sealed sections of bamboo.

[34] The standard accounts of Indonesian economic history in the post-1945 period are: B. Dahm, *History of Indonesia in the Twentieth Century* (London, 1971); A. Gelb and Associates, *Oil Windfalls: Blessing or Curse* (New York, 1988), esp. ch. 12; B. Glassburner (ed.), *The Economy of Indonesia* (Ithaca, NY, 1971); B. Grant, *Indonesia* (Melbourne, 1964); Hill, *Foreign Investment*; G. McT. Kahin, *Nationalism and Revolution in Indonesia* (Ithaca, NY, 1952); J. D. Legge, *Sukarno* (London, 1972); I. Palmer, *The Indonesian Economy since 1965* (London, 1978).

further disincentive. Thus between 1950 and 1965 net private capital flows totalled only $450 million, from 1956 to 1965 they were only $84 million, consisting entirely of investment by foreign oil companies. Western aid also dried up. Indonesia therefore relied largely on East European capital and technology: one estimate puts this at some $600 million, half from Russia in the form of large capital projects. Much also was borrowed to pay for military equipment for the Confrontation.

Seen in the round, the Indonesian economic experience before 1965 and the effective fall of Sukarno closely resembled the worst of many other LDCs, particularly in Africa. It was based on economic nationalism coupled with export pessimism, on faith in the primacy of the state and on the need to create a capital-goods industry. In Indonesia this widely unsuccessful strategy proved disastrous sooner than in many other countries. This was due mainly to the fact that Sukarno appeared after 1957 to have no interest in economic or fiscal realities. Earlier governments had at least attempted, with limited success, to combat inflation and to control overseas indebtedness. Thereafter Sukarno made no effort to do this. Despite strong advice from the central bank, the state created credit as it needed it. The exchange rate for the rupiah (replacing the guilder) was originally fixed at $1 = Rp11.4. It was devalued in 1959 to $1 = Rp45, and to $1 = Rp315 in 1963. But this was quite unrealistic. By 1963 the black market rate was $1 = Rp1,500. By 1965 the inflation rate had reached 1,000 per cent and the currency was virtually worthless. By 1963 Indonesia owed some $2.5 billion abroad and foreign-exchange reserves had virtually disappeared. Indonesia was effectively bankrupt.

How great an impact deterioration in the formal economy had on the national income is unclear. The World Bank states that per capita incomes in 1965 were 15 per cent lower than in 1958. Glassburner, however, calculated that at constant prices (1958 = 100) the index never fell below 93.1, in 1963.[35] If he was right, this was mainly because more than half the national product came from agriculture, and this was not greatly affected by domestic inflation and foreign indebtedness. Thus the main effects of inflation, import shortages and controls fell on the small modern sector of the economy. In effect this meant that Indonesia had done almost nothing to create an efficient industrial system in the first fifteen years of independence. It was one of the least industrialized of the larger Third World countries.

There is little doubt that economic decline was the immediate reason for public discontent and the army intervention of 1965–7. The new regime that came into power in 1967 under General Suharto proved the turning point. Suharto's 'New Order' was politically autocratic and acquired a very bad reputation for ignoring human rights. But in

[35] Glassburner (ed.), *The Economy of Indonesia*, p. 11.

economic terms the regime did many of the things the IMF and World Bank were to press on distressed Third World countries from the 1970s. The exchange rate was progressively reduced. It was pegged to the US dollar from 1971 to 1986 (with devaluations in 1978, 1983 and 1986), and thereafter closely aligned with it until the crisis of 1997. Exchange controls were gradually removed, leading to a free-exchange market that was exceptional in the Third World. Inflation was brought down to 84 per cent in 1968, 9 per cent in 1970, and 4 per cent in 1971. Interest rates were raised until positive real rates were reached in 1969. It was accepted that budgets must be balanced, though in practice this was for some time achieved only by using foreign aid and loans as income. The Foreign Investment Law of 1967 was passed to encourage foreign investors with promises of security or full compensation for nationalization. Sequestered Dutch, British and American enterprises were returned, though, at least in the case of Unilever, with no compensation for damage or loss.

But, for all its apparent acceptance of economic liberalism, the New Order was never fully converted to the concept of an open economy, though there was extensive liberalization after 1986. Both domestic and foreign investment was tightly controlled by the planning ministry, Bappenas, and more specifically by the BKPM, the Capital Investment Coordinating Board, which could refuse to license a new industrial enterprise or allow expansion on the ground that a particular market was saturated. Thousands of ordinances regulated production. Trade, also, was strictly regulated, by both tariffs and QRs. The result was a very variable level of effective protection. In the mid-1970s it was estimated, for example, that the effective rate for the automobile tyre and tube industry was 4,315 per cent, for the car industry 718 per cent. On the other hand, the system perversely handicapped some important export industries by insisting on their using expensive domestic inputs: for example, the batik industry had negative protection of 35 per cent. Thus the system gave very high protection to ISI enterprises and encouraged them to be capital intensive. At one point the capital intensity of protected ISI industries was four times that of exporting sectors.

By contrast, however, with many other LDCs that embarked on an ISI policy, the Suharto regime made improvement in agriculture a main objective. Until the mid-1960s food production had not kept pace with population growth. It now became a government priority, helped by the oil windfall of the post-1973 period. By the extension of harvested acreage by 10 per cent, the introduction of improved strains of rice, and greater use of fertilizers (a major element in the industrial programme), food output was increased on average by 3.6 per cent a year between 1969–71 and 1979–81. Agriculture as a whole grew by an average of 4.3 per cent in 1965–80, 3.4 per cent in 1980–90, and

3.0 per cent in 1990–4. Rice output rose 53 per cent by 1979, though rice imports also increased as national income made increased consumption affordable. Non-food agricultural production also increased. In the decade after 1971/2 rubber exports grew by an average of 1.8 per cent, palm oil by 6.6 per cent, coffee by 13.9 per cent. Meantime the percentage of the economically active population engaged in agriculture fell from 75 in 1960 to 49 in 1990.[36]

Indonesia was thus by about 1970 launched onto a more liberal, financially orthodox, but largely conventional strategy of import-substituting industrialization. This might have proceeded relatively slowly had it not been for the oil bonanza of the post-1973 period. Indonesia, in common with Nigeria and other Third World countries, became primarily an oil-exporting economy.

Oil had been exported from Indonesia from the 1880s, but large-scale exploitation began only in the early 1950s, when the American firm Caltex developed the fields in Central Sumatra, and was further expanded after 1967 when a profit-sharing agreement was made based on those of Venezuela and the Gulf a decade earlier. In terms of volume there was a limited increase, from some 500 to 600 million barrels a year between the early and late 1970s; but the new profit-sharing agreement, coupled with the OPEC price increase, resulted in a very large increase in government revenues. At current prices the received value of oil exports rose from $641 million in 1973/4 to a peak of $9,345 million in 1980/1, falling to $6,016 million in 1983/4.[37]

Using this windfall and avoiding its potentially serious economic and social effects was a test of governmental competence in all oil-exporting countries. Gelb argues that Indonesia did unusually well.[38] In the mid-1970s Jakarta allocated about half the additional public income to investment, only 18 per cent to consumption (half public, half private). The largest share of development spending was on infrastructure, including, unusually in LDCs, much to improve agriculture and rural facilities. Devaluation of the rupiah avoided the danger to exporters of high currency revaluation.

This caution continued during the economic downturn of the early 1980s. Indonesia avoided the fiscal and debt crisis of many other Third World countries by drastic cost-cutting and devaluations. Domestic subsidies and planned capital investment, much of it in highly capital-intensive

---

[36] L. G. Reynolds, *Economic Growth in the Third World, 1850–1980* (New Haven and London, 1985) p. 364; World Bank, *World Development Report, 1990* and *World Development Report 1996*; Colman and Nixon, *Economics of Change*, table 7.1, p. 209.
[37] Gelb et al., *Oil Windfalls*, table 12.3, p. 210.
[38] The following section in based mainly on ibid., ch. 12.

industries, were cut. More investment went to labour–intensive activities with lower import requirements. Overall Gelb concluded that Indonesia had avoided the 'Dutch Disease', the contraction of traded sectors and the expansion of non–trade sectors of the economy.[39] During the critical period between 1969 and 1985, and despite a low level of private capital formation, manufacturing, agriculture and food production all grew reasonably fast. Most importantly, Indonesia increased its non–oil exports: all the normal commodities did well until the post–1981 recession bit. Thereafter, non–commodity exports, mainly manufactures, became relatively more important, taking up the slack left by the deteriorating terms of trade of commodities.

This raises two questions. Does this later expansion of manufactured exports imply that Indonesian industry had experienced a dramatic expansion both in size and international competitiveness? How important was foreign capital in the process?

The answer to the first question is that, until about 1985, manufacturing grew quite rapidly, both absolutely and as a proportion of total production. The rate of growth between 1973 and 1984 was 14.9 per cent and manufacturing reached 13 per cent of GDP, or 50 per cent of the output of agriculture, in 1984. But this concealed major limitations, when compared with the East Asian 'Tigers'. In 1984 manufactures provided only 8 per cent of exports and exports were worth only $11 a head. Moreover, the main expansion in exports had taken place in two very labour–intensive areas – clothing and textiles – and in one processing industry – plywood – owing largely to governmental restrictions on the export of timber. In 1985 exports of electronic products, although much greater than in 1975, were less than they had been in 1980. Clearly there had been no great surge in technical development.

In fact, the main industrial expansion had occurred in a range of highly protected and in some cases state–owned industries producing intermediate goods for domestic consumption. The biggest increases were iron and steel, cement and fertilizer (all state dominated), with lesser though significant increases in paper, basic chemicals and glass.[40] All this indicates that Indonesian industrialization during the oil–boom period had been primarily for domestic consumption. In 1984 manufactured exports were only $11 per capita, ahead of India at $7, but very far behind Malaysia at $236. After 1986, however, this changed significantly. By 1992 manufactures provided more than 50 per cent of merchandise exports.

---

[39] For a definition of the 'Dutch Disease', see ibid., p. 22, so–called because of the Netherlands alleged overdependence on revenues from natural gas, and coined by *The Economist*, 26 Nov. 1977.

[40] Hill, *Foreign Investment*, table 2.2, p. 15; table 2.3, p. 18.

Secondly, what part did FDI play in this skewed industrial growth?[41] Statistically, at least, FDI was relatively very unimportant. If the official figures are reliable, in 1983 wholly owned foreign firms provided only 1.5 per cent of value added and 1.1 per cent of employment. Joint foreign–private ventures, however, provided 21.1 per cent of value added and 9.4 per cent of employment. The figures for joint government–foreign firms were 4.2 and 1.1 per cent. Private indigenous firms provided 56.7 per cent of value added and 74 per cent of the employment. When measured by the value added per firm and per worker, foreign and joint foreign and indigenous enterprises were far bigger than either government of private firms. The largest value added and value added per worker was in joint foreign–government firms, followed by joint foreign–government–private enterprises. But these figures are to some extent misleading. Measured by ownership shares (including joint ventures), foreign firms provided more than 50 per cent of value added in only four major products: beverages, footwear, non-industrial chemicals and glass.[42] None of these was a major export industry.

There were many reasons for this limited FDI achievement. The most important was that, despite the relatively liberal terms of the 1967 Investment Law, and several subsequent changes in its terms, in practice foreign firms could invest only by permission of a very complex bureaucratic process. This system was infused by economic nationalism: from 1974, after anti-foreign riots, no foreign firm could have 100 per cent ownership, though there were no precise limits below that, as there were in India from the 1950s and Nigeria from the 1970s. But, in practice, in most important areas of production, particularly of capital goods and intermediates such as fertilizer, the state would insist on a partnership with the foreign firm, and in other areas also the authorities would insist on this. The oil boom financed a major extension in the state enterprise sector between 1978 and 1986.

The general result, at least between 1967 and 1985, was that by far the largest foreign investment in Indonesia was not in manufacturing but in petroleum: $15.7 billion out of a total of $21.8 billion, 78 per cent of it from the United States. In the industrial sector controlled by BKPM, total investment was only $6.0 billion. Of that, Japan, by far the largest foreign investor in manufacturing in Indonesia, had invested $4.1 billion, or 68 per cent of the total FDI in this field. Japan concentrated on three main sectors: basic metals (50 per cent), textiles (24 per cent) and metal goods (13 per cent). Significantly, in 1973 96 per cent of the sales of Japanese subsidiaries in Indonesia were in the

---

[41] The following section is based mainly on Hill, *Foreign Investment*.
[42] Ibid., table 2.4, p. 20; table 2.5, p. 21; table 2.6, p. 23.

domestic market, whereas in Taiwan the home market took only 47
per cent of such sales, in Korea 52 per cent. Moreover, there was virtually no foreign-owned offshore manufacture or assembly of imported
components for export in Indonesia by the mid-1980s.[43]

It seems clear, in fact, that in Indonesia FDI did not play a dominant
or even very dynamic role in economic or industrial development, though
it was critical for oil and gas. The reason was simply that the regime did
not permit it to do so. The trade regime attracted FDI by providing a
sheltered market and relatively high profits, with free remittance of
dividends and capital. It also made it difficult for foreign firms to develop
export markets by the high cost of local inputs and the tariffs and
restrictions on imports, though there was major liberalization between
1986 and 1990. Moreover, the very limited scientific and educational
infrastructure seriously limited the technological spin-off of foreign enterprise. These factors largely explain not only the limited achievement of
FDI but also the comparatively small growth of Indonesian manufacturing
before the mid-1980s. Seen in the wider context of the Third World,
Indonesia was a typical case of FDI attracted by protected markets which
excluded manufactured imports. But it was in marked contrast with the
more dynamic parts of South-east and East Asia.

According to the World Bank this inward orientation changed sharply
in the mid-1980s.[44] Facing deteriorating terms of trade (due to declining
real oil prices) and a large balance-of-payments deficit, the government
began to experiment with orthodox macroeconomic reforms: two
devaluations (1983 and 1986) and postponement of large-scale investments in state-owned capital-intensive projects. This resulted in a
depression and low growth. But for the first time in and after 1986 the
government also tried economic liberalization as a means of stimulating the economy without high inflation. Major exporters were given
unrestricted duty-free access to imports. Conditions for foreign investment were liberalized. Between 1986 and 1991 officially approved
foreign investments increased tenfold, and between 1980 and 1994 private capital flows increased from $987 million to $7.4 billion. Domestic
capital investment continued to rise by over 7 per cent of GNP a year.
The financial sector was freed from many earlier restraints in 1988.
Government cut back on directed credit and reduced the value of credit
concessions to those sectors still receiving them, with the result that
credit became much more generally available to entrepreneurs.

The short-run results were generally encouraging. Manufacturing
almost doubled, from 13 to 24 per cent of GNP. The growth rate of

[43] The data on which this paragraph is based come mainly from ibid., ch. 4.
[44] The following summary is based on *TEAM*, pp. 118–19, 138–9, 238–9, and
on World Bank, *World Development Report 1996*, various tables.

exports, which had been sluggish at 2.9 per cent between 1980 and 1988, rose to 10.8 per cent in the early 1990s. Some 70 per cent of new approved FDI was export oriented rather than for domestic consumption, compared with 38 per cent in 1986. The proportion of manufactured goods in total exports rose from 2 to 53 per cent between 1980 and 1993. The share of metal products, electronics and machinery in total manufacturing value added almost trebled between 1973 and 1988, though still only 18 per cent of the total.[45] Thus it seemed that Indonesia was at last heading in the same direction as the already highly successful export-oriented East Asian countries.

The extent of this conversion from an inward-looking to an outward-looking economy must, however, not be exaggerated. Indonesia had, like Taiwan and Korea at an earlier stage of their industrial and exporting development, become a dual economy. Export industries, apart from textiles, cloth and footwear, were by the 1990s receiving virtually no effective protection. On the other hand, the old staple industries for the domestic market still had very high levels of effective protection. Overall the manufacturing sector (excluding oil) had 59 per cent ERP in 1990.[46]

More serious, the new export and industrial drive had its costs. Total external debt had increased nearly five times between 1980 and 1994. It rose most steeply between 1982/3 and 1986/7, after which it was stabilized, but still represented 57.4 per cent of GNP and 211.3 per cent of the value of exports of goods and services in 1994. The comparable figures for Korea in 1994 were 15.3 and 48.1, though the Korean position had been nearer to that of Indonesia in 1980. This left Indonesia extremely vulnerable to international loss of confidence in its ability to service its overseas debts and to its being perhaps the worst hit of all the Asian countries by the 1997–8 economic and political crisis. Hence, the ultimate outcome of the Indonesian attempt to follow the example of the very successful export-oriented East Asian economies remained very uncertain in the later 1990s. Indonesia remained a very poor country, still heavily dependent on the export of oil (which represented more than half the value of both exports and government revenues in the mid-1980s) and of low-technology processed or unprocessed commodities. It had a very large rural population, which provided some 55 per cent of the labour force, but generated only about 17 per cent of GDP. The question was still whether Indonesia would be able to transform its economy as the 'Tigers' and Malaysia had done, or whether it would continue to be a rather more prosperous fellow of India and many African countries.

[45] *TEAM*, table 6.14, p. 305.
[46] Ibid., table 6.11, p. 399.

3   The World Bank and the East Asian 'Miracle'

What, then, was the East Asian 'miracle', what was special about these
high-performing Asian economies (HPAE), and what light does their
varying success throw on the general problem of modern Third World
development? One answer can be found in the opening chapter of the
World Bank's *The East Asian Miracle (TEAM)*, which is an exact summary of the main text and, though published well before the economic
crisis of 1997–8, provides a clear exposition of the Bank's basic approach
to economic development.

The basic argument is that, in very varying degrees, the seven states
included in that analysis followed what the World Bank would regard
as sound growth strategies. At the root of their success lay high rates of
investment, averaging over 20 per cent of GDP between 1960 and 1990,
and rising endowment of human capital owing to universal primary and
high secondary education. These achievements were clearly not accidental, but there had been much debate over the role of the state in
producing them. Did governments in these HPAEs limit their activities
to providing a sound macroeconomic and legal framework plus the
provision of infrastructure, education, etc.; or were they constructively
interventionist, acting against market forces when they saw this as
necessary?

The answer is said to have been that governments in these states were
both market oriented and interventionist. While maintaining 'sound'
open-market macroeconomic policies, they were prepared to intervene
where the market appeared to fail. Intervention took many forms. In
the early stage of post-war growth all these states, except for Hong
Kong, were highly protectionist, aiming at import substitution. This
was the common strategy of most Third World states. What made the
original HPAES exceptional was that (with the exception of Hong
Kong) they coupled protectionism with export promotion. In this way
the first wave of successful HPAEs was able to operate what were in
effect dual economies, gradually shifting from highly protectionist ISI
to moderately open competitive economies. It was this transition that
enabled these states to maintain the momentum of industrialization once
the limits of ISI had been reached.

On the political side, it was accepted that these were for the most
part authoritarian states in which democracy as understood in the West
was limited. The key to their success in maintaining such systems lay
in two things: close links between the state and the business and technological elite, commonly through a corporative system of negotiation;
and a relatively equitable distribution of rewards throughout the society
to achieve legitimacy in the eyes of the general public.

Clearly, then, these HPAEs were not *laissez-faire* economies. Why, then, did they not suffer the same fate as other highly interventionist economies, as in Black Africa and South Asia? The *TEAM* answer is in part the competence of these governments. In these Asian states the bureaucracy was exceptionally efficient at economic management. It was this exceptional ability that enabled these states to juggle between interventionist and free-market strategies so successfully. In part, also, success resulted from openness to foreign technology. All these states welcomed technology via licensing, training and import of capital goods. Japan, Taiwan and Korea restricted FDI, mainly because they were able to raise capital at home or by foreign borrowing, and because they were able rapidly to acquire the necessary know-how and operational skills. Other HPAEs welcomed FDI, though with different degrees of control. All, except Hong Kong, shifted sooner or later from ISI to export-oriented industry and gradually opened their domestic markets to foreign competition, though those in the northern tier, again except for Hong Kong, were prepared to halt liberalization of imports if this seemed to endanger domestic production. But state interventionism was not invariably good for growth. *TEAM* argues that state promotion of specific industries, notably heavy capital goods production, was not always successful. Broadly, growth was greatest in sectors in which these countries had a comparative advantage, which for most meant labour- rather than capital-intensive enterprises.

The conclusions drawn are as follows. The success of the HPAEs was basically the result of 'getting the fundamentals right' in macro-economic policy: high rates of capital accumulation, limited price distortions and broadly based human capital. Most of the growth was created by private enterprise, but state intervention helped considerably where it was cautious and, above all, flexible, recognizing when strategies were failing and altering them. The most important single factor was the adoption of export-push strategies, which 'have been by far the most successful combination of fundamentals and policy interventions and hold the most promise for other developing economies'.[47] Nevertheless, there were major differences within East Asia, for example between North and South. These reflected different resource endowments, degrees of bureaucratic competence, ethnic schisms and the human-resource base.

But the strategies that helped these HPAEs from the 1950s to the 1980s might not work so well in other parts of the world in the 1990s and beyond. Repression of interest rates, critical for these states, was less possible in the new global financial framework, and might lead to capital flight. The export push was still valuable, but the use

[47] Ibid., p. 24.

of export-subsidies was no longer acceptable under GATT and WTO rules, and might lead to retribution. Many LDCs could not provide the same essential high level of official export promotion. But other devices used successfully by these states should still be useful, as was demonstrated by the later HPAEs, notably Malaysia, Thailand and Indonesia. Among these were providing free-trade zones, duty-free imports and financial help for exporters, courting export-oriented FDI, improving the infrastructure and concentrating on those export products in which a country has comparative advantage, particularly in labour costs. But state interventionism of the East Asian variety was unlikely in itself to enable other states to copy their success. As *TEAM* puts it, 'the prerequisites for success were so rigorous that policymakers seeking to follow similar paths in other developing countries have often met with failure'.[48]

What light does the experience of Black African states, India and the East and South-east Asian states after about 1950 throw on the three general questions posed at the start of chapter 10?

First, it is clear that the period after about 1950 was one of unprecedented growth and development for most Third World countries. Despite limited information on national incomes before the 1960s, it seems clear that, at least until the middle 1980s and the international recession, there was considerable growth of both the GDP and per capita incomes. How equally this increase in incomes was distributed within societies is a different and contested issue. But there appears to be no statistical correlation between high growth and increased income inequality: this depended on the particular social and economic characteristics of individual countries.[49]

Secondly, how important was trade in Third World development after 1945? It is immediately clear that the export pessimism of the early theorists was exaggerated. Between 1953 and 1982 the volume index of world exports (1963 = 100) increased from 54 to 300 and unit values from 100 to 403. Agricultural exports, about which there was most pessimism, did not increase as fast as this: but their volume index rose from an estimated 64 in 1955 to 209 in 1982, their unit value from 100 in 1953 to 292 in 1982.

To this extent, then, the export pessimists were right: exports of agricultural commodities and raw materials grew less fast than exports of manufactures, and food and agricultural raw materials formed a declining proportion of total western imports. But this did not necessarily imply

[48] Ibid., p. 6.
[49] For a useful discussion of this issue, see Colman and Nixson, *Economics of Change*, ch. 3.

that specialization in producing these export commodities was unrewarding for Third World countries. A number of these did in fact achieve impressive rates of growth based on efficient commodity exporting down to the early 1980s, and some continued to prosper during and after the depression of the mid-1980s. The most successful were normally those whose exports were reasonably balanced between different crops or industrial raw materials so as to offset market fluctuations in a particular product, and which also used earnings from these exports to diversify into manufacturing exports. Moreover, it can be argued that the declining proportion of commodity exports and income in some states was at least partly the result of producer inefficiency. It is significant that both the volume and the purchasing power of the exports of the least developed and most heavily indebted LDCs increased far less than those of the average non-petroleum-producing LDCs between 1960 and 1989.[50]

But, while international trade in non-petroleum commodities became relatively less important, world trade in manufactures grew very fast. Between 1953 and 1982 the volume grew from 51 to 410 and the unit value from 95 to 314, though this was not much more than the increase for agricultural products. The biggest value increase was, of course, in minerals, including petroleum, whose index rose from 99 to 1,234 in the same years. Clearly, if one could not export petroleum, the best strategy was to export manufactures.[51]

This, in fact, is what the more successful LDCs increasingly did. In 1955 the share of manufactures in non-fuel exports from LDCs was 11.9 per cent; in 1989 it was 75.3 per cent. While the share of LDCs in all industrialized countries' imports was much the same in 1987 as in 1965, falling only from 20.6 to 19.0 per cent (with a rise to 28.9 in 1980 at the height of the oil-price boom), the share of LDCs in the imports of manufactures to industrialized countries rose from 4.1 to 13.6 per cent between 1965 and 1987.[52] Manufacturing for export would thus seem to be the logical solution for the Third World. The example of the NICs of Asia seemed to demonstrate that agricultural countries could gradually convert themselves into industrialized and exporting economies and raise their income levels to near those of the West.

In principle this must be true. There were, however, two major problems, one on the supply, the other on the demand side. On the supply side it was quite uncertain whether the conditions described in the section above on the East and South-east Asian countries could be

[50] Ibid., table 5.6, p. 168.
[51] L. Moore, *The Growth and Structure of International Trade since the Second World War* (Brighton, 1985), table 8.1, p. 148; table 8.2, p. 149.
[52] Colman and Nixson, *Economics of Change*, table 5.1, p. 143; table 5.2, p. 156.

replicated throughout the Third World. In Black Africa, for example, industrialization was largely for the domestic market and heavily protected: very little was truly competitive at international prices. The comparative advantage stemming from relatively low real wages was commonly counterbalanced by inefficiencies of scale and production techniques.

The demand side, however, might prove a more serious obstacle to Third World industrial exports. First, since the majority of Third World manufactured exports to the West were in raw-material-intensive and labour-intensive products, often components for final assembly in the West, it was possible that the market or these things would prove as inelastic as that for food and industrial raw materials. Secondly, in so far as Third World exports seriously competed with industrial products in the West, there was a wide range of methods used to protect western domestic markets without breaking the rules of GATT and the WTO, ranging from formal tariffs to quotas, such as the Multi-Fibre Arrangements of the 1970s and 1980s. In short, while exporting had proved its value as the best route to rapid growth for a small group of LDCs since the 1950s, and might well be the most effective route for the generality of Third World countries in the future, the residual protectionism of virtually all countries, both developed and underdeveloped, might provide an obstacle that the exporting countries of the pre-1914 free-trading era did not have to face.

Finally, what does the evidence of these chapters suggest were the features that distinguished the more from the less successful countries after 1950? The simple answer must be that it was the quality of governments and the wisdom of their economic and social policies. Most Black African states were 'soft', weak in their ability to govern, let alone construct and carry through complex development policies. Their planning was unrealistic and their execution ineffectual. India was not a soft state. It possessed a strong government, alone among all these states deeply committed to democracy, and experienced no revolutions. Unfortunately it also remained, at least until early in the 1980s, hamstrung by commitment to a dogmatic economic strategy based on the concept of the big push, Soviet-style planning, and hostility to exporting as a means to growth. The result was that ISI reached the limits of a restricted market and the growth of industry and its ability to absorb the growing rural surplus population were circumscribed. By contrast, except for Japan and Malaysia, the East Asian 'Tigers' and South-east Asian NICs had little concern for democracy. But they were all strong governments with very considerable bureaucratic abilities. In all of them the state was able to dictate or determine the pattern of economic activity with varying degrees of competence, often learning flexibly from experience. All, in different degrees, followed the dictates of comparative advantage in developing by stages, from economies based on production and export of primary commodities, through ISI, to processing, assembly and manufacture for export. This progression was no accident. It flowed from the ability of a government to rationalize economic problems and take constructive remedial action. Ultimately, therefore, it would seem that it is primarily the quality of government that enables a Third World country to move up the escalator to affluence.[53]

[53] For a valuable summary of the role of government in a range of Third World countries from the early 1970s to the 1990s, see I. M. D. Little, R. N. Cooper, W. M. Corden and S. Rajapatirana, *Boom, Crisis, and Adjustment: The Macroeconomic Experience of Developing Countries* (New York, 1993), esp. chs 12 and 13.

12

Some Conclusions

Two basic questions were posed in the Preface. Have the Third World countries benefited or suffered from close economic relationships with the more developed countries of the West? Conversely, would they have done better if they had been able to maintain their autonomy and keep the West at arm's length? It was admitted that no definite or universally acceptable answer is possible to either of these questions, and it is not now proposed to attempt to provide one. On the other hand, the evidence surveyed in earlier chapters makes it possible at least to suggest on which side the balance of the argument has swung.

Consider first the second of these questions, what may be called the autonomy option. Historically, of course, this was never a genuine possibility. The combined economic and military resources of the West from the sixteenth century can be seen, in retrospect, to have been certain sooner or later to incorporate the rest of the world into a single 'world system', to use Wallerstein's term. Evasion was possible only for a very large state, such as China, mainly because it was so big and potentially resistant that it escaped formal colonial rule; and even its escape was partial, since the western powers and Japan obtained extensive rights of commercial access and control of treaty ports, customs duties and other aspects of the economy. Japan also was never colonized; but it was first propelled into the international economy from the 1850s, and then willingly collaborated with it.

Nevertheless, it was common ground after 1945 among many of the 'pessimists' surveyed in chapter 2 that, once a Third World country obtained political freedom, it was in its best interests to cut or restrict its links with the international capitalist economy and develop in its own way. Although reasons for such pessimism varied widely, the common ground was belief that all indigenous societies at some stage possessed the potential to develop successfully, but that this potential had been blocked, arrested or checked by the effects of incorporation into the single 'world system'. Satisfactory development therefore required disengagement from the international system, rejection of capitalism and, for many, adoption of socialism.

It is important that from the 1940s to the 1980s, when most of these arguments were being generated, this socialist alternative did seem both desirable and feasible. The Soviet Union appeared to many, not only in the Third World but also in the West, to provide a far better model of development than capitalism. Moreover, in practical terms, a country which wanted to opt out of the international capitalist economy could, for that half century, rely on the USSR, its east European satellites and also the post-1949 China to substitute for the West by providing the capital, consumer goods and export markets needed in the transition to sustained development. The prescription of socialism for the Third World in much of the more radical development literature of the period after about 1950 commonly assumed that this option existed and that it offered the only route to true development.

By the 1990s, however, it had become clear that this had been a mirage. Hitherto the communist states had given considerable support to nationalist movements and new Third World states, and this aid had encouraged some Third World countries to proclaim their independence of capitalism. But, even at its peak, it had serious limitations.

First, the USSR lacked the economic, and in some respects the technical, ability to fill the role of the far more affluent West.

Secondly, in accepting Third World commodity exports in return for capital and consumer goods, the USSR was merely replicating the role of the western market. In most places it did little or nothing to enable these countries to transform themselves into developed industrial economies. The consequences are difficult to judge, because few of the USSR's Third World clients provided useful information to the World Bank. But in 1994 two of these in West Africa that did so, Guinea and Guinea-Bissau, had clearly not made much progress in this direction. In that year the proportion of Guinea's labour force said to be in agriculture was still 87 per cent, that of Guinea-Bissau 85 per cent. The corresponding shares of manufactures in GDP were 5 and 7 per cent.[1] Both remained among the poorest states of the Third World. One suspects that countries such as Cuba, for which no such statistics are available, would show comparably limited structural change. In short, the shift from

[1] World Bank, *World Development Report 1996: From Plan to Market* (Oxford, 1996) table 1, p. 188; table 12, p. 210.

dependence on the capitalist West to dependence on the non-capitalist East seems to have made little difference.

Finally, however, the real moment of truth came with the effective collapse of state socialism in the USSR and its European satellites in the late 1980s. Even in China the economy was being rapidly switched towards capitalism. For all practical purposes there was no longer a 'Second World' in which dissenters from the western-dominated international system could take refuge. More importantly, the ideological option of state socialism could no longer be held up as a successful model for Third World countries to adopt.

This meant that the Third World was left to make its way as best it could in the single world system dominated by the capitalist West. That in turn brings us to the central issue of this book. Does the evidence suggest that the pessimists or the optimists were nearer the truth in their assessment of the effects of this integrated international capitalist system on the Third World during the twentieth century? Were the LDCs richer or poorer in the 1990s than they had been a century earlier? Did they do well or badly from the operation of comparative advantage? Should they still concentrate on export-led growth and rely on the principle of comparative advantage?

Any answers must, of course, be heavily qualified; moreover, we have no reliable statistics on national or per capita incomes before the mid-twentieth century for most Third World countries. But, at least on the more reliable evidence of the last half of the twentieth century, there seems no doubt that virtually every Third World country that has not been devastated by war, civil war or crass governmental incompetence is now richer in real terms than it was before its integration. By other standards also there has been very considerable improvement, notably in life expectancy, health and literacy. That progress was not continuous. Adverse trends in international economic conditions in the 1930s, and again in the period after about 1980, may have set it back. But at least there is little evidence to support belief in the general or inevitable immiseration of the Third World as a result of its incorporation into the international division of labour.

What of the role of trade and exporting and the operation of comparative advantage in this economic advance? How much correlation has there been between growth and specialization in export production? What qualifications seem necessary in stating that trade was a generally successful engine of development?

First, the evidence suggests that, in the initial stage at least, the establishment of an export trade was almost invariably the starting point of greater economic growth. This was true of most of Latin America, of North America, Australasia, Asia and Africa. I have come across no example of such a trade, normally in the first instance based on exploitation of indigenous factors such as timber or minerals, later also of agricultural and other products, that did not enable the inhabitants of an LDC to increase their incomes. This was the classic early form of both comparative advantage and vent for surplus. The main qualification is that, if it was to provide the maximum benefits, such trade had to be fair, not handicapped by unequal regulations, as most colonial trades were under pre-nineteenth-century 'mercantilist' conditions, and again under the protectionism of some imperial systems during the period between about 1880 and the 1950s.

This, however, leaves the more important question of how far such a strategy enabled these countries to develop. Was there, as the 'export pessimists' argued, an impassable limit beyond which exporting, particularly of commodities, could not take Third World economies? Was it a dead end, leaving them as a poorly rewarded proletariat in the international division of labour? Alternatively, what factors differentiated countries that were able to maintain the momentum of growth, through commodity exporting to industrialization and sustained development, from those that did not?

The limited evidence surveyed above seems to suggest that the critical factor was the extent to which a newly established export–import sector was able to permeate and transform the rest of a country's economy. The great success stories of the nineteenth and early twentieth centuries were the settler societies of North America and Australasia. Starting as exporters of natural resources such as timber, skins and easily accessible minerals, they moved to intensive production of agricultural exports, and thence to investment in infrastructure and industry. In the process, virtually all sectors became part of a single capitalist economy, based on high levels of education and skills and relatively high wages. Conversely, average national incomes were not held down by the existence of large numbers of people whose productivity was very much smaller than that of the modern sector: there was never a significant dual economy. In the later twentieth century a comparable pattern can be seen in parts of East and South-east Asia.

It is important also that much of this development was based on foreign technology and capital. None of these countries, nor those of Latin America, hesitated to borrow extensively in their earlier development phase. Heavy borrowing caused serious problems when international recessions reduced foreign-exchange earnings, but none of the anglophone and few of the Latin American countries ever reneged on their liabilities. Direct foreign investment also played an important role in development. Its main advantage, as always, was that it brought with it technology and know-how. Moreover, international transfers were conditional on profitability, whereas other forms of foreign borrowing had to be serviced irrespective of economic conditions. Its concomitant disadvantage was that FDI might take vital sectors of the host economy out of the control of the indigenous society. Over time, however, most foreign enterprises came under local control, either by state action or by purchase of shares.

But, if incorporation of these New World, Australasian and Asian countries into the international economy proved generally beneficial, most Latin American states remain on the margins of the Third World. Furtado and other Latin American analysts, particularly dependency theorists, suggest special reasons for this, including foreign control of key sectors, excessive protectionism for import-substituting industry, and improvident government control of money supply. But a common and probably more fundamental problem was the inability of the modernized, mainly industrial and urban, sector to raise the general level of productivity and incomes in the rural sector. This was often due to archaic landownership and employment patterns. The result was economic dualism, a key factor in much dependency theory. This provides a key to the comparable, though usually far worse problems of Black Africa and other less-developed Third World countries.

It was argued in chapter 7 that the fundamental reason for the limited economic growth of the Gold Coast/Ghana, taken as a model of development based on commodity production in Black Africa both during and after the colonial period, was that a very dynamic, innovatory and largely capitalist sector producing cocoa for the international market failed to transform the economy as a whole: this was in marked contrast with the role of wool and other export commodities in Australia and New Zealand. The reasons lay partly in limited technical and productivity development in the cocoa industry, still more in the failure of the rest of the economy to respond to the new opportunities opened up. This failure can be explained in many ways. Under the colonial regime, governments did little to use the increased national income to improve education and only spasmodically to invest in infrastructure. Because exports were mostly unprocessed, there was little stimulus to downstream activity, apart perhaps from that of the courts of law. There was equally little encouragement to upstream activity, because there was no great increase in demand for marketed food, and most of the few requirements of cocoa production were met by imports. Because the trade was dominated by expatriate companies, cocoa did little to generate an African capitalist class, so that there was little indigenous investment in the modern sector. Because Britain insisted on a free-trade policy until the early 1950s, and because the government was hostile to urbanization and any threat to peasant industries, virtually no manufacturing developed. Thus, until independence, cocoa merely enabled sections of the Gold Coast society to enjoy a higher standard of living than they might otherwise have done. The bulk of the society was little affected, remaining mostly outside the range of capitalist enterprise.

Comparable patterns of limited sectoral growth could be described in most other parts of Black Africa and pre-1945 Asia. India, however, differed in one major respect from most African countries. Trade was never a major factor in Indian economic life. Though there were isolated areas of commodity export production, notably of tea, wheat, cotton and jute, these had a limited effect on the economy as a whole. Yet, paradoxically, India was the first Asian country, apart from Japan, that generated a significant industrial sector, and it did so largely on Indian, not expatriate, initiative. In absolute terms, Indian industry was very large; yet, in common with the exporting commodity sector, it was very small in relation to both the domestic product and the labour force. Moreover, although in the earlier years manufactured textiles, particularly cotton and jute, found important export markets, this did not lead to an export-oriented industrial system. With protection from the 1920s, Indian industry became increasingly import substituting, unable to compete internationally with rivals such as Japan. The Indian example, both before and after independence, therefore, throws little light on the potential of an export-oriented development strategy.

The best modern examples of the potential of such a strategy in the Third World were obviously the states of East and later South-east Asia. All began their modern development by exporting: Japan initially with simple labour-intensive manufactures, leading to the highest technical levels; the others from conventional commodity exports, again leading to simple labour-intensive manufactures and ultimately high technology. All, bar Hong Kong, went through periods of very severe protectionism, but most found means of combining domestic protection with virtual free trade for the export sector. All, in varying degrees, relied on imported technology, foreign loans and FDI. All ran the same risk of over-borrowing, with attendant debt-servicing dangers, which, for example, forced South Korea, Thailand and Indonesia to depend on the IMF help in 1997–8. But basically all had demonstrated the value of exploiting comparative advantage, which in their cases consisted mainly of a supply of increasingly educated and hard-working people who were able to spot where the opportunities lay and move flexibly to exploit them.

What general conclusion should be drawn? This book started with the concept of development through specialization and trade, and will end with it. The limited evidence of these chapters suggests the following tentative conclusions.

1 There is no strong evidence to suggest that the Third World was made poorer by the creation of a single world economy and market,

though there may well have been undesirable side effects, particularly in cultures and lifestyles.

2 The concept of 'dependence', though superficially very attractive as a description of the resulting relationship between more and less economically developed trading partners, in fact, as Little has argued, has little explanatory power. All economies in a world system are to some extent dependent on others for markets and sources of imports. Any adverse effects of such interdependence must stem from the inability of a particular country to adjust its economic and social structures to the challenge of internal and external markets, as T. dos Santos was seen to argue in chapter 2.

3 Colonialism played a complex and in some ways paradoxical role. On the one hand, it facilitated the evolution of a world market by opening up territories to trade through improved transport and by integrating regions politically. In some territories it promoted the transition to capitalism by the use of state compulsion to overcome indigenous resistance, though, as in East Africa, the transition was commonly partial, producing 'straddling' or 'articulation' rather than a conventional capitalist bourgeoisie and proletariat. On the other hand, colonialism can be seen as an obstacle to sustained development. The interests of the metropolis were often incompatible with those of the subject people, as over the establishment of local industries. Colonial governments had conservative attitudes to development, more concerned with political stability than growth. Neither they, nor expatriate private enterprise, provided much opportunity for indigenous people to gain experience in the higher levels of administration or the economy. The concept of intra-imperial 'cooperation', as preached by the French and others, was valid in so far as it reflected a genuine complementarity between economies, and may have been mutually beneficial in times of acute recession. But it often concealed selfish imperial stratagems and, in the longer term, might perpetuate archaic patterns of production in Third World countries. In short, while colonialism was not an insuperable obstacle to growth, and may have helped it up to a certain point, it might also become an obstacle to sustained development.

4 Trade, and the concept of development based on the exploitation of comparative advantage, come well out of this survey. Most Third World societies willingly adapted to the possibilities offered by international trade because exchange offered them tangible material benefits. For all the countries considered here, and for many others, Furtado's critique of Latin America holds good: sustained growth often began with the establishment of large-scale export–import trades. On the other hand, it is also clear that, if trade was a necessary starting point, it was not by itself a sufficient condition for sustained growth or

development. This depended on the ability of a particular society to exploit the gains from trade to the full, which in practice meant employing the profits from trade to transform the society as a whole. In practice it also meant that the capitalist relations implicit in the trading sector had to be extended throughout the economy.

5 The logic of this developmental process, as the development economists correctly saw, was that commodity production and export must lead to industrialization, since this alone could break through both the Malthusian obstacle of limited land and the barrier of an inelastic and unpredictable world commodity market. The first step to industrialization was almost always ISI. But the evidence everywhere suggests that this could also prove an economic dead end, since, as early Marxists predicted, highly protected industries will eventually come up against the limits of a domestic market, sooner in small states, such as those of Black Africa, later in large countries such as the United States or even India. In the long run, therefore, industrialization will lead to sustained growth only if a substantial part of the manufacturing sector becomes internationally competitive. Exporting was as critical for manufactures as for commodities.

My conclusion, therefore, must be that, in principle, Adam Smith, Ricardo and their later disciples were right. Trade, specialization and comparative advantage have always led to growth, not to underdevelopment or immiseration. But trade alone has not been sufficient for sustained development. This depended on the ability of a society to exploit and invest the benefits of trade, so that each stage of specialized production led to higher technical levels and to the ability to compete in international markets.

Select Bibliography

Abbott, G. J., and Nairn, N. B. (eds), *Economic Growth of Australia 1788–1821* (Melbourne, 1969).

Albertini, R. von, *European Colonial Rule, 1880–1940: The Impact of the West on India, Southeast Asia, and Africa* (Oxford, 1982).

Allen, G. C., and Donnithorne, A. G., *Indonesia and Malaya: A Study in Economic Development* (New York, 1954).

Allen, G. C., and Donnithorne, A.G., *Western Enterprise in Indonesia and Malaya* (London, 1957).

Amin, S., *L'Afrique de l'ouest bloquée: L'Économie politique de la colonisation, 1880–1970* (Paris, 1971).

Amin, S., *Neo-colonialism in West Africa* (New York and London, 1973).

Amin, S., *Accumulation on a World Scale* (Paris, 1970; Eng. edn, New York, 1974).

Annuaire Statistique de la France (Paris, 1966).

Apter, D. E., *Ghana in Transition* (2nd rev. edn, Princeton, 1972).

Ariff, M., *The Malaysian Economy: Pacific Connections* (Singapore, 1991).

Arndt, H. W., 'Overseas Borrowing – the New Model', *Economic Record*, 33 (1957), pp. 247–61.

Aruda, M., de Souza, H., and Alfonso, C., *Multinationals in Brazil* (Toronto, 1975).

Austin, D., *Politics in Ghana 1946–1960* (London, 1964).

Avinieri, S. (ed.), *Karl Marx on Colonialism and Modernisation* (Moscow, 1971).

Bacon, C. (ed.), *Technology, Employment, and Basic Needs in Food Processing* (Oxford, 1979).

Bagchi, A. K., *Private Investment in India 1900–1939* (Cambridge, 1972).

Bairoch, P., *The Economic Development of the Third World since 1900* (London, 1975).

Balasubramanyam, V. N., *Multinational Enterprises in the Third World* (London, 1980).

Balasubramanyam, V. N., *The Economy of India* (London, 1984).

Balinsky, A., *Marx's Economics: Origin and Development* (Lexington, Mass., 1970).

Baran, P., *The Political Economy of Growth* (New York, 1957).

Baran, P., and Sweezy, P., *Monopoly Capitalism* (New York, 1966).

Barker, Lady, *Station Amusements in New Zealand* (Auckland, 1870).

Barker, Lady, *Station Life in New Zealand* (Auckland, 1870).

Barlow, C., *The Natural Rubber Industry: Its Development, Technology and Economy in Malaysia* (Kuala Lumpur, 1978).

Barnard, A., *The Australian Wool Market 1840–1900* (Melbourne, 1958).

Barnard, A. (ed.), *The Simple Fleece: Studies in the Australian Wool Industry* (Melbourne, 1962).

Barnet, R. J., and Muller, R. E., *Global Reach* (New York, 1974).

Bates, R. H., *Markets and States in Tropical Africa* (Berkeley and Los Angeles, 1981).

Bates, R. H., *Essays on the Political Economy of Rural Africa* (Cambridge, 1983).

Bauer, (Lord) P. T., *The Rubber Industry: A Study in Competition and Monopoly* (London, 1948).

Bauer, (Lord) P. T., *West African Trade* (Cambridge, 1954).

Bauer, (Lord) P. T., *United States Aid and Indian Economic Development* (Washington, 1959).

Bauer, (Lord) P. T., *Dissent on Development* (London, 1971).

Bauer, (Lord) P. T., *Equality, the Third World and Economic Delusion* (London, 1981).

Bauer, (Lord) P. T., *Reality and Rhetoric: Studies in the Economics of Development* (London, 1984).

Bauer, (Lord) P. T., *The Development Frontier* (Cambridge, 1991).

Bayart, J.-F., *The State in Africa: The Politics of the Belly* (Paris, 1989; Eng. edn, London, 1993).

Beckford, G. L., *Persistent Poverty: Underdevelopment in Plantation Economies of the Third World* (New York, 1972).

Beckman, B., *Organising the Farmers: Cocoa Politics and National Development in Ghana* (Uppsala, 1976).

Behrman, J. N., *Some Patterns in the Rise of the Multinational Enterprise* (Chapel Hill, NC, 1968).

Bergsten, C. F., Horst, T., and Moran, T. H., *American Multinationals and American Interests* (Washington, 1978).

Berman, B., and Lonsdale, J., *Unhappy Valley: Conflict in Kenya and Africa* (2 vols, London, 1992).

Bernstein, H. (ed.), *Underdevelopment and Development* (Harmondsworth, 1973).

Bernstein, H., 'Capital and Peasantry in the Epoch of Imperialism' (Occasional Paper 7(2), Economic Research Bureau, University of Dar es Salaam, 1977).

Bethell, L. (ed.), *The Cambridge History of Latin America* (5 vols, Cambridge, 1984–6).

Bhagwati, J. N., and Desai, P., *India: Planning for Industrialization: Industrialization and Trade Policies since 1951* (Oxford, 1970).

Bhagwati, J. N., and Srinivasan, T. N., *Foreign Trade Regimes and Economic Development: India* (Delhi, 1976).

Biersteker, T. J., *Distortion or Development? Contending Perspectives on the Multinational Corporation* (Cambridge, Mass., 1978).

Biersteker, T. J., *Multinationals, the State, and Control of the Nigerian Economy* (Princeton, 1987).

Bird, G., *IMF Lending to Developing Countries* (London, 1995).

Blainey, G., *The Tyranny of Distance: How Distance Shaped Australia's History* (Melbourne, 1966).

Bloch-Lainé, F., *La Zone franc* (Paris, 1965).

Board of Trade Journal, 187 (July–Dec. 1964); 189 (July–Dec. 1965).

Boeke, J. H., *The Evolution of the Netherlands Indian Economy* (New York, 1942).

Boeke, J. H., *Economics and Economic Policy of Dual Societies* (New York, 1953).

Brading, D., *The First America: The Spanish Monarchy, Creole Patriots, and the Liberal State, 1492–1867* (Cambridge, 1993).

Brash, D. T., 'Australia as Host to the International Corporation' in C. P. Kindleberger (ed.), *The International Corporation* (Cambridge, Mass., 1970).

Brewer, A., *Marxist Theories of Imperalism: A Critical Survey* (London, 1980).

Brown, M. B., *Africa's Choices: After Thirty Years of the World Bank* (London, 1995).

Brunschwig, H., *French Colonialism 1871–1914* (London, 1966).

Butler, L. J., *Industrialisation and the British Colonial State: West Africa 1939–1951* (London, 1997).

Butlin, N. G., *Australian Domestic Product, Investment and Foreign Borrowing, 1861–1938/9* (Cambridge, 1962).

Butlin, N. G., *Investment in Australian Economic Development 1861–1900* (Cambridge, 1964).

Butlin, N. G., *Forming a Colonial Economy: Australia 1810–1850* (Cambridge, 1994).

Butlin, S. J., *Foundations of the Australian Monetary System* (Melbourne, 1953).

Byé, M., 'Self-financed Multiterritorial Units and their Time Horizon', *International Economic Papers*, 8 (London, 1958), pp. 147–78.

Cain, P. J., and Hopkins, A. G., *British Imperialism* (2 vols, London, 1993).

Callis, H. G., *Foreign Capital in South East Asia* (New York, 1942).

Cardoso, F. H., 'Dependent Capitalist Development in Latin America', *New Left Review*, 74 (1972), pp. 83–95.

Cassen, R., and Associates, *Does Aid Work? Report to an Intergovernmental Task Force* (2nd edn, Oxford, 1994).

Casson, M. (ed.), *The Growth of International Business* (London, 1983).

Caves, R. E., *Multinational Enterprise and Economic Analysis* (Cambridge, 1982).

Chambers, E. J., and Gordon, D. F., 'Primary Products and Economic Growth: an Empirical Measurement', *Journal of Political Economy*, 74 (1966), pp. 315–32.

Chandler, A. D., *Strategy and Structure* (Cambridge, Mass., 1962).

Chandra, B., *The Rise and Growth of Economic Nationalism in India* (New Delhi, 1966).

Chapman, J. K., *The Career of Sir Arthur Hamilton Gordon, First Lord Stanmore, 1829–1912* (Toronto, 1964).

Clark, G., *The Balance Sheets of Imperialism* (New York, 1936).

Clarke, P., *Liberals and Social Democrats* (Cambridge, 1978).

Cohen, R. B. et al. (eds), *The Multinational: A Radical Approach* (Cambridge, 1979).

Colman, D., and Nixson, F., *Economics of Change in Less Developed Countries* (New York, 1994).

Commonwealth Secretariat, *Commonwealth Trade 1966* (London, 1967).

Constantine, S., *The Making of British Colonial Development Policy 1914–1940* (London, 1984).

Dahm, B., *History of Indonesia in the Twentieth Century* (London, 1971).

Davidson, B., *The Black Man's Burden: Africa and the Curse of the Nation State* (London, 1992).

Denoon, D., *Settler Capitalism: The Dynamics of Dependent Development in the Southern Hemisphere* (Oxford, 1983).

Desai, A. V., 'Factors Underlying the Slow Growth of Indian Industry', *Economic and Political Weekly* (Mar. 1981), pp. 381–92.

Diaz Alejandro, C. F., *Essays on the Economic History of the Argentine Republic* (New Haven, 1970).

Dos Santos, T., 'The Crisis of Development Theory and the Problem of Dependence in Latin America', in H. Bernstein (ed.), *Underdevelopment and Development* (London, 1973), pp. 57–69.

Drabble, J. H., *Rubber in Malaya, 1876–1922* (Oxford, 1973).

Drabble, J. H., *Malayan Rubber: The Interwar Years* (London, 1991).

Drummond, I. M., *Imperial Economic Policy 1917–1939: Studies in Expansion and Protection* (London, 1974).

Duchêne, A., *Histoire des finances coloniales de la France* (Paris, 1938).

Duignan, P., and Gann, L. (eds), *Colonialism in Africa*, vol. 4: *The Economics of Colonialism* (Cambridge, 1975).

Dunning, J. H., *American Investment in British Manufacturing Industry* (London, 1958).

Dunning, J. H., 'Changes in the Level and Structure of International Production: The Last One Hundred Years', in M. Casson (ed.), *The Growth of International Business* (London, 1983).

Dutt, R. C., *The Economic History of India in the Victorian Age* (London, 1906).

Dutt, R. Palme, *Modern India* (London, 1927).

Dyster, B., and Meredith, D., *Australia in the International Economy in the Twentieth Century* (Cambridge, 1990).

Elliot, H. (ed.), *John Stuart Mill: Letters* (2 vols, London, 1910).

Ellis, H. S. (ed.), *Economic Development for Latin America* (London, 1961).

Emmanuel, A., *Unequal Exchange: A Study of the Imperialism of Trade* (Paris, 1969; Eng. edn, London and New York, 1972).

Emmanuel, A., *Appropriate or Underdeveloped Technology?* (Paris, 1981; Eng. edn, Chichester, 1982).

Etheringon, N., *Theories of Imperialism* (London, 1984).

Fieldhouse, D. K., ' "Imperialism": An Historiographical Revision', *Economic History Review*, 2nd ser. 14 (1961), pp. 187–209.

Fieldhouse, D. K., 'The Economic Exploitation of Africa: Some British and French Comparisons', in P. Gifford and Wm. R. Louis (eds), *France and Britain in Africa: Imperial Rivalry and Colonial Rule* (New Haven and London, 1971).

Fieldhouse, D. K., *Unilever Overseas: The Anatomy of a Multinational* (London, 1978).

Fieldhouse, D. K., *Black Africa 1945–1980: Economic Decolonization and Arrested Development* (London, 1986).

Fieldhouse, D. K., 'A New Imperial System? The Role of the Multinational Reconsidered', in W. J. Mommsen and J. Osterhammel (eds), *Imperialism and After: Continuities and Discontinuities* (London, 1986).

Fieldhouse, D. K., 'The Multinational: A Critique of a Concept', in A. Teichova, M. Levy-Leboyer and H. Nussbaum (eds), *Multilateral Enterprise in Historical Perspective* (Cambridge, 1986).

Fieldhouse, D. K., 'War and the Origins of the Gold Coast Marketing Board, 1929–40', in M. Twaddle (ed.), *Imperialism, the State and the Third World* (London, 1992).

Fieldhouse, D. K., *Merchant Capital and Economic Decolonization: The United Africa Company 1929–1987* (Oxford, 1994).

Findlay, R., 'Primary Exports, Manufacturing, and Development', in M. Lundahl (ed.), *The Primary Sector in Economic Development* (London, 1985).

Findlay, R., and Lundahl, M., 'Natural Resources, "Vent-for-Surplus", and the Staples Theory', in G. M. Meier (ed.), *From Classical Economics to Development Economics* (London, 1994).

Fitzpatrick, B., *The British Empire in Australia* (London, 1939).

Frank, A. G., *Capitalism and Underdevelopment in Latin America* (London and New York, 1967; 2nd edn, London and New York, 1969).

Frank, A. G., *Dependent Accumulation and Underdevelopment* (London and New York, 1978).

Frankel, F., *India's Political Economy, 1947–1977: The Gradual Revolution* (Princeton, 1978).

Frankel, S. H., *Capital Investment in Africa: Its Course and Effects* (London, 1938).

Frankel, S. H., *Investment and the Return to Equity Capital in the South African Gold Mining Industry, 1887–1965* (Oxford, 1967).

Furnivall, J. S., *Colonial Policy and Practice* (Cambridge, 1948).

Furtado, C., *Development and Underdevelopment* (Eng. edn, Berkeley and Los Angeles, 1964; Harmondsworth, 1973).

Furtado, C., *Economic Development of Latin America* (1970; 2nd edn, Cambridge, 1976).

Galenson, W. (ed.), *Economic Growth and Structural Change in Taiwan: The Postwar Experience of the Republic of China* (Ithaca, NY, and London, 1979).

Gallagher, J., and Robinson, R. E., 'The Imperialism of Free Trade', *Economic History Review*, 2nd ser. 6 (1953), pp. 1–15.

Geertz, C., *Agricultural Involution: The Process of Ecological Change in Indonesia* (Berkeley and Los Angeles, 1963).

Gelb, A., and Associates, *Oil Windfalls: Blessing or Curse* (New York, 1988).

Gifford, P., and Louis, Wm. R. (eds.), *France and Britain in Africa: Imperial Rivalry and Colonial Rule* (New Haven and London, 1971).

Girault, A., *The Colonial Tariff Policy of France* (Oxford, 1916).

Girault, A., *Principes de colonisation et de legislation coloniale* (5th edn, 3 vols, Paris, 1927–30; 6th edn, vol. 4, Paris, 1933).

Glassburner, B. (ed.), *The Economy of Indonesia* (Ithaca, NY, 1971).

Glezer, L., *Tariff Policies: Australian Policy-making 1960–80* (Carlton, 1982).

Goldthorpe, J. E., *The Sociology of Post-colonial Societies* (Cambridge, 1996).

Graham, E. G., with Floering, I., *The Modern Plantation in the Third World* (London, 1984).

Graham, J., *Frederick Weld* (Auckland, 1983).

Grant, B., *Indonesia* (Melbourne, 1964).

Griffin, K., 'Foreign Capital, Domestic Savings and Economic Development', *Bulletin of Oxford Institute of Economics and Statistics*, 32, 2 (1970).

Hancock, (Sir) W. K., *Survey of British Commonwealth Affairs* (2 vols, London, 1937, 1942).

Harmond, J., *Domination et colonisation* (Paris, 1910).

Havinden, M., and Meredith, D., *Colonialism and Development: Britain and its Tropical Colonies, 1850–1960* (London, 1993).

Hawke, G. R., *The Making of New Zealand: An Economic History* (Cambridge, 1985).

Hayter, T., *French Aid* (London, 1966).

Hayter, T., *Aid as Imperialism* (Harmondsworth, 1971).

Headrick, D. R., *The Tentacles of Progress: Technology Transfer in the Age of Imperialism, 1850–1940* (Oxford, 1988).

Helleiner, G. K., 'The Fiscal Role of the Marketing Boards in Nigerian Economic Development, 1947–61', *Economic Journal*, 74 (1964), pp. 582–610.

Henderson, D., *New Zealand in an International Perspective* (Wellington, 1996).

Herring, R. J., *Land to the Tiller* (New Haven and London, 1983).

Hewitt, A., 'The Lomé Convention: Myth and Substance of the "Partnership of Equals"', in M. Cornell (ed.), *Europe and Africa: Issues in Post-colonial Relations* (London, 1981).

Hilferding, R., *Finance Capital* (1910; Eng. edn, London, 1981).

Hill, H., *Foreign Investment and Industrialization in Indonesia* (Singapore, Oxford and New York, 1988).

Hill, H., *The Indonesian Economy since 1966: Southeast Asia's Emerging Giant* (Cambridge, 1996).

Hill, Polly, *The Gold Coast Cocoa Farmer* (London, 1957).

Hill, Polly, *The Migrant Cocoa Farmers of Southern Ghana: A Study in Rural Capitalism* (Cambridge, 1963).

Hirschman, A., *The Strategy of Economic Development* (New Haven, 1958).

Hobson, J. A., *Imperialism: A Study* (London, 1902).

Hodgkin, T., 'Where the Paths Began', in C. Fyfe (ed.), *African Studies since 1945* (London, 1976).

Hogendorn, J. S., 'Economic Initiative and African Cash Farming', in P. Duignan and L. Gann (eds), *Colonialism in Africa*, vol. 4: *The Economics of Colonialism* (Cambridge, 1975).

Hood, N., and Young, S., *The Economics of Multinational Enterprise* (London, 1979).

Hopkins, A. G., *An Economic History of West Africa* (London, 1973).

Howe, S., *Anticolonialism in British Politics: The Left and the End of Empire, 1918–1964* (Oxford, 1993).

Hyden, G., *Beyond Ujamaa in Tanzania: Underdevelopment and an Uncaptured Peasantry* (London, 1980).

Hymer, S., *The International Operations of National Firms: A Study of Direct Foreign Investment* (Cambridge, Mass., 1976).

Iliffe, J., *Africans: The History of a Continent* (Cambridge, 1995).

IMF, *Direction of Trade* (Washington, 1963–).

Innis, H. A., *The Fur Trade in Canada: An Introduction to Canadian Economic History* (New Haven, 1930; rev. edn, Toronto, 1956).

Jha, P. S., *India: A Political Economy of Stagnation* (Bombay, 1980).

Joshi, V., and Little, I. M. D., *India: Macroeconomics and Political Economy, 1964–1991* (Delhi, 1994).

Kahin, G. McT., *Nationalism and Revolution in Indonesia* (Ithaca, NY, 1952).

Kay, G. B., *The Political Economy of Colonialism in Ghana: A Collection of Documents and Statistics, 1900–1960* (Cambridge, 1972).

Kesner, R. M., *Economic Control and Colonial Development: Crown Colony Financial Management in the Age of Joseph Chamberlain* (Westport, Conn., 1981).

Keynes, (Lord) J. M., *General Theory of Employment, Interest, and Money* (London, 1936).

Kidron, M., *Foreign Investments in India* (London, 1965).

Killick, T., *Development Economics in Action: A Study of Economic Policies in Ghana* (London, 1978).

Kindleberger, C. P., *American Business Abroad* (New Haven, 1969).

Kindleberger, C. P. (ed.), *The International Corporation: A Symposium* (Cambridge, Mass., 1970).

Klein, L., and Ohkawa, K. (eds), *Economic Growth: The Japanese Experience since the Meiji Era* (Homewood, Ill., 1968).

Kumar, D. (ed.), *The Cambridge Economic History of India*, vol. 2: c.*1757*–c.*1970* (Cambridge, 1983).

Lal, D., *The Poverty of 'Development Economics'* (London, 1983).

Lal, D., 'In Praise of the Classics', in G. M. Meier (ed.), *From Classical Economics to Development Economics* (London, 1994).

Lall, S., 'Private Foreign Investment and the Transfer of Technology in Food Processing', in C. Bacon (ed.), *Technology, Employment, and Basic Needs in Food Processing* (Oxford, 1979).

Lall, S., *The Multinational Corporation: Nine Essays* (London, 1980).

Lall, S., *Developing Countries and the International Economy* (London, 1981).

Lall, S. and Streeten, R. *Foreign Investment, Transnationals and Developing Countries* (London, 1977).

Law, R. (ed.), *From Slave Trade to 'Legitimate' Commerce: The Commercial Transition in Nineteenth Century West Africa* (Cambridge, 1995).

League of Nations, *Industrialization and Foreign Trade* (Geneva, 1945).

Leduc, M., *Les Institutions monétaires africaines, pays francophones* (Paris, 1965).

Lee, J. M., and Petter, M., *The Colonial Office, War and Development Policy: Organization and the Planning of a Metropolitan Initiative, 1939–1945* (London, 1982).

Legge, J. D., *Britain in Fiji, 1858–1880* (London, 1958).

Legge, J. D., *Sukarno* (London, 1972).

Leibenstein, H., *Economic Backwardness and Economic Growth* (New York, 1957).

Lenin, V. I., *Imperialism: The Highest Stage of Capitalism* (1917; Eng. edn, Moscow, 1947).

Leroy-Beaulieu, P., *De la colonisation chez les peuples modernes* (Paris, 1874).

Levitt, K., *Silent Surrender: The Multinationals and Canada* (Toronto, 1970).

Lewis, (Sir) W. A., 'Economic Development with Unlimited Supplies of Labour', *Manchester School* (May 1954).

Lewis, (Sir) W. A., *The Theory of Economic Growth* (London, 1955).

Leys, C., *Underdevelopment in Kenya* (London, 1975).

Liefmann, R. W., *International Cartels, Combines and Trusts* (London, 1927).

Liefmann, R. W., *Cartels, Concerns and Trusts* (London, 1932).

Lilienthal, D. E., *The Harvest years 1959–63* (New York, 1971).

Lipson, C., *Standing Guard: Protecting Foreign Capital in the Nineteenth and Twentieth Centuries* (Berkeley and Los Angeles, and London, 1985).

List, F., *The National System of Political Economy* (1841; Eng. trans., London, 1904).

Little, I. M. D., 'An Economic Reconnaissance', in W. Galenson (ed.), *Economic Growth and Structural Change in Taiwan: The Postwar Experience of the Republic of China* (Ithaca, NY, and London, 1979).

Little, I. M. D., *Economic Development: Theory, Policy and International Relations* (New York, 1982).

Little, I. M. D., and Tipping, D. G., *Social Cost Benefit Analysis of the Kulai Oil Palm Estate* (Paris, 1972).

Little, I. M. D., Cooper, R. N., Corden, W. M., and Rajapatirana, S., *Boom, Crisis, and Adjustment: The Macroeconomic Experience of Developing Countries* (New York, 1993).

Lonsdale, J., 'The European Scramble and Conquest in African History', in R. Oliver and G. N. Sanderson (eds.), *The Cambridge History of Africa*, vol. 6: *From 1870 to 1905* (Cambridge, 1985).

Louis, Wm. R., *Imperialism at Bay 1941–1945: The United States and the Decolonization of the British Empire* (Oxford, 1977).

Low, D. A., and Smith, A. (eds), *History of East Africa*, vol. 3 (Oxford, 1976).

Lugard, (Lord) F. D., *The Dual Mandate in British Tropical Africa* (1922; 3rd edn, London, 1926).

Luxemburg, R., *The Accumulation of Capital* (1913; Eng. edn, London, 1951).

Lynn, M., *Commerce and Economic Change in West Africa: The Palm Oil Industry in the Nineteenth Century* (Cambridge, 1997).

MacDougall, (Sir) D., 'The Benefits and Costs of Private Foreign Investment from Abroad', *Economic Record*, 36 (1960), pp. 13–35.

Madden, A. F., and Darwin, J. (eds), *The Dependent Empire, 1900–1948* (Westport, Conn., and London, 1994).

Maddison, A., *Class Structure and Economic Growth: India and Pakistan since the Moghuls* (New York, 1972).

Mandel, F., 'International Capitalism and "Supra-Nationality"', in R. Miliband and J. Savile (eds), *The Socialist Reporter* (London, 1967).

Mandel, F., *Late Capitalism* (1972; Eng. edn, London, 1975).

Mansergh, N., *Survey of British Commonwealth Affairs: Problems of External Policy 1931–1939* (London, 1952).

Marseille, J., *Empire colonial et capitalisme français: Histoire d'un divorce* (Paris, 1984).

Marshall, P. J., *Problems of Empire: Britain and India 1757–1813* (London, 1968).

Marshall, P. J. (ed.), *The Writings and Speeches of Edmund Burke,* vol. 5: *Madras and Bengal, 1774–85* (Oxford, 1981).

Marshall, P. J. (ed.), *The Cambridge Illustrated History of the British Empire* (Cambridge, 1996).

Martin, S. M., 'The Long Depression: West African Export Producers and the World Economy, 1914–45', in I. Brown (ed.), *The Economies of Africa and Asia in the Inter-War Depression* (London, 1989).

Martinnez-Acier, J., *Haciendas, Plantations, and Collective Farms* (London, 1977).

Martyn, H., 'Development of the Multinational Corporation', in A. A. Said and L. R. Simons (eds), *The New Sovereigns: Multinational Corporations as World Powers* (Englewood Cliffs, NJ, 1975).

Marx, K., *Capital* (3 vols, 1867, 1885, 1894; Eng. edn, 3 vols, Moscow, 1957–62).

Marx, K., and Engels, F., *On Colonialism* (Moscow, n.d.).

Meier, G. M., 'External Trade and Internal Development', in P. Duignan and L. Gann (eds), *Colonialism in Africa*, vol. 4: *The Economics of Colonialism* (Cambridge, 1975).

Meyer, F. V., *Britain's Colonies in World Trade* (London, 1948).

Miksell, R. F. (ed.), *Foreign Investment in Petroleum and Mineral Industries: Case Studies of Investor–Host Relations* (Baltimore, 1971).

Mill, J. S., *Principles of Political Economy* (1848; London, 1898).

Miller, J. D. B., *Survey of Commonwealth Affairs: Problems of Expansion and Attrition 1953–1969* (London, 1974).

Mitchell, B. R., *British Historical Statistics* (Cambridge, 1994).

Mommsen, W. J., and Osterhammel, J., *Imperialism and After: Continuities and Discontinuities* (London, 1986).

Montavon, R., *The Role of Multinational Companies in Latin America: A Case Study in Mexico* (Farnborough, 1979).

Moon, P. T., *Imperialism and World Politics* (New York, 1926).

Moore, L., *The Growth and Structure of International Trade since the Second World War* (Brighton, 1985).

Morgan, D. J., *The Official History of Colonial Development* (5 vols, London, 1980).

Morris, Morris D., 'The Growth of Large-scale Industry', in D. Kumar (ed.), *Cambridge Economic History of India*, vol. 2: *c.1757–c.1970* (Cambridge, 1983).

Morrison, D. G., Mitchell, R. M., and Paden, J. N., *Black Africa: A Comparative Handbook* (London, 1989).

Mosely, P., Harrigan, J., and Toye, J., *Aid and Power: The World Bank and Policy-based Lending* (2 vols, 2nd edn, London, 1991).

Myers, R. H., and Peattie, M. R. (eds), *The Japanese Colonial Empire, 1895–1945* (Princeton, 1984).

Myint, H., 'The "Classical Theory" of International Trade and the Underdeveloped Countries', *Economic Journal*, 68 (1958), pp. 317–37.

Myint, H., *The Economics of Developing Countries* (New York, 1965).

Myrdal, G., *Development and Underdevelopment* (Cairo, 1956).

Myrdal, G., *Economic Theory and Underdeveloped Regions* (London, 1957).

Nabudere, W., *Essays on the Theory and Practice of Imperialism* (London and Dar es Salaam, 1979).

Naoroji, D., *Poverty and Un-British Rule* (London, 1901).

Nayyar, D., 'Industrial Development in India; Growth or Stagnation', in A. Baggchi and N. Banerjee (eds), *Change and Choice in Indian Industry* (Calcutta, 1981).

Nurkse, R., *Problems of Capital Formation in Underdeveloped Countries* (Oxford, 1953).

Nurkse, R., *Patterns of Trade and Development* (Wicksell Lectures; Stockholm, 1959), reproduced in Nurkse, R., *Equilibrium and Growth in the World Economy* (Cambridge, Mass., 1961).

O'Brien, P. J., 'A Critique of Latin American Theories of Dependency', in I. Oxall et al. (eds), *Beyond the Sociology of Development* (London, 1975).

Oliver, R., *The African Experience* (London, 1991).

Oliver, R., and Sanderson, G. N. (eds), *The Cambridge History of Africa*, vol. 6: *From 1870 to 1905* (Cambridge, 1985).

Oliver, W. H., with Williams, B. R. (eds), *The Oxford History of New Zealand* (Oxford, 1981).

Ord, H. W., and Livingstone, I., *An Introduction to West African Economics* (London, 1971).

Pagden, A., *Spanish Imperialism and the Political Imagination* (New Haven and London, 1990).

Palmer, I., *The Indonesian Economy since 1965* (London, 1978).

Pao-San Ho, S., 'Colonialism and Development: Korea, Taiwan, and Kwantung', in R. H. Myers and M. R. Peatie (eds), *The Japanese Colonial Empire, 1895–1945* (Princeton, NJ, 1984).

Parkinson, Sir Cosmo, *The Colonial Office from Within, 1909–1945* (London, 1947).

Parry, J. H., *The Age of Reconnaissance* (London, 1963).

Penrose, E. T., 'Limits to the Size and Growth of the Firm', *American Economic History Review*, 45, 2 (1955), pp. 531–43.

Penrose, E. T., 'Foreign Investment and the Growth of the Firm', *Economic Journal*, 66 (1956), pp. 64–99.

Penrose, E. T., *Theory of the Growth of the Firm* (Oxford, 1959).

Penrose, E. T., *The Large International Firm in Developing Countries: The International Petroleum Industry* (London, 1968).

Pheby, J., *J. A. Hobson after Fifty Years: Freethinker of the Social Sciences* (London, 1994).

Phillips, A., *The Enigma of Colonialism: British Policy in West Africa* (London and Bloomington, Ind., 1989).

Platt, C. (ed.), *Business Imperialism 1840–1930: An Inquiry Based on British Experience in Latin America* (Oxford, 1977).

Plummer, A., *International Combines in Modern History* (London, 1934).

Porter, B., *Critics of Empire* (London, 1968).

Prebisch, R., 'The Role of Commercial Policies in Underdeveloped Countries', *American Economic Review*, 49 (1958), pp. 251–73.

Prebisch, R., *Towards a New Trade Policy for Development* (New York, 1964).

Radice, H. (ed.), *International Firms and Modern Imperialism* (Harmondsworth, 1975).

Ramachandran, N., *Foreign Plantation Investment in Ceylon, 1889–1958* (Colombo, 1963).

Ranis, G. (ed.), *Government and Economic Development* (New Haven, 1971).

Raynal, G. T. F., *A Philosophical and Political History of the Settlements and Trade of the Europeans in the East and West Indies* (London, 1798).

Reuber, G. L., and Associates, *Private Foreign Investment in Development* (Oxford, 1973).

Rey, P. P., *Colonialisme, neo-colonialisme et transition au capitalisme* (Paris, 1971).

Rey, P. P., *Les Alliances de classes* (Paris, 1973).

Reynolds, L. G., *Economic Growth in the Third World, 1850–1980* (New Haven and London, 1985).

Ricardo, D., *Principles of Political Economy and Taxation* (1817; ed. M. P. Fogarty, London, 1969).

Rimmer, D., *The Economies of West Africa* (London, 1984).

Rimmer, D., *Staying Poor: Ghana's Political Economy 1950–1990* (Oxford, 1992).

Robbins, L., *The Theory of Economic Development in the History of Economic Thought* (London, 1968).

Rodney, W., *How Europe Underdeveloped Africa* (London, 1973).

Rolfe, R. E., *The International Corporation* (Paris, 1969).

Rooth, T., *British Protectionism and the International Economy: Overseas Commercial Policy in the 1930s* (Cambridge, 1993).

Rosenstein Rodan, P. N., 'Problems of Industrialization of Eastern and South-Eastern Europe', *Economic Journal*, 53 (1943), pp. 202–11.

Rostow, W. W., *The Stages of Economic Growth* (Cambridge, 1960).

Rowthorn, R. E., and Hymer, S., *International Big Business: A Study of Comparative Growth* (Cambridge, 1971).

Said, A. A., and Simons, L. R. (eds), *The New Sovereigns: Multinational Corporations as World Powers* (Englewood Cliffs, NJ, 1975).

Sampson, A., *The Sovereign State of I.T.&T.* (London, 1973).

Samuelson, P. A., 'The Illogic of Neo-Marxian Doctrine of Unequal Exchange', in D. A. Belsey, E. J. Kane, P. A. Samuelson and R. M. Slow (eds), *Inflation, Trade and Taxes* (Ohio, 1976).

Sarraut, A., *La Mise en valeur des colonies françaises* (Paris, 1923).

Schenk, C. R., 'Decolonization and European Economic Integration: The Free Trade Area Negotiations, 1956–8, *Journal of Imperial and Commonwealth History*, 24, 3 (Sept. 1996), pp. 444–63.

Scitovsky, T., 'Economic Development in Taiwan and South Korea: 1965–81', (first published in 1985, repr. in his *Economic Theory and Reality* (Aldershot, 1995)).

Scott, M. FG, 'Foreign Trade', in W. Galenson (ed.), *Economic Growth and Structural Change in Taiwan: The Postwar Experience of the Republic of China* (Ithaca, NY, and London, 1979).

Servan Schreiber, J.-J., *Le Défi américain* (Paris, 1967; Eng. edn, *The American Challenge* (New York, 1968)).

Shetty, S. L., *Structural Retrogression in the Indian Economy since the Mid-Sixties* (Bombay, 1979).

Simkin, C. G. F., *The Instability of a Dependent Economy* (Oxford, 1951).

Simkin, C. G. F., *The Sugarbag Years* (Wellington, 1974).

Singer, H., 'The Distribution of Gains between Investing and Borrowing Countries', *American Economic Review*, 40 (1950), pp. 473–85.

Sitsen, P. W. H., *Industrial Development of the Netherlands Indies* (New York, 1944).

Skidelsky, (Lord) R., *John Maynard Keynes*, vol. 2: *The Economist as Saviour 1920–1937* (London, 1992).

Smith, A., *An Inquiry into the Nature and Causes of the Wealth of Nations* (1776; Everyman's Library edn, 2 vols, London and New York, 1964).

Snodgrass, D. N., *Inequality and Economic Development in Malaysia* (Kuala Lumpur, 1980).

Stevens, C., and van Themaat, J. V. (eds), *Europe and the International Division of Labour: New Patterns of Trade and Investment with Developing Countries: EEC and the Third World: A Survey 6* (London, 1987).

Stokes, E., 'Late Nineteenth Century Colonial Expansion and the Attack on the Theory of economic Imperialism: A Case of Mistaken Identity?', *Historical Journal*, 12 (1969), pp. 285–301.

Sunkel, O., 'Big Business and *dependencia*: A Latin American View', *Foreign Affairs*, 50, 3 (1972), pp. 517–31.

Suret-Canale, J., *Afrique noire: L'Ère coloniale* (2 vols, Paris, 1964; Eng. edn, *French Colonialism in Tropical Africa* (New York, 1971)).

Sutch, W. B., *Poverty and Progress in New Zealand: A Reassessment* (Wellington, 1941).

Sutch, W. B., *The Quest for Security in New Zealand 1840–1966* (Wellington, 1942).

Swamy, S., 'The Economic Distance between China and India, 1955–73', *China Quarterly*, 70 (June 1977), pp. 371–82.

Sweezy, P., *The Theory of Capitalist Development* (New York, 1942; 2nd edn, London, 1946).

Taylor, J. G., *Form Modernization of Modes of Production* (London, 1979).

Tendler, J., *Inside Foreign Aid* (Baltimore, Md, 1975).

Thorbecke, E., 'Agricultural Development', in W. Galenson (ed.), *Economic Growth and Structural Change in Taiwan: The Postwar Experience of the Republic of China* (Ithaca, NY, and London, 1979).

Tomlinson, B. R., *The Economy of Modern India, 1860–1970* (Cambridge, 1993).

Tomlinson, B. R. 'British Business in India', in R. P. T. Davenport-Hines and G. Jones (eds), *British Business in Asia since 1860* (Cambridge, 1989).

Toye, J., *Dilemmas of Development* (2nd edn, Oxford, 1993).

Tsokhas, K., *Beyond Dependence: Companies, Labour Processes and Australian Mining* (Melbourne, 1986).

Tungendhat, (Lord) C., *The Multinationals* (London, 1973).

Turner, L., *Invisible Empires* (London, 1970).

UN, *Relative Prices of Exports and Imports of Under-developed Countries* (New York, 1949).

United Africa Company, *Statistical and Economic Review* (London, 1948–9).

Urquhart, M. C. (ed.), *Historical Statistics of Canada* (Cambridge, 1965).

Vaitsos, C. V., 'Bargaining and the Distribution of Returns in the Purchase of Technology by Developing Countries', *Institute of Development Studies Bulletin*, 3, 1 (1970), pp. 16–23.

Vaitsos, C. V., 'The Changing Policies of Latin American Governments towards Economic Development and Direct Foreign Investment', in

R. B. Williams, W. P. Glade and K. M. Schmitt (eds), *Latin-American–US Economic Interactions* (Washington, 1974).

van der Hoeven, R., and van der Kraaj, F. (eds), *Structural Adjustment and Beyond in Sub-Saharan Africa* (The Hague, 1994).

van Helten, J.-J., and Jones, G. 'British Business in Malaysia and Singapore since the 1870s', in R. P. T. Davenport-Hines and G. Jones (eds), *British Business in Asia since 1860* (Cambridge, 1989)

Vandewalle, G., *De conjoncturele evolutie in Kongo en Ruanda-Urundi van 1920 tot 1939 en van 1949 tot 1958* (Antwerp, 1966).

Vernon, R., *Sovereignty at Bay: The Multinational Spread of US Enterprises* (New York, 1971).

Vernon, R., *Restrictive Business Practices* (New York, 1972).

Vernon, R., *Storm over the Multinationals: The Real Issues* (London, 1977).

Wakefield, E. G., *A View of the Art of Colonization* (1849; Oxford, 1914).

Wallerstein, I., *The Modern World System* (3 vols, New York, 1974, 1980, 1989).

Warren, B., *Imperialism: Pioneer of Capitalism*, ed. J. Sender (London, 1980).

Watkins, M. H., 'A Staple Theory of Economic Growth', *Canadian Journal of Economics and Political Science*, 29 (1963), pp. 141–58.

White, J., *The Politics of Foreign Aid* (London, 1974).

Wilkins, M., *The Emergence of Multinational Enterprise: American Business Abroad from the Colonial Era to 1914* (Cambridge, Mass., 1970).

Wilkins, M., *The Maturing of Multinational Enterprise: American Business Abroad from 1914 to 1970* (Cambridge, Mass., 1976).

Williams, R. B., Glade, W. P. and Schmitt, K. M. (eds), *Latin-American–US Interactions* (Washington, 1974).

Wilson, C. H., *History of Unilever* (2 vols, London, 1954).

Wolf, M., *India's Exports* (London, 1982).

Wolff, R. D., *The Economics of Colonialism: Britain and Kenya 1870–1930* (New Haven and London, 1974).

Wong Lin Ken, *The Malayan Tin Industry to 1914* (Tucson, Ariz., 1965).

Woolf, L., *Empire and Commerce in Africa: A Study in Economic Imperialism* (London, 1920; 2nd edn, London, 1968).

World Bank, *Accelerated Development in Sub-Saharan Africa: An Agenda for Action* (Washington, 1981).

World Bank, *Toward Sustained Development in Sub-Saharan Africa* (Washington, 1984).

World Bank, *World Development Report 1990: Poverty* (Oxford, 1990).

World Bank, *The East Asian Miracle* (Oxford, 1993).

World Bank, *Adjustment in Africa: Reforms, Results, and the Road Ahead* (Oxford, 1994).

World Bank, *World Development Report 1996: From Plan to Market* (Oxford, 1996).

Yip Yat Hoong, *The Development of the Tin Mining Industry in Malaya* (Kuala Lumpur, 1969).

Young, Crawford, *The African Colonial State in Comparative Perspective* (New Haven and London, 1994).

Index